Book Club

an Unshelved® collection
by Bill Barnes and Gene Ambaum

**OVERDUE
MEDIA**
Seattle

Reprinting *Unshelved* comic strips originally published on the Overdue Media LLC website from February 16, 2005 to February 19, 2006, the American Library Association website, and *ALA CogNotes* newspapers in June 2005 and January 2006.

ISBN: 0-9740353-3-5

First printing: June 2006

Printed in Canada.

Our story so far

Dewey, young adult librarian at the **Mallville Public Library**, has an encyclopedic knowledge of pop culture and a snappy answer to every stupid question. His coworker **Colleen** struggles against newfangled technology and is raising her adopted daughter **Doreen** on a strict diet of reference books and classification systems. Idealistic, health-conscious children's librarian **Tamara** writes and mourns worn-out stuffed animals. She is secretly adored by **Buddy the Book Beaver**, summer reading mascot turned library page. Their beleaguered manager **Mel** is at her most effective when ordering office supplies.

Now read on

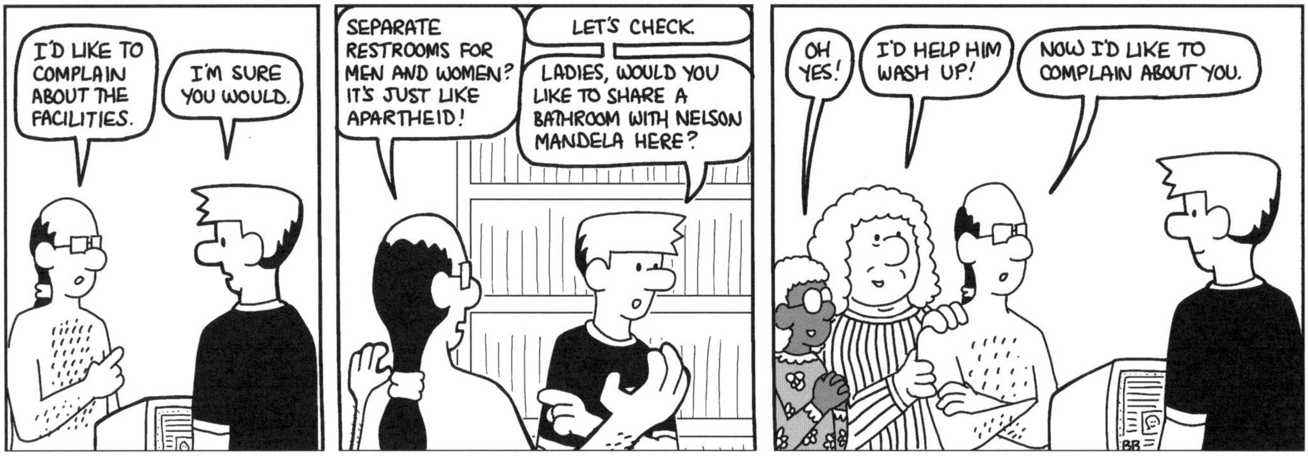
I'D LIKE TO COMPLAIN ABOUT THE FACILITIES.
I'M SURE YOU WOULD.
SEPARATE RESTROOMS FOR MEN AND WOMEN? IT'S JUST LIKE APARTHEID!
LET'S CHECK.
LADIES, WOULD YOU LIKE TO SHARE A BATHROOM WITH NELSON MANDELA HERE?
OH YES!
I'D HELP HIM WASH UP!
NOW I'D LIKE TO COMPLAIN ABOUT YOU.

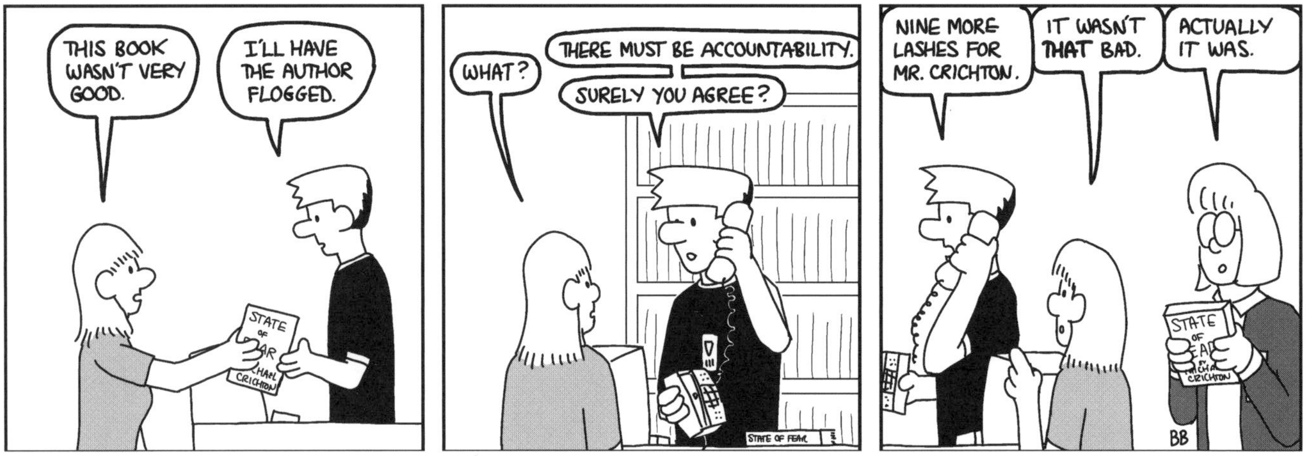
THIS BOOK WASN'T VERY GOOD.
I'LL HAVE THE AUTHOR FLOGGED.
WHAT?
THERE MUST BE ACCOUNTABILITY.
SURELY YOU AGREE?
STATE OF FEAR
NINE MORE LASHES FOR MR. CRICHTON.
IT WASN'T **THAT** BAD.
ACTUALLY IT WAS.

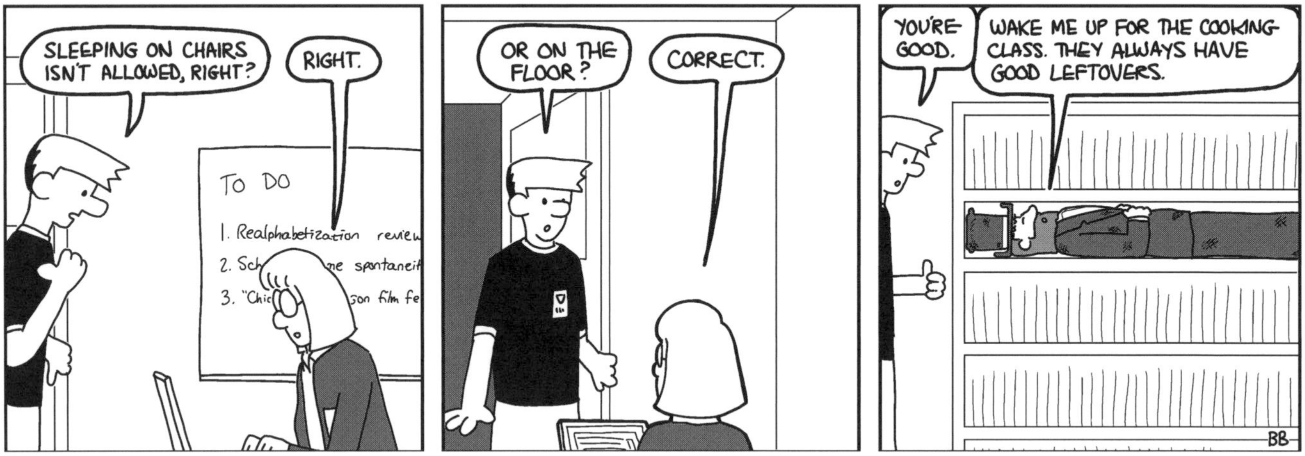
SLEEPING ON CHAIRS ISN'T ALLOWED, RIGHT?
RIGHT.
To Do
1. Realphabetization review
OR ON THE FLOOR?
CORRECT.
YOU'RE GOOD.
WAKE ME UP FOR THE COOKING CLASS. THEY ALWAYS HAVE GOOD LEFTOVERS.

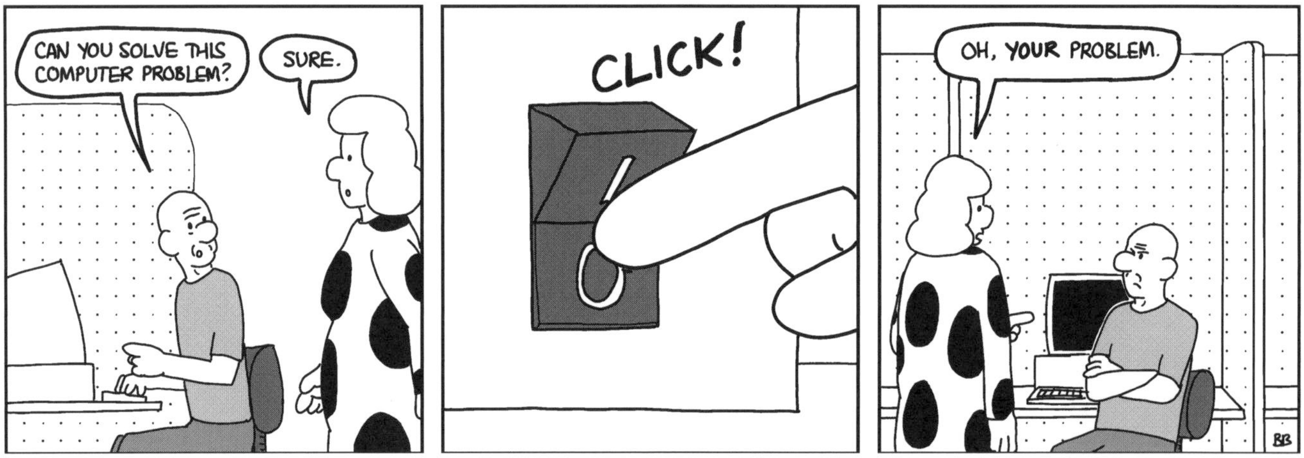
CAN YOU SOLVE THIS COMPUTER PROBLEM?
SURE.
CLICK!
OH, **YOUR** PROBLEM.

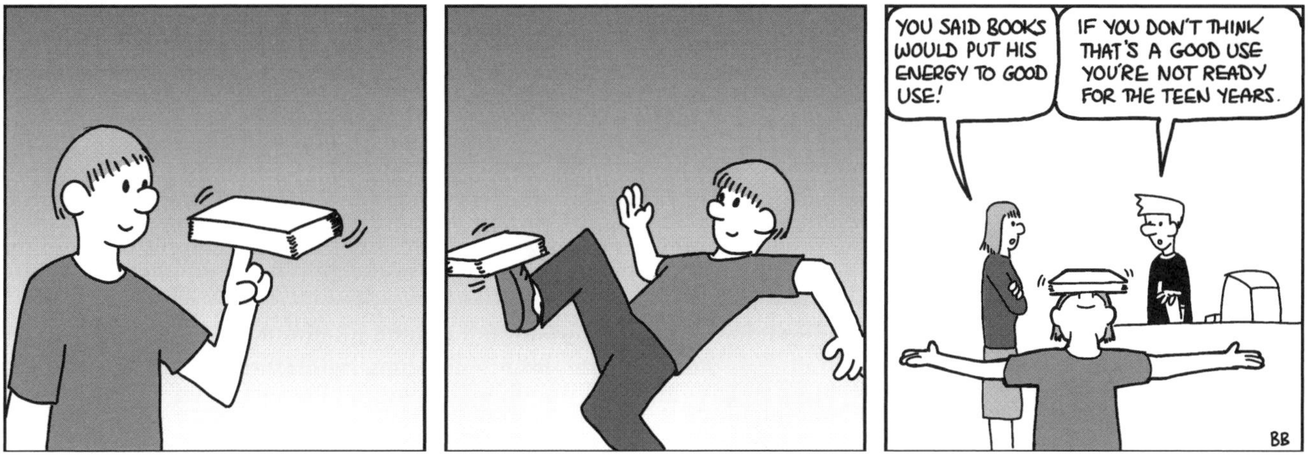
YOU SAID BOOKS WOULD PUT HIS ENERGY TO GOOD USE!
IF YOU DON'T THINK THAT'S A GOOD USE YOU'RE NOT READY FOR THE TEEN YEARS.
BB

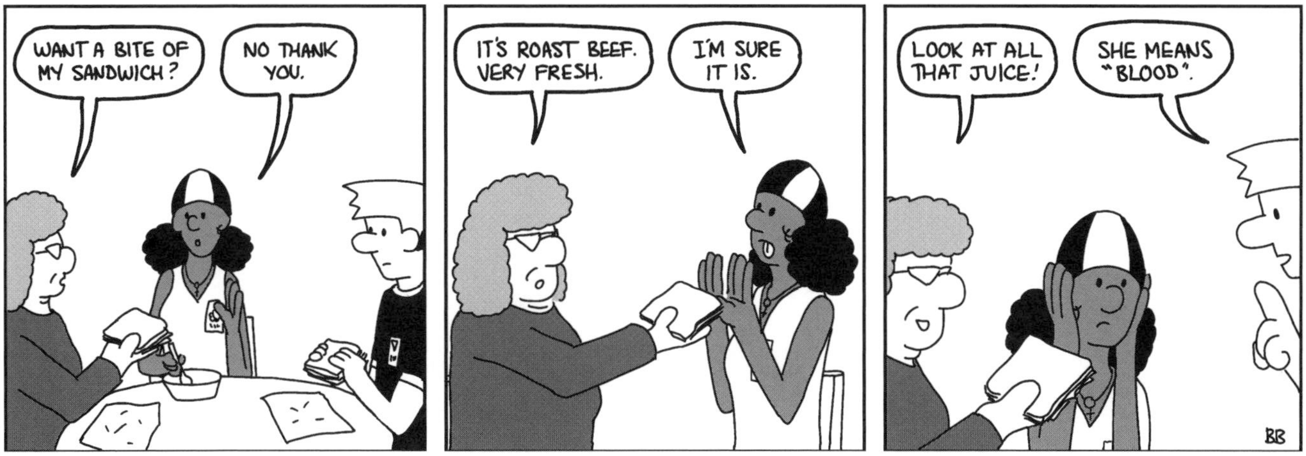
WANT A BITE OF MY SANDWICH?
NO THANK YOU.
IT'S ROAST BEEF. VERY FRESH.
I'M SURE IT IS.
LOOK AT ALL THAT JUICE!
SHE MEANS "BLOOD".
BB

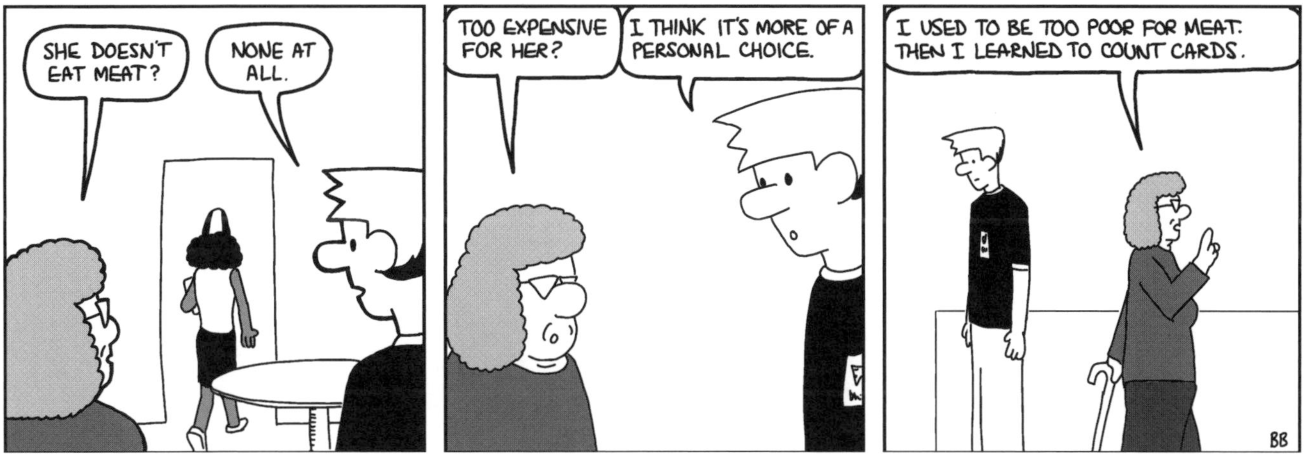
SHE DOESN'T EAT MEAT?
NONE AT ALL.
TOO EXPENSIVE FOR HER?
I THINK IT'S MORE OF A PERSONAL CHOICE.
I USED TO BE TOO POOR FOR MEAT. THEN I LEARNED TO COUNT CARDS.
BB

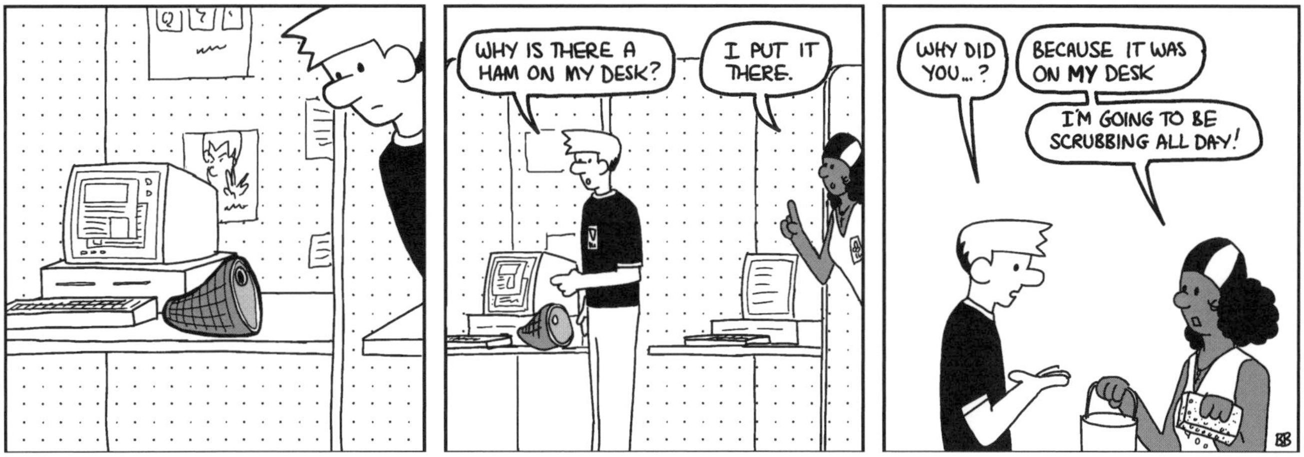
WHY IS THERE A HAM ON MY DESK?
I PUT IT THERE.
WHY DID YOU...?
BECAUSE IT WAS ON MY DESK
I'M GOING TO BE SCRUBBING ALL DAY!
BB

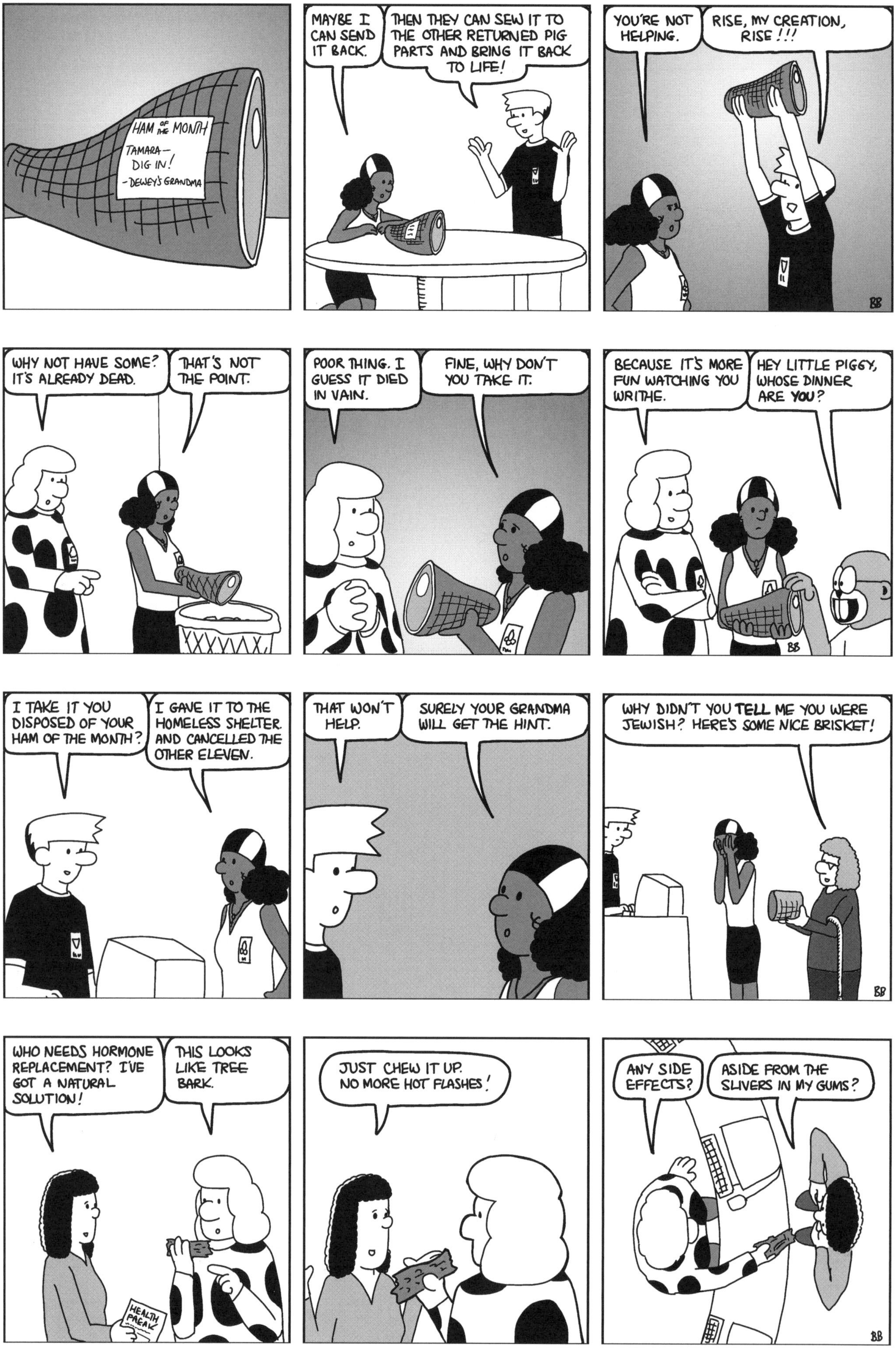
HAM OF THE MONTH
TAMARA— DIG IN!
-DEWEY'S GRANDMA
MAYBE I CAN SEND IT BACK.
THEN THEY CAN SEW IT TO THE OTHER RETURNED PIG PARTS AND BRING IT BACK TO LIFE!
YOU'RE NOT HELPING.
RISE, MY CREATION, RISE!!!
BB
WHY NOT HAVE SOME? IT'S ALREADY DEAD.
THAT'S NOT THE POINT.
POOR THING. I GUESS IT DIED IN VAIN.
FINE, WHY DON'T YOU TAKE IT.
BECAUSE IT'S MORE FUN WATCHING YOU WRITHE.
HEY LITTLE PIGGY, WHOSE DINNER ARE YOU?
BB
I TAKE IT YOU DISPOSED OF YOUR HAM OF THE MONTH?
I GAVE IT TO THE HOMELESS SHELTER. AND CANCELLED THE OTHER ELEVEN.
THAT WON'T HELP.
SURELY YOUR GRANDMA WILL GET THE HINT.
WHY DIDN'T YOU TELL ME YOU WERE JEWISH? HERE'S SOME NICE BRISKET!
BB
WHO NEEDS HORMONE REPLACEMENT? I'VE GOT A NATURAL SOLUTION!
THIS LOOKS LIKE TREE BARK.
HEALTH FREAK
JUST CHEW IT UP. NO MORE HOT FLASHES!
ANY SIDE EFFECTS?
ASIDE FROM THE SLIVERS IN MY GUMS?
BB

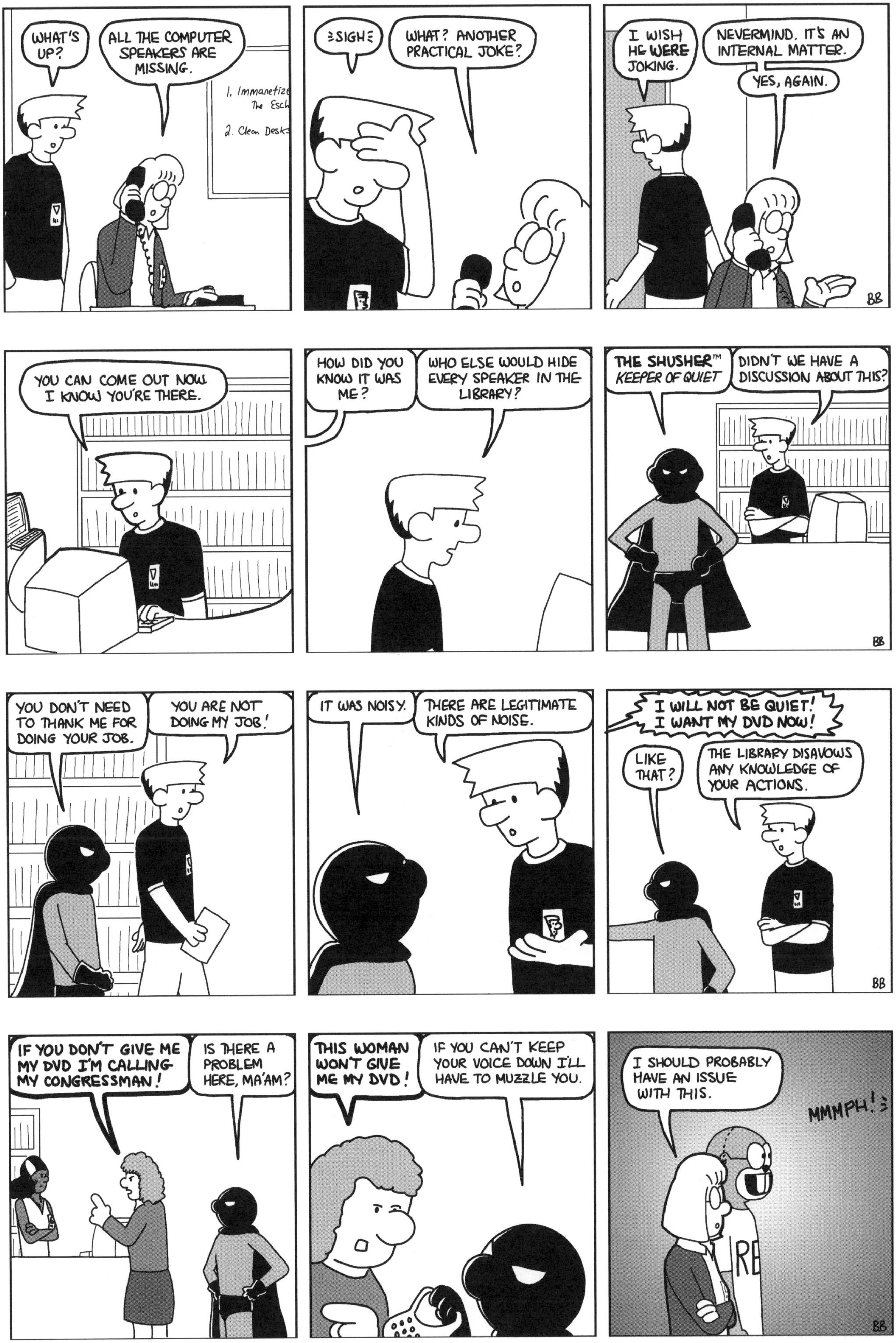
WHAT'S UP?
ALL THE COMPUTER SPEAKERS ARE MISSING.
1. Immanetize The Esch
2. Clean Desks
SIGH
WHAT? ANOTHER PRACTICAL JOKE?
I WISH HE WERE JOKING.
NEVERMIND. IT'S AN INTERNAL MATTER.
YES, AGAIN.
BB
YOU CAN COME OUT NOW. I KNOW YOU'RE THERE.
HOW DID YOU KNOW IT WAS ME?
WHO ELSE WOULD HIDE EVERY SPEAKER IN THE LIBRARY?
THE SHUSHER™ KEEPER OF QUIET
DIDN'T WE HAVE A DISCUSSION ABOUT THIS?
BB
YOU DON'T NEED TO THANK ME FOR DOING YOUR JOB.
YOU ARE NOT DOING MY JOB!
IT WAS NOISY.
THERE ARE LEGITIMATE KINDS OF NOISE.
I WILL NOT BE QUIET! I WANT MY DVD NOW!
LIKE THAT?
THE LIBRARY DISAVOWS ANY KNOWLEDGE OF YOUR ACTIONS.
BB
IF YOU DON'T GIVE ME MY DVD I'M CALLING MY CONGRESSMAN!
IS THERE A PROBLEM HERE, MA'AM?
THIS WOMAN WON'T GIVE ME MY DVD!
IF YOU CAN'T KEEP YOUR VOICE DOWN I'LL HAVE TO MUZZLE YOU.
I SHOULD PROBABLY HAVE AN ISSUE WITH THIS.
MMMPH!
BB

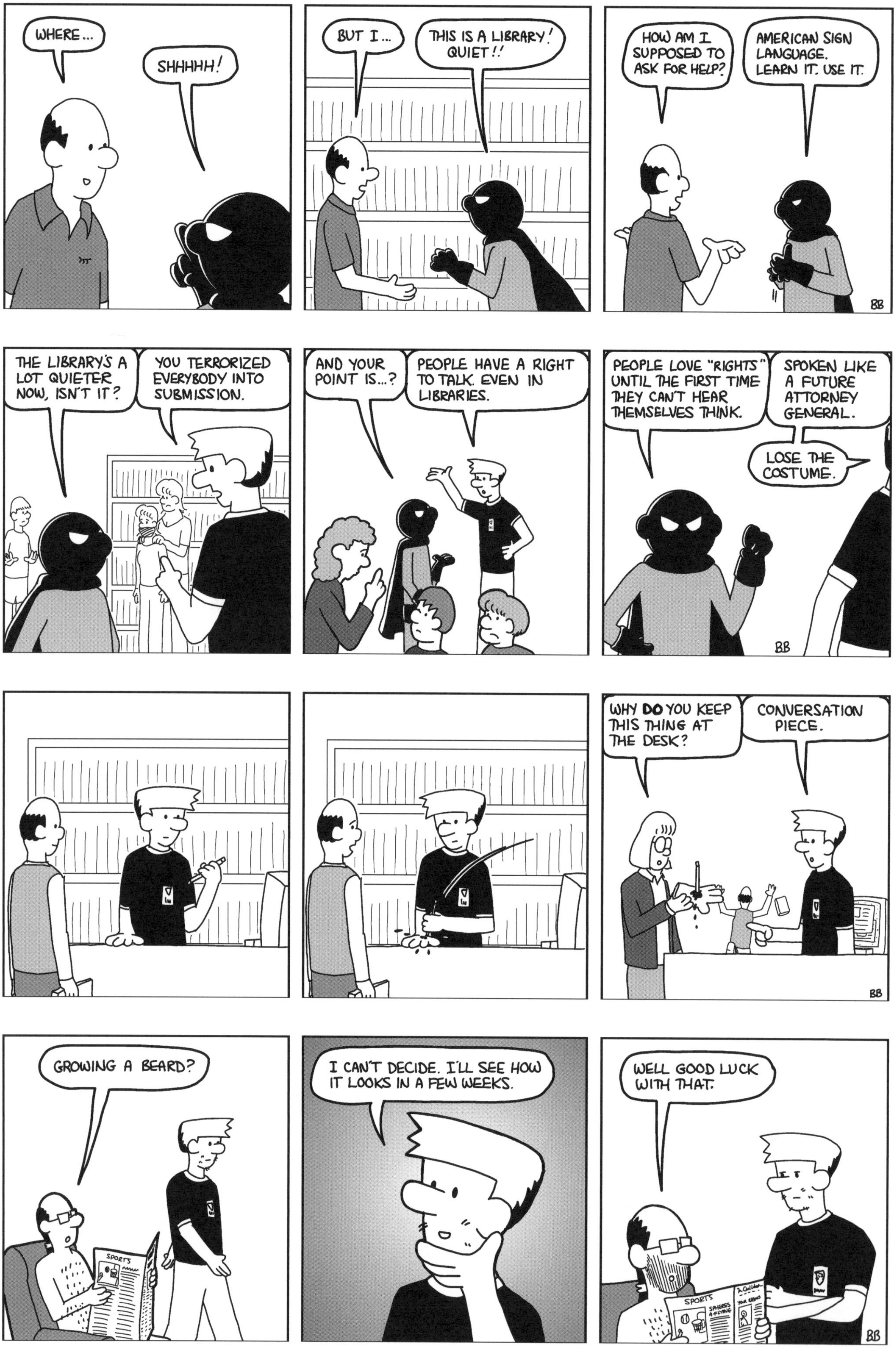
WHERE...
SHHHHH!
BUT I...
THIS IS A LIBRARY! QUIET!!
HOW AM I SUPPOSED TO ASK FOR HELP?
AMERICAN SIGN LANGUAGE. LEARN IT. USE IT.
BB
THE LIBRARY'S A LOT QUIETER NOW, ISN'T IT?
YOU TERRORIZED EVERYBODY INTO SUBMISSION.
AND YOUR POINT IS...?
PEOPLE HAVE A RIGHT TO TALK. EVEN IN LIBRARIES.
PEOPLE LOVE "RIGHTS" UNTIL THE FIRST TIME THEY CAN'T HEAR THEMSELVES THINK.
SPOKEN LIKE A FUTURE ATTORNEY GENERAL.
LOSE THE COSTUME.
BB
WHY DO YOU KEEP THIS THING AT THE DESK?
CONVERSATION PIECE.
BB
GROWING A BEARD?
I CAN'T DECIDE. I'LL SEE HOW IT LOOKS IN A FEW WEEKS.
WELL GOOD LUCK WITH THAT.
BB

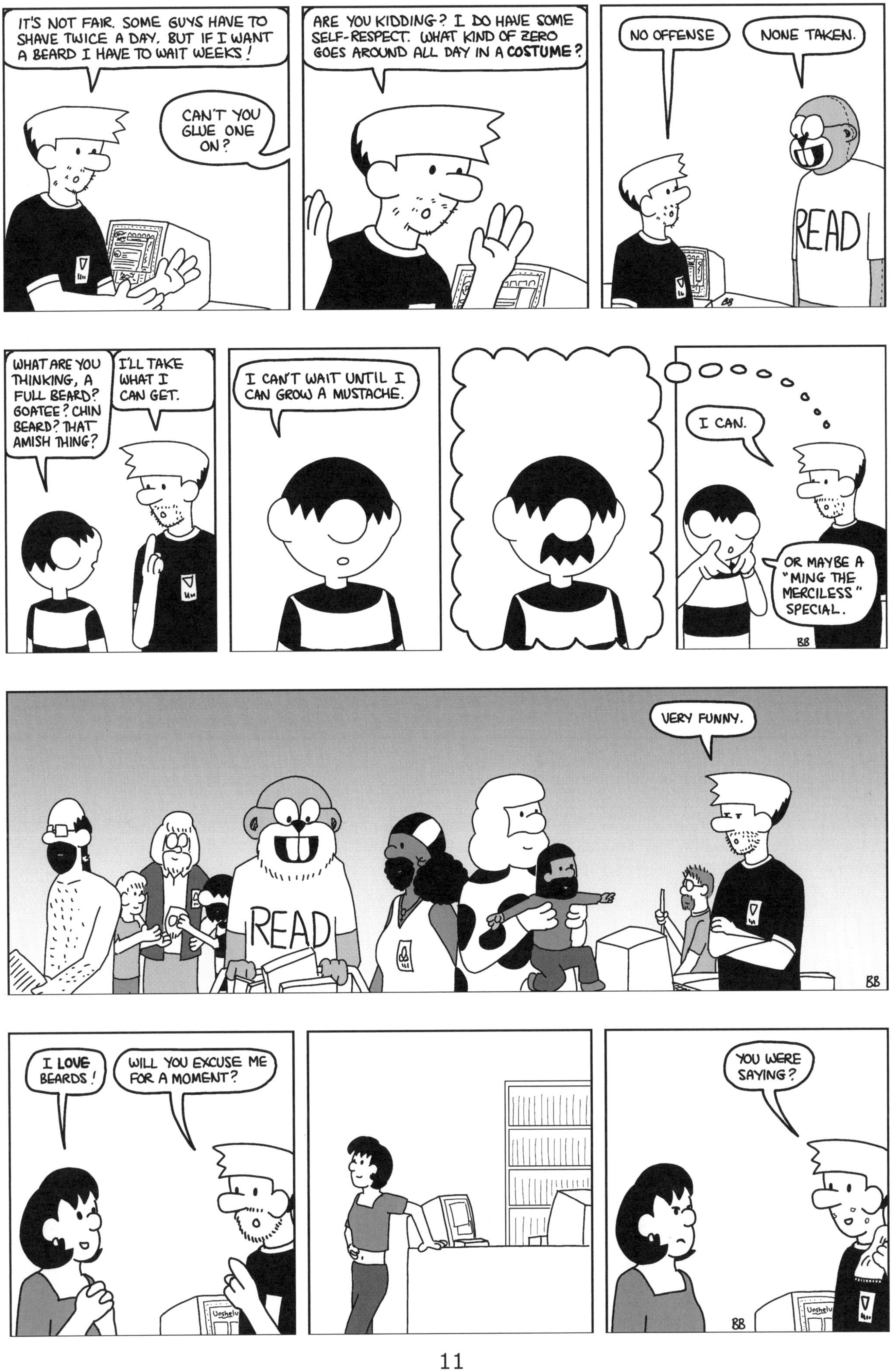
IT'S NOT FAIR. SOME GUYS HAVE TO SHAVE TWICE A DAY. BUT IF I WANT A BEARD I HAVE TO WAIT WEEKS!
CAN'T YOU GLUE ONE ON?
ARE YOU KIDDING? I DO HAVE SOME SELF-RESPECT. WHAT KIND OF ZERO GOES AROUND ALL DAY IN A **COSTUME**?
NO OFFENSE
NONE TAKEN.
READ
WHAT ARE YOU THINKING, A FULL BEARD? GOATEE? CHIN BEARD? THAT AMISH THING?
I'LL TAKE WHAT I CAN GET.
I CAN'T WAIT UNTIL I CAN GROW A MUSTACHE.
I CAN.
OR MAYBE A "MING THE MERCILESS" SPECIAL.
VERY FUNNY.
READ
I **LOVE** BEARDS!
WILL YOU EXCUSE ME FOR A MOMENT?
YOU WERE SAYING?

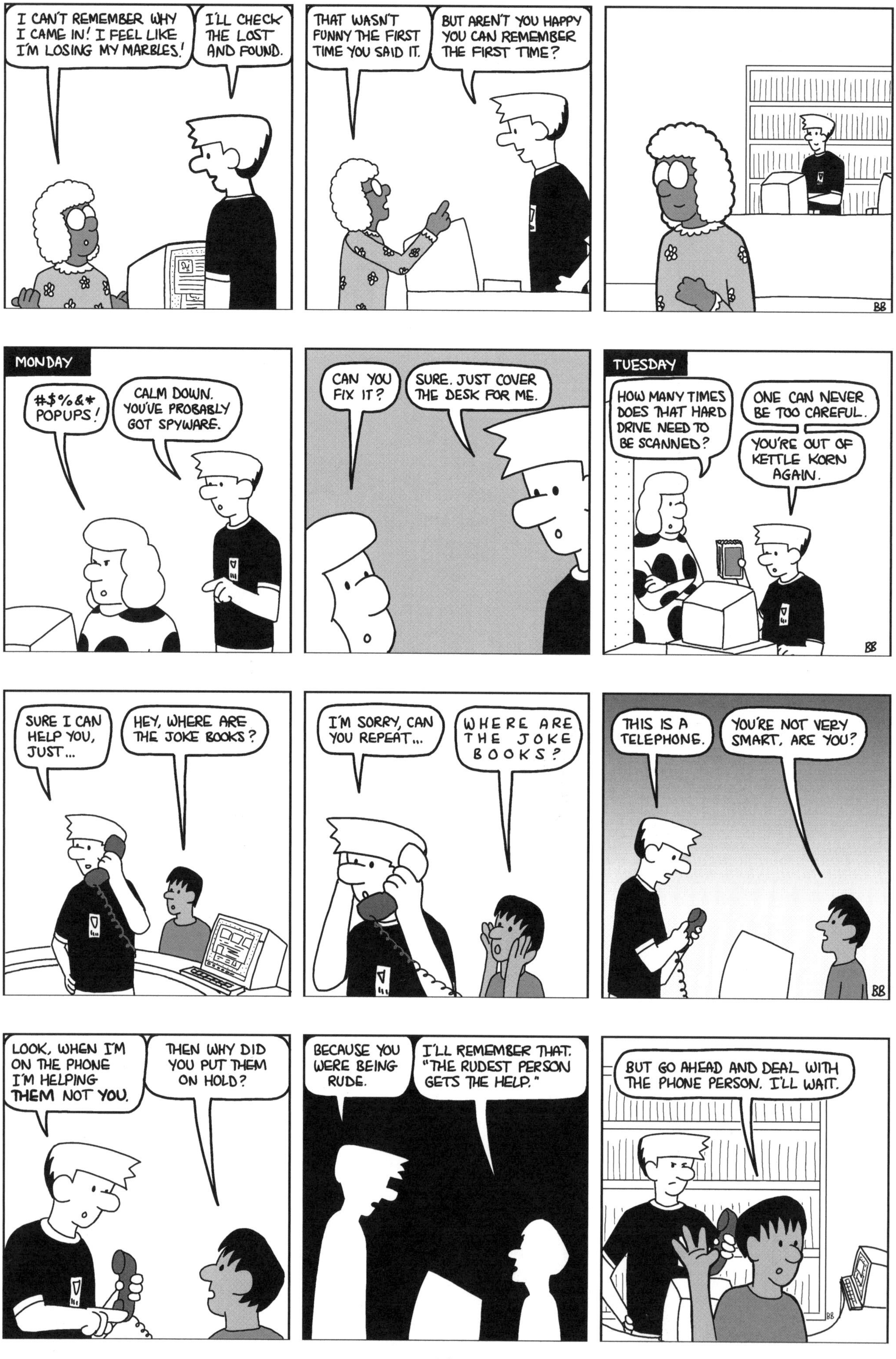

I CAN'T REMEMBER WHY I CAME IN! I FEEL LIKE I'M LOSING MY MARBLES!
I'LL CHECK THE LOST AND FOUND.
THAT WASN'T FUNNY THE FIRST TIME YOU SAID IT.
BUT AREN'T YOU HAPPY YOU CAN REMEMBER THE FIRST TIME?
BB
MONDAY
#$%&* POPUPS!
CALM DOWN. YOU'VE PROBABLY GOT SPYWARE.
CAN YOU FIX IT?
SURE. JUST COVER THE DESK FOR ME.
TUESDAY
HOW MANY TIMES DOES THAT HARD DRIVE NEED TO BE SCANNED?
ONE CAN NEVER BE TOO CAREFUL.
YOU'RE OUT OF KETTLE KORN AGAIN.
BB
SURE I CAN HELP YOU, JUST...
HEY, WHERE ARE THE JOKE BOOKS?
I'M SORRY, CAN YOU REPEAT...
WHERE ARE THE JOKE BOOKS?
THIS IS A TELEPHONE.
YOU'RE NOT VERY SMART, ARE YOU?
BB
LOOK, WHEN I'M ON THE PHONE I'M HELPING THEM NOT YOU.
THEN WHY DID YOU PUT THEM ON HOLD?
BECAUSE YOU WERE BEING RUDE.
I'LL REMEMBER THAT. "THE RUDEST PERSON GETS THE HELP."
BUT GO AHEAD AND DEAL WITH THE PHONE PERSON. I'LL WAIT.
BB

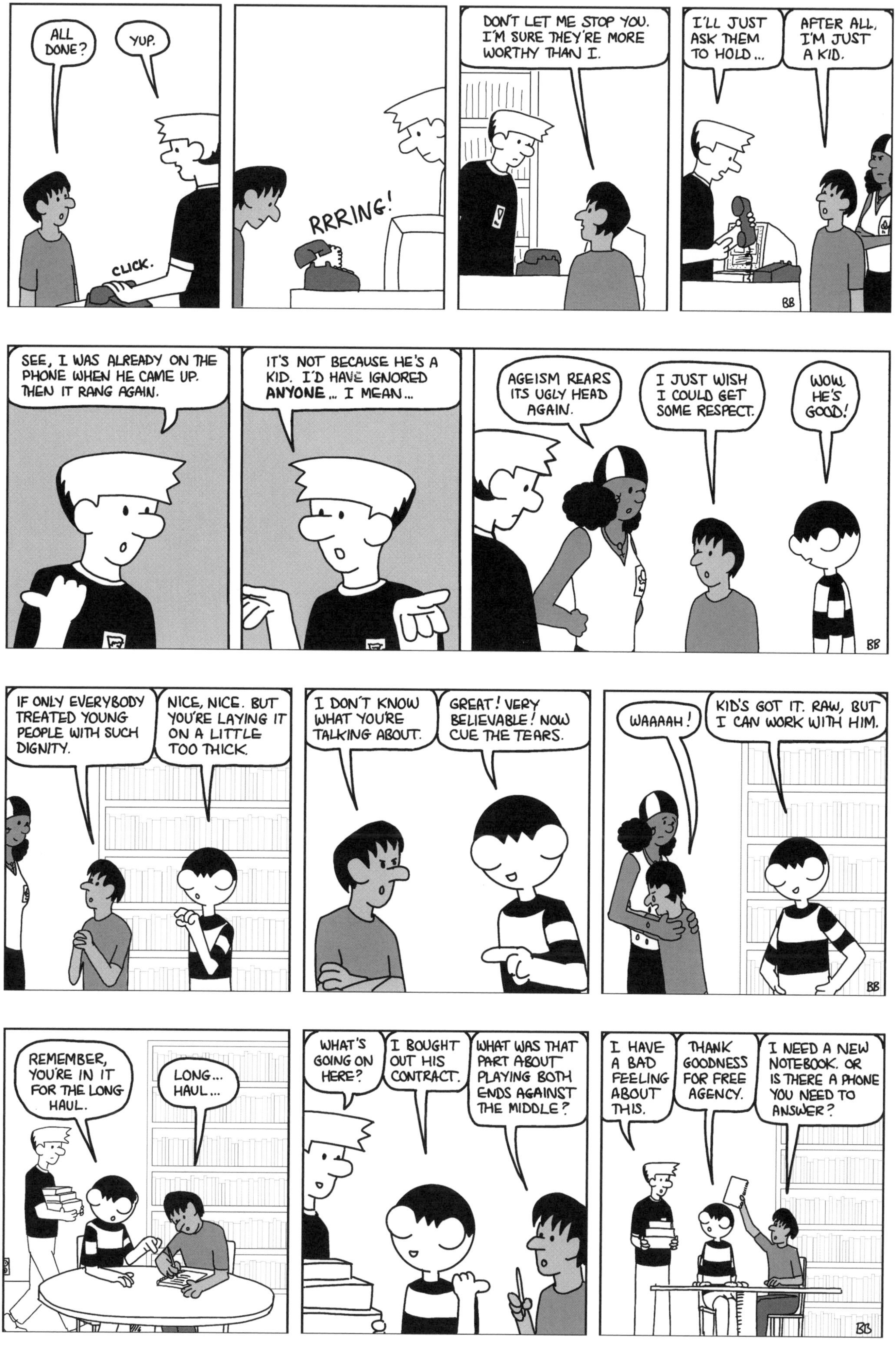
ALL DONE?
YUP.
CLICK.
RRRING!
DON'T LET ME STOP YOU. I'M SURE THEY'RE MORE WORTHY THAN I.
I'LL JUST ASK THEM TO HOLD...
AFTER ALL, I'M JUST A KID.
BB
SEE, I WAS ALREADY ON THE PHONE WHEN HE CAME UP. THEN IT RANG AGAIN.
IT'S NOT BECAUSE HE'S A KID. I'D HAVE IGNORED ANYONE... I MEAN...
AGEISM REARS ITS UGLY HEAD AGAIN.
I JUST WISH I COULD GET SOME RESPECT.
WOW, HE'S GOOD!
BB
IF ONLY EVERYBODY TREATED YOUNG PEOPLE WITH SUCH DIGNITY.
NICE, NICE. BUT YOU'RE LAYING IT ON A LITTLE TOO THICK.
I DON'T KNOW WHAT YOU'RE TALKING ABOUT.
GREAT! VERY BELIEVABLE! NOW CUE THE TEARS.
WAAAAH!
KID'S GOT IT. RAW, BUT I CAN WORK WITH HIM.
BB
REMEMBER, YOU'RE IN IT FOR THE LONG HAUL.
LONG... HAUL...
WHAT'S GOING ON HERE?
I BOUGHT OUT HIS CONTRACT.
WHAT WAS THAT PART ABOUT PLAYING BOTH ENDS AGAINST THE MIDDLE?
I HAVE A BAD FEELING ABOUT THIS.
THANK GOODNESS FOR FREE AGENCY.
I NEED A NEW NOTEBOOK. OR IS THERE A PHONE YOU NEED TO ANSWER?
BB

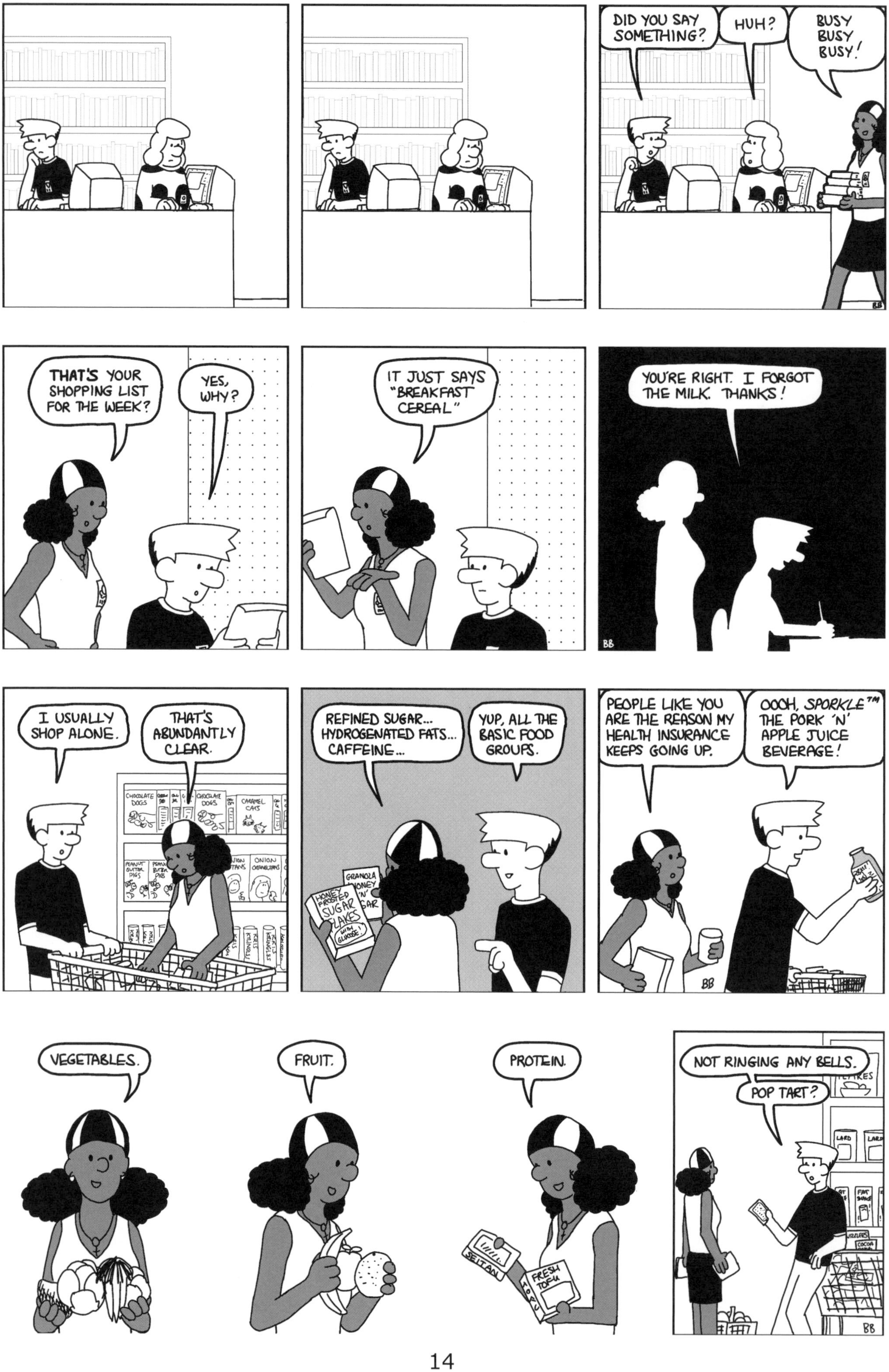
DID YOU SAY SOMETHING?
HUH?
BUSY BUSY BUSY!
THAT'S YOUR SHOPPING LIST FOR THE WEEK?
YES, WHY?
IT JUST SAYS "BREAKFAST CEREAL"
YOU'RE RIGHT. I FORGOT THE MILK. THANKS!
I USUALLY SHOP ALONE.
THAT'S ABUNDANTLY CLEAR.
CHOCOLATE DOGS
CARAMEL CATS
REFINED SUGAR... HYDROGENATED FATS... CAFFEINE...
YUP, ALL THE BASIC FOOD GROUPS.
HONEY FROSTED SUGAR FLAKES
WITH GLUCOSE!
PEOPLE LIKE YOU ARE THE REASON MY HEALTH INSURANCE KEEPS GOING UP.
OOOH, SPORKLE™ THE PORK 'N' APPLE JUICE BEVERAGE!
VEGETABLES.
FRUIT.
PROTEIN.
SEITAN
FRESH TOFU
NOT RINGING ANY BELLS.
POP TART?
LARD

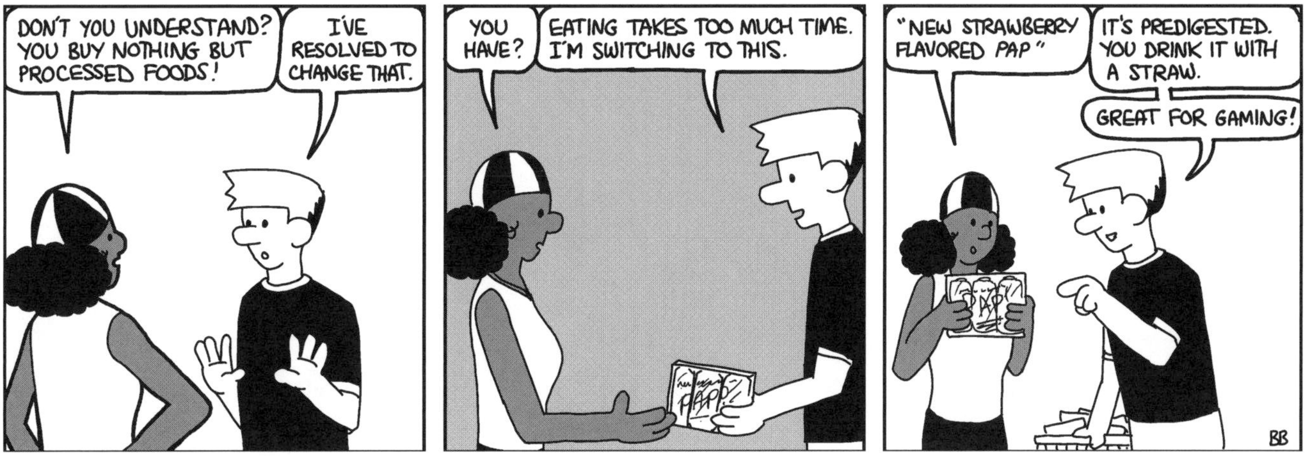
DON'T YOU UNDERSTAND? YOU BUY NOTHING BUT PROCESSED FOODS!
I'VE RESOLVED TO CHANGE THAT.
YOU HAVE?
EATING TAKES TOO MUCH TIME. I'M SWITCHING TO THIS.
PAP
"NEW STRAWBERRY FLAVORED *PAP*"
IT'S PREDIGESTED. YOU DRINK IT WITH A STRAW.
GREAT FOR GAMING!
BB

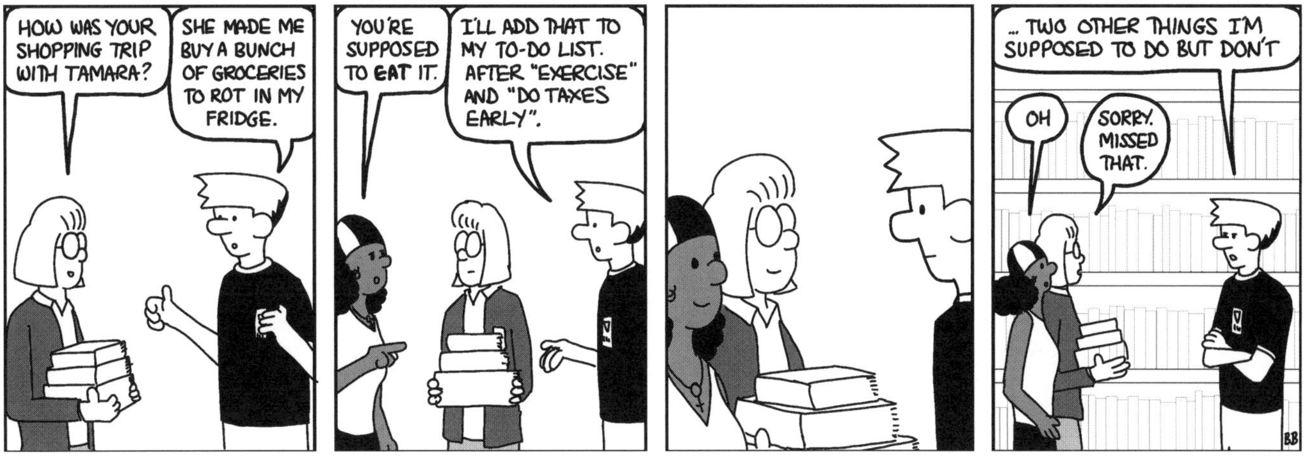
HOW WAS YOUR SHOPPING TRIP WITH TAMARA?
SHE MADE ME BUY A BUNCH OF GROCERIES TO ROT IN MY FRIDGE.
YOU'RE SUPPOSED TO **EAT** IT.
I'LL ADD THAT TO MY TO-DO LIST. AFTER "EXERCISE" AND "DO TAXES EARLY".
... TWO OTHER THINGS I'M SUPPOSED TO DO BUT DON'T
OH
SORRY. MISSED THAT.
BB

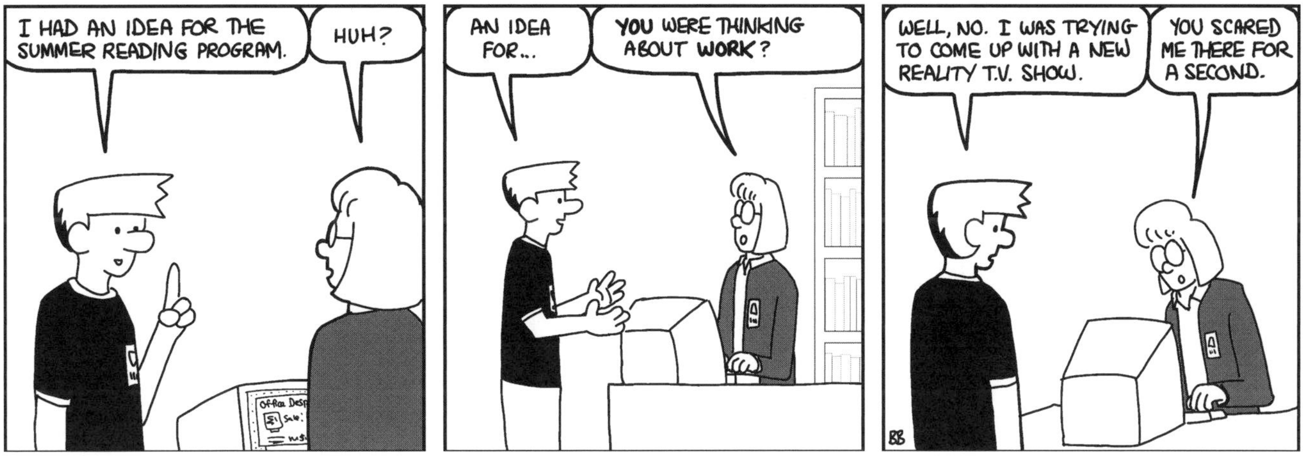
I HAD AN IDEA FOR THE SUMMER READING PROGRAM.
HUH?
AN IDEA FOR...
YOU WERE THINKING ABOUT **WORK**?
WELL, NO. I WAS TRYING TO COME UP WITH A NEW REALITY T.V. SHOW.
YOU SCARED ME THERE FOR A SECOND.
BB

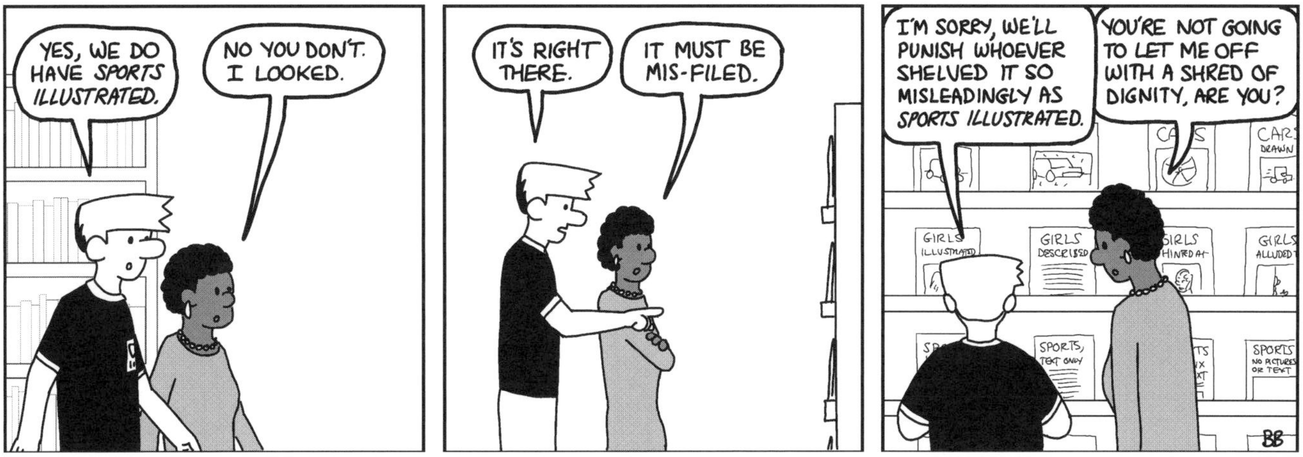
YES, WE DO HAVE *SPORTS ILLUSTRATED*.
NO YOU DON'T. I LOOKED.
IT'S RIGHT THERE.
IT MUST BE MIS-FILED.
I'M SORRY, WE'LL PUNISH WHOEVER SHELVED IT SO MISLEADINGLY AS *SPORTS ILLUSTRATED*.
YOU'RE NOT GOING TO LET ME OFF WITH A SHRED OF DIGNITY, ARE YOU?
CARS DRAWN
GIRLS ILLUSTRATED
GIRLS DESCRIBED
GIRLS HINTED AT
SPORTS, TEXT ONLY
SPORTS NO PICTURES OR TEXT
BB

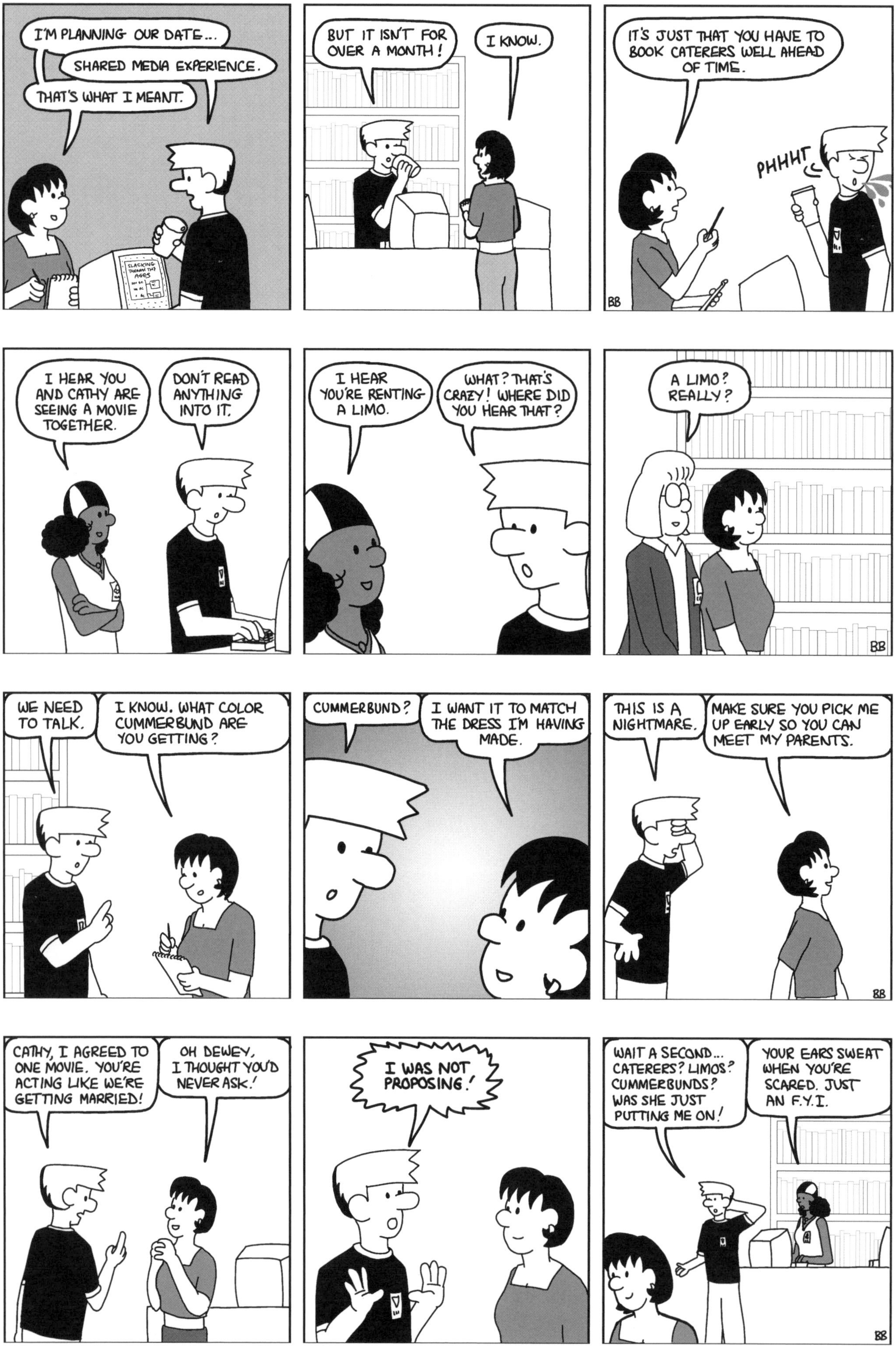
I'M PLANNING OUR DATE...
SHARED MEDIA EXPERIENCE.
THAT'S WHAT I MEANT.
BUT IT ISN'T FOR OVER A MONTH!
I KNOW.
IT'S JUST THAT YOU HAVE TO BOOK CATERERS WELL AHEAD OF TIME.
PHHHT
BB
I HEAR YOU AND CATHY ARE SEEING A MOVIE TOGETHER.
DON'T READ ANYTHING INTO IT.
I HEAR YOU'RE RENTING A LIMO.
WHAT? THAT'S CRAZY! WHERE DID YOU HEAR THAT?
A LIMO? REALLY?
BB
WE NEED TO TALK.
I KNOW. WHAT COLOR CUMMERBUND ARE YOU GETTING?
CUMMERBUND?
I WANT IT TO MATCH THE DRESS I'M HAVING MADE.
THIS IS A NIGHTMARE.
MAKE SURE YOU PICK ME UP EARLY SO YOU CAN MEET MY PARENTS.
BB
CATHY, I AGREED TO ONE MOVIE. YOU'RE ACTING LIKE WE'RE GETTING MARRIED!
OH DEWEY, I THOUGHT YOU'D NEVER ASK!
I WAS NOT PROPOSING!
WAIT A SECOND... CATERERS? LIMOS? CUMMERBUNDS? WAS SHE JUST PUTTING ME ON!
YOUR EARS SWEAT WHEN YOU'RE SCARED. JUST AN F.Y.I.
BB

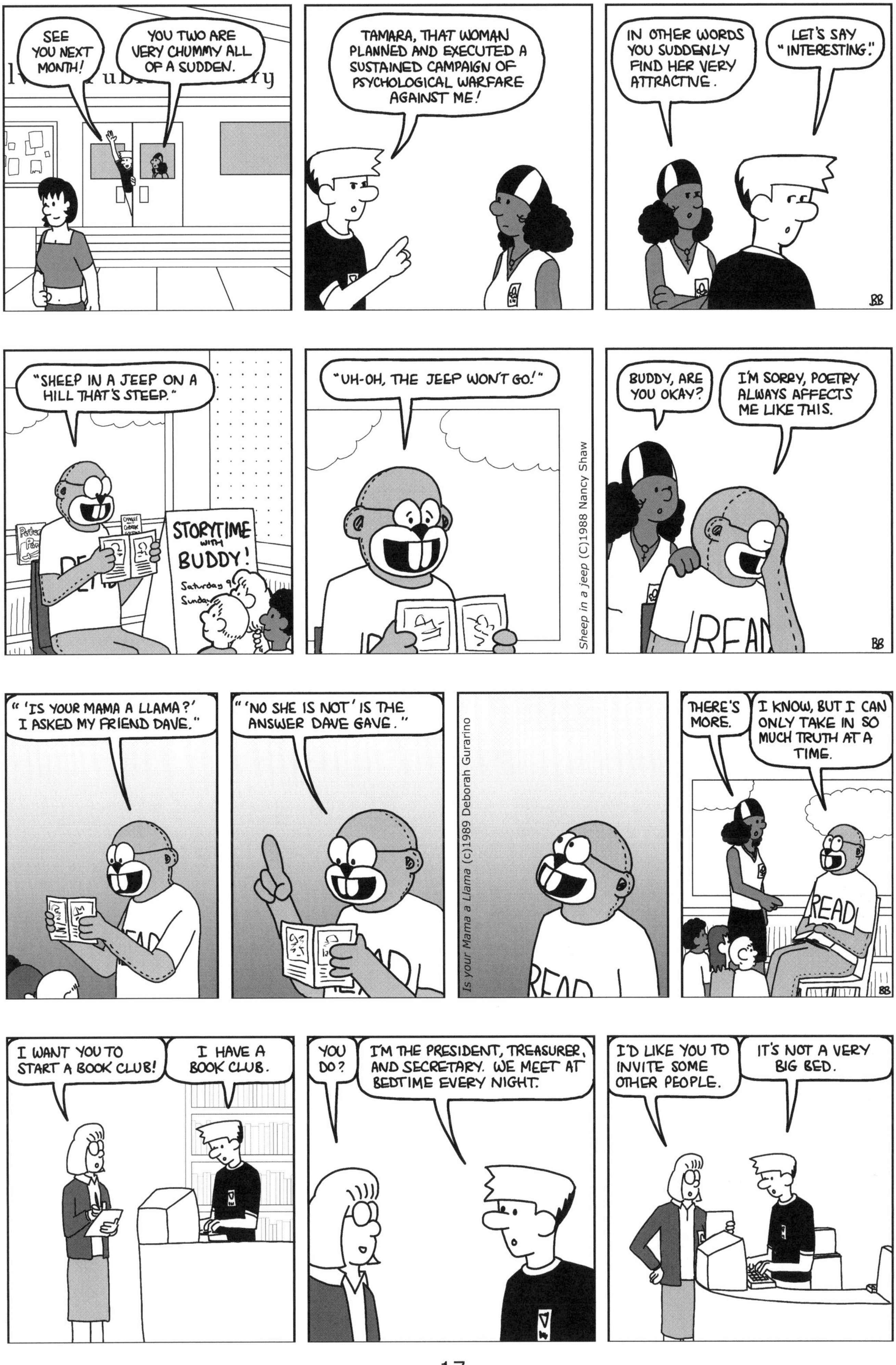
SEE YOU NEXT MONTH!
YOU TWO ARE VERY CHUMMY ALL OF A SUDDEN.
TAMARA, THAT WOMAN PLANNED AND EXECUTED A SUSTAINED CAMPAIGN OF PSYCHOLOGICAL WARFARE AGAINST ME!
IN OTHER WORDS YOU SUDDENLY FIND HER VERY ATTRACTIVE.
LET'S SAY "INTERESTING."
BB
"SHEEP IN A JEEP ON A HILL THAT'S STEEP."
STORYTIME with BUDDY!
Saturday 9
Sunday
"UH-OH, THE JEEP WON'T GO!"
Sheep in a jeep (C)1988 Nancy Shaw
BUDDY, ARE YOU OKAY?
I'M SORRY, POETRY ALWAYS AFFECTS ME LIKE THIS.
READ
BB
" 'IS YOUR MAMA A LLAMA?' I ASKED MY FRIEND DAVE."
" 'NO SHE IS NOT' IS THE ANSWER DAVE GAVE."
Is your Mama a Llama (c)1989 Deborah Gurarino
THERE'S MORE.
I KNOW, BUT I CAN ONLY TAKE IN SO MUCH TRUTH AT A TIME.
READ
BB
I WANT YOU TO START A BOOK CLUB!
I HAVE A BOOK CLUB.
YOU DO?
I'M THE PRESIDENT, TREASURER, AND SECRETARY. WE MEET AT BEDTIME EVERY NIGHT.
I'D LIKE YOU TO INVITE SOME OTHER PEOPLE.
IT'S NOT A VERY BIG BED.

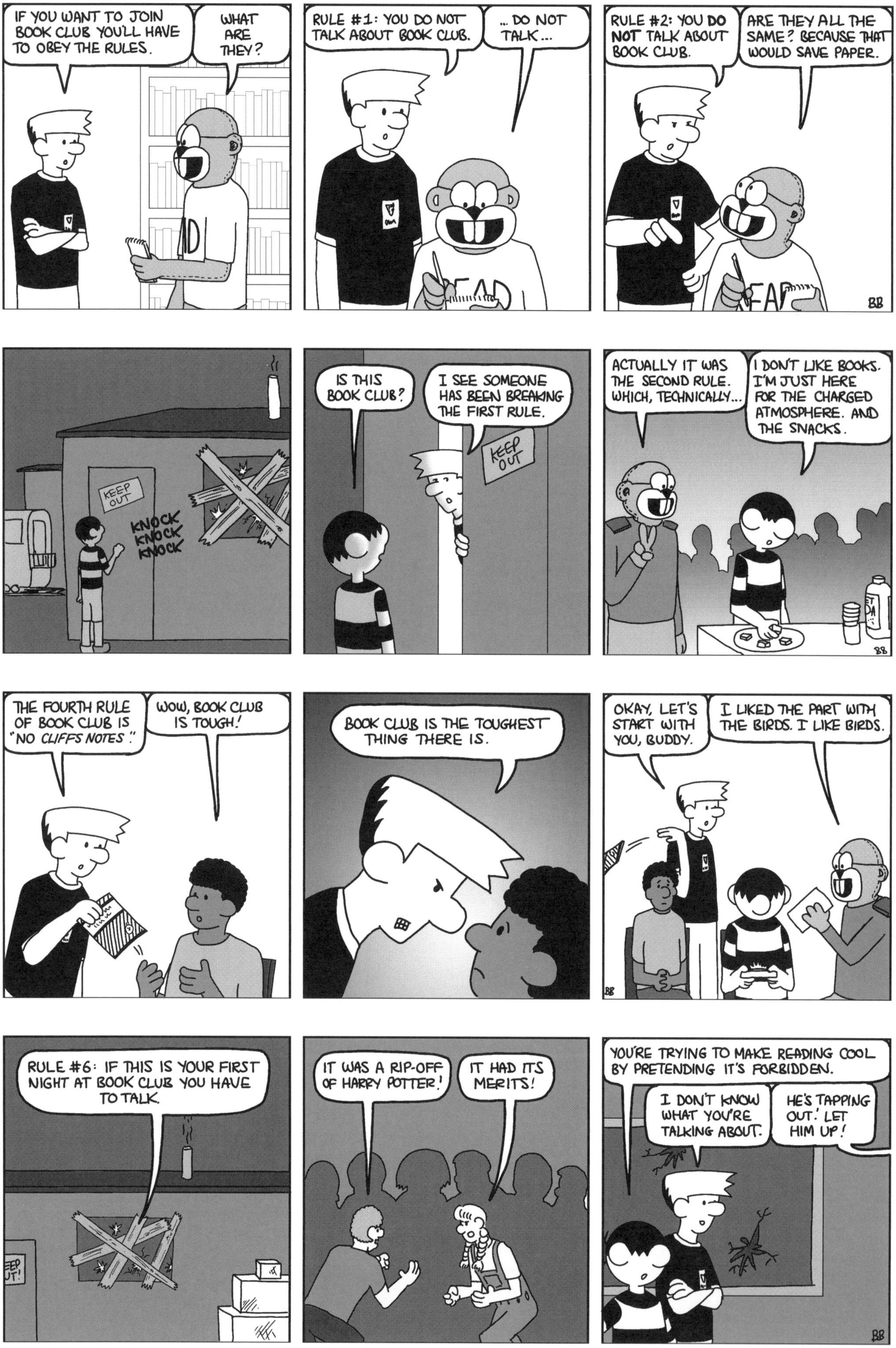
IF YOU WANT TO JOIN BOOK CLUB YOU'LL HAVE TO OBEY THE RULES.
WHAT ARE THEY?
RULE #1: YOU DO NOT TALK ABOUT BOOK CLUB.
... DO NOT TALK...
RULE #2: YOU DO NOT TALK ABOUT BOOK CLUB.
ARE THEY ALL THE SAME? BECAUSE THAT WOULD SAVE PAPER.
KEEP OUT
KNOCK KNOCK KNOCK
IS THIS BOOK CLUB?
I SEE SOMEONE HAS BEEN BREAKING THE FIRST RULE.
KEEP OUT
ACTUALLY IT WAS THE SECOND RULE. WHICH, TECHNICALLY...
I DON'T LIKE BOOKS. I'M JUST HERE FOR THE CHARGED ATMOSPHERE. AND THE SNACKS.
THE FOURTH RULE OF BOOK CLUB IS "NO CLIFFS NOTES."
WOW, BOOK CLUB IS TOUGH!
BOOK CLUB IS THE TOUGHEST THING THERE IS.
OKAY, LET'S START WITH YOU, BUDDY.
I LIKED THE PART WITH THE BIRDS. I LIKE BIRDS.
RULE #6: IF THIS IS YOUR FIRST NIGHT AT BOOK CLUB YOU HAVE TO TALK.
IT WAS A RIP-OFF OF HARRY POTTER!
IT HAD ITS MERITS!
YOU'RE TRYING TO MAKE READING COOL BY PRETENDING IT'S FORBIDDEN.
I DON'T KNOW WHAT YOU'RE TALKING ABOUT.
HE'S TAPPING OUT! LET HIM UP!

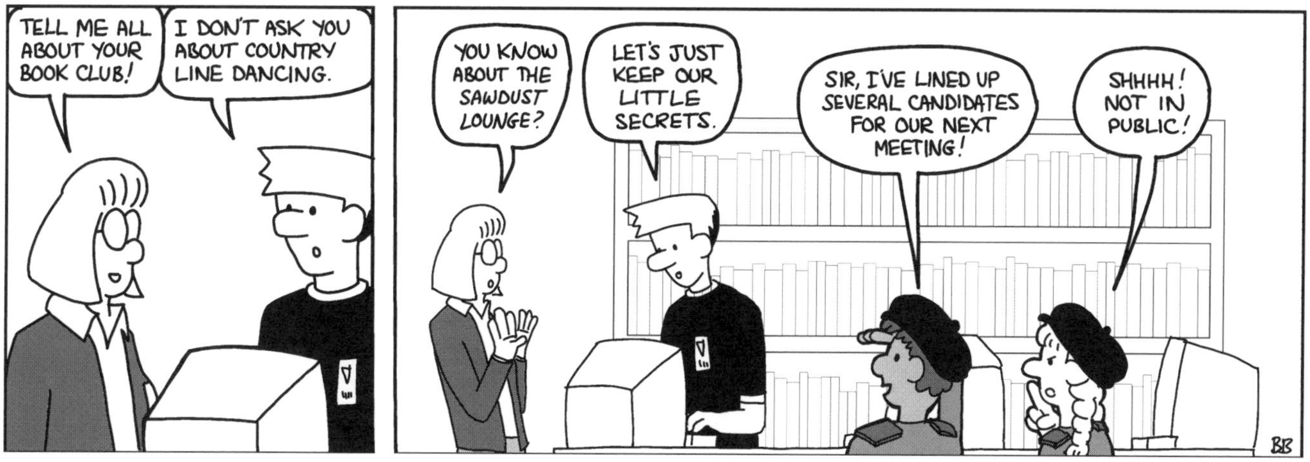
TELL ME ALL ABOUT YOUR BOOK CLUB!
I DON'T ASK YOU ABOUT COUNTRY LINE DANCING.
YOU KNOW ABOUT THE SAWDUST LOUNGE?
LET'S JUST KEEP OUR LITTLE SECRETS.
SIR, I'VE LINED UP SEVERAL CANDIDATES FOR OUR NEXT MEETING!
SHHHH! NOT IN PUBLIC!

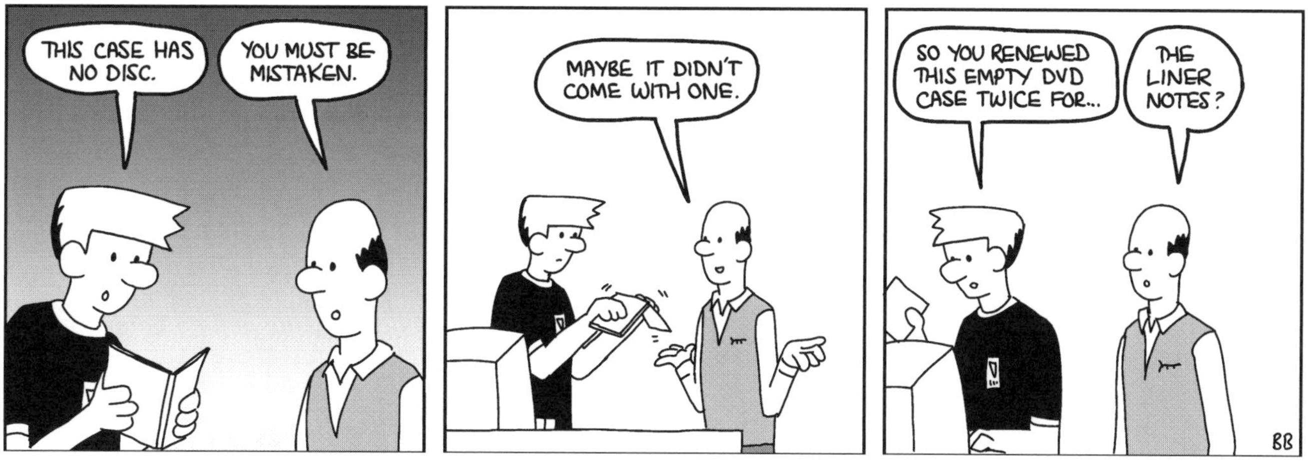
THIS CASE HAS NO DISC.
YOU MUST BE MISTAKEN.
MAYBE IT DIDN'T COME WITH ONE.
SO YOU RENEWED THIS EMPTY DVD CASE TWICE FOR...
THE LINER NOTES?

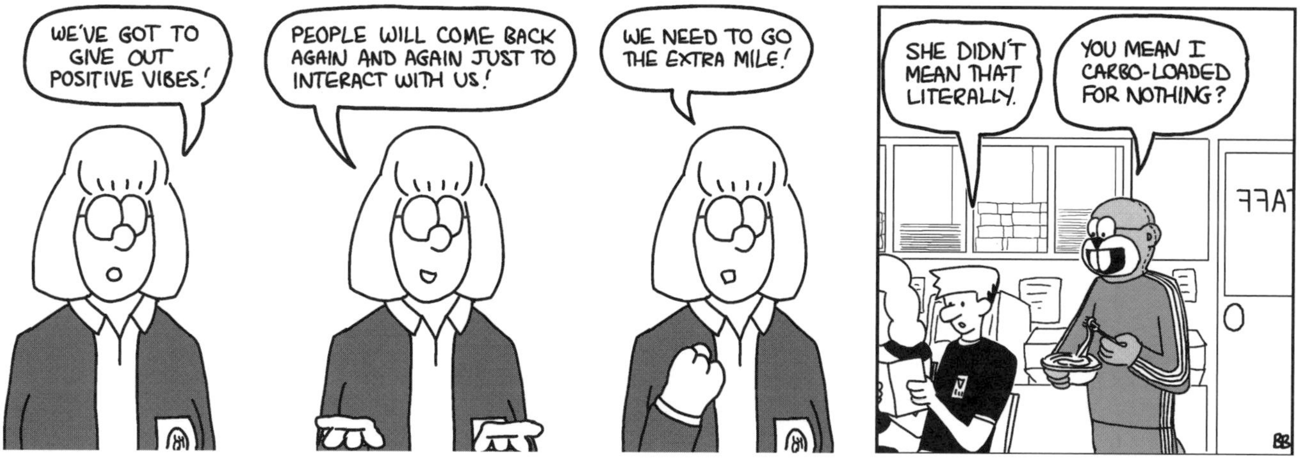
WE'VE GOT TO GIVE OUT POSITIVE VIBES!
PEOPLE WILL COME BACK AGAIN AND AGAIN JUST TO INTERACT WITH US!
WE NEED TO GO THE EXTRA MILE!
SHE DIDN'T MEAN THAT LITERALLY.
YOU MEAN I CARBO-LOADED FOR NOTHING?

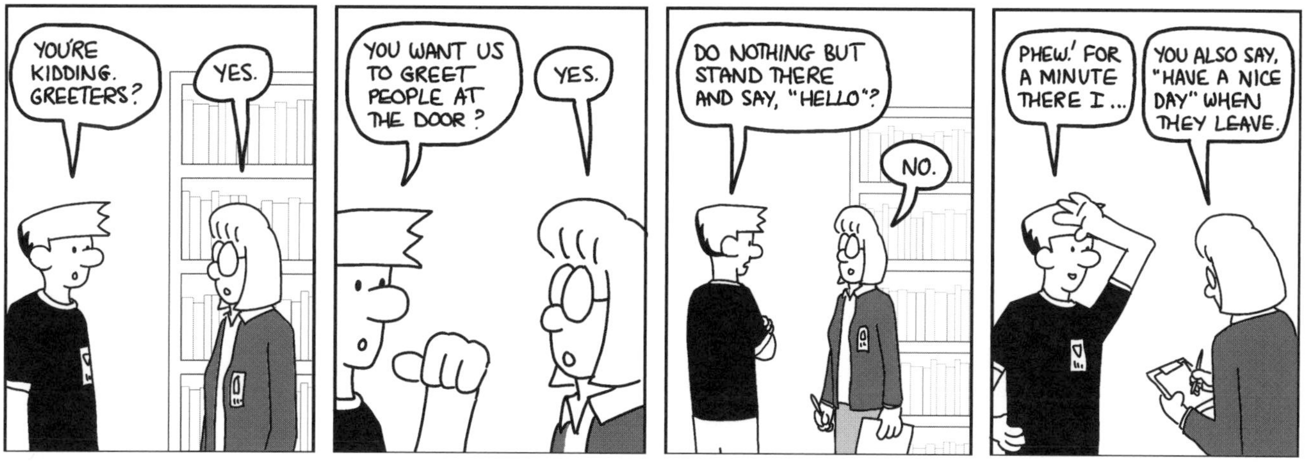
YOU'RE KIDDING. GREETERS?
YES.
YOU WANT US TO GREET PEOPLE AT THE DOOR?
YES.
DO NOTHING BUT STAND THERE AND SAY, "HELLO"?
NO.
PHEW! FOR A MINUTE THERE I...
YOU ALSO SAY, "HAVE A NICE DAY" WHEN THEY LEAVE.

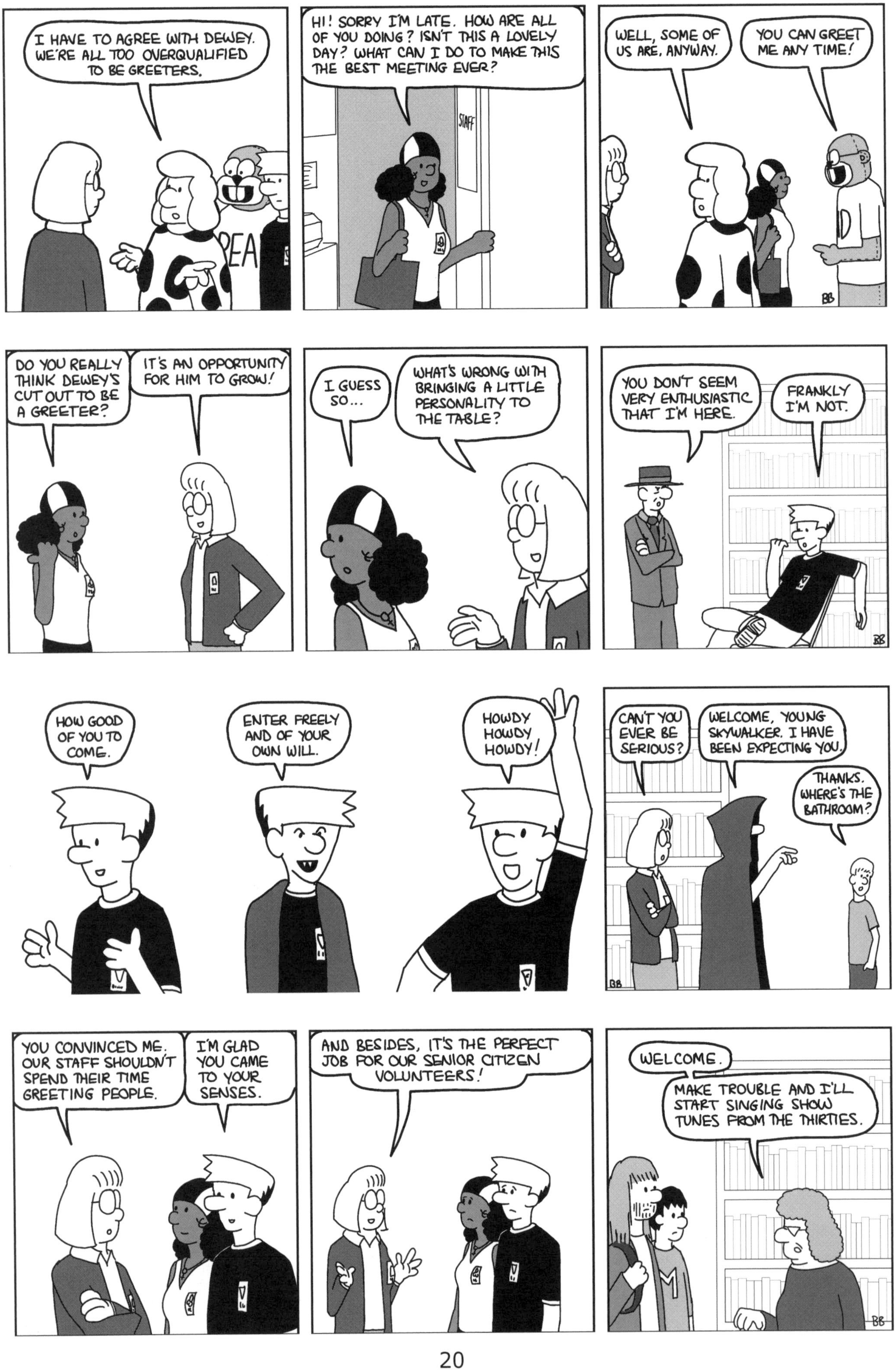

I HAVE TO AGREE WITH DEWEY. WE'RE ALL TOO OVERQUALIFIED TO BE GREETERS.
HI! SORRY I'M LATE. HOW ARE ALL OF YOU DOING? ISN'T THIS A LOVELY DAY? WHAT CAN I DO TO MAKE THIS THE BEST MEETING EVER?
STAFF
WELL, SOME OF US ARE, ANYWAY.
YOU CAN GREET ME ANY TIME!
BB
DO YOU REALLY THINK DEWEY'S CUT OUT TO BE A GREETER?
IT'S AN OPPORTUNITY FOR HIM TO GROW!
I GUESS SO...
WHAT'S WRONG WITH BRINGING A LITTLE PERSONALITY TO THE TABLE?
YOU DON'T SEEM VERY ENTHUSIASTIC THAT I'M HERE.
FRANKLY I'M NOT.
BB
HOW GOOD OF YOU TO COME.
ENTER FREELY AND OF YOUR OWN WILL.
HOWDY HOWDY HOWDY!
CAN'T YOU EVER BE SERIOUS?
WELCOME, YOUNG SKYWALKER. I HAVE BEEN EXPECTING YOU.
THANKS. WHERE'S THE BATHROOM?
BB
YOU CONVINCED ME. OUR STAFF SHOULDN'T SPEND THEIR TIME GREETING PEOPLE.
I'M GLAD YOU CAME TO YOUR SENSES.
AND BESIDES, IT'S THE PERFECT JOB FOR OUR SENIOR CITIZEN VOLUNTEERS!
WELCOME.
MAKE TROUBLE AND I'LL START SINGING SHOW TUNES FROM THE THIRTIES.
BB

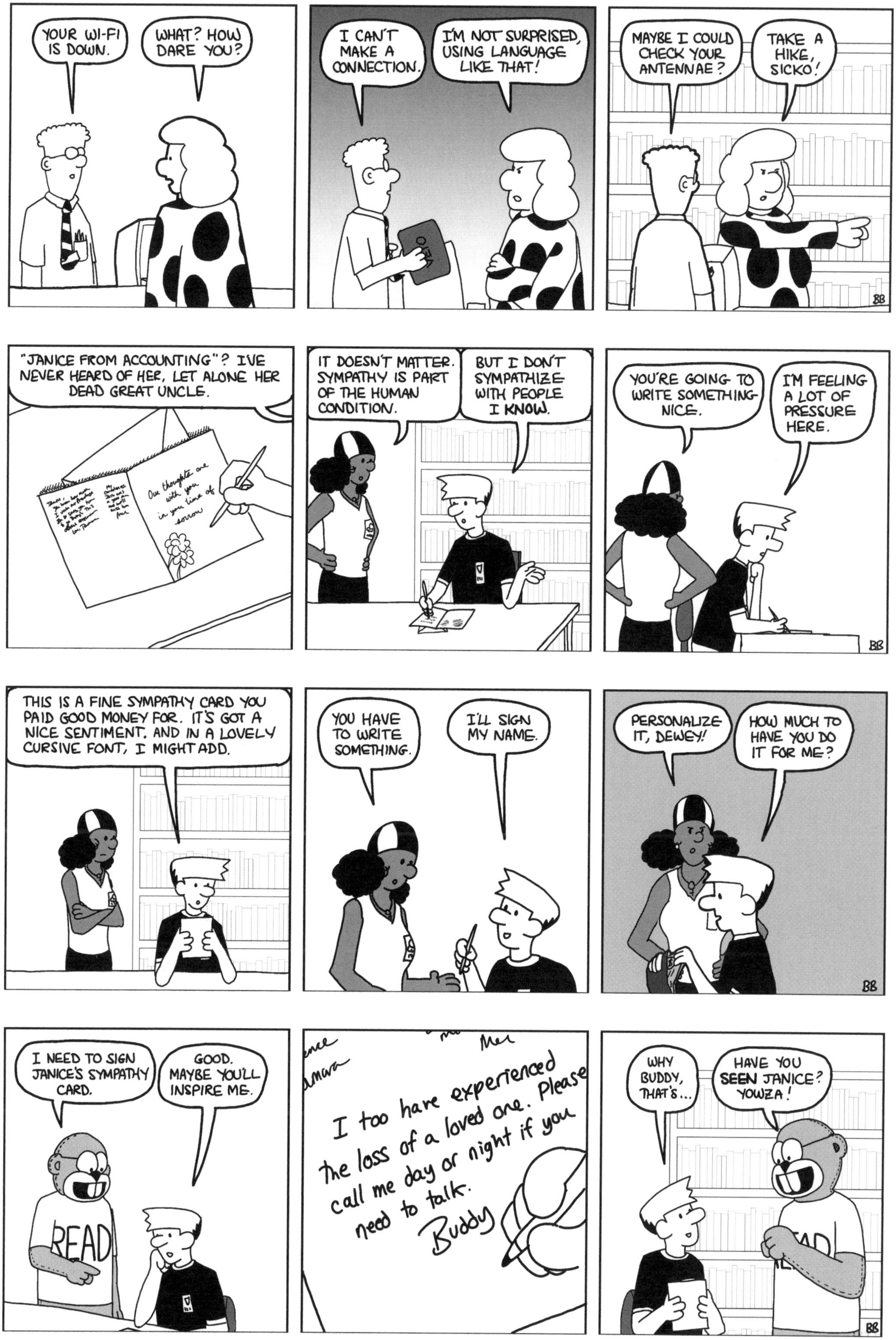

YOUR WI-FI IS DOWN.
WHAT? HOW DARE YOU?
I CAN'T MAKE A CONNECTION.
I'M NOT SURPRISED, USING LANGUAGE LIKE THAT!
MAYBE I COULD CHECK YOUR ANTENNAE?
TAKE A HIKE, SICKO!
"JANICE FROM ACCOUNTING"? I'VE NEVER HEARD OF HER, LET ALONE HER DEAD GREAT UNCLE.
Our thoughts are with you in your time of sorrow
IT DOESN'T MATTER. SYMPATHY IS PART OF THE HUMAN CONDITION.
BUT I DON'T SYMPATHIZE WITH PEOPLE I KNOW.
YOU'RE GOING TO WRITE SOMETHING NICE.
I'M FEELING A LOT OF PRESSURE HERE.
THIS IS A FINE SYMPATHY CARD YOU PAID GOOD MONEY FOR. IT'S GOT A NICE SENTIMENT. AND IN A LOVELY CURSIVE FONT, I MIGHT ADD.
YOU HAVE TO WRITE SOMETHING.
I'LL SIGN MY NAME.
PERSONALIZE IT, DEWEY!
HOW MUCH TO HAVE YOU DO IT FOR ME?
I NEED TO SIGN JANICE'S SYMPATHY CARD.
GOOD. MAYBE YOU'LL INSPIRE ME.
READ
I too have experienced the loss of a loved one. Please call me day or night if you need to talk.
Buddy
WHY BUDDY, THAT'S...
HAVE YOU SEEN JANICE? YOWZA!

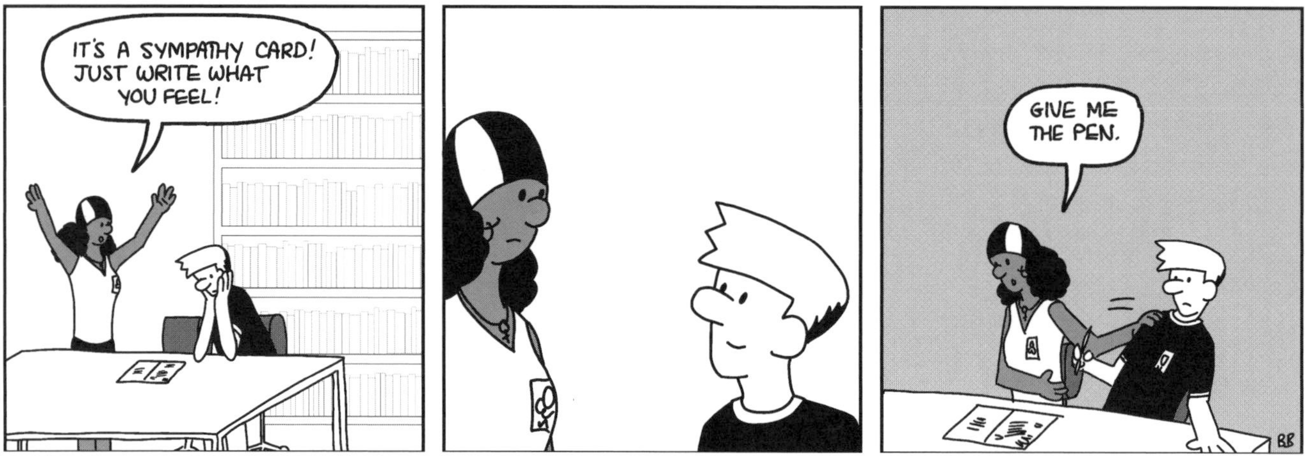
IT'S A SYMPATHY CARD! JUST WRITE WHAT YOU FEEL!
GIVE ME THE PEN.

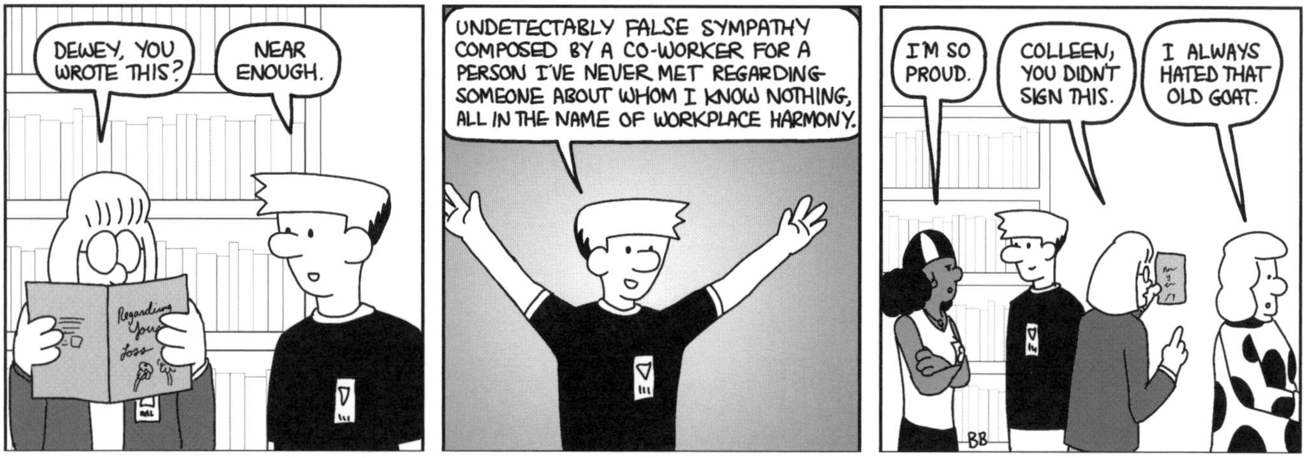
DEWEY, YOU WROTE THIS?
NEAR ENOUGH.
Regarding Your Loss
UNDETECTABLY FALSE SYMPATHY COMPOSED BY A CO-WORKER FOR A PERSON I'VE NEVER MET REGARDING SOMEONE ABOUT WHOM I KNOW NOTHING, ALL IN THE NAME OF WORKPLACE HARMONY.
I'M SO PROUD.
COLLEEN, YOU DIDN'T SIGN THIS.
I ALWAYS HATED THAT OLD GOAT.

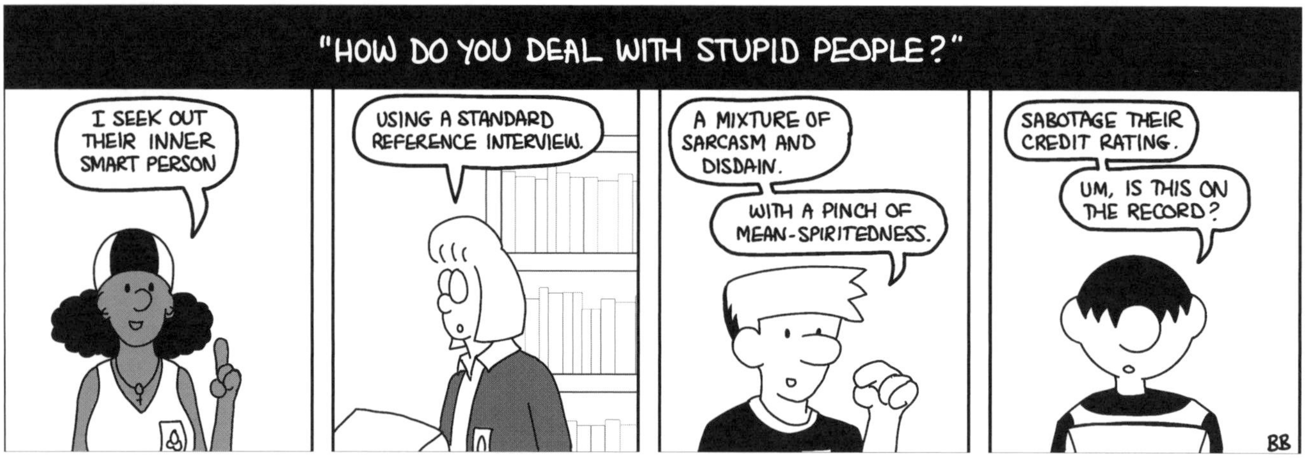
"HOW DO YOU DEAL WITH STUPID PEOPLE?"
I SEEK OUT THEIR INNER SMART PERSON
USING A STANDARD REFERENCE INTERVIEW.
A MIXTURE OF SARCASM AND DISDAIN.
WITH A PINCH OF MEAN-SPIRITEDNESS.
SABOTAGE THEIR CREDIT RATING.
UM, IS THIS ON THE RECORD?

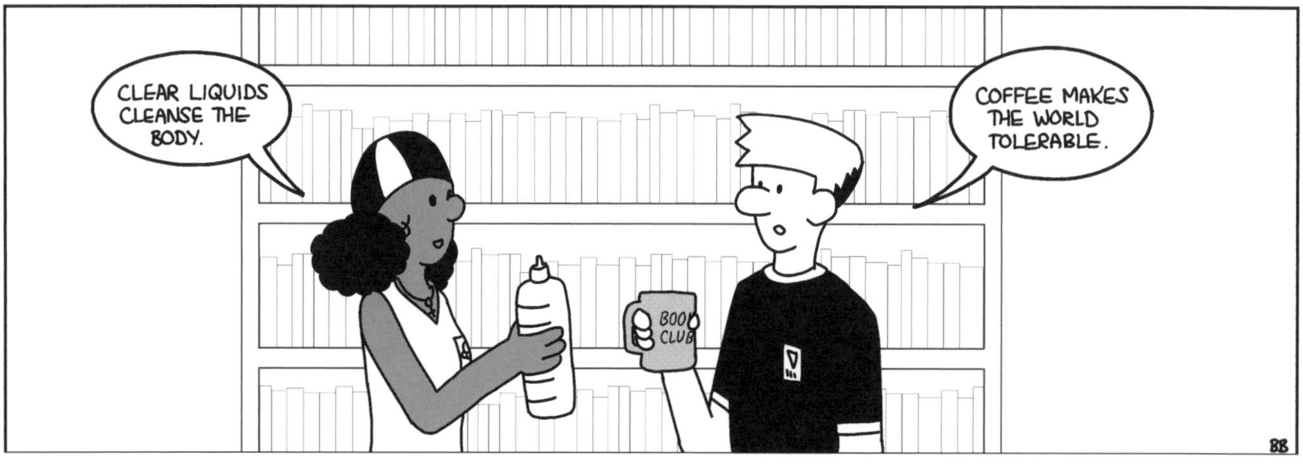
CLEAR LIQUIDS CLEANSE THE BODY.
COFFEE MAKES THE WORLD TOLERABLE.

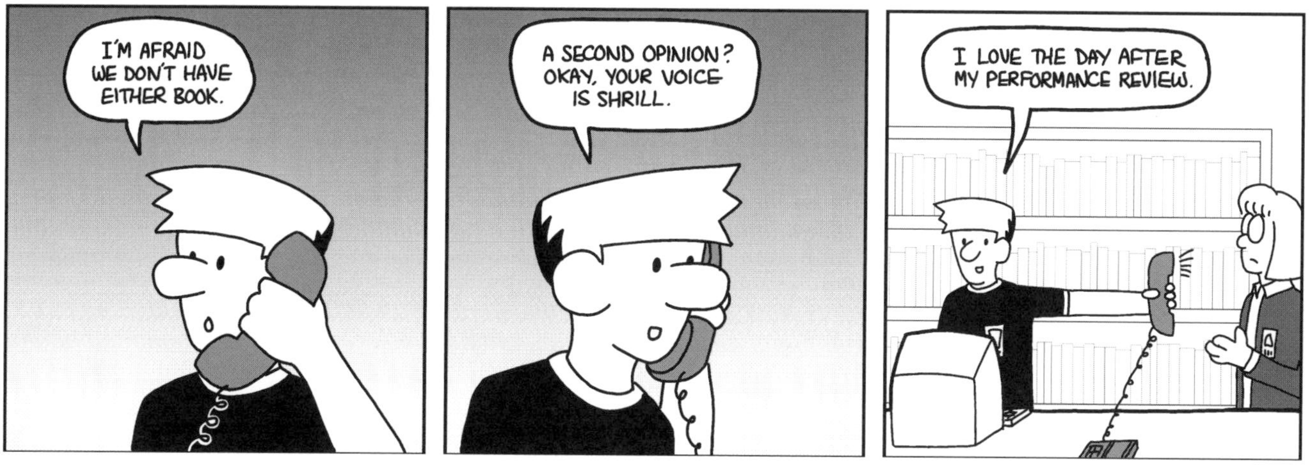
I'M AFRAID WE DON'T HAVE EITHER BOOK.
A SECOND OPINION? OKAY, YOUR VOICE IS SHRILL.
I LOVE THE DAY AFTER MY PERFORMANCE REVIEW.

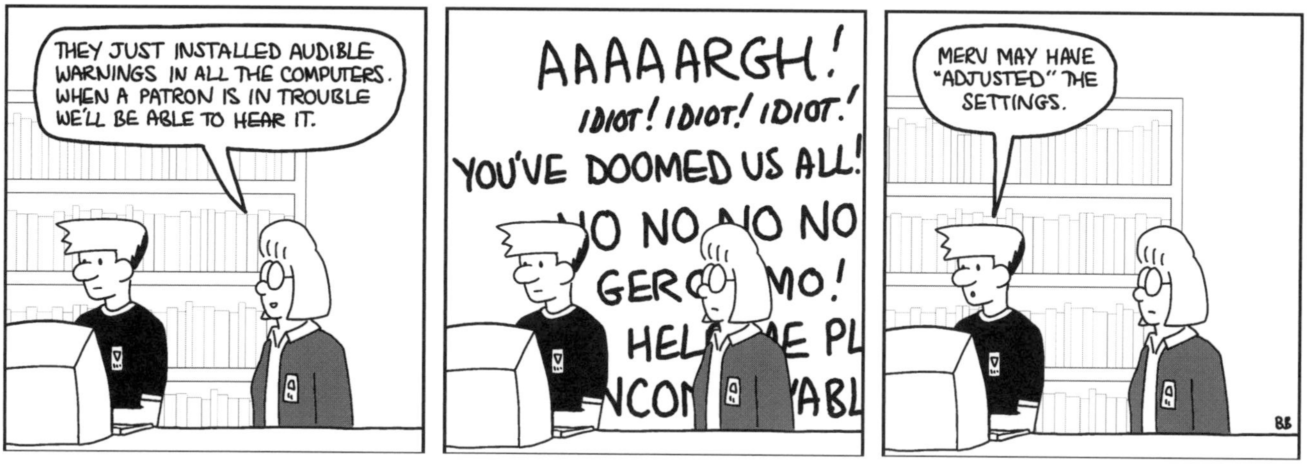
THEY JUST INSTALLED AUDIBLE WARNINGS IN ALL THE COMPUTERS. WHEN A PATRON IS IN TROUBLE WE'LL BE ABLE TO HEAR IT.
AAAAARGH!
IDIOT! IDIOT! IDIOT!
YOU'VE DOOMED US ALL!
MERV MAY HAVE "ADJUSTED" THE SETTINGS.
BB

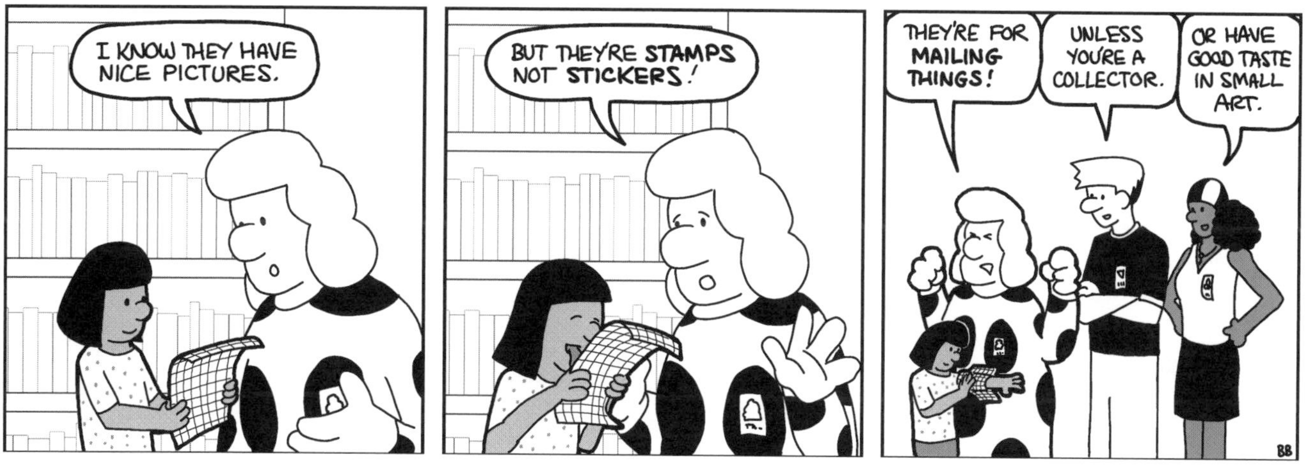
I KNOW THEY HAVE NICE PICTURES.
BUT THEY'RE STAMPS NOT STICKERS!
THEY'RE FOR MAILING THINGS!
UNLESS YOU'RE A COLLECTOR.
OR HAVE GOOD TASTE IN SMALL ART.
BB

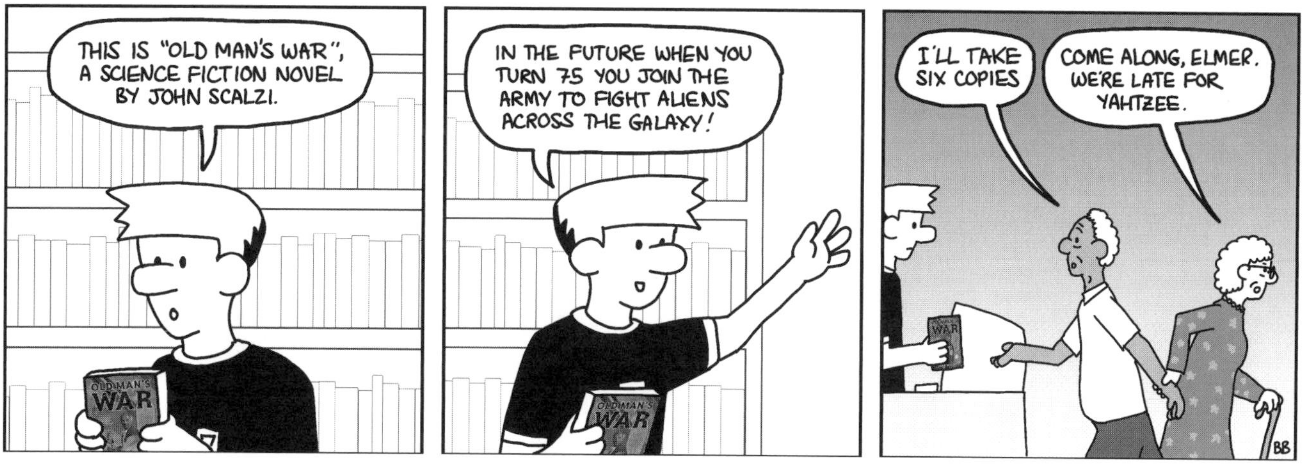
THIS IS "OLD MAN'S WAR", A SCIENCE FICTION NOVEL BY JOHN SCALZI.
OLD MAN'S WAR
IN THE FUTURE WHEN YOU TURN 75 YOU JOIN THE ARMY TO FIGHT ALIENS ACROSS THE GALAXY!
OLD MAN'S WAR
I'LL TAKE SIX COPIES
COME ALONG, ELMER. WE'RE LATE FOR YAHTZEE.
BB

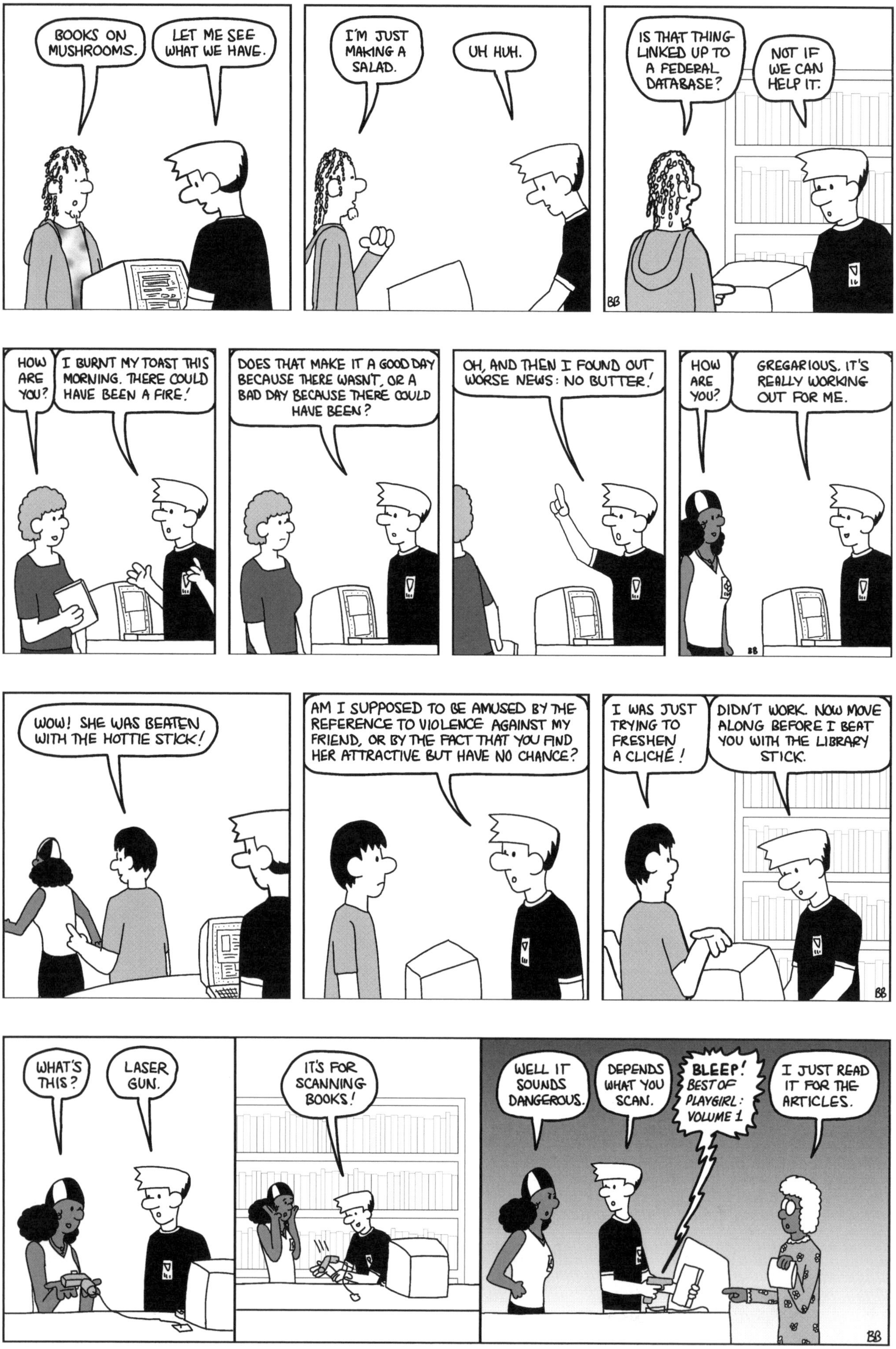
BOOKS ON MUSHROOMS.
LET ME SEE WHAT WE HAVE.
I'M JUST MAKING A SALAD.
UH HUH.
IS THAT THING LINKED UP TO A FEDERAL DATABASE?
NOT IF WE CAN HELP IT.
BB
HOW ARE YOU?
I BURNT MY TOAST THIS MORNING. THERE COULD HAVE BEEN A FIRE!
DOES THAT MAKE IT A GOOD DAY BECAUSE THERE WASN'T, OR A BAD DAY BECAUSE THERE COULD HAVE BEEN?
OH, AND THEN I FOUND OUT WORSE NEWS: NO BUTTER!
HOW ARE YOU?
GREGARIOUS. IT'S REALLY WORKING OUT FOR ME.
BB
WOW! SHE WAS BEATEN WITH THE HOTTIE STICK!
AM I SUPPOSED TO BE AMUSED BY THE REFERENCE TO VIOLENCE AGAINST MY FRIEND, OR BY THE FACT THAT YOU FIND HER ATTRACTIVE BUT HAVE NO CHANCE?
I WAS JUST TRYING TO FRESHEN A CLICHÉ!
DIDN'T WORK. NOW MOVE ALONG BEFORE I BEAT YOU WITH THE LIBRARY STICK.
BB
WHAT'S THIS?
LASER GUN.
IT'S FOR SCANNING BOOKS!
WELL IT SOUNDS DANGEROUS.
DEPENDS WHAT YOU SCAN.
BLEEP! BEST OF PLAYGIRL: VOLUME 1
I JUST READ IT FOR THE ARTICLES.
BB

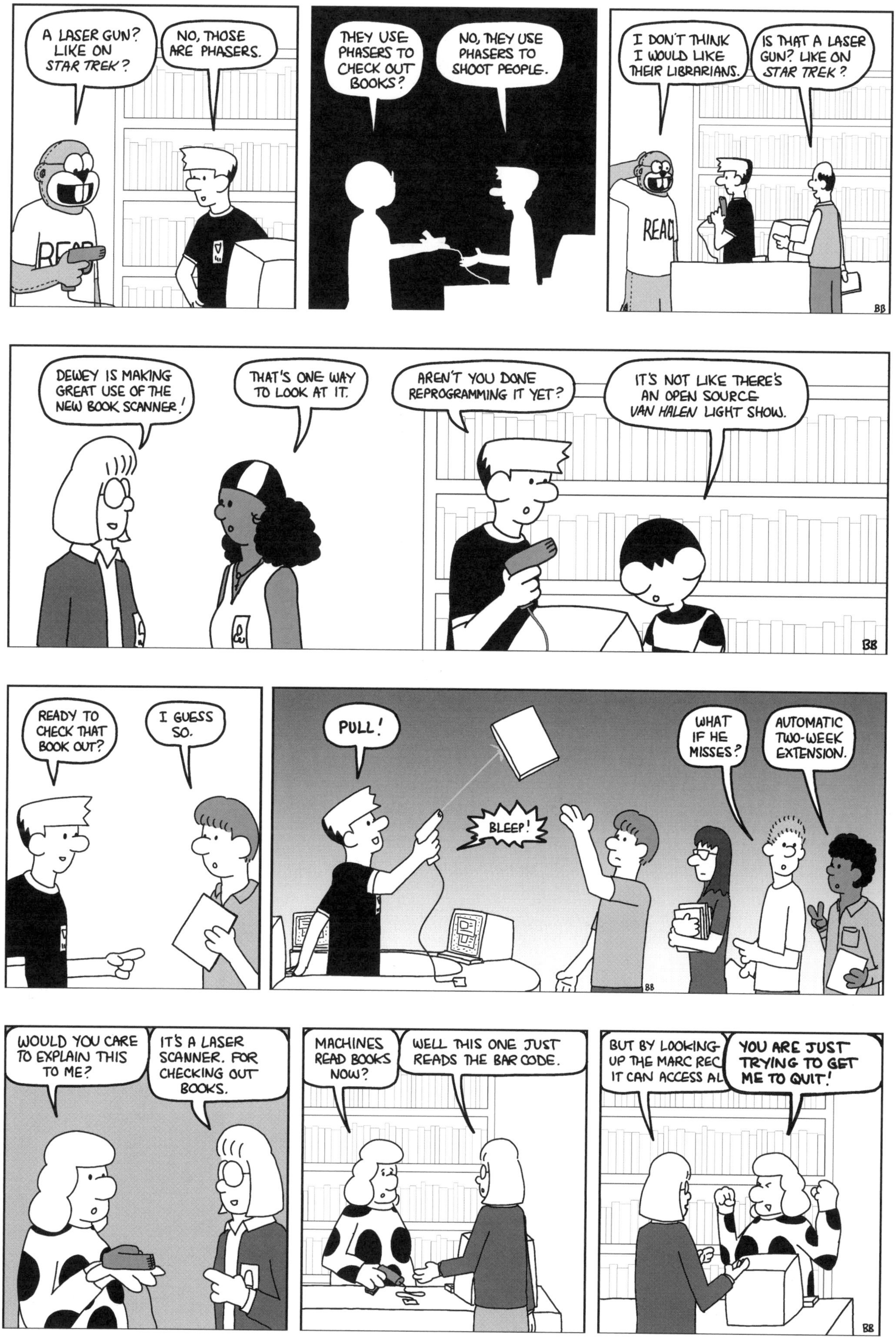
A LASER GUN? LIKE ON *STAR TREK*?
NO, THOSE ARE PHASERS.
THEY USE PHASERS TO CHECK OUT BOOKS?
NO, THEY USE PHASERS TO SHOOT PEOPLE.
I DON'T THINK I WOULD LIKE THEIR LIBRARIANS.
IS THAT A LASER GUN? LIKE ON *STAR TREK*?
READ
BB
DEWEY IS MAKING GREAT USE OF THE NEW BOOK SCANNER!
THAT'S ONE WAY TO LOOK AT IT.
AREN'T YOU DONE REPROGRAMMING IT YET?
IT'S NOT LIKE THERE'S AN OPEN SOURCE *VAN HALEN* LIGHT SHOW.
BB
READY TO CHECK THAT BOOK OUT?
I GUESS SO.
PULL!
BLEEP!
WHAT IF HE MISSES?
AUTOMATIC TWO-WEEK EXTENSION.
BB
WOULD YOU CARE TO EXPLAIN THIS TO ME?
IT'S A LASER SCANNER. FOR CHECKING OUT BOOKS.
MACHINES READ BOOKS NOW?
WELL THIS ONE JUST READS THE BAR CODE.
BUT BY LOOKING UP THE MARC REC IT CAN ACCESS AL
YOU ARE JUST TRYING TO GET ME TO QUIT!
BB

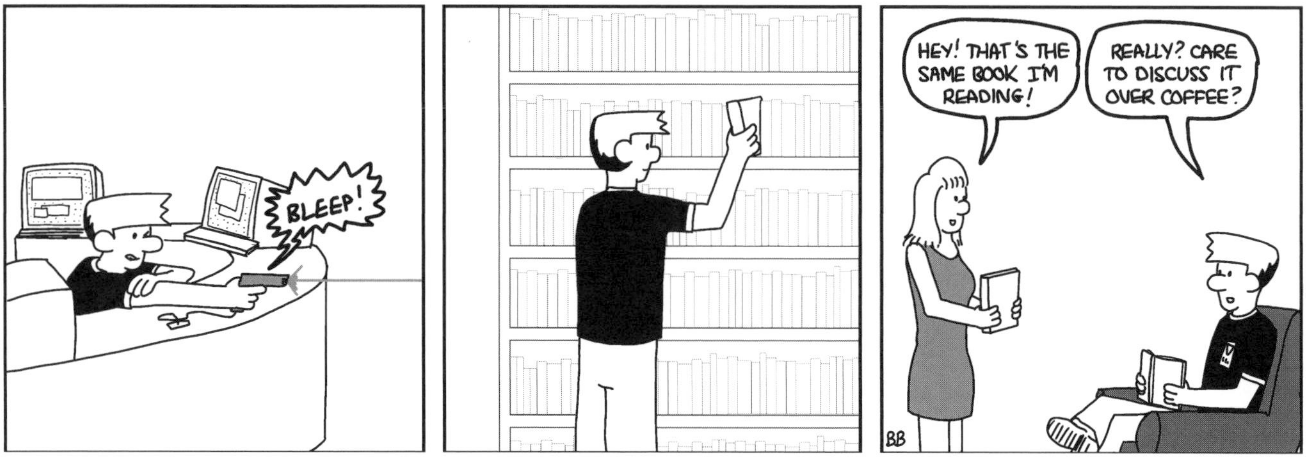
BLEEP!
HEY! THAT'S THE SAME BOOK I'M READING!
REALLY? CARE TO DISCUSS IT OVER COFFEE?
BB

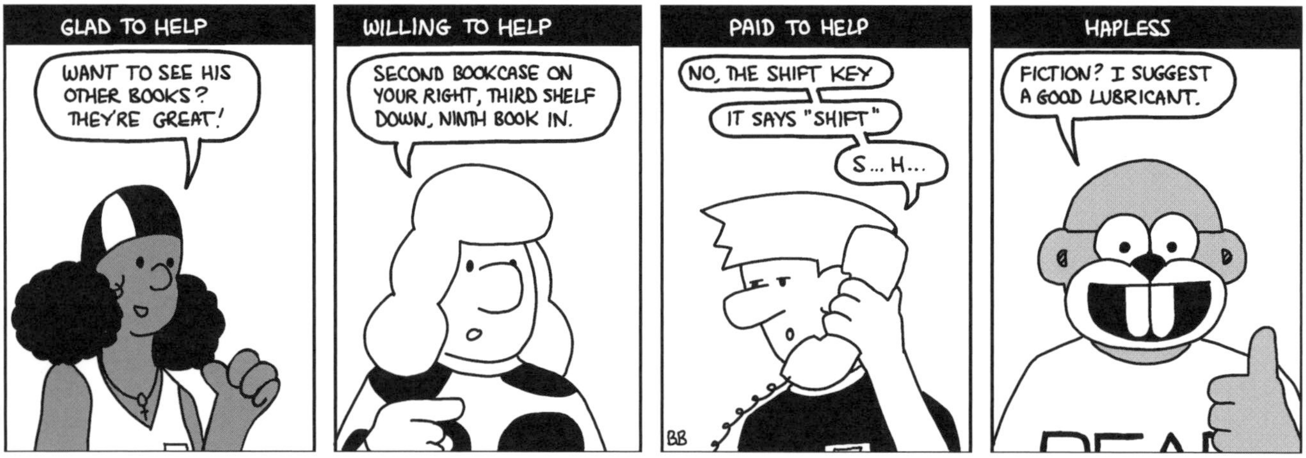
GLAD TO HELP
WANT TO SEE HIS OTHER BOOKS? THEY'RE GREAT!
WILLING TO HELP
SECOND BOOKCASE ON YOUR RIGHT, THIRD SHELF DOWN, NINTH BOOK IN.
PAID TO HELP
NO, THE SHIFT KEY
IT SAYS "SHIFT"
S... H...
BB
HAPLESS
FICTION? I SUGGEST A GOOD LUBRICANT.

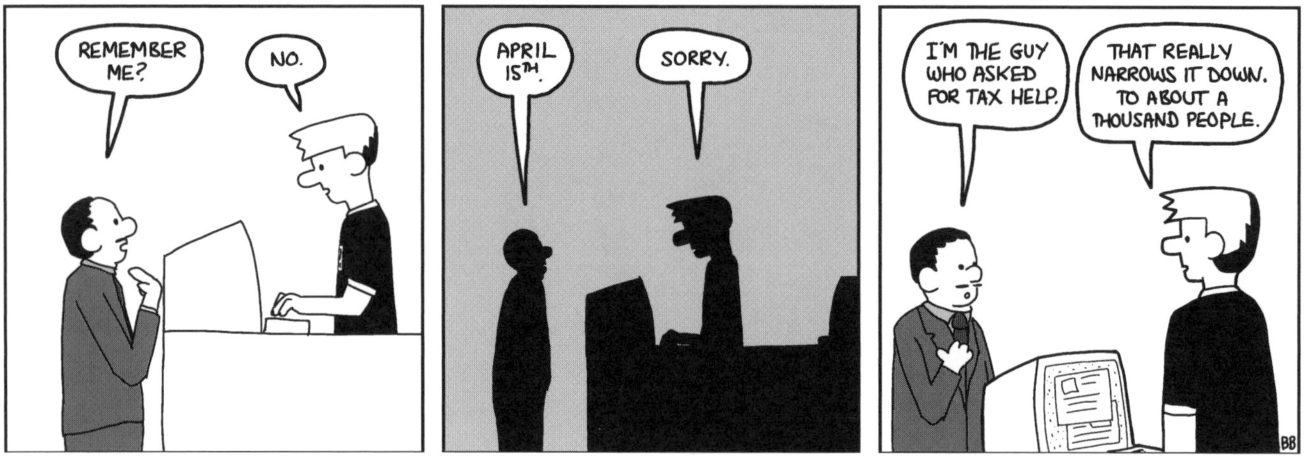
REMEMBER ME?
NO.
APRIL 15TH.
SORRY.
I'M THE GUY WHO ASKED FOR TAX HELP.
THAT REALLY NARROWS IT DOWN. TO ABOUT A THOUSAND PEOPLE.
BB

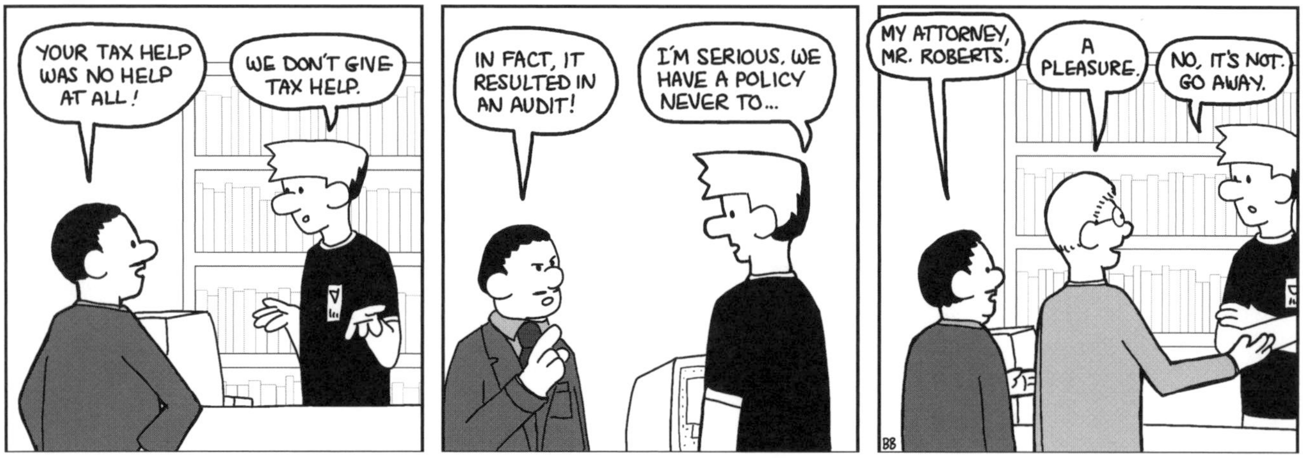
YOUR TAX HELP WAS NO HELP AT ALL!
WE DON'T GIVE TAX HELP.
IN FACT, IT RESULTED IN AN AUDIT!
I'M SERIOUS. WE HAVE A POLICY NEVER TO...
MY ATTORNEY, MR. ROBERTS.
A PLEASURE.
NO, IT'S NOT. GO AWAY.
BB

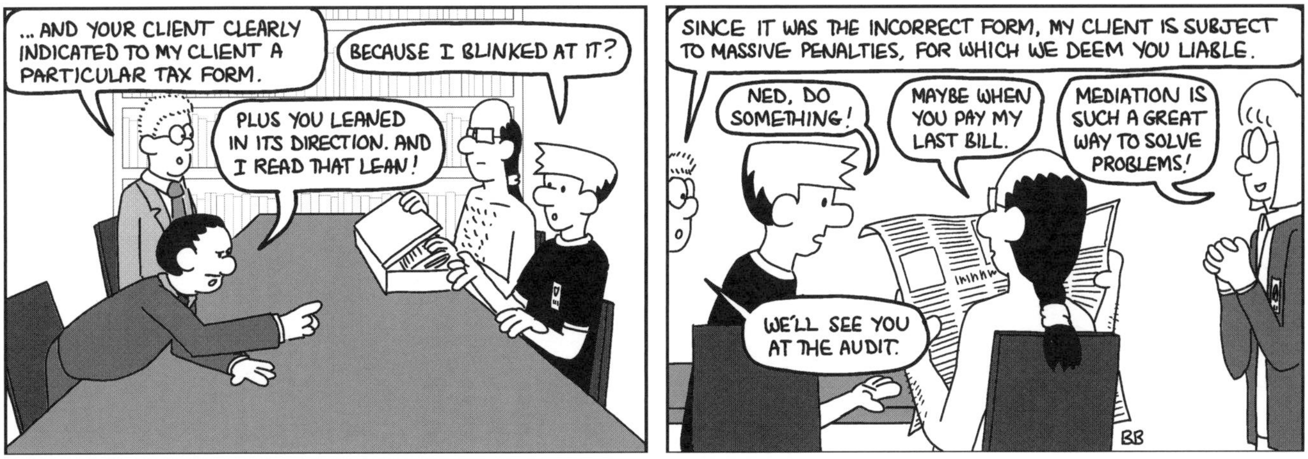
... AND YOUR CLIENT CLEARLY INDICATED TO MY CLIENT A PARTICULAR TAX FORM.
BECAUSE I BLINKED AT IT?
PLUS YOU LEANED IN ITS DIRECTION. AND I READ THAT LEAN!
SINCE IT WAS THE INCORRECT FORM, MY CLIENT IS SUBJECT TO MASSIVE PENALTIES, FOR WHICH WE DEEM YOU LIABLE.
NED, DO SOMETHING!
MAYBE WHEN YOU PAY MY LAST BILL.
MEDIATION IS SUCH A GREAT WAY TO SOLVE PROBLEMS!
WE'LL SEE YOU AT THE AUDIT.
BB

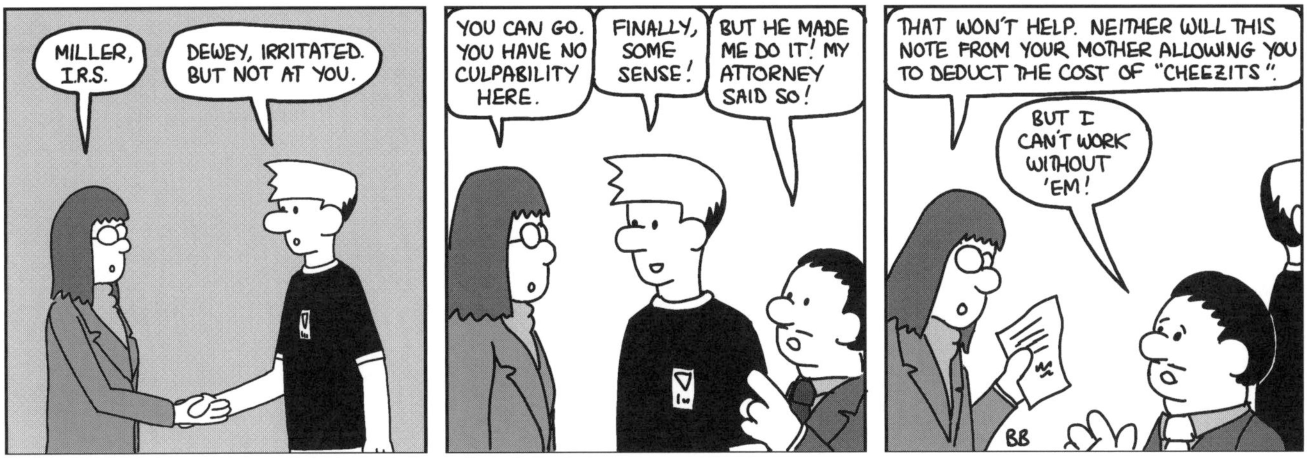
MILLER, I.R.S.
DEWEY, IRRITATED. BUT NOT AT YOU.
YOU CAN GO. YOU HAVE NO CULPABILITY HERE.
FINALLY, SOME SENSE!
BUT HE MADE ME DO IT! MY ATTORNEY SAID SO!
THAT WON'T HELP. NEITHER WILL THIS NOTE FROM YOUR MOTHER ALLOWING YOU TO DEDUCT THE COST OF "CHEEZITS".
BUT I CAN'T WORK WITHOUT 'EM!
BB

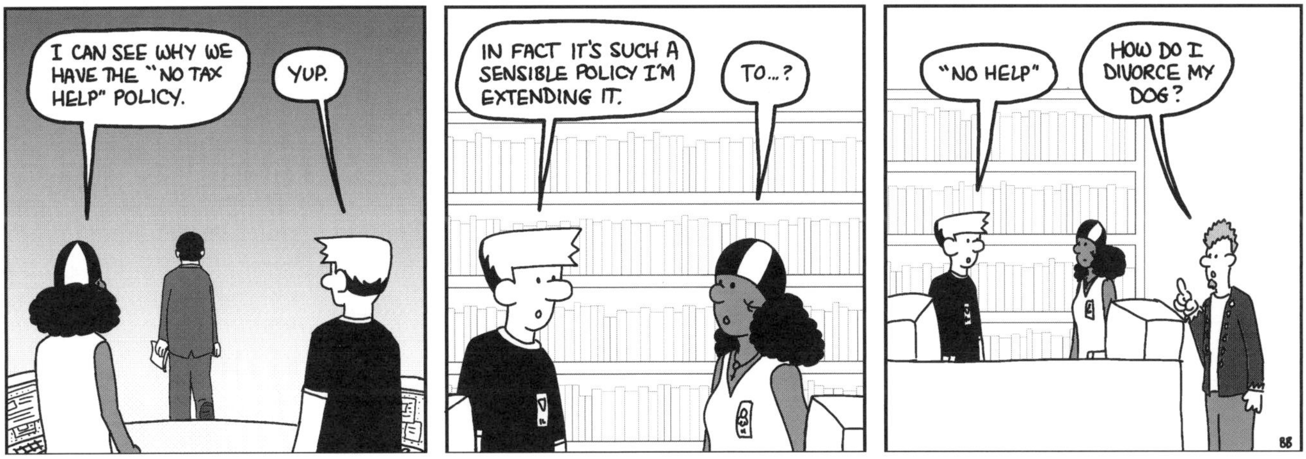
I CAN SEE WHY WE HAVE THE "NO TAX HELP" POLICY.
YUP.
IN FACT IT'S SUCH A SENSIBLE POLICY I'M EXTENDING IT.
TO...?
"NO HELP"
HOW DO I DIVORCE MY DOG?
BB

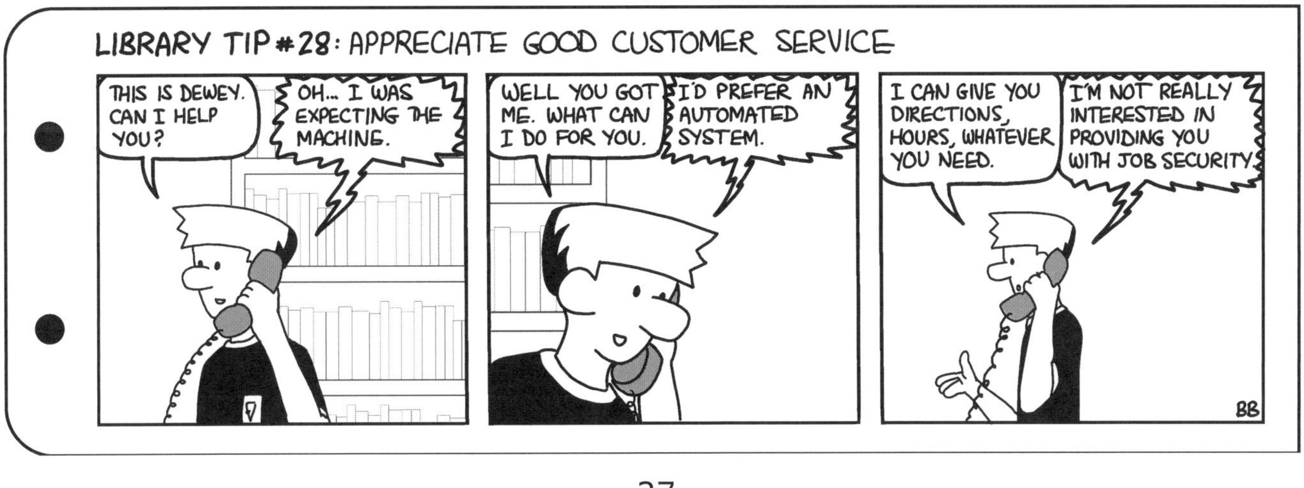
LIBRARY TIP #28: APPRECIATE GOOD CUSTOMER SERVICE
THIS IS DEWEY. CAN I HELP YOU?
OH... I WAS EXPECTING THE MACHINE.
WELL YOU GOT ME. WHAT CAN I DO FOR YOU.
I'D PREFER AN AUTOMATED SYSTEM.
I CAN GIVE YOU DIRECTIONS, HOURS, WHATEVER YOU NEED.
I'M NOT REALLY INTERESTED IN PROVIDING YOU WITH JOB SECURITY.
BB

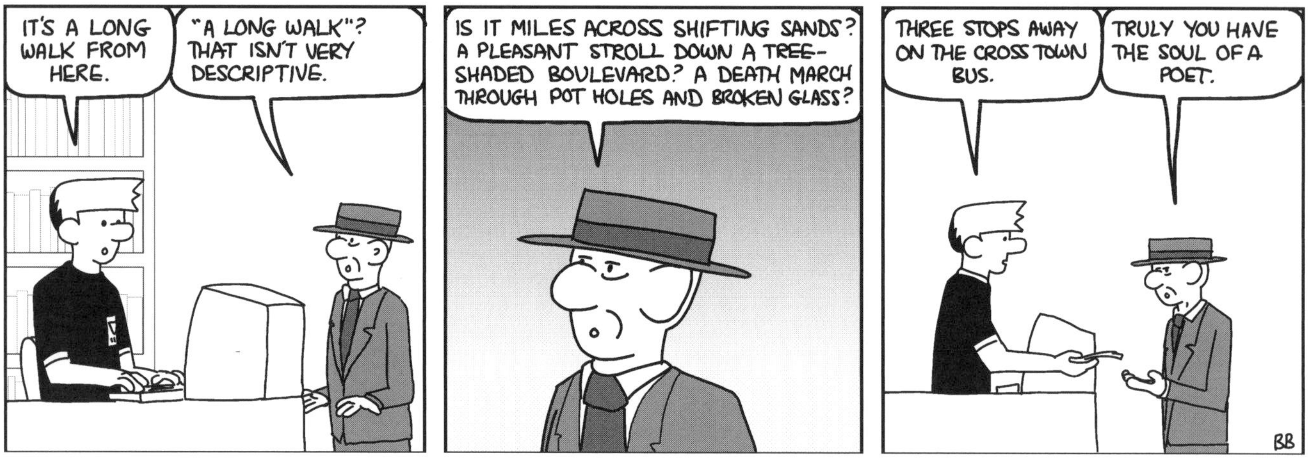
IT'S A LONG WALK FROM HERE.
"A LONG WALK"? THAT ISN'T VERY DESCRIPTIVE.
IS IT MILES ACROSS SHIFTING SANDS? A PLEASANT STROLL DOWN A TREE-SHADED BOULEVARD? A DEATH MARCH THROUGH POT HOLES AND BROKEN GLASS?
THREE STOPS AWAY ON THE CROSS TOWN BUS.
TRULY YOU HAVE THE SOUL OF A POET.
BB

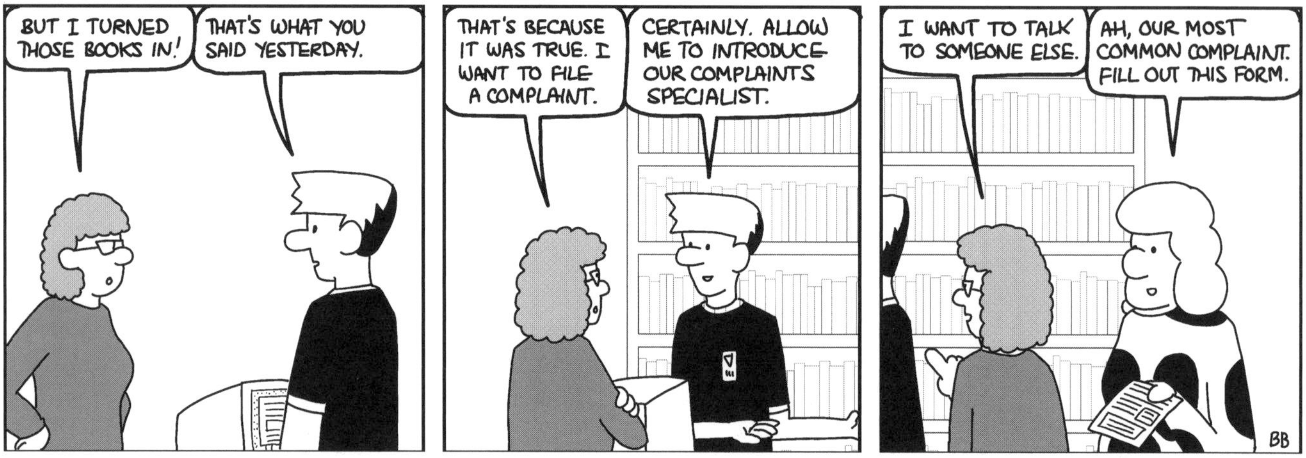
BUT I TURNED THOSE BOOKS IN!
THAT'S WHAT YOU SAID YESTERDAY.
THAT'S BECAUSE IT WAS TRUE. I WANT TO FILE A COMPLAINT.
CERTAINLY. ALLOW ME TO INTRODUCE OUR COMPLAINTS SPECIALIST.
I WANT TO TALK TO SOMEONE ELSE.
AH, OUR MOST COMMON COMPLAINT. FILL OUT THIS FORM.
BB

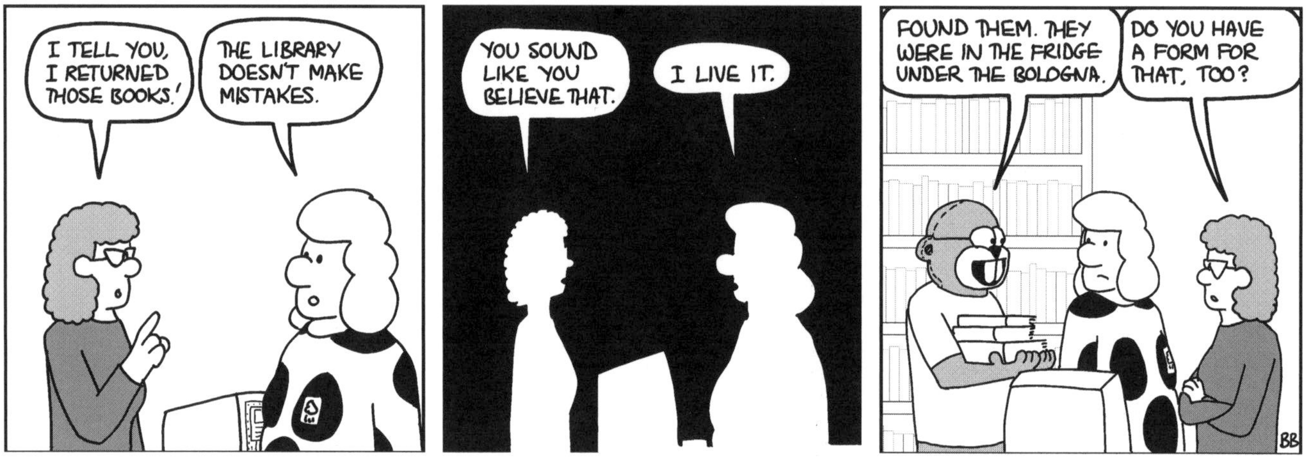
I TELL YOU, I RETURNED THOSE BOOKS!
THE LIBRARY DOESN'T MAKE MISTAKES.
YOU SOUND LIKE YOU BELIEVE THAT.
I LIVE IT.
FOUND THEM. THEY WERE IN THE FRIDGE UNDER THE BOLOGNA.
DO YOU HAVE A FORM FOR THAT, TOO?
BB

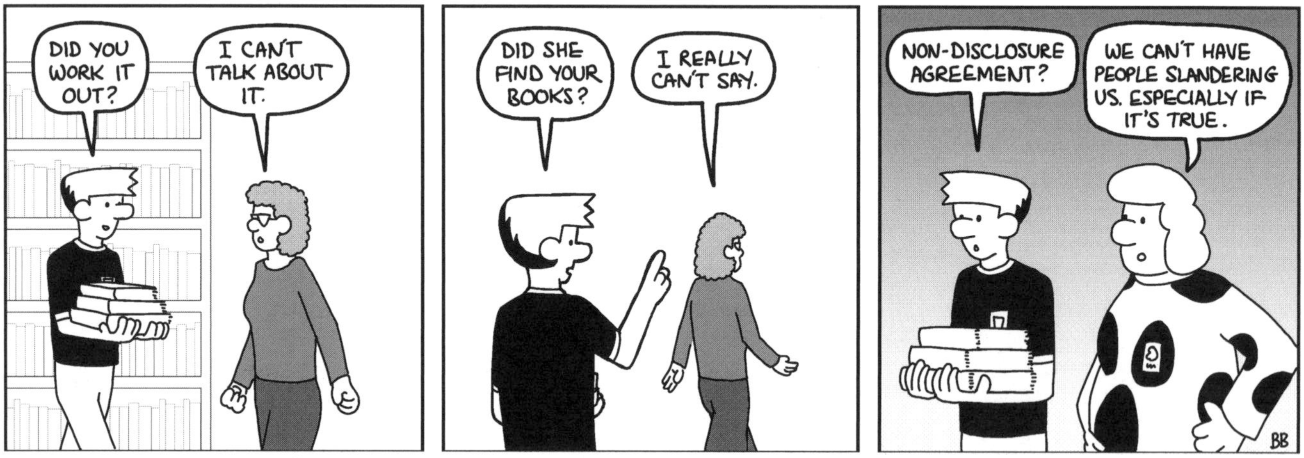
DID YOU WORK IT OUT?
I CAN'T TALK ABOUT IT.
DID SHE FIND YOUR BOOKS?
I REALLY CAN'T SAY.
NON-DISCLOSURE AGREEMENT?
WE CAN'T HAVE PEOPLE SLANDERING US. ESPECIALLY IF IT'S TRUE.
BB

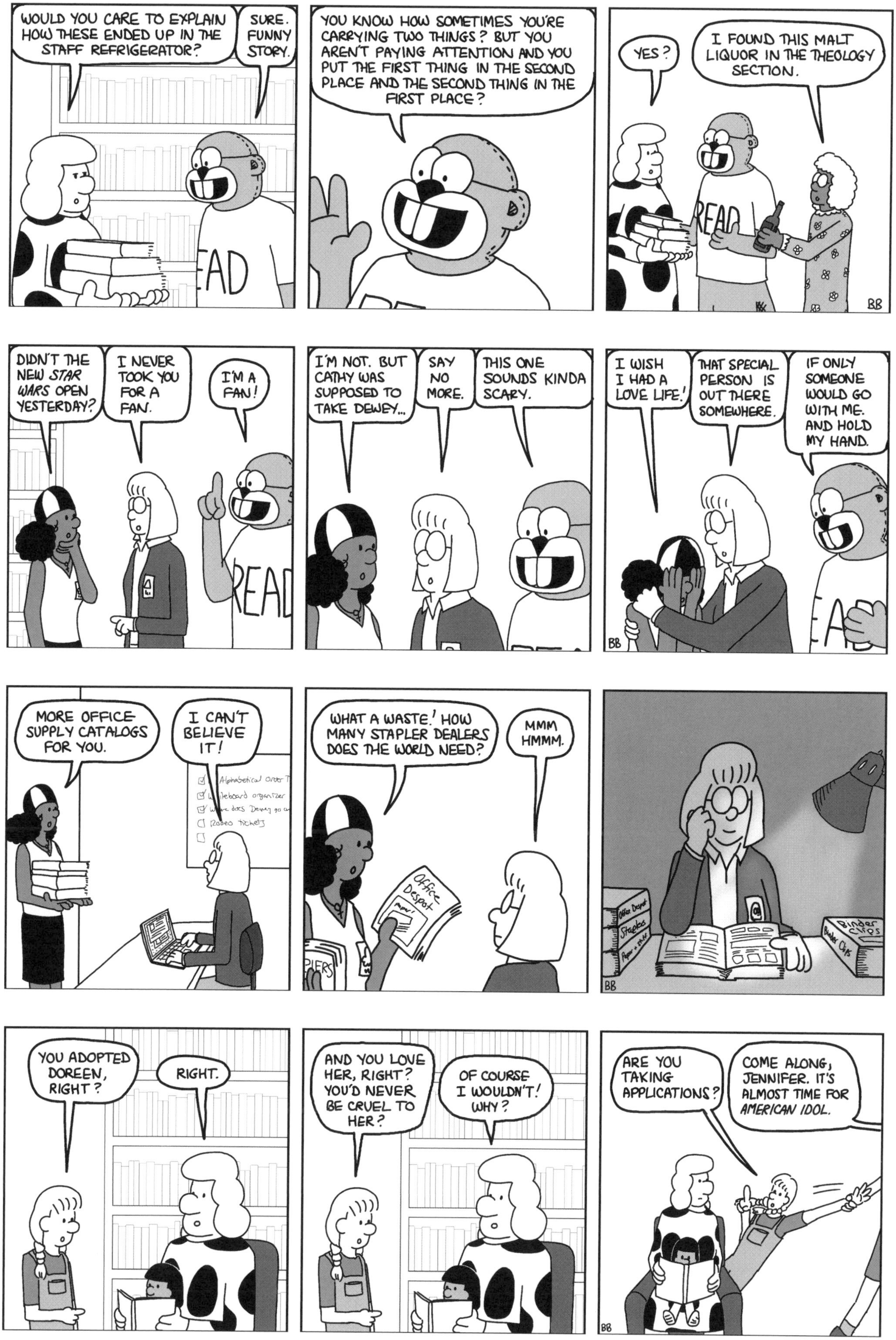
WOULD YOU CARE TO EXPLAIN HOW THESE ENDED UP IN THE STAFF REFRIGERATOR?
SURE. FUNNY STORY.
YOU KNOW HOW SOMETIMES YOU'RE CARRYING TWO THINGS? BUT YOU AREN'T PAYING ATTENTION AND YOU PUT THE FIRST THING IN THE SECOND PLACE AND THE SECOND THING IN THE FIRST PLACE?
YES?
I FOUND THIS MALT LIQUOR IN THE THEOLOGY SECTION.
READ
BB
DIDN'T THE NEW STAR WARS OPEN YESTERDAY?
I NEVER TOOK YOU FOR A FAN.
I'M A FAN!
I'M NOT. BUT CATHY WAS SUPPOSED TO TAKE DEWEY...
SAY NO MORE.
THIS ONE SOUNDS KINDA SCARY.
I WISH I HAD A LOVE LIFE!
THAT SPECIAL PERSON IS OUT THERE SOMEWHERE.
IF ONLY SOMEONE WOULD GO WITH ME. AND HOLD MY HAND.
BB
MORE OFFICE SUPPLY CATALOGS FOR YOU.
I CAN'T BELIEVE IT!
Rodeo tickets
WHAT A WASTE! HOW MANY STAPLER DEALERS DOES THE WORLD NEED?
MMM HMMM.
Office Despot
Office Despot
Staples
Binder Clips
BB
YOU ADOPTED DOREEN, RIGHT?
RIGHT.
AND YOU LOVE HER, RIGHT? YOU'D NEVER BE CRUEL TO HER?
OF COURSE I WOULDN'T! WHY?
ARE YOU TAKING APPLICATIONS?
COME ALONG, JENNIFER. IT'S ALMOST TIME FOR AMERICAN IDOL.
BB

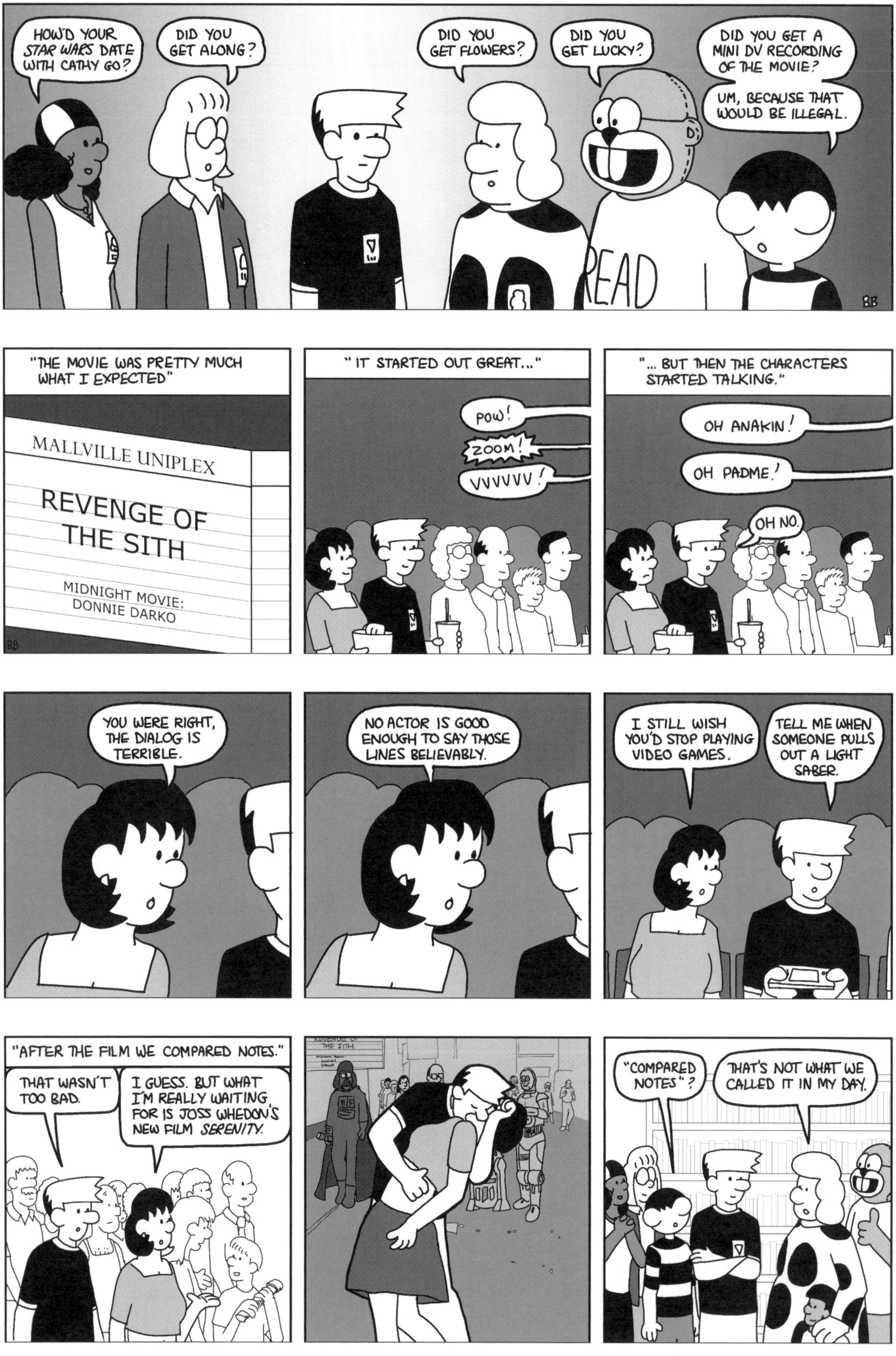
HOW'D YOUR STAR WARS DATE WITH CATHY GO?
DID YOU GET ALONG?
DID YOU GET FLOWERS?
DID YOU GET LUCKY?
DID YOU GET A MINI DV RECORDING OF THE MOVIE?
UM, BECAUSE THAT WOULD BE ILLEGAL.
READ
BB
"THE MOVIE WAS PRETTY MUCH WHAT I EXPECTED"
MALLVILLE UNIPLEX
REVENGE OF THE SITH
MIDNIGHT MOVIE: DONNIE DARKO
BB
"IT STARTED OUT GREAT..."
POW!
ZOOM!
VVVVVV!
"... BUT THEN THE CHARACTERS STARTED TALKING."
OH ANAKIN!
OH PADME!
OH NO.
YOU WERE RIGHT, THE DIALOG IS TERRIBLE.
NO ACTOR IS GOOD ENOUGH TO SAY THOSE LINES BELIEVABLY.
I STILL WISH YOU'D STOP PLAYING VIDEO GAMES.
TELL ME WHEN SOMEONE PULLS OUT A LIGHT SABER.
"AFTER THE FILM WE COMPARED NOTES."
THAT WASN'T TOO BAD.
I GUESS. BUT WHAT I'M REALLY WAITING FOR IS JOSS WHEDON'S NEW FILM SERENITY.
"COMPARED NOTES"?
THAT'S NOT WHAT WE CALLED IT IN MY DAY.

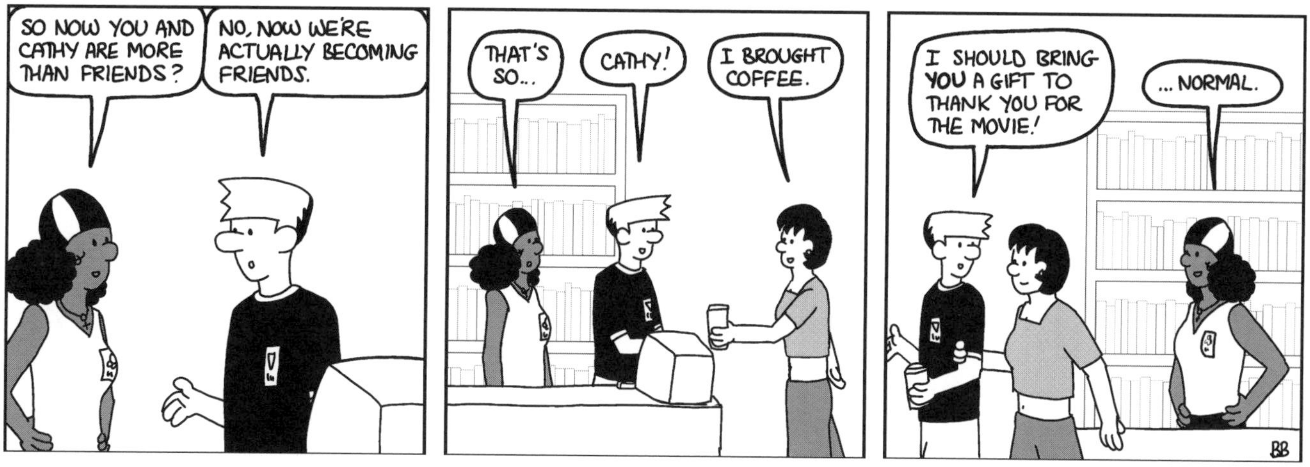
SO NOW YOU AND CATHY ARE MORE THAN FRIENDS?
NO, NOW WE'RE ACTUALLY BECOMING FRIENDS.
THAT'S SO...
CATHY!
I BROUGHT COFFEE.
I SHOULD BRING **YOU** A GIFT TO THANK YOU FOR THE MOVIE!
... NORMAL.
BB

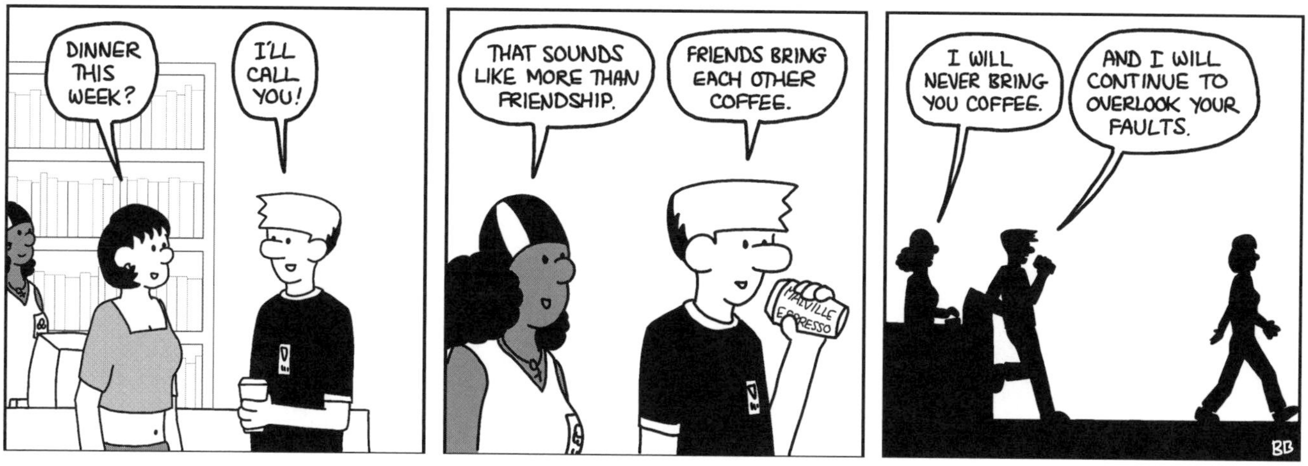
DINNER THIS WEEK?
I'LL CALL YOU!
THAT SOUNDS LIKE MORE THAN FRIENDSHIP.
FRIENDS BRING EACH OTHER COFFEE.
MANVILLE ESPRESSO
I WILL NEVER BRING YOU COFFEE.
AND I WILL CONTINUE TO OVERLOOK YOUR FAULTS.
BB

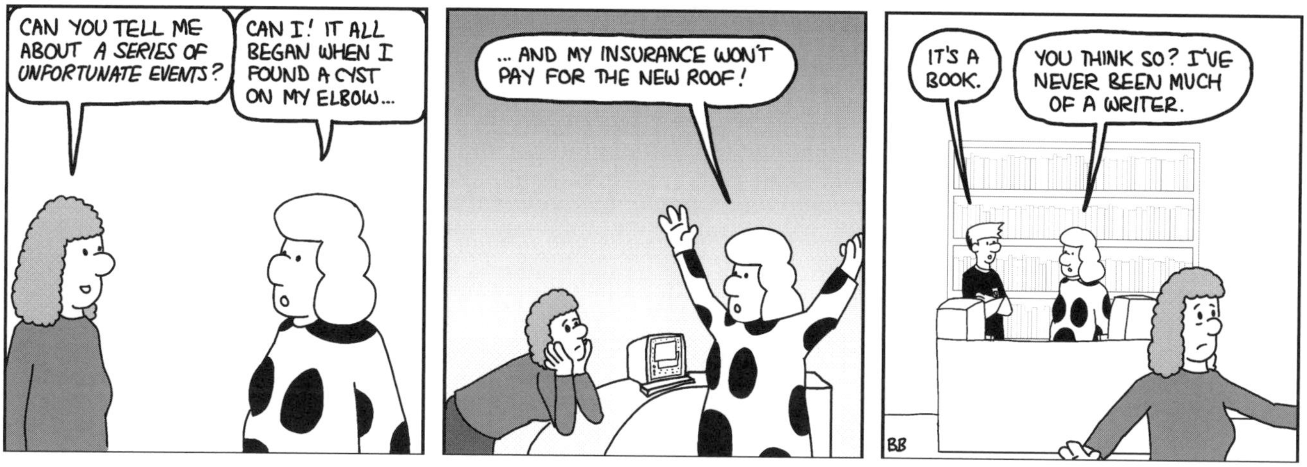
CAN YOU TELL ME ABOUT *A SERIES OF UNFORTUNATE EVENTS*?
CAN I! IT ALL BEGAN WHEN I FOUND A CYST ON MY ELBOW...
... AND MY INSURANCE WON'T PAY FOR THE NEW ROOF!
IT'S A BOOK.
YOU THINK SO? I'VE NEVER BEEN MUCH OF A WRITER.
BB

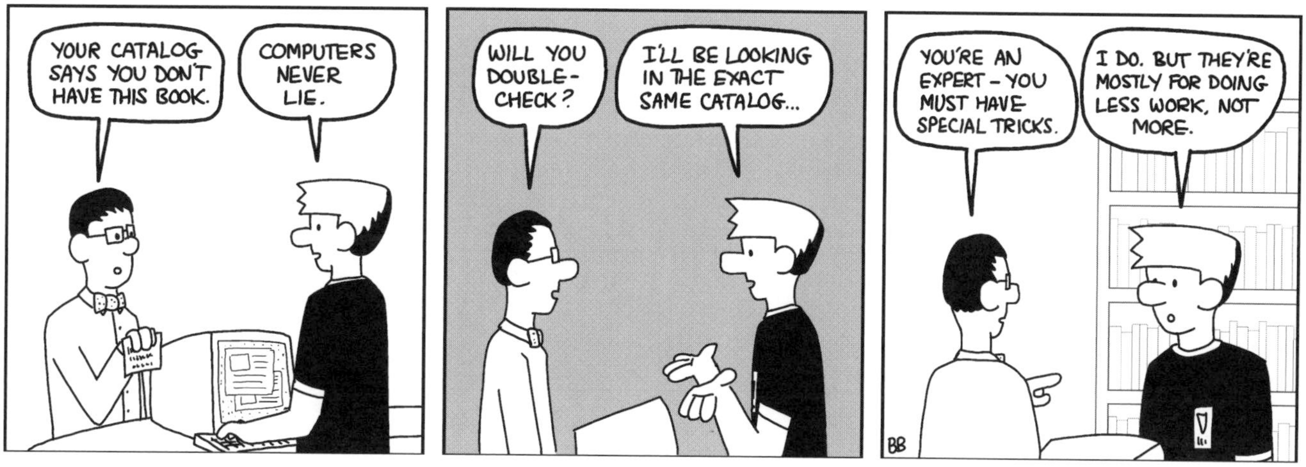
YOUR CATALOG SAYS YOU DON'T HAVE THIS BOOK.
COMPUTERS NEVER LIE.
WILL YOU DOUBLE-CHECK?
I'LL BE LOOKING IN THE EXACT SAME CATALOG...
YOU'RE AN EXPERT - YOU MUST HAVE SPECIAL TRICKS.
I DO. BUT THEY'RE MOSTLY FOR DOING LESS WORK, NOT MORE.
BB

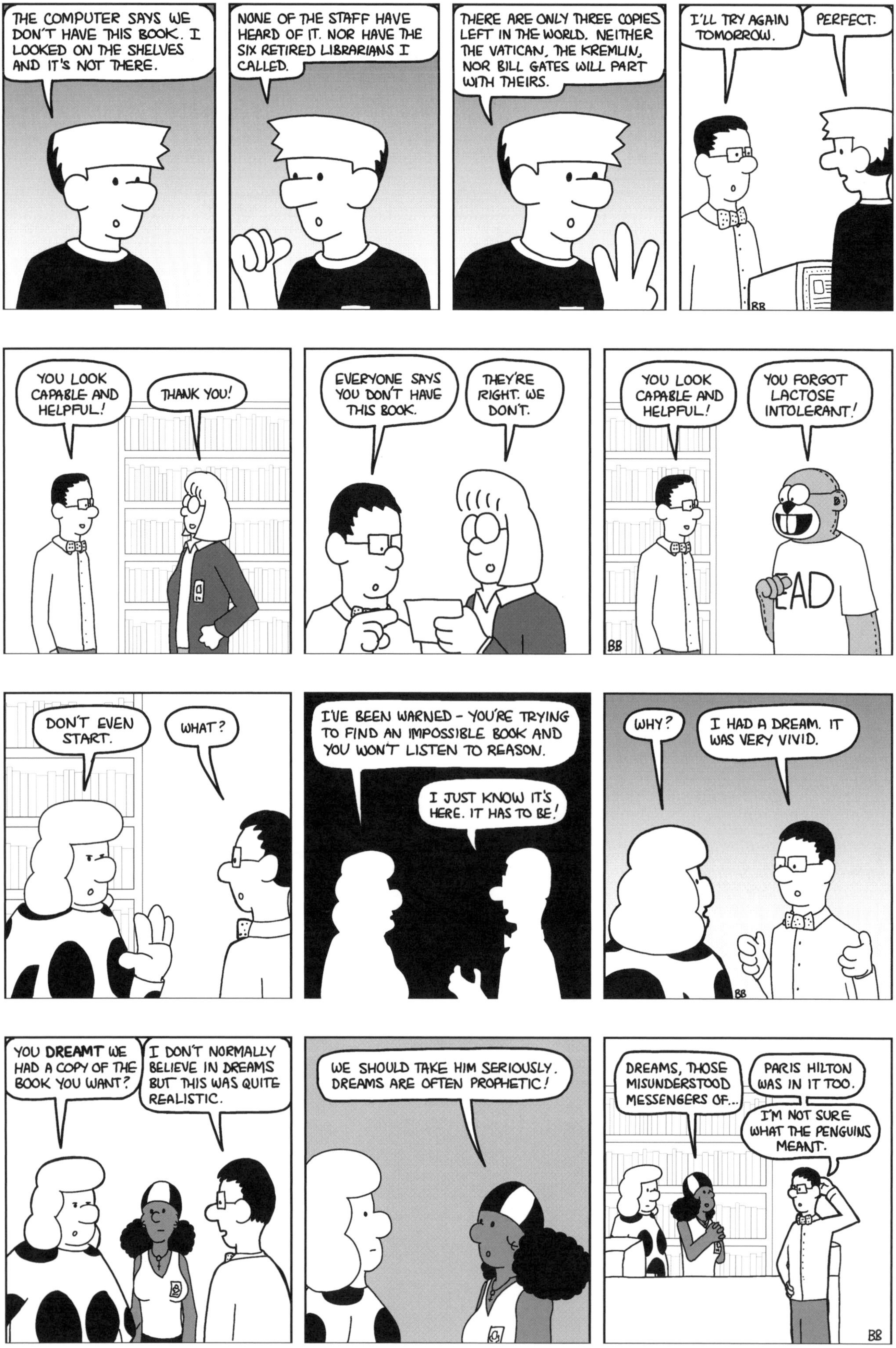
THE COMPUTER SAYS WE DON'T HAVE THIS BOOK. I LOOKED ON THE SHELVES AND IT'S NOT THERE.
NONE OF THE STAFF HAVE HEARD OF IT. NOR HAVE THE SIX RETIRED LIBRARIANS I CALLED.
THERE ARE ONLY THREE COPIES LEFT IN THE WORLD. NEITHER THE VATICAN, THE KREMLIN, NOR BILL GATES WILL PART WITH THEIRS.
I'LL TRY AGAIN TOMORROW.
PERFECT.
YOU LOOK CAPABLE AND HELPFUL!
THANK YOU!
EVERYONE SAYS YOU DON'T HAVE THIS BOOK.
THEY'RE RIGHT. WE DON'T.
YOU LOOK CAPABLE AND HELPFUL!
YOU FORGOT LACTOSE INTOLERANT!
EAD
DON'T EVEN START.
WHAT?
I'VE BEEN WARNED - YOU'RE TRYING TO FIND AN IMPOSSIBLE BOOK AND YOU WON'T LISTEN TO REASON.
I JUST KNOW IT'S HERE. IT HAS TO BE!
WHY?
I HAD A DREAM. IT WAS VERY VIVID.
YOU **DREAMT** WE HAD A COPY OF THE BOOK YOU WANT?
I DON'T NORMALLY BELIEVE IN DREAMS BUT THIS WAS QUITE REALISTIC.
WE SHOULD TAKE HIM SERIOUSLY. DREAMS ARE OFTEN PROPHETIC!
DREAMS, THOSE MISUNDERSTOOD MESSENGERS OF...
PARIS HILTON WAS IN IT TOO.
I'M NOT SURE WHAT THE PENGUINS MEANT.

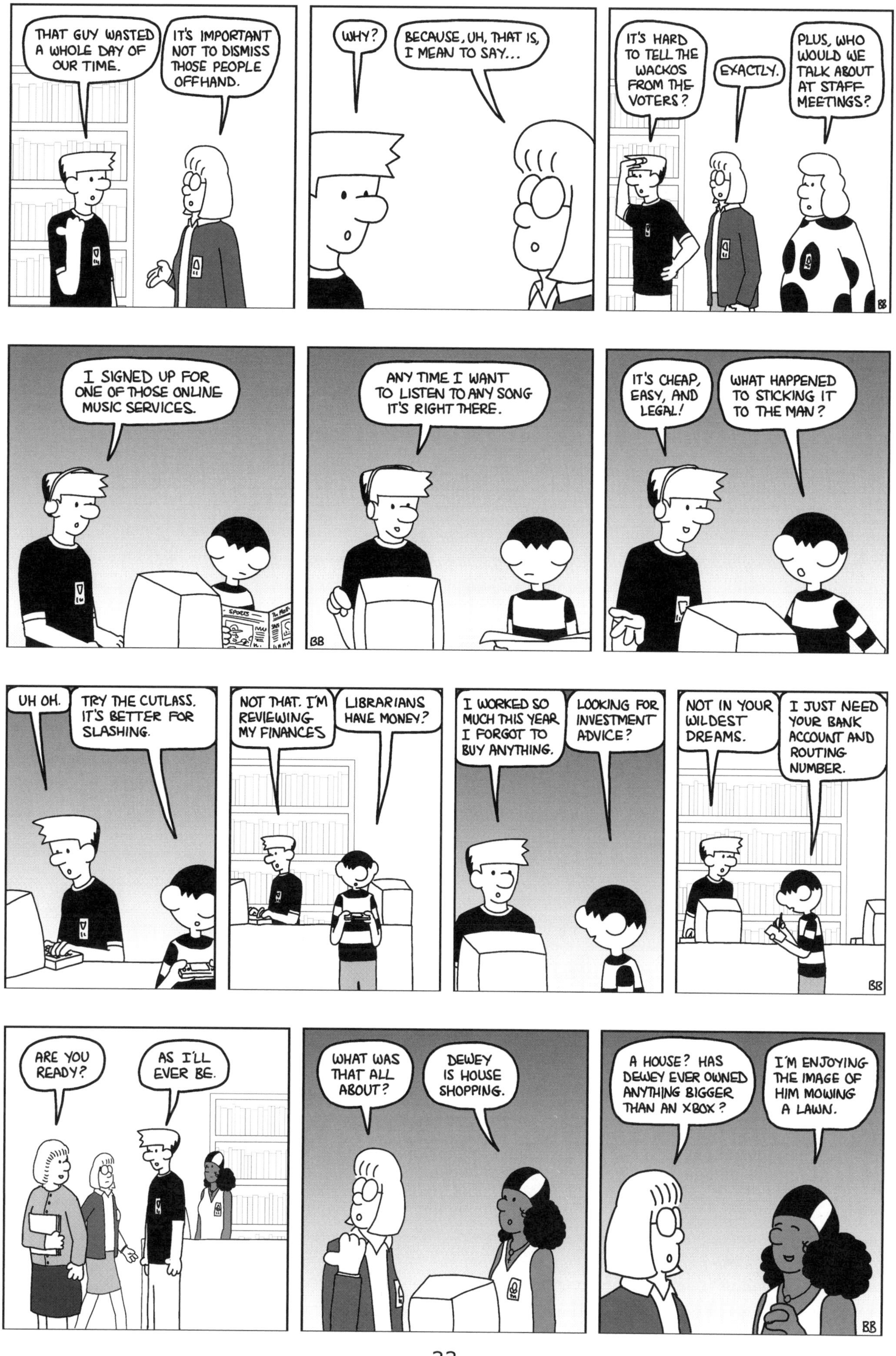
THAT GUY WASTED A WHOLE DAY OF OUR TIME.
IT'S IMPORTANT NOT TO DISMISS THOSE PEOPLE OFFHAND.
WHY?
BECAUSE, UH, THAT IS, I MEAN TO SAY...
IT'S HARD TO TELL THE WACKOS FROM THE VOTERS?
EXACTLY.
PLUS, WHO WOULD WE TALK ABOUT AT STAFF MEETINGS?
BB
I SIGNED UP FOR ONE OF THOSE ONLINE MUSIC SERVICES.
SPORTS
ANY TIME I WANT TO LISTEN TO ANY SONG IT'S RIGHT THERE.
BB
IT'S CHEAP, EASY, AND LEGAL!
WHAT HAPPENED TO STICKING IT TO THE MAN?
UH OH.
TRY THE CUTLASS. IT'S BETTER FOR SLASHING.
NOT THAT. I'M REVIEWING MY FINANCES
LIBRARIANS HAVE MONEY?
I WORKED SO MUCH THIS YEAR I FORGOT TO BUY ANYTHING.
LOOKING FOR INVESTMENT ADVICE?
NOT IN YOUR WILDEST DREAMS.
I JUST NEED YOUR BANK ACCOUNT AND ROUTING NUMBER.
BB
ARE YOU READY?
AS I'LL EVER BE.
WHAT WAS THAT ALL ABOUT?
DEWEY IS HOUSE SHOPPING.
A HOUSE? HAS DEWEY EVER OWNED ANYTHING BIGGER THAN AN XBOX?
I'M ENJOYING THE IMAGE OF HIM MOWING A LAWN.
BB

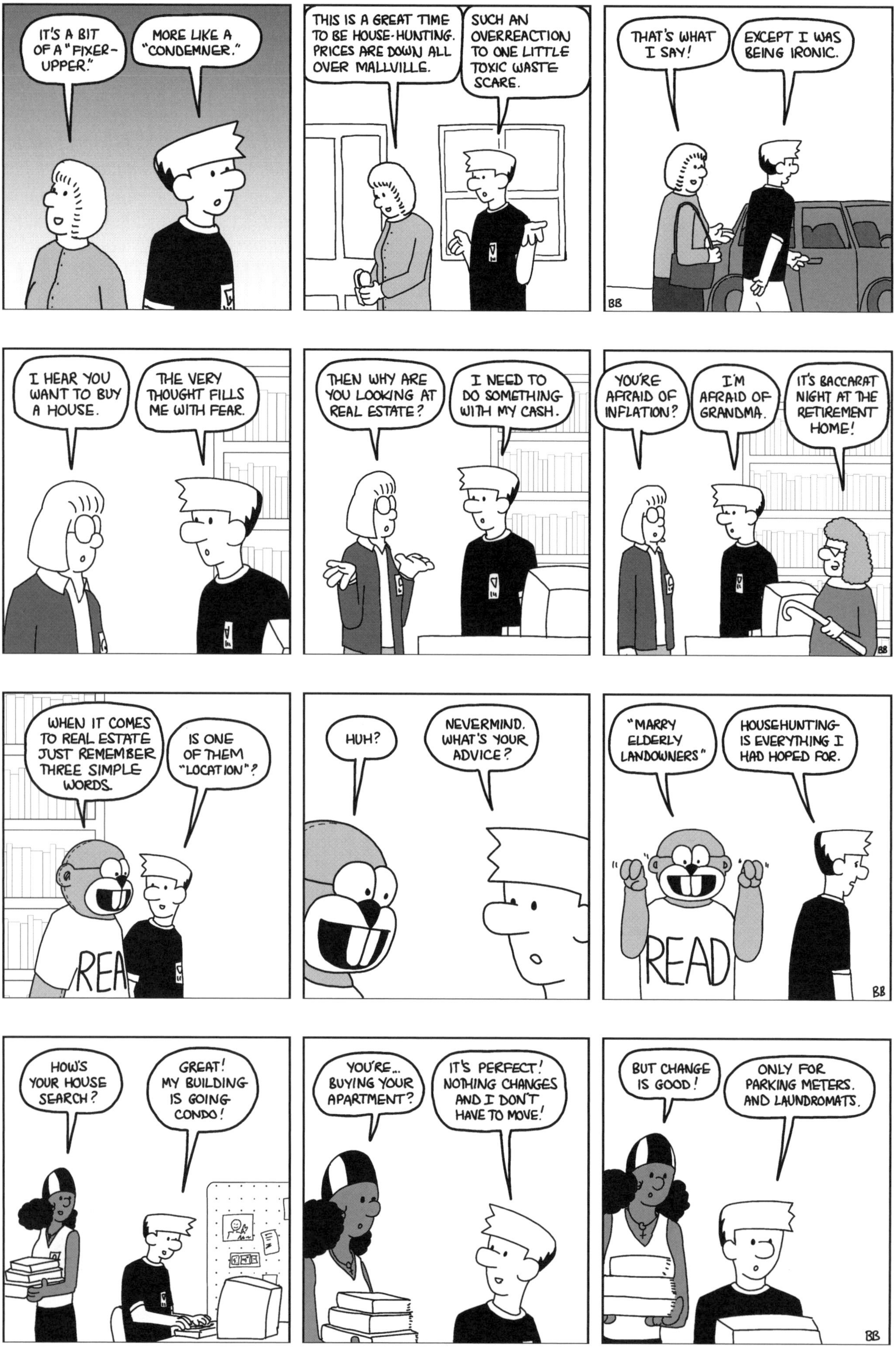
IT'S A BIT OF A "FIXER-UPPER."
MORE LIKE A "CONDEMNER."
THIS IS A GREAT TIME TO BE HOUSE-HUNTING. PRICES ARE DOWN ALL OVER MALLVILLE.
SUCH AN OVERREACTION TO ONE LITTLE TOXIC WASTE SCARE.
THAT'S WHAT I SAY!
EXCEPT I WAS BEING IRONIC.
BB
I HEAR YOU WANT TO BUY A HOUSE.
THE VERY THOUGHT FILLS ME WITH FEAR.
THEN WHY ARE YOU LOOKING AT REAL ESTATE?
I NEED TO DO SOMETHING WITH MY CASH.
YOU'RE AFRAID OF INFLATION?
I'M AFRAID OF GRANDMA.
IT'S BACCARAT NIGHT AT THE RETIREMENT HOME!
BB
WHEN IT COMES TO REAL ESTATE JUST REMEMBER THREE SIMPLE WORDS.
IS ONE OF THEM "LOCATION"?
REA
HUH?
NEVERMIND. WHAT'S YOUR ADVICE?
"MARRY ELDERLY LANDOWNERS"
HOUSEHUNTING IS EVERYTHING I HAD HOPED FOR.
READ
BB
HOW'S YOUR HOUSE SEARCH?
GREAT! MY BUILDING IS GOING CONDO!
YOU'RE... BUYING YOUR APARTMENT?
IT'S PERFECT! NOTHING CHANGES AND I DON'T HAVE TO MOVE!
BUT CHANGE IS GOOD!
ONLY FOR PARKING METERS. AND LAUNDROMATS.
BB

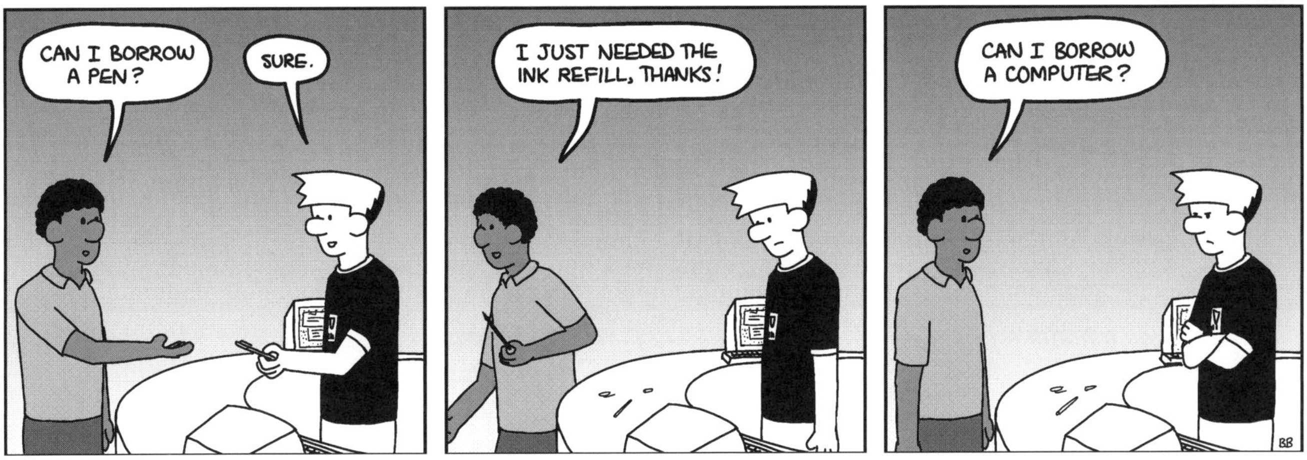
CAN I BORROW A PEN?
SURE.
I JUST NEEDED THE INK REFILL, THANKS!
CAN I BORROW A COMPUTER?
BB

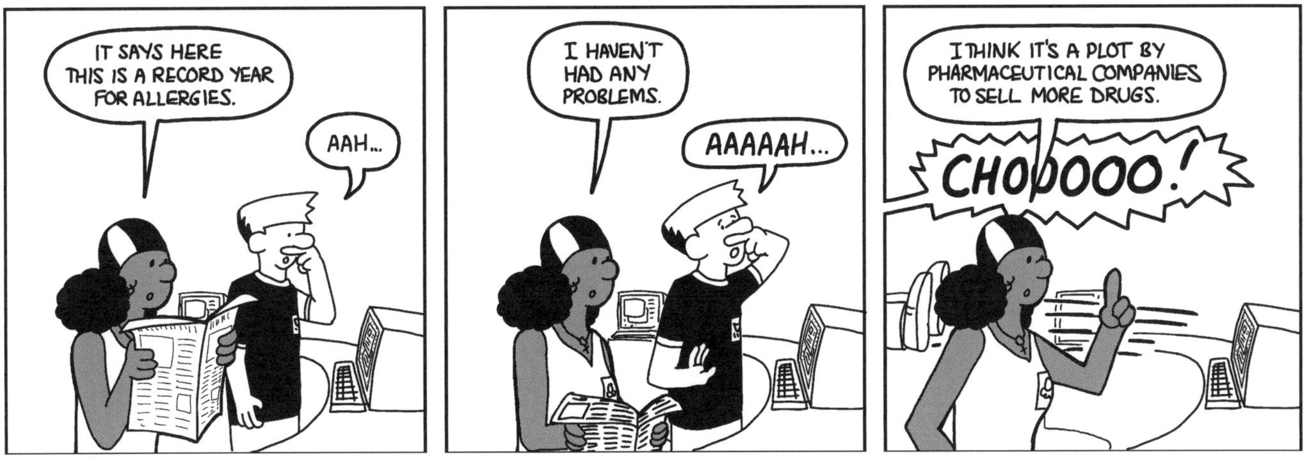
IT SAYS HERE THIS IS A RECORD YEAR FOR ALLERGIES.
AAH...
I HAVEN'T HAD ANY PROBLEMS.
AAAAAH...
I THINK IT'S A PLOT BY PHARMACEUTICAL COMPANIES TO SELL MORE DRUGS.
CHOOOOO!

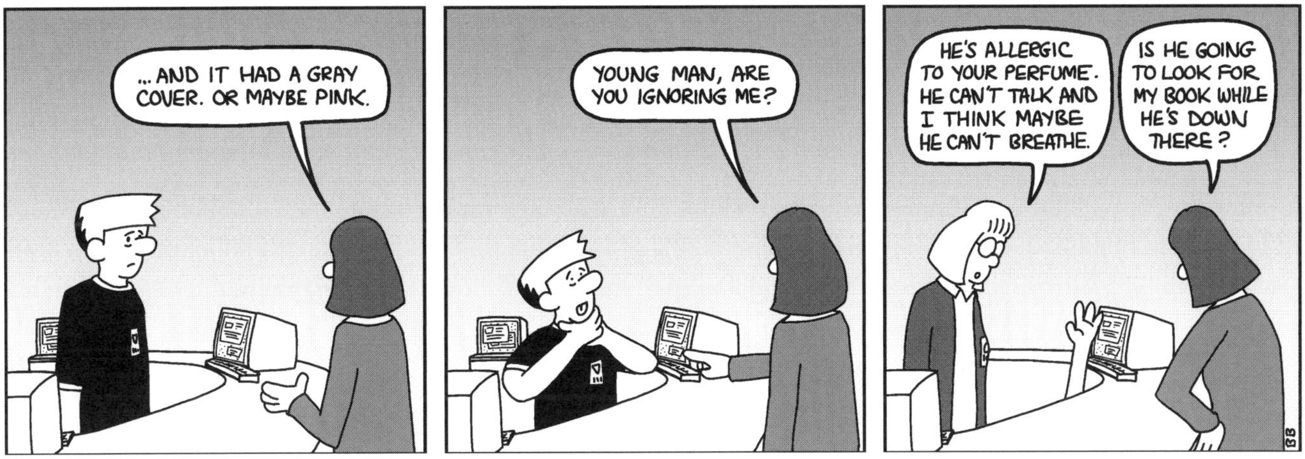
...AND IT HAD A GRAY COVER. OR MAYBE PINK.
YOUNG MAN, ARE YOU IGNORING ME?
HE'S ALLERGIC TO YOUR PERFUME. HE CAN'T TALK AND I THINK MAYBE HE CAN'T BREATHE.
IS HE GOING TO LOOK FOR MY BOOK WHILE HE'S DOWN THERE?
BB

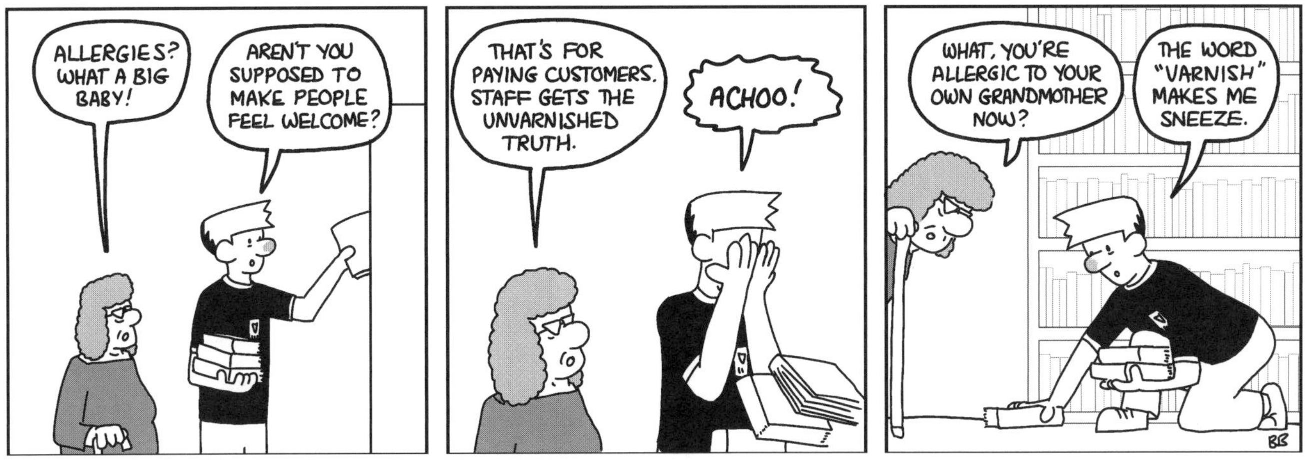
ALLERGIES? WHAT A BIG BABY!
AREN'T YOU SUPPOSED TO MAKE PEOPLE FEEL WELCOME?
THAT'S FOR PAYING CUSTOMERS. STAFF GETS THE UNVARNISHED TRUTH.
ACHOO!
WHAT, YOU'RE ALLERGIC TO YOUR OWN GRANDMOTHER NOW?
THE WORD "VARNISH" MAKES ME SNEEZE.
BB

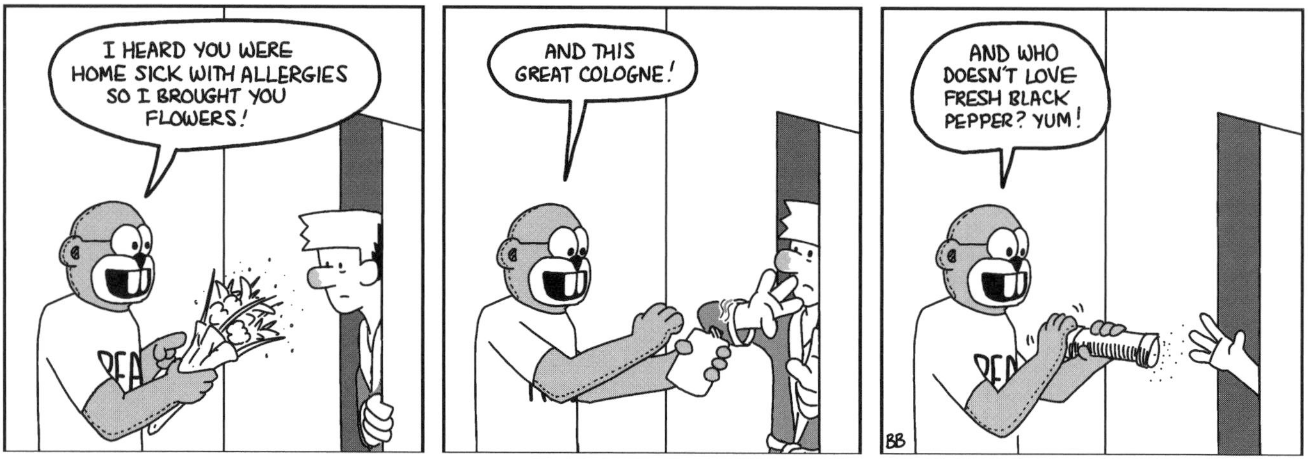
I HEARD YOU WERE HOME SICK WITH ALLERGIES SO I BROUGHT YOU FLOWERS!
AND THIS GREAT COLOGNE!
AND WHO DOESN'T LOVE FRESH BLACK PEPPER? YUM!
BB

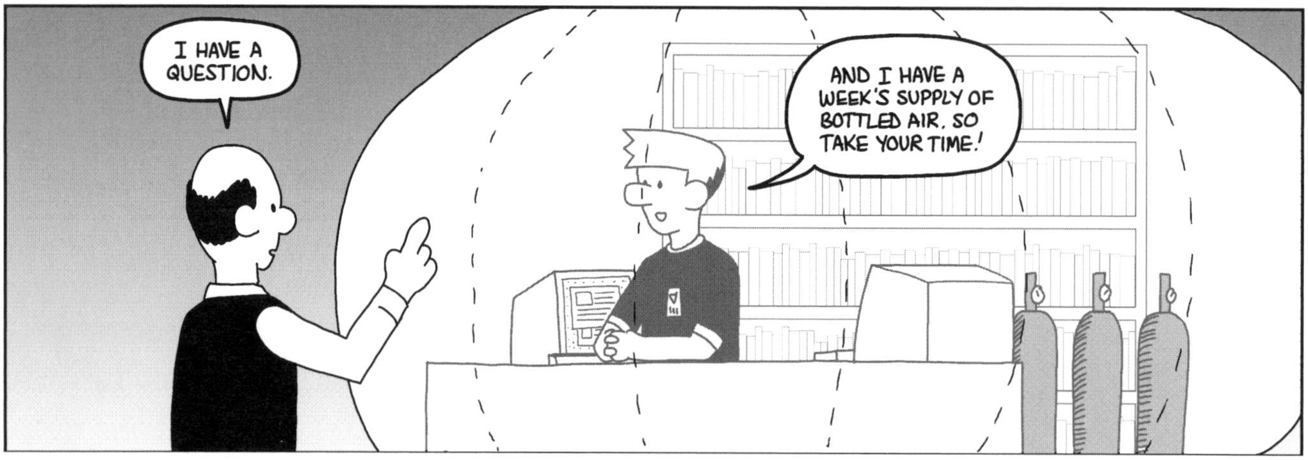
I HAVE A QUESTION.
AND I HAVE A WEEK'S SUPPLY OF BOTTLED AIR, SO TAKE YOUR TIME!

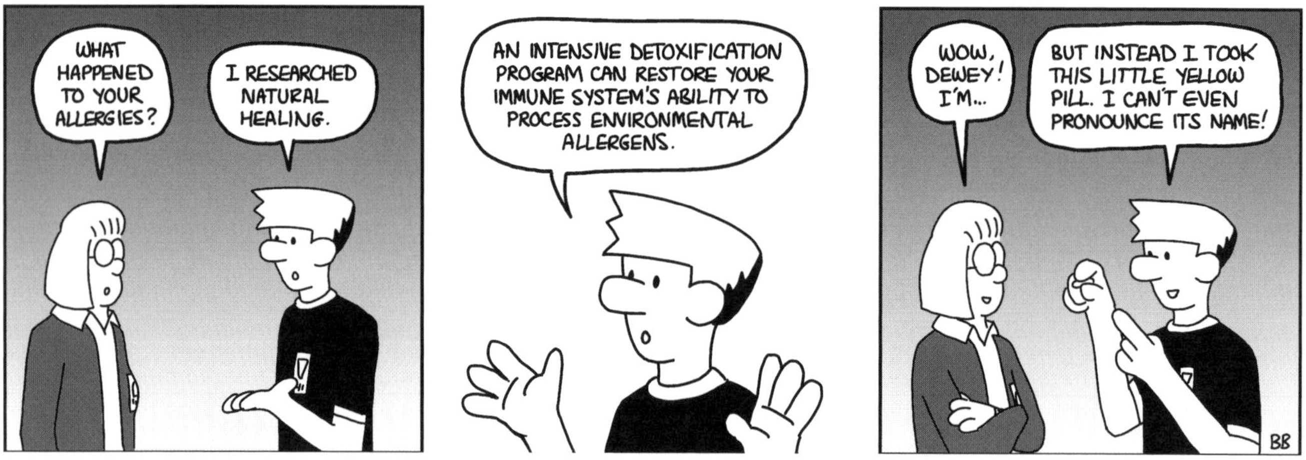
WHAT HAPPENED TO YOUR ALLERGIES?
I RESEARCHED NATURAL HEALING.
AN INTENSIVE DETOXIFICATION PROGRAM CAN RESTORE YOUR IMMUNE SYSTEM'S ABILITY TO PROCESS ENVIRONMENTAL ALLERGENS.
WOW, DEWEY! I'M...
BUT INSTEAD I TOOK THIS LITTLE YELLOW PILL. I CAN'T EVEN PRONOUNCE ITS NAME!
BB

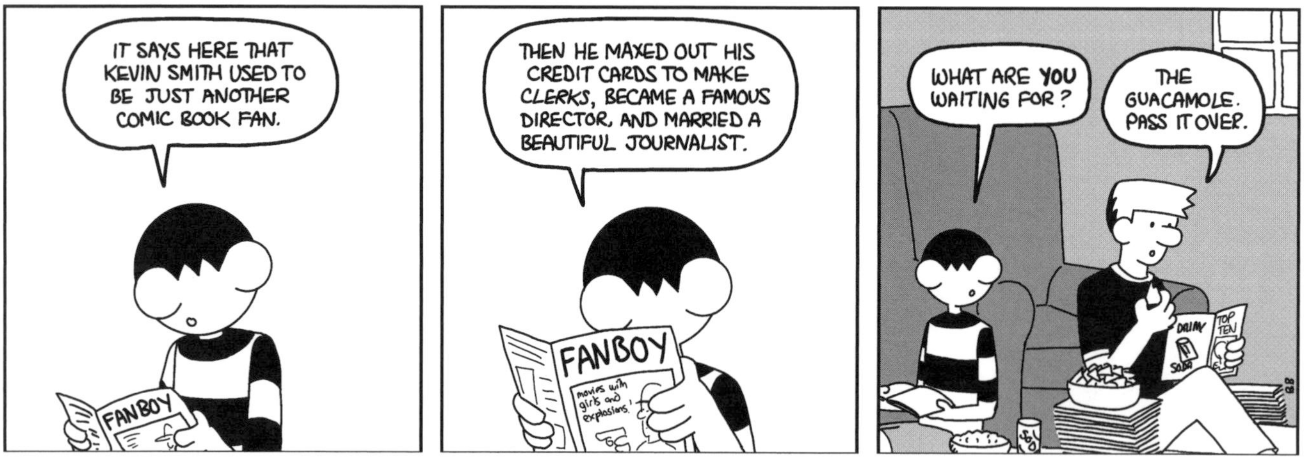
IT SAYS HERE THAT KEVIN SMITH USED TO BE JUST ANOTHER COMIC BOOK FAN.
FANBOY
THEN HE MAXED OUT HIS CREDIT CARDS TO MAKE CLERKS, BECAME A FAMOUS DIRECTOR, AND MARRIED A BEAUTIFUL JOURNALIST.
FANBOY
movies with girls and explosions!
WHAT ARE YOU WAITING FOR?
THE GUACAMOLE. PASS IT OVER.
TOP TEN

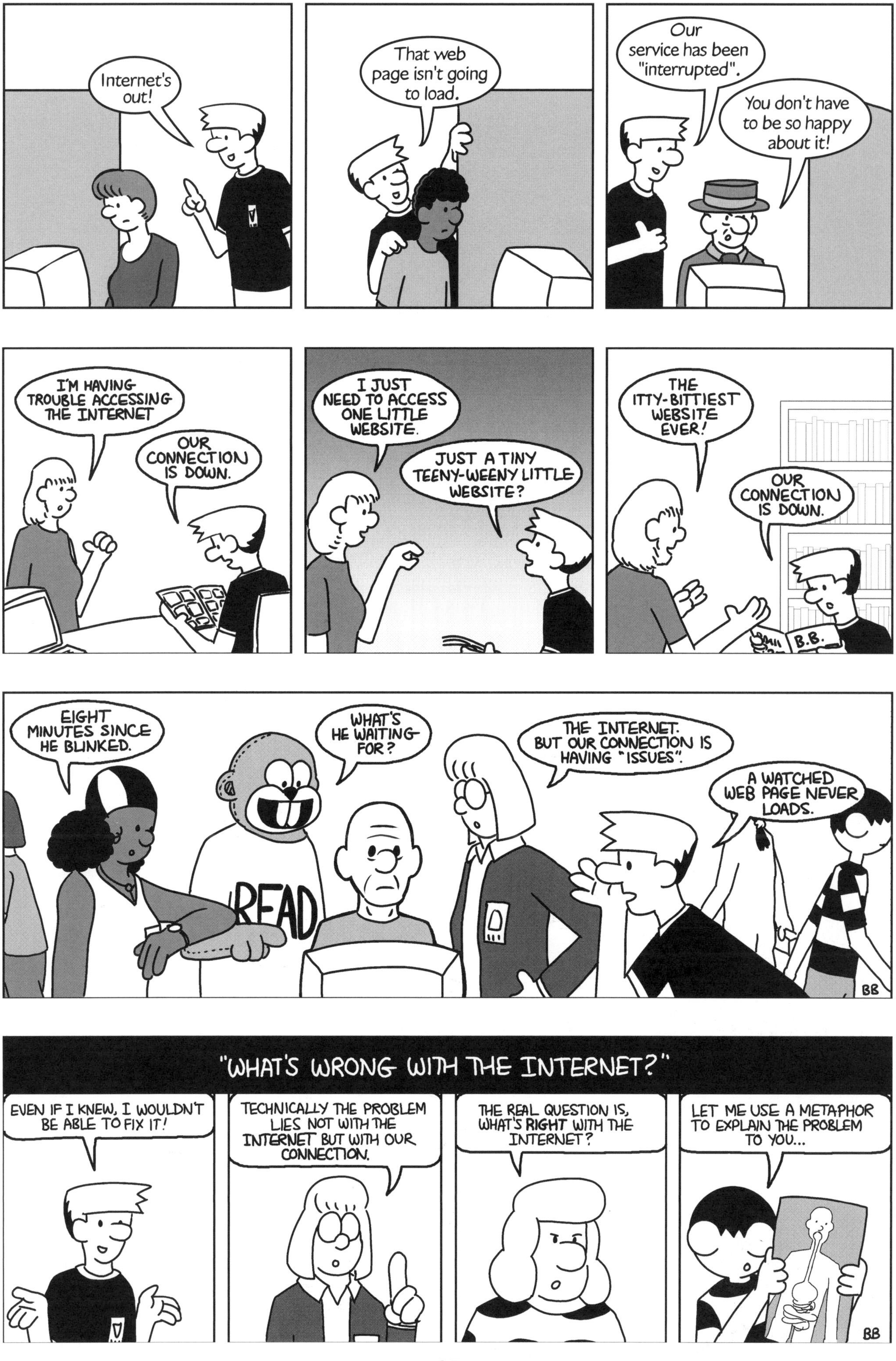
Internet's out!
That web page isn't going to load.
Our service has been "interrupted".
You don't have to be so happy about it!
I'M HAVING TROUBLE ACCESSING THE INTERNET
OUR CONNECTION IS DOWN.
I JUST NEED TO ACCESS ONE LITTLE WEBSITE.
JUST A TINY TEENY-WEENY LITTLE WEBSITE?
THE ITTY-BITTIEST WEBSITE EVER!
OUR CONNECTION IS DOWN.
EIGHT MINUTES SINCE HE BLINKED.
WHAT'S HE WAITING FOR?
THE INTERNET. BUT OUR CONNECTION IS HAVING "ISSUES".
A WATCHED WEB PAGE NEVER LOADS.
READ
"WHAT'S WRONG WITH THE INTERNET?"
EVEN IF I KNEW, I WOULDN'T BE ABLE TO FIX IT!
TECHNICALLY THE PROBLEM LIES NOT WITH THE INTERNET BUT WITH OUR CONNECTION.
THE REAL QUESTION IS, WHAT'S RIGHT WITH THE INTERNET?
LET ME USE A METAPHOR TO EXPLAIN THE PROBLEM TO YOU...

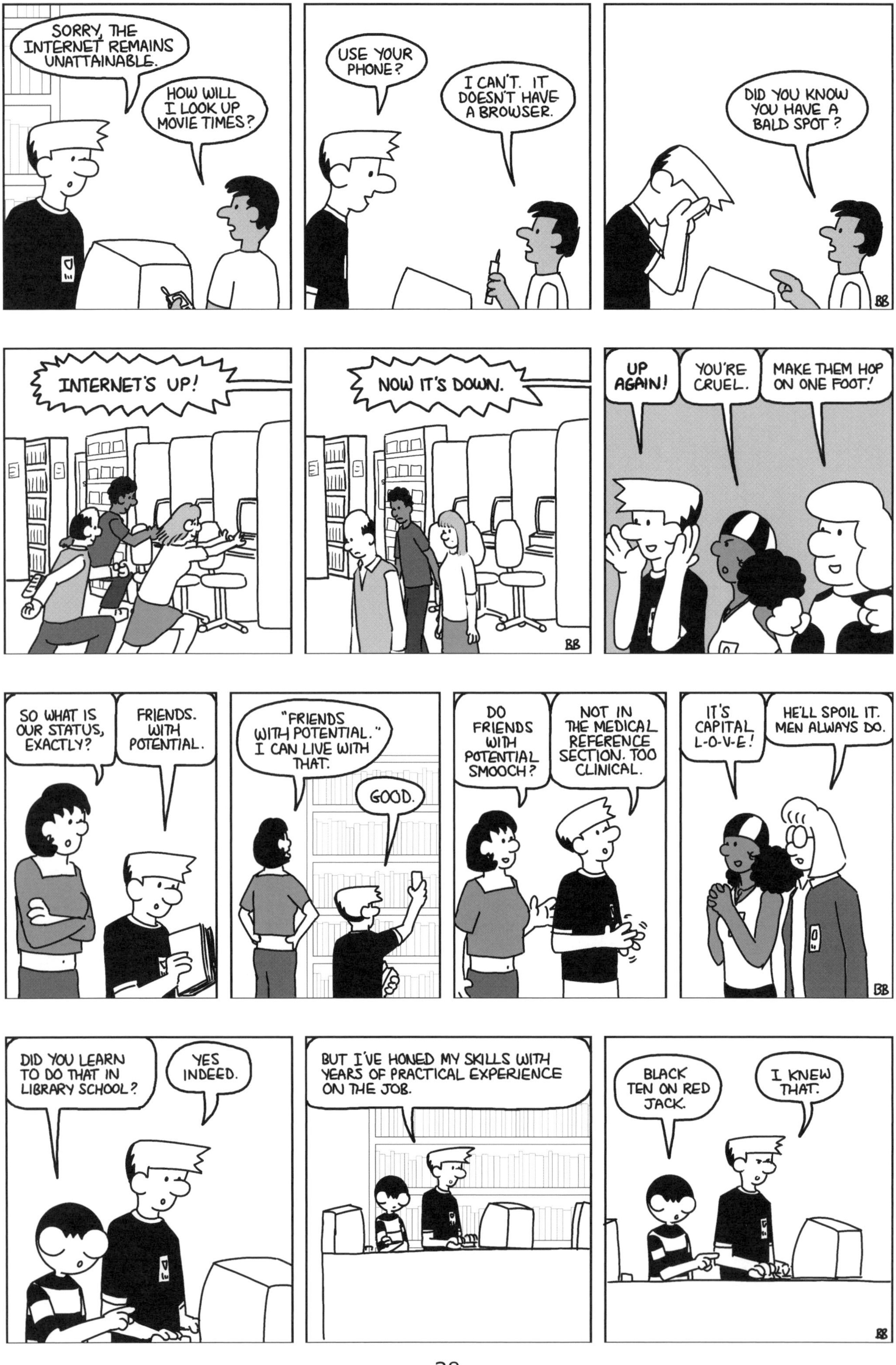
SORRY, THE INTERNET REMAINS UNATTAINABLE.
HOW WILL I LOOK UP MOVIE TIMES?
USE YOUR PHONE?
I CAN'T. IT DOESN'T HAVE A BROWSER.
DID YOU KNOW YOU HAVE A BALD SPOT?
BB
INTERNET'S UP!
NOW IT'S DOWN.
UP AGAIN!
YOU'RE CRUEL.
MAKE THEM HOP ON ONE FOOT!
BB
SO WHAT IS OUR STATUS, EXACTLY?
FRIENDS. WITH POTENTIAL.
"FRIENDS WITH POTENTIAL." I CAN LIVE WITH THAT.
GOOD.
DO FRIENDS WITH POTENTIAL SMOOCH?
NOT IN THE MEDICAL REFERENCE SECTION. TOO CLINICAL.
IT'S CAPITAL L-O-V-E!
HE'LL SPOIL IT. MEN ALWAYS DO.
BB
DID YOU LEARN TO DO THAT IN LIBRARY SCHOOL?
YES INDEED.
BUT I'VE HONED MY SKILLS WITH YEARS OF PRACTICAL EXPERIENCE ON THE JOB.
BLACK TEN ON RED JACK.
I KNEW THAT.
BB

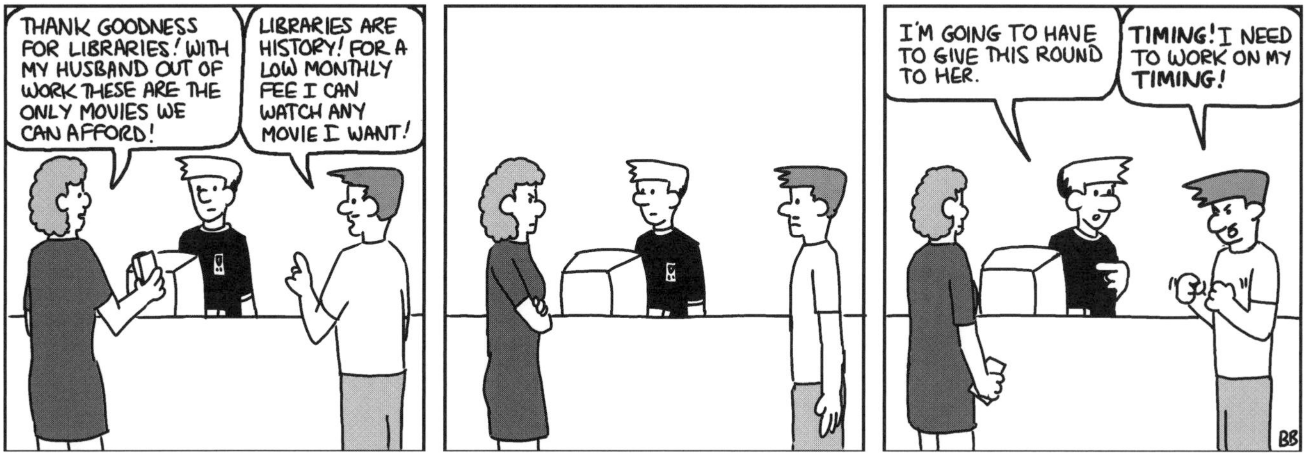
THANK GOODNESS FOR LIBRARIES! WITH MY HUSBAND OUT OF WORK THESE ARE THE ONLY MOVIES WE CAN AFFORD!
LIBRARIES ARE HISTORY! FOR A LOW MONTHLY FEE I CAN WATCH ANY MOVIE I WANT!
I'M GOING TO HAVE TO GIVE THIS ROUND TO HER.
TIMING! I NEED TO WORK ON MY TIMING!
BB

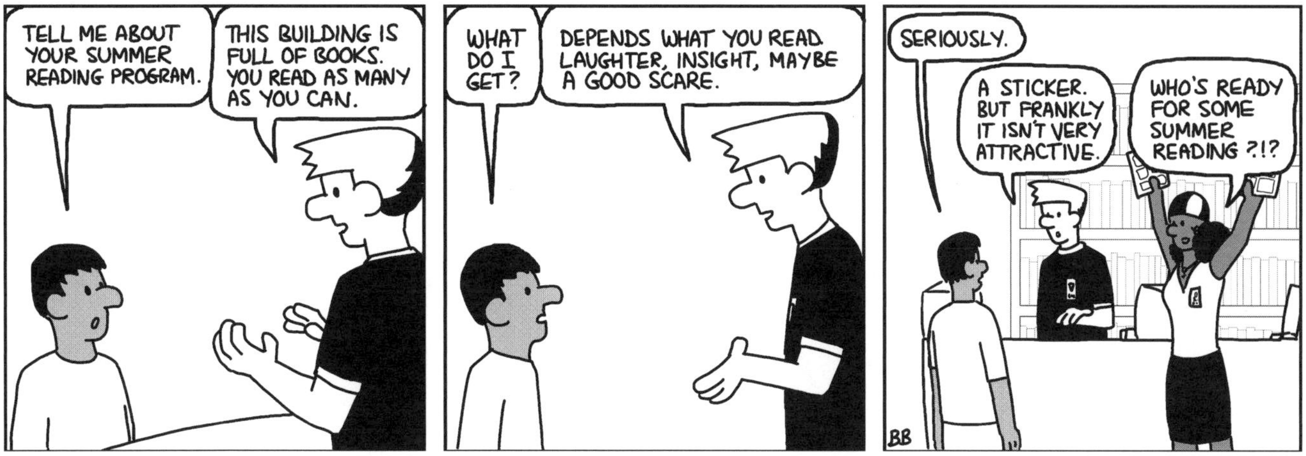
TELL ME ABOUT YOUR SUMMER READING PROGRAM.
THIS BUILDING IS FULL OF BOOKS. YOU READ AS MANY AS YOU CAN.
WHAT DO I GET?
DEPENDS WHAT YOU READ. LAUGHTER, INSIGHT, MAYBE A GOOD SCARE.
SERIOUSLY.
A STICKER. BUT FRANKLY IT ISN'T VERY ATTRACTIVE.
WHO'S READY FOR SOME SUMMER READING ?!?
BB

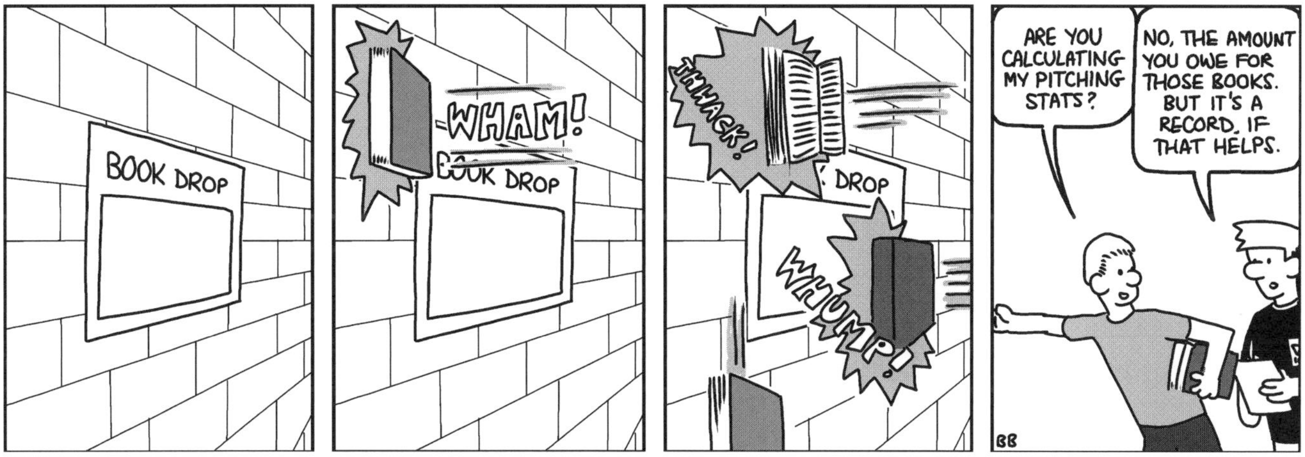
BOOK DROP
WHAM!
THWACK!
WHUMP!
ARE YOU CALCULATING MY PITCHING STATS?
NO, THE AMOUNT YOU OWE FOR THOSE BOOKS. BUT IT'S A RECORD, IF THAT HELPS.
BB

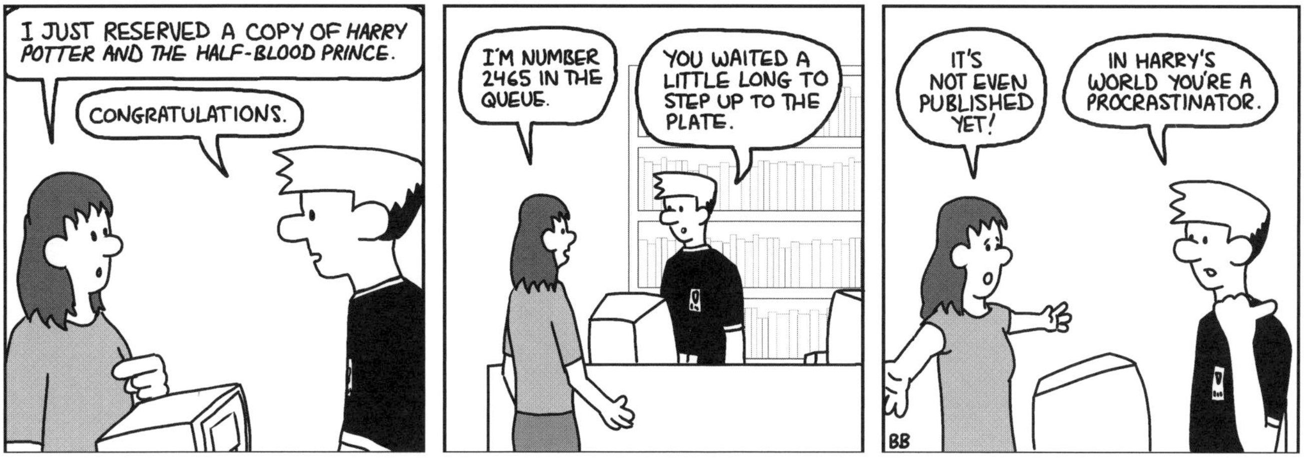
I JUST RESERVED A COPY OF *HARRY POTTER AND THE HALF-BLOOD PRINCE*.
CONGRATULATIONS.
I'M NUMBER 2465 IN THE QUEUE.
YOU WAITED A LITTLE LONG TO STEP UP TO THE PLATE.
IT'S NOT EVEN PUBLISHED YET!
IN HARRY'S WORLD YOU'RE A PROCRASTINATOR.
BB

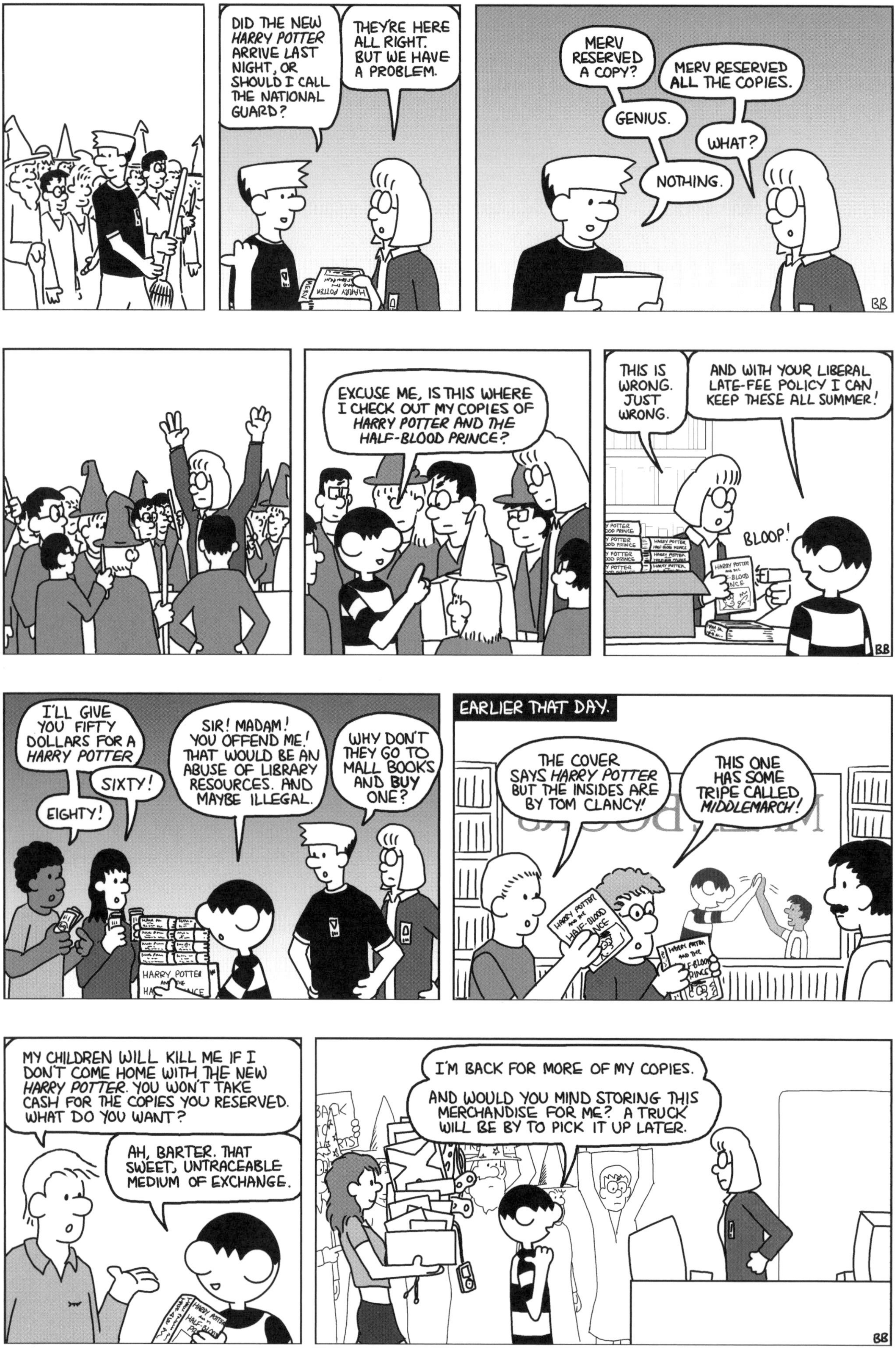
DID THE NEW *HARRY POTTER* ARRIVE LAST NIGHT, OR SHOULD I CALL THE NATIONAL GUARD?
THEY'RE HERE ALL RIGHT. BUT WE HAVE A PROBLEM.
MERV RESERVED A COPY?
GENIUS.
NOTHING.
MERV RESERVED **ALL** THE COPIES.
WHAT?
BB
EXCUSE ME, IS THIS WHERE I CHECK OUT MY COPIES OF *HARRY POTTER AND THE HALF-BLOOD PRINCE?*
THIS IS WRONG. JUST WRONG.
AND WITH YOUR LIBERAL LATE-FEE POLICY I CAN KEEP THESE ALL SUMMER!
BLOOP!
BB
I'LL GIVE YOU FIFTY DOLLARS FOR A *HARRY POTTER*
SIXTY!
EIGHTY!
SIR! MADAM! YOU OFFEND ME! THAT WOULD BE AN ABUSE OF LIBRARY RESOURCES. AND MAYBE ILLEGAL.
WHY DON'T THEY GO TO MALL BOOKS AND **BUY** ONE?
EARLIER THAT DAY.
THE COVER SAYS *HARRY POTTER* BUT THE INSIDES ARE BY TOM CLANCY!
THIS ONE HAS SOME TRIPE CALLED *MIDDLEMARCH!*
MY CHILDREN WILL KILL ME IF I DON'T COME HOME WITH THE NEW *HARRY POTTER*. YOU WON'T TAKE CASH FOR THE COPIES YOU RESERVED. WHAT DO YOU WANT?
AH, BARTER. THAT SWEET, UNTRACEABLE MEDIUM OF EXCHANGE.
I'M BACK FOR MORE OF MY COPIES.
AND WOULD YOU MIND STORING THIS MERCHANDISE FOR ME? A TRUCK WILL BE BY TO PICK IT UP LATER.
BB

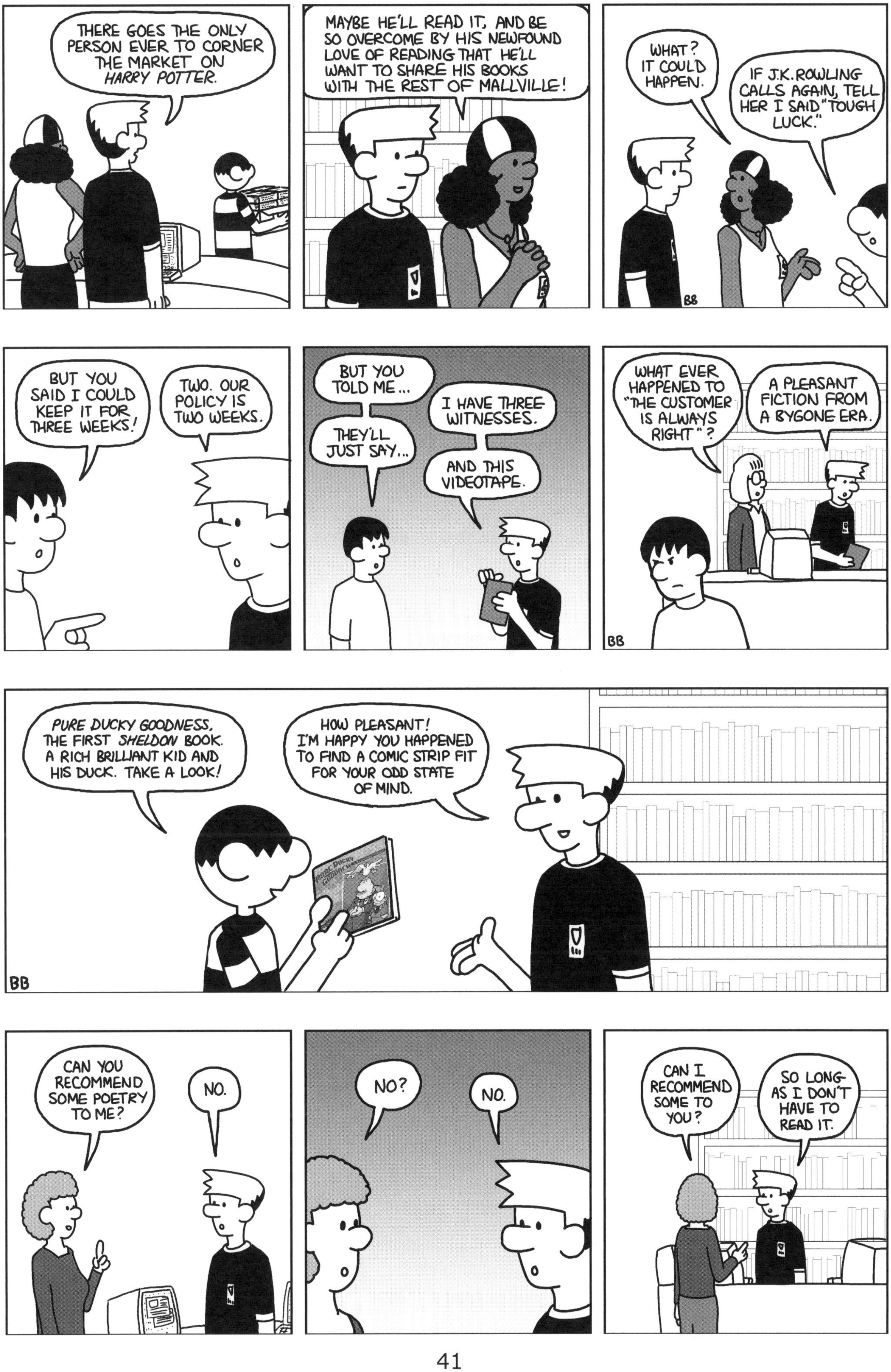
THERE GOES THE ONLY PERSON EVER TO CORNER THE MARKET ON *HARRY POTTER*.
MAYBE HE'LL READ IT, AND BE SO OVERCOME BY HIS NEWFOUND LOVE OF READING THAT HE'LL WANT TO SHARE HIS BOOKS WITH THE REST OF MALLVILLE!
WHAT? IT COULD HAPPEN.
IF J.K. ROWLING CALLS AGAIN, TELL HER I SAID "TOUGH LUCK."
BUT YOU SAID I COULD KEEP IT FOR THREE WEEKS!
TWO. OUR POLICY IS TWO WEEKS.
BUT YOU TOLD ME...
THEY'LL JUST SAY...
I HAVE THREE WITNESSES.
AND THIS VIDEOTAPE.
WHAT EVER HAPPENED TO "THE CUSTOMER IS ALWAYS RIGHT"?
A PLEASANT FICTION FROM A BYGONE ERA.
PURE DUCKY GOODNESS, THE FIRST *SHELDON* BOOK. A RICH BRILLIANT KID AND HIS DUCK. TAKE A LOOK!
HOW PLEASANT! I'M HAPPY YOU HAPPENED TO FIND A COMIC STRIP FIT FOR YOUR ODD STATE OF MIND.
CAN YOU RECOMMEND SOME POETRY TO ME?
NO.
NO?
NO.
CAN I RECOMMEND SOME TO YOU?
SO LONG AS I DON'T HAVE TO READ IT.

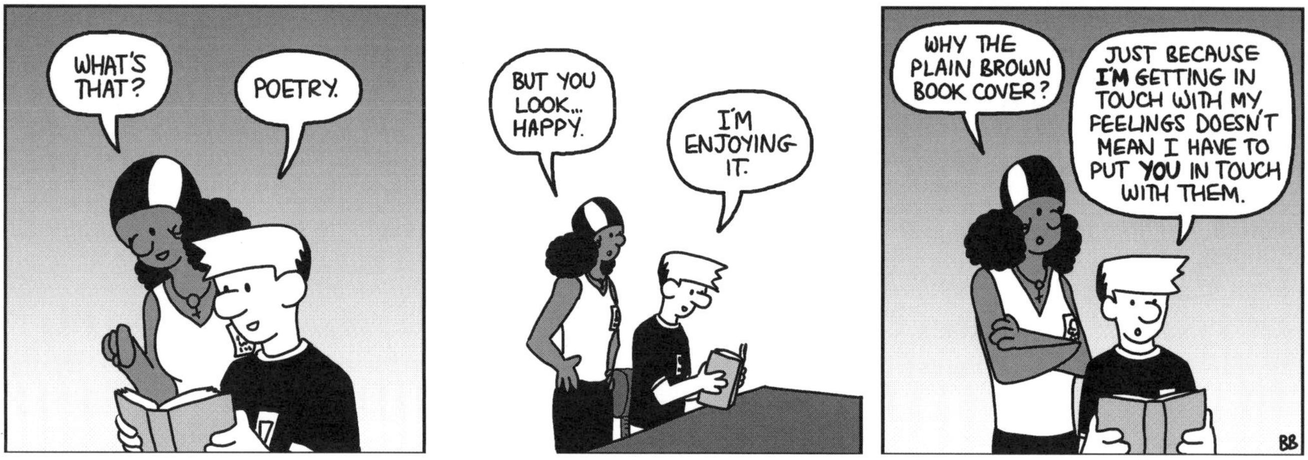
WHAT'S THAT?
POETRY.
BUT YOU LOOK... HAPPY.
I'M ENJOYING IT.
WHY THE PLAIN BROWN BOOK COVER?
JUST BECAUSE I'M GETTING IN TOUCH WITH MY FEELINGS DOESN'T MEAN I HAVE TO PUT YOU IN TOUCH WITH THEM.
BB

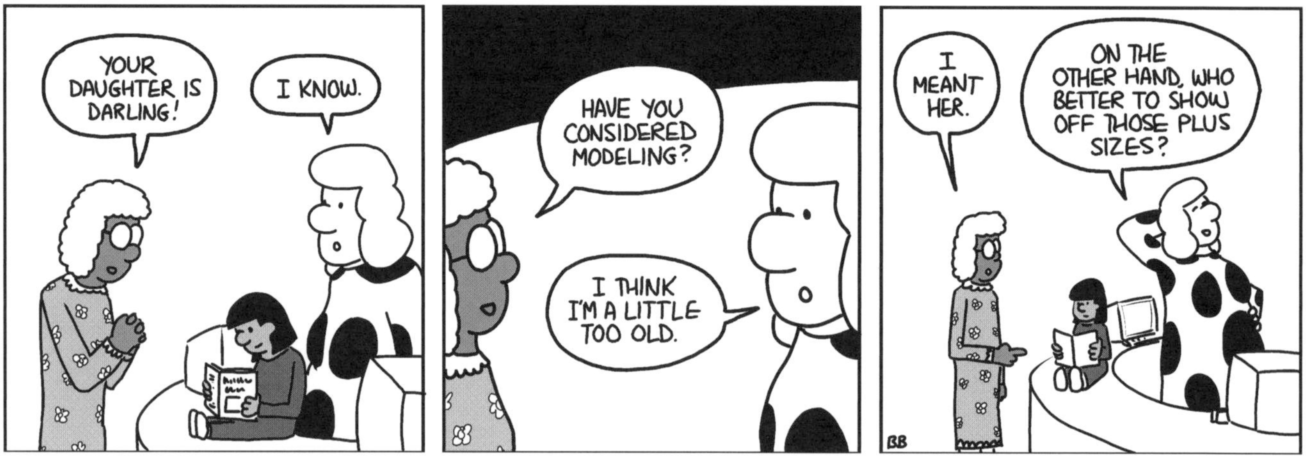
YOUR DAUGHTER IS DARLING!
I KNOW.
HAVE YOU CONSIDERED MODELING?
I THINK I'M A LITTLE TOO OLD.
I MEANT HER.
ON THE OTHER HAND, WHO BETTER TO SHOW OFF THOSE PLUS SIZES?
BB

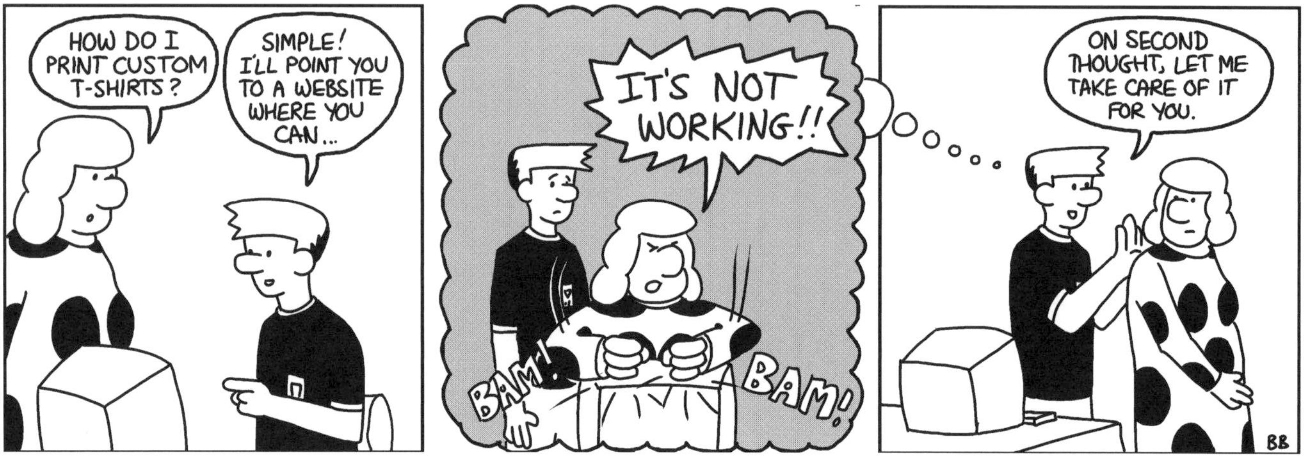
HOW DO I PRINT CUSTOM T-SHIRTS?
SIMPLE! I'LL POINT YOU TO A WEBSITE WHERE YOU CAN...
IT'S NOT WORKING!!
BAM!
BAM!
ON SECOND THOUGHT, LET ME TAKE CARE OF IT FOR YOU.
BB

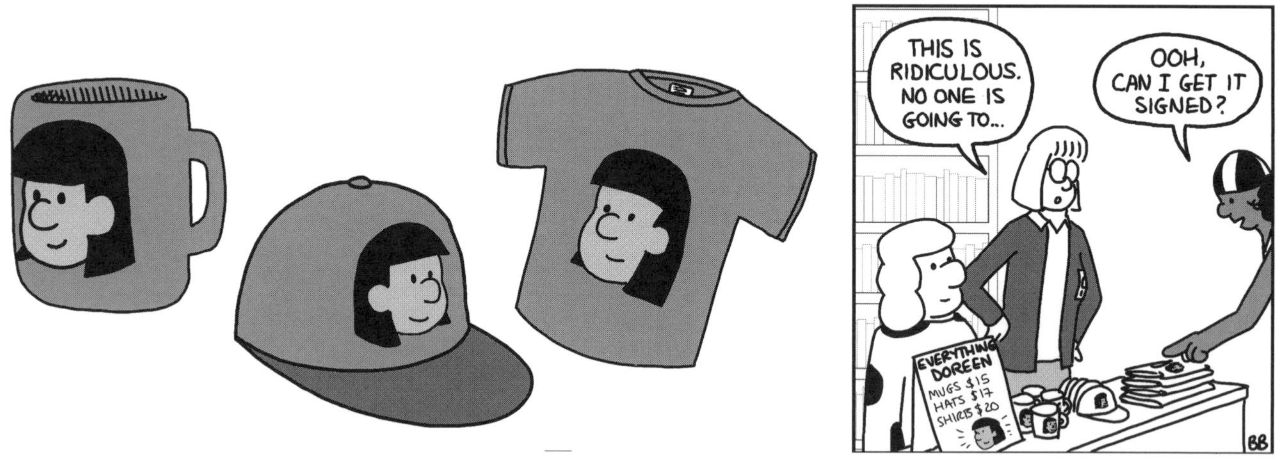
THIS IS RIDICULOUS. NO ONE IS GOING TO...
OOH, CAN I GET IT SIGNED?
EVERYTHING DOREEN
MUGS $15
HATS $17
SHIRTS $20
BB

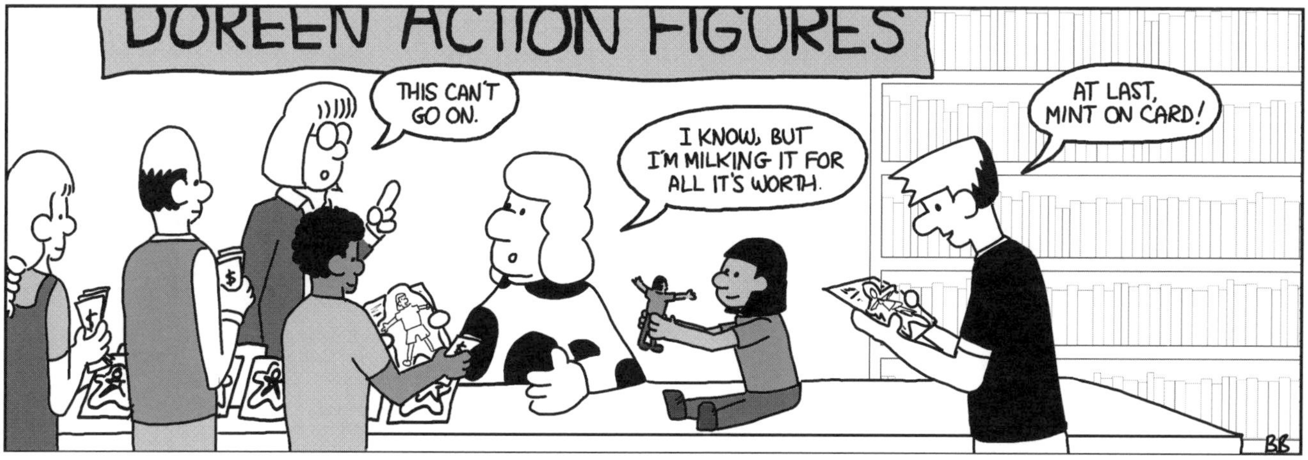
DOREEN ACTION FIGURES
THIS CAN'T GO ON.
I KNOW, BUT I'M MILKING IT FOR ALL IT'S WORTH.
AT LAST, MINT ON CARD!

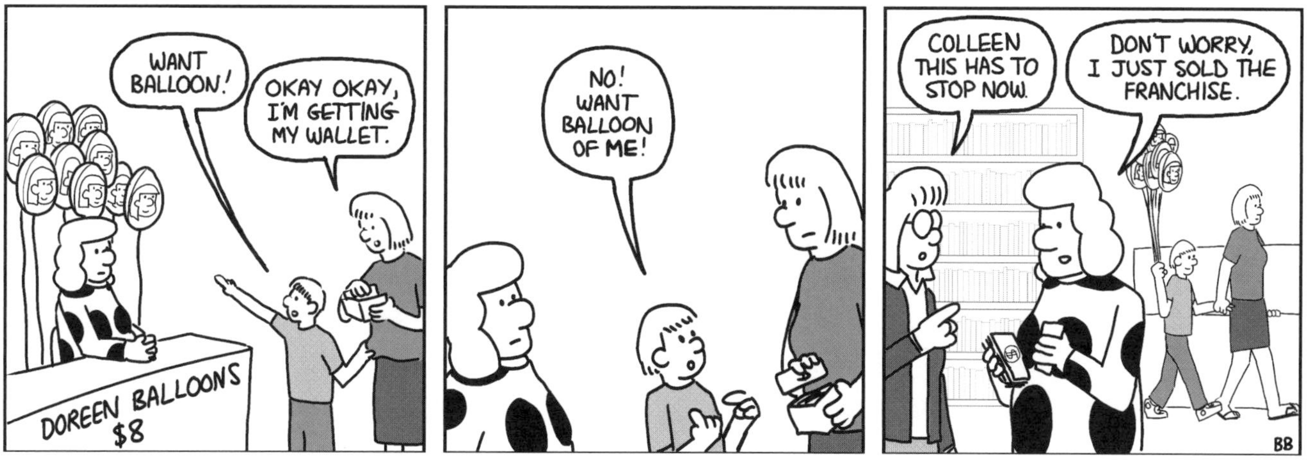
WANT BALLOON!
OKAY OKAY, I'M GETTING MY WALLET.
DOREEN BALLOONS $8
NO! WANT BALLOON OF ME!
COLLEEN THIS HAS TO STOP NOW.
DON'T WORRY, I JUST SOLD THE FRANCHISE.

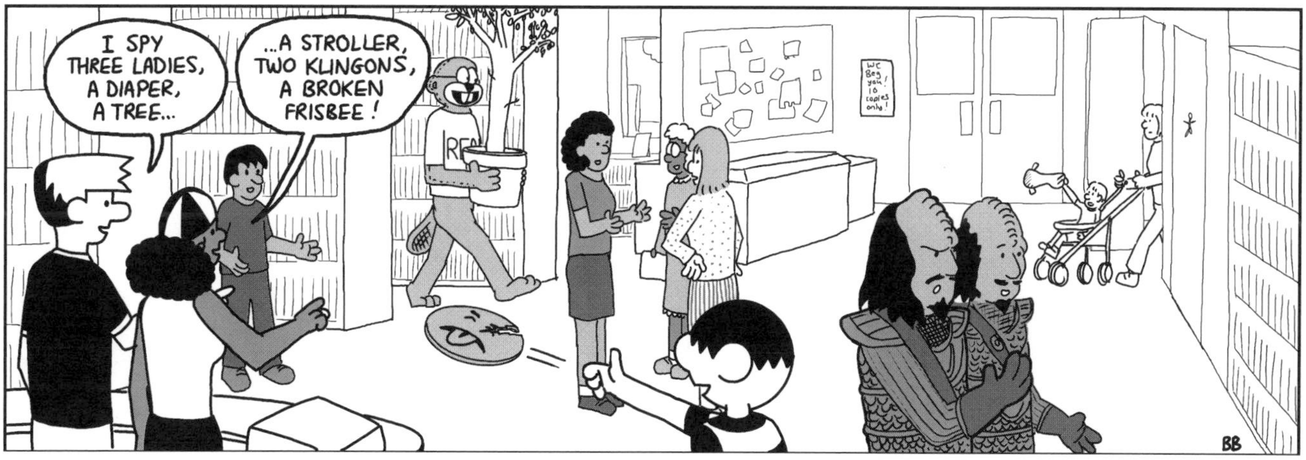
I SPY THREE LADIES, A DIAPER, A TREE...
...A STROLLER, TWO KLINGONS, A BROKEN FRISBEE!

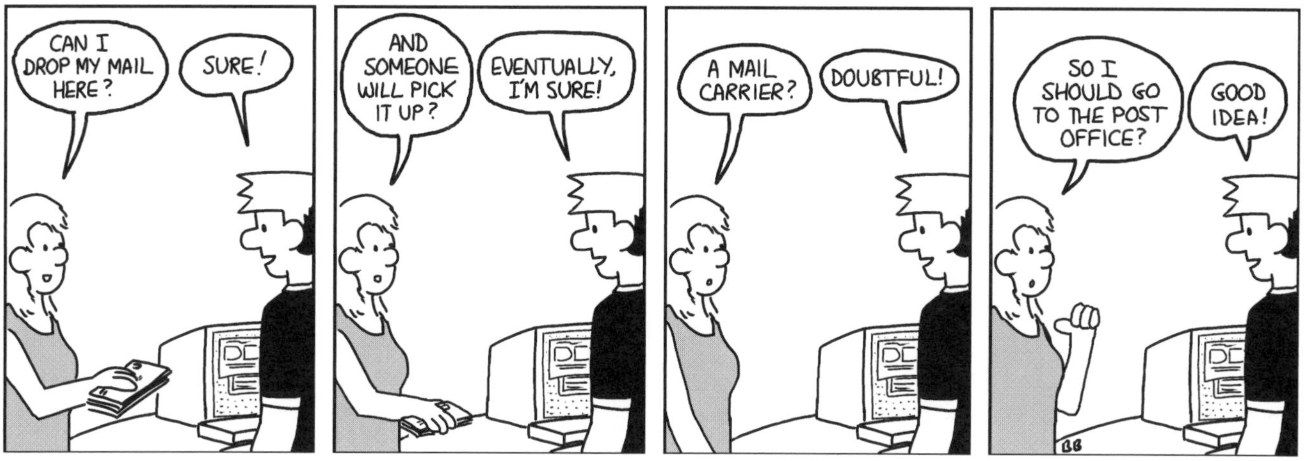
CAN I DROP MY MAIL HERE?
SURE!
AND SOMEONE WILL PICK IT UP?
EVENTUALLY, I'M SURE!
A MAIL CARRIER?
DOUBTFUL!
SO I SHOULD GO TO THE POST OFFICE?
GOOD IDEA!

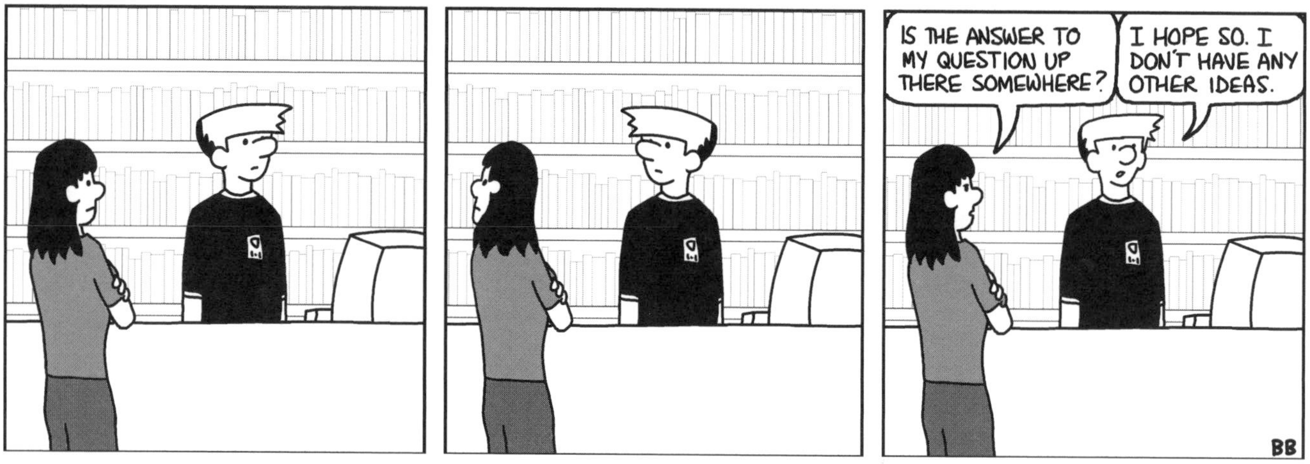
IS THE ANSWER TO MY QUESTION UP THERE SOMEWHERE?
I HOPE SO. I DON'T HAVE ANY OTHER IDEAS.

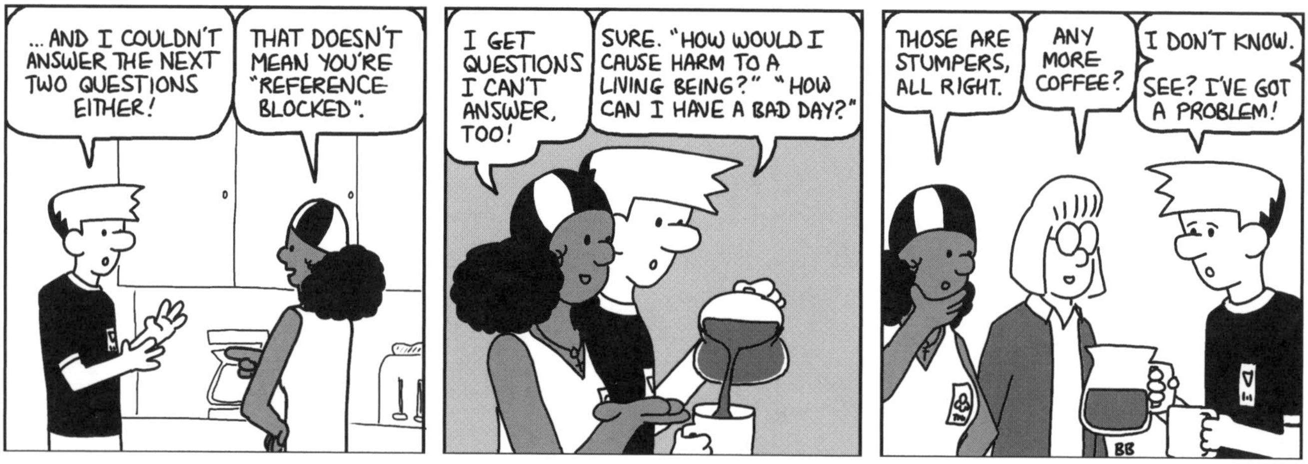
... AND I COULDN'T ANSWER THE NEXT TWO QUESTIONS EITHER!
THAT DOESN'T MEAN YOU'RE "REFERENCE BLOCKED".
I GET QUESTIONS I CAN'T ANSWER, TOO!
SURE. "HOW WOULD I CAUSE HARM TO A LIVING BEING?" "HOW CAN I HAVE A BAD DAY?"
THOSE ARE STUMPERS, ALL RIGHT.
ANY MORE COFFEE?
I DON'T KNOW.
SEE? I'VE GOT A PROBLEM!

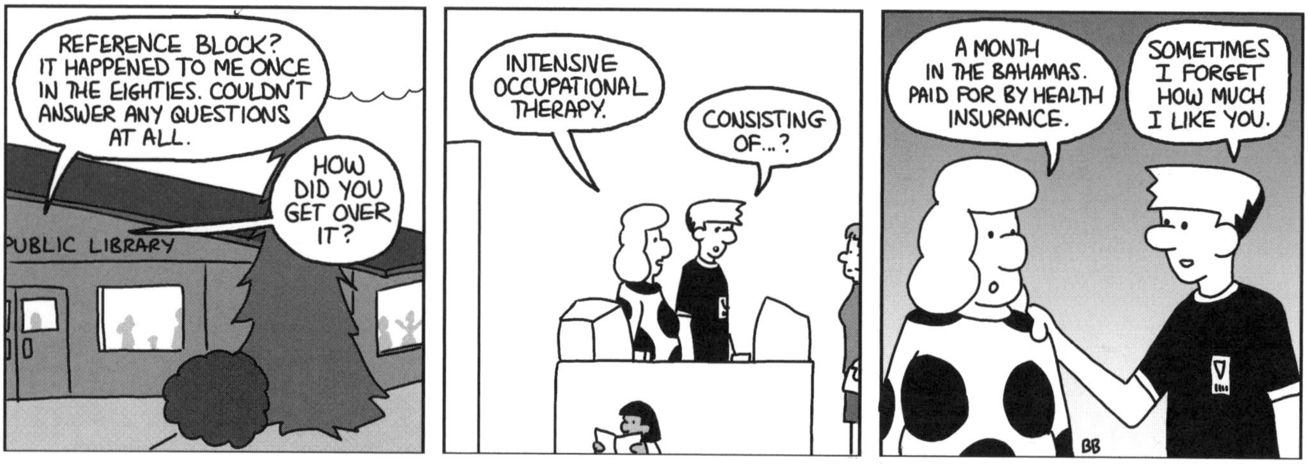
REFERENCE BLOCK? IT HAPPENED TO ME ONCE IN THE EIGHTIES. COULDN'T ANSWER ANY QUESTIONS AT ALL.
HOW DID YOU GET OVER IT?
PUBLIC LIBRARY
INTENSIVE OCCUPATIONAL THERAPY.
CONSISTING OF...?
A MONTH IN THE BAHAMAS. PAID FOR BY HEALTH INSURANCE.
SOMETIMES I FORGET HOW MUCH I LIKE YOU.

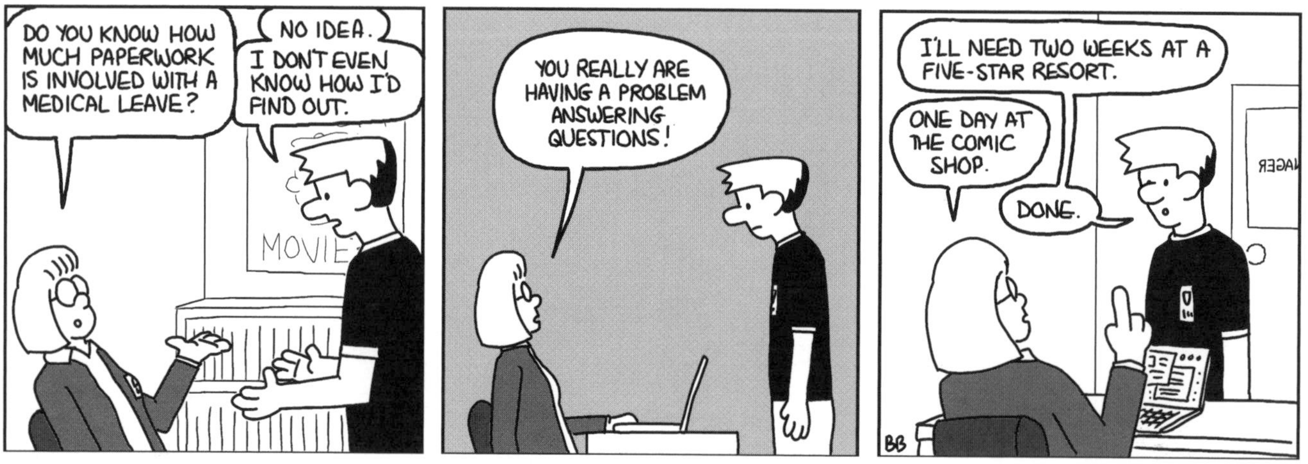
DO YOU KNOW HOW MUCH PAPERWORK IS INVOLVED WITH A MEDICAL LEAVE?
NO IDEA. I DON'T EVEN KNOW HOW I'D FIND OUT.
MOVIE
YOU REALLY ARE HAVING A PROBLEM ANSWERING QUESTIONS!
I'LL NEED TWO WEEKS AT A FIVE-STAR RESORT.
ONE DAY AT THE COMIC SHOP.
DONE.

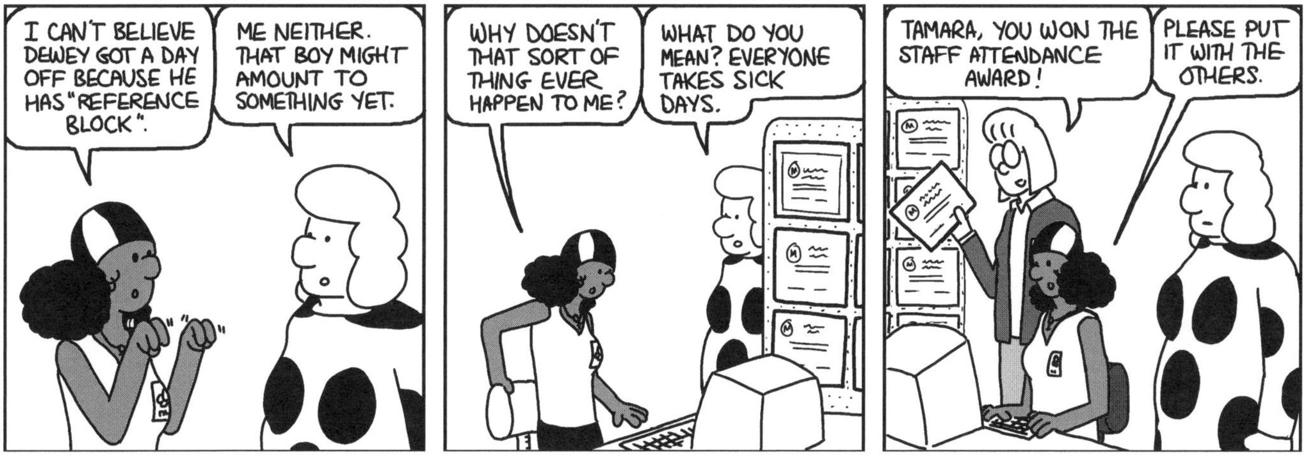
I CAN'T BELIEVE DEWEY GOT A DAY OFF BECAUSE HE HAS "REFERENCE BLOCK".
ME NEITHER. THAT BOY MIGHT AMOUNT TO SOMETHING YET.
WHY DOESN'T THAT SORT OF THING EVER HAPPEN TO ME?
WHAT DO YOU MEAN? EVERYONE TAKES SICK DAYS.
TAMARA, YOU WON THE STAFF ATTENDANCE AWARD!
PLEASE PUT IT WITH THE OTHERS.

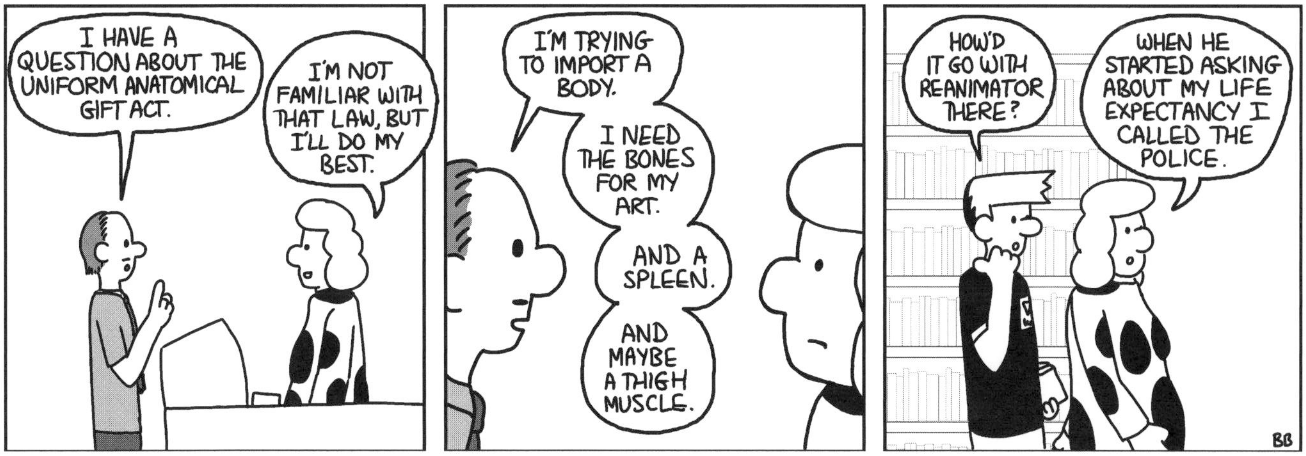
I HAVE A QUESTION ABOUT THE UNIFORM ANATOMICAL GIFT ACT.
I'M NOT FAMILIAR WITH THAT LAW, BUT I'LL DO MY BEST.
I'M TRYING TO IMPORT A BODY.
I NEED THE BONES FOR MY ART.
AND A SPLEEN.
AND MAYBE A THIGH MUSCLE.
HOW'D IT GO WITH REANIMATOR THERE?
WHEN HE STARTED ASKING ABOUT MY LIFE EXPECTANCY I CALLED THE POLICE.
BB

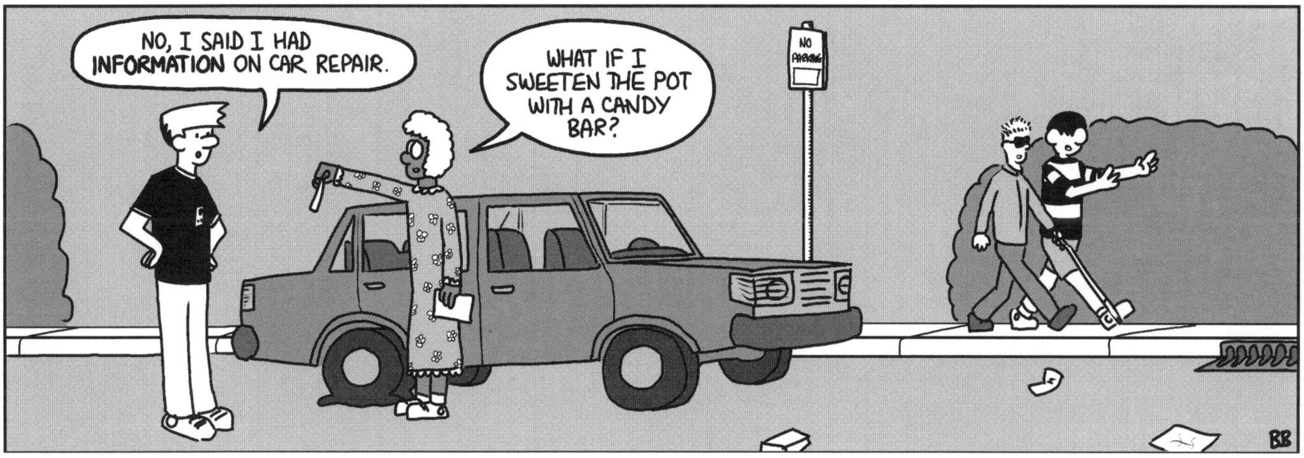
NO, I SAID I HAD INFORMATION ON CAR REPAIR.
WHAT IF I SWEETEN THE POT WITH A CANDY BAR?
NO PARKING
BB

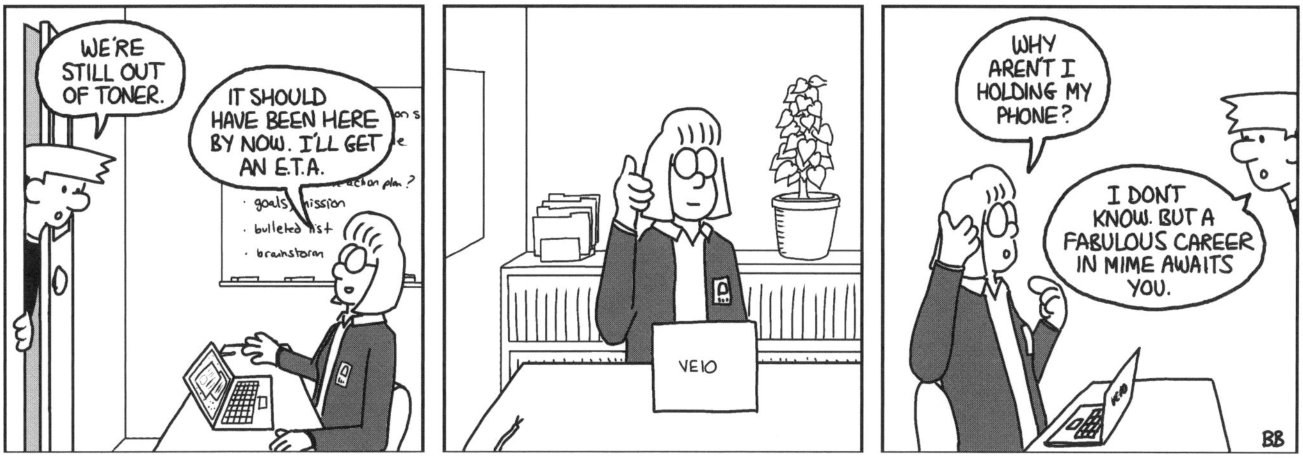
WE'RE STILL OUT OF TONER.
IT SHOULD HAVE BEEN HERE BY NOW. I'LL GET AN E.T.A.
· goals/mission
· bulleted list
· brainstorm
WHY AREN'T I HOLDING MY PHONE?
I DON'T KNOW. BUT A FABULOUS CAREER IN MIME AWAITS YOU.
BB

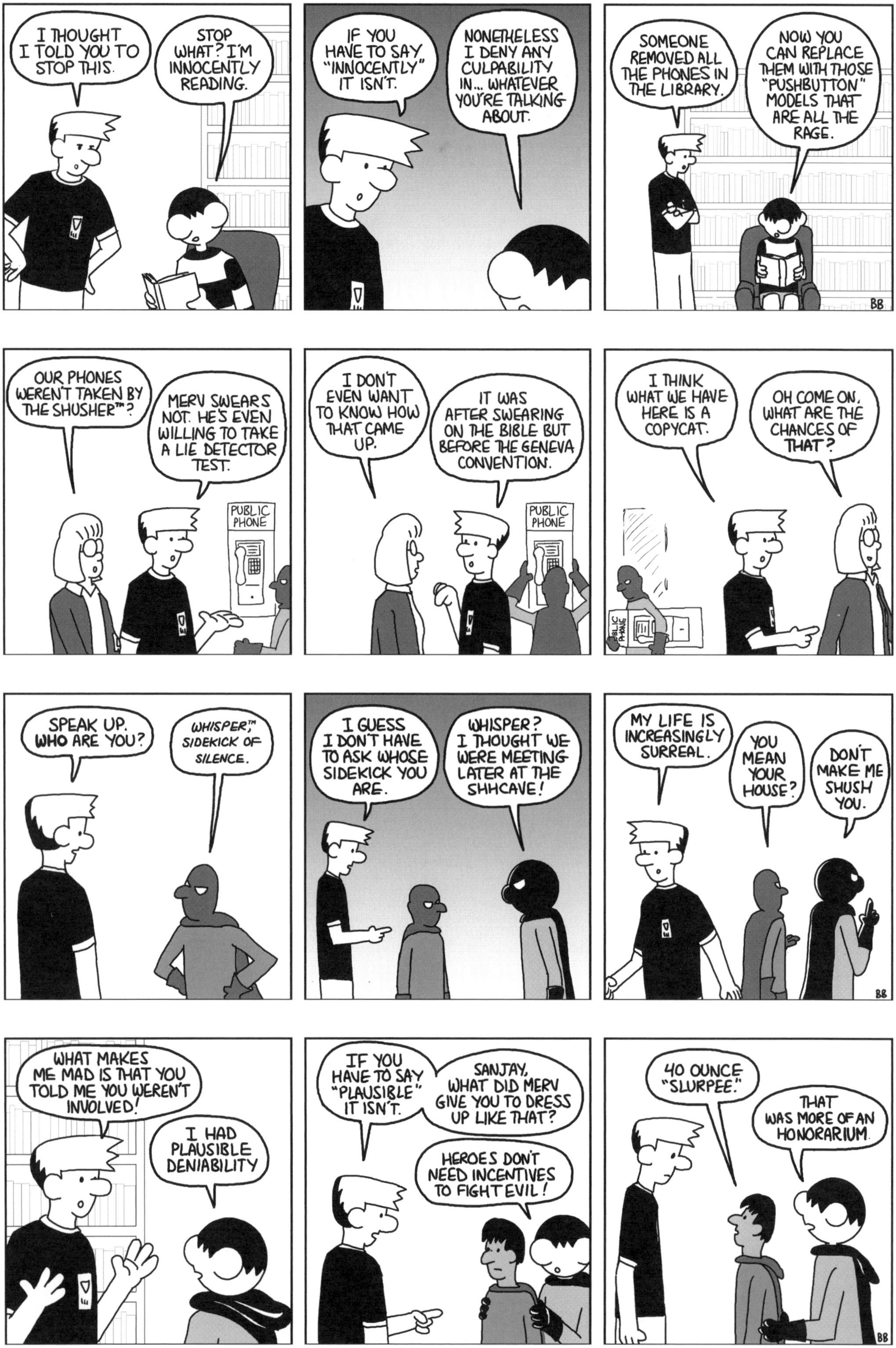
I THOUGHT I TOLD YOU TO STOP THIS.
STOP WHAT? I'M INNOCENTLY READING.
IF YOU HAVE TO SAY "INNOCENTLY" IT ISN'T.
NONETHELESS I DENY ANY CULPABILITY IN... WHATEVER YOU'RE TALKING ABOUT.
SOMEONE REMOVED ALL THE PHONES IN THE LIBRARY.
NOW YOU CAN REPLACE THEM WITH THOSE "PUSHBUTTON" MODELS THAT ARE ALL THE RAGE.
BB
OUR PHONES WEREN'T TAKEN BY THE SHUSHER™?
MERV SWEARS NOT. HE'S EVEN WILLING TO TAKE A LIE DETECTOR TEST.
PUBLIC PHONE
I DON'T EVEN WANT TO KNOW HOW THAT CAME UP.
IT WAS AFTER SWEARING ON THE BIBLE BUT BEFORE THE GENEVA CONVENTION.
PUBLIC PHONE
I THINK WHAT WE HAVE HERE IS A COPYCAT.
OH COME ON, WHAT ARE THE CHANCES OF THAT?
PUBLIC PHONE
SPEAK UP. WHO ARE YOU?
WHISPER,™ SIDEKICK OF SILENCE.
I GUESS I DON'T HAVE TO ASK WHOSE SIDEKICK YOU ARE.
WHISPER? I THOUGHT WE WERE MEETING LATER AT THE SHHCAVE!
MY LIFE IS INCREASINGLY SURREAL.
YOU MEAN YOUR HOUSE?
DON'T MAKE ME SHUSH YOU.
BB
WHAT MAKES ME MAD IS THAT YOU TOLD ME YOU WEREN'T INVOLVED!
I HAD PLAUSIBLE DENIABILITY
IF YOU HAVE TO SAY "PLAUSIBLE" IT ISN'T.
SANJAY, WHAT DID MERV GIVE YOU TO DRESS UP LIKE THAT?
HEROES DON'T NEED INCENTIVES TO FIGHT EVIL!
40 OUNCE "SLURPEE."
THAT WAS MORE OF AN HONORARIUM.
BB

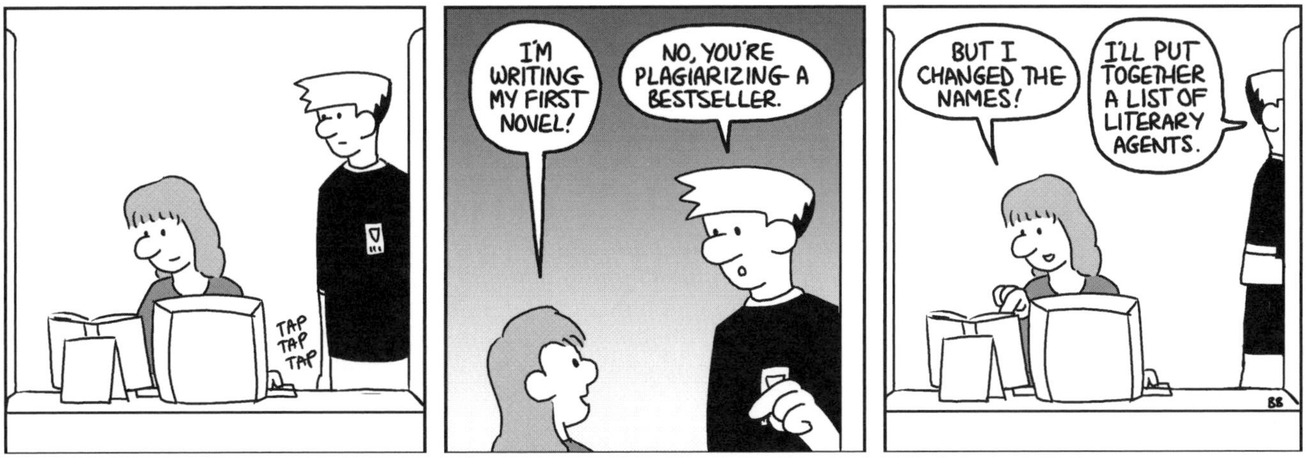
TAP
TAP
TAP
I'M WRITING MY FIRST NOVEL!
NO, YOU'RE PLAGIARIZING A BESTSELLER.
BUT I CHANGED THE NAMES!
I'LL PUT TOGETHER A LIST OF LITERARY AGENTS.
BB

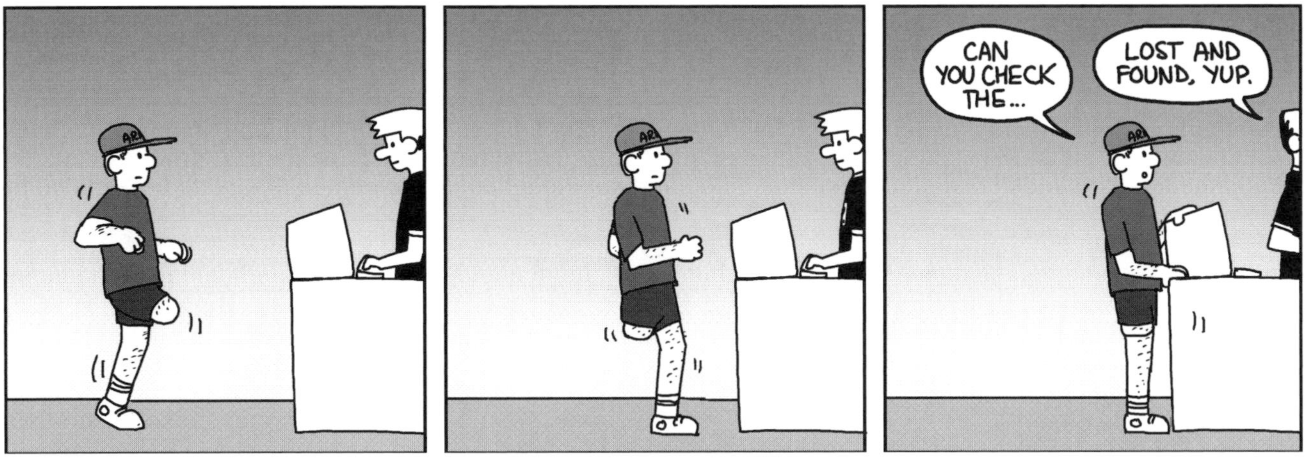
CAN YOU CHECK THE...
LOST AND FOUND, YUP.

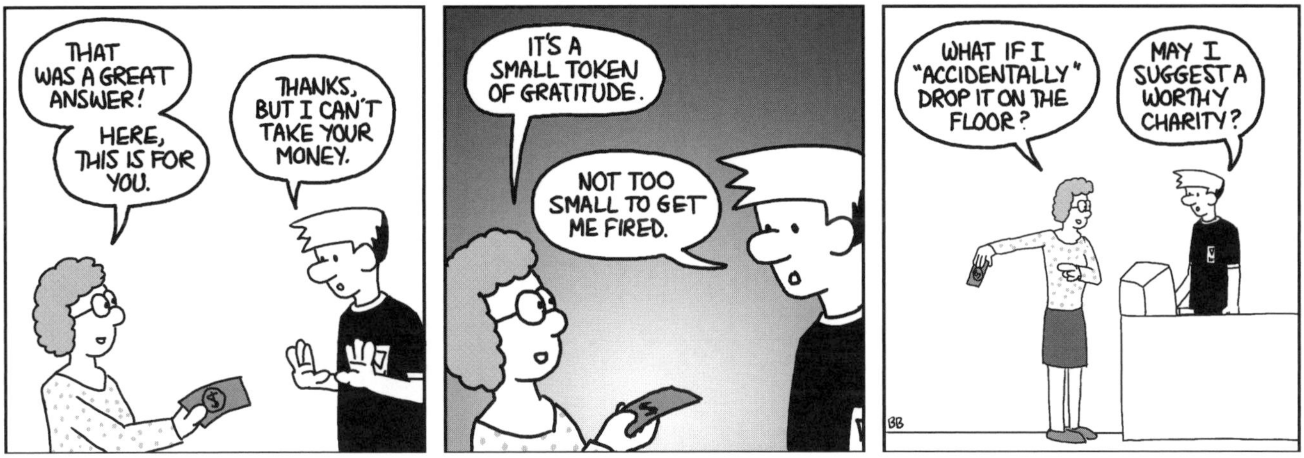
THAT WAS A GREAT ANSWER!
HERE, THIS IS FOR YOU.
THANKS, BUT I CAN'T TAKE YOUR MONEY.
IT'S A SMALL TOKEN OF GRATITUDE.
NOT TOO SMALL TO GET ME FIRED.
WHAT IF I "ACCIDENTALLY" DROP IT ON THE FLOOR?
MAY I SUGGEST A WORTHY CHARITY?
BB

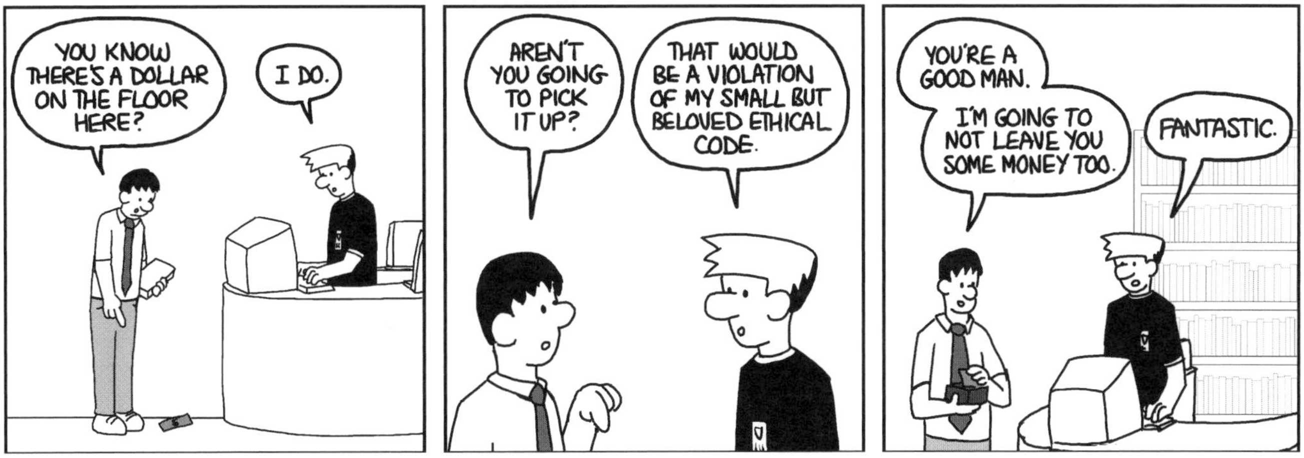
YOU KNOW THERE'S A DOLLAR ON THE FLOOR HERE?
I DO.
AREN'T YOU GOING TO PICK IT UP?
THAT WOULD BE A VIOLATION OF MY SMALL BUT BELOVED ETHICAL CODE.
YOU'RE A GOOD MAN.
I'M GOING TO NOT LEAVE YOU SOME MONEY TOO.
FANTASTIC.

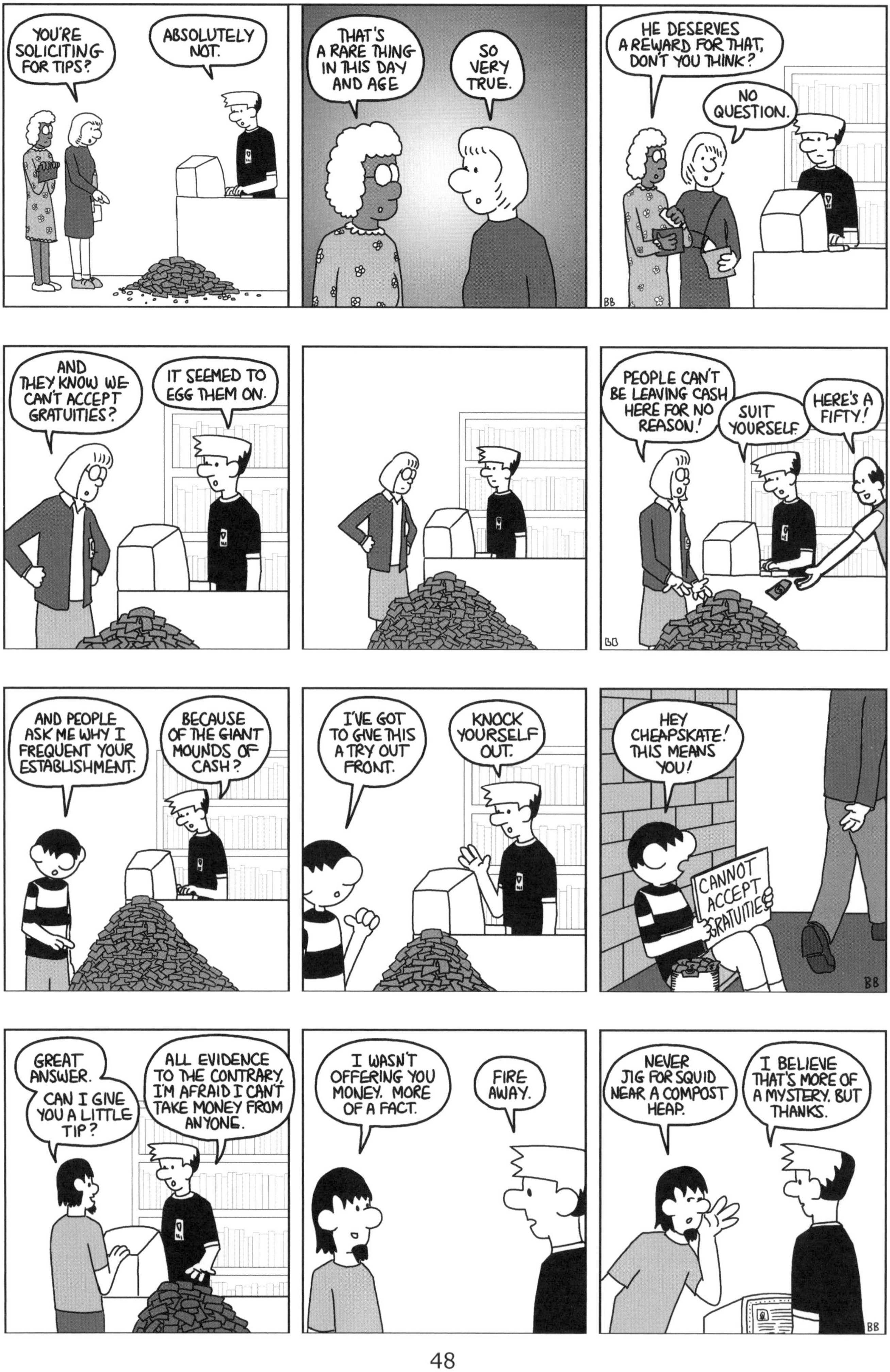
YOU'RE SOLICITING FOR TIPS?
ABSOLUTELY NOT.
THAT'S A RARE THING IN THIS DAY AND AGE
SO VERY TRUE.
HE DESERVES A REWARD FOR THAT, DON'T YOU THINK?
NO QUESTION.
BB
AND THEY KNOW WE CAN'T ACCEPT GRATUITIES?
IT SEEMED TO EGG THEM ON.
PEOPLE CAN'T BE LEAVING CASH HERE FOR NO REASON!
SUIT YOURSELF.
HERE'S A FIFTY!
BB
AND PEOPLE ASK ME WHY I FREQUENT YOUR ESTABLISHMENT.
BECAUSE OF THE GIANT MOUNDS OF CASH?
I'VE GOT TO GIVE THIS A TRY OUT FRONT.
KNOCK YOURSELF OUT.
HEY CHEAPSKATE! THIS MEANS YOU!
CANNOT ACCEPT GRATUITIES
BB
GREAT ANSWER.
CAN I GIVE YOU A LITTLE TIP?
ALL EVIDENCE TO THE CONTRARY, I'M AFRAID I CAN'T TAKE MONEY FROM ANYONE.
I WASN'T OFFERING YOU MONEY. MORE OF A FACT.
FIRE AWAY.
NEVER JIG FOR SQUID NEAR A COMPOST HEAP.
I BELIEVE THAT'S MORE OF A MYSTERY. BUT THANKS.
BB

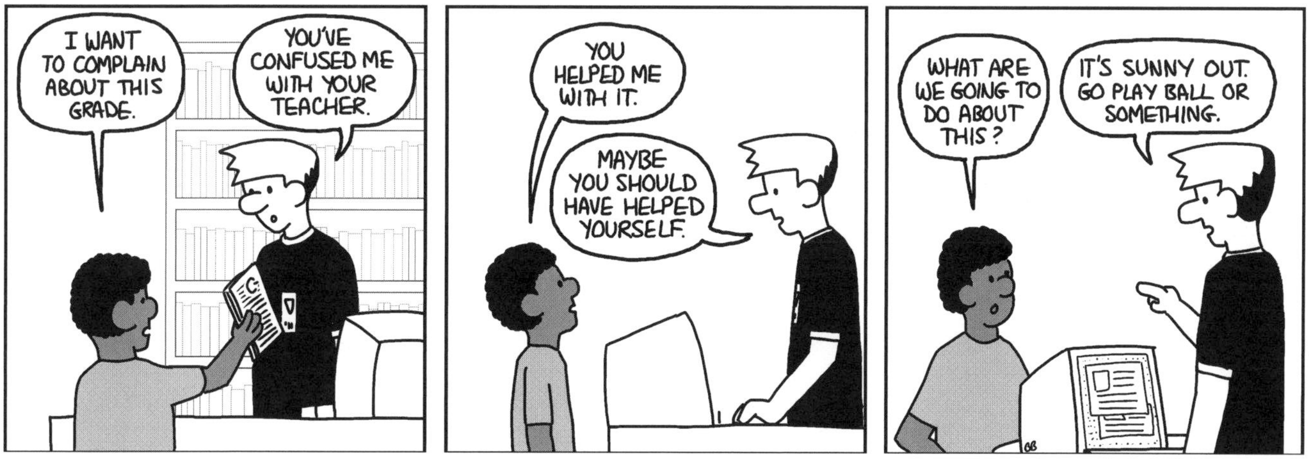
I WANT TO COMPLAIN ABOUT THIS GRADE.
YOU'VE CONFUSED ME WITH YOUR TEACHER.
YOU HELPED ME WITH IT.
MAYBE YOU SHOULD HAVE HELPED YOURSELF.
WHAT ARE WE GOING TO DO ABOUT THIS?
IT'S SUNNY OUT. GO PLAY BALL OR SOMETHING.

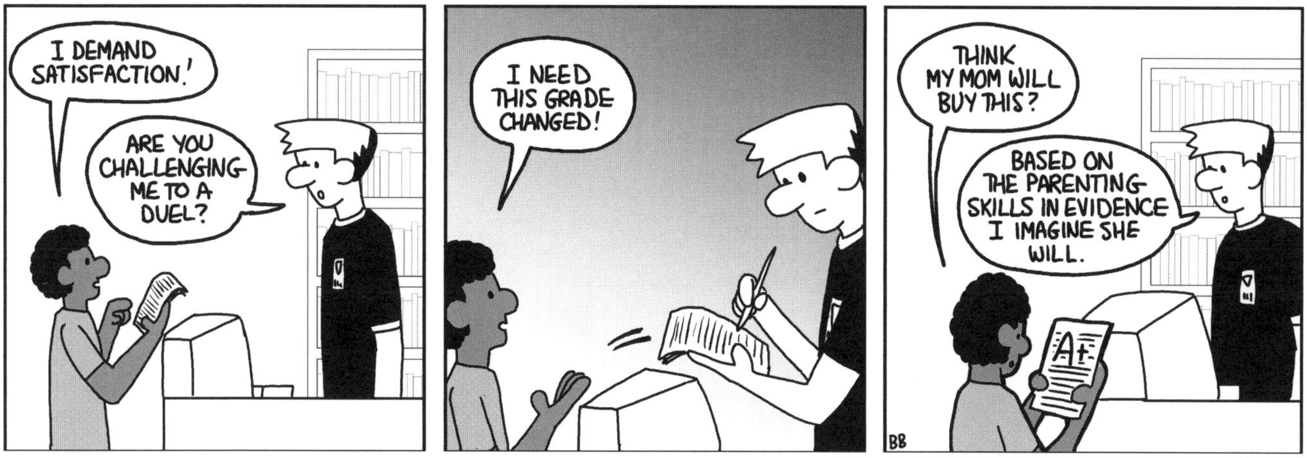
I DEMAND SATISFACTION!
ARE YOU CHALLENGING ME TO A DUEL?
I NEED THIS GRADE CHANGED!
THINK MY MOM WILL BUY THIS?
BASED ON THE PARENTING SKILLS IN EVIDENCE I IMAGINE SHE WILL.
A+
BB

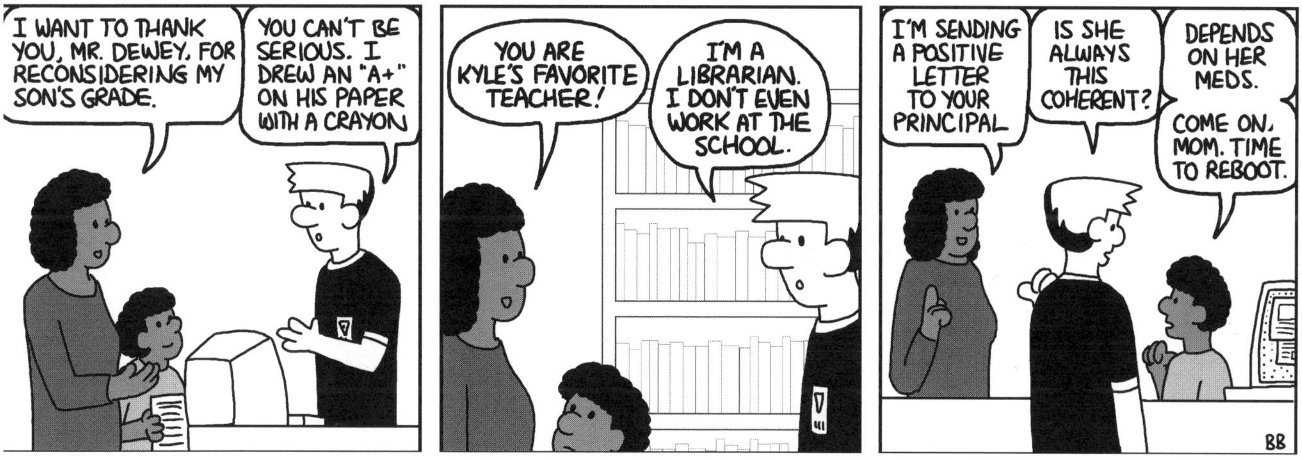
I WANT TO THANK YOU, MR. DEWEY, FOR RECONSIDERING MY SON'S GRADE.
YOU CAN'T BE SERIOUS. I DREW AN "A+" ON HIS PAPER WITH A CRAYON
YOU ARE KYLE'S FAVORITE TEACHER!
I'M A LIBRARIAN. I DON'T EVEN WORK AT THE SCHOOL.
I'M SENDING A POSITIVE LETTER TO YOUR PRINCIPAL
IS SHE ALWAYS THIS COHERENT?
DEPENDS ON HER MEDS.
COME ON, MOM. TIME TO REBOOT.
BB

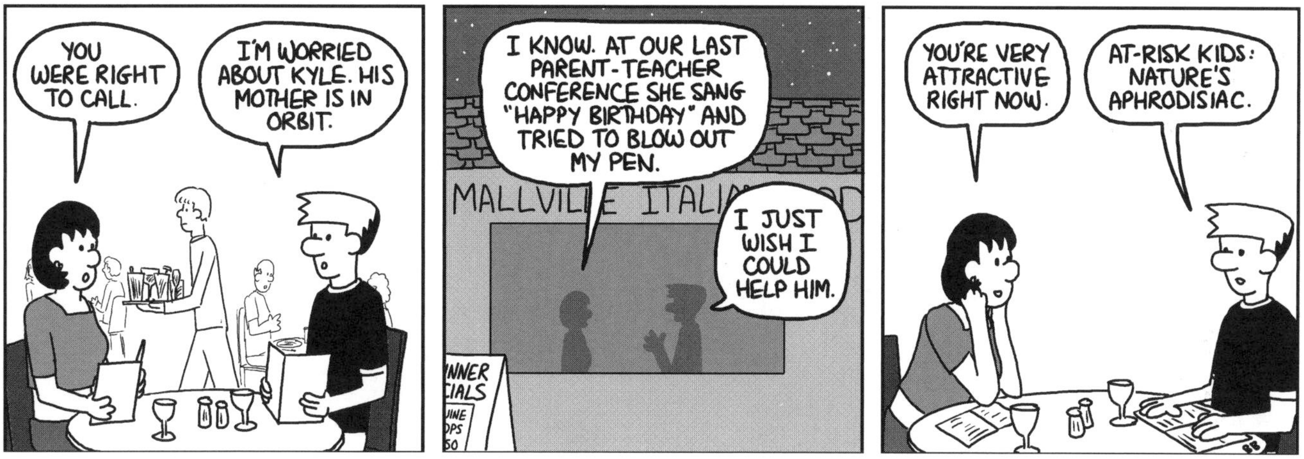
YOU WERE RIGHT TO CALL.
I'M WORRIED ABOUT KYLE. HIS MOTHER IS IN ORBIT.
I KNOW. AT OUR LAST PARENT-TEACHER CONFERENCE SHE SANG "HAPPY BIRTHDAY" AND TRIED TO BLOW OUT MY PEN.
I JUST WISH I COULD HELP HIM.
YOU'RE VERY ATTRACTIVE RIGHT NOW.
AT-RISK KIDS: NATURE'S APHRODISIAC.

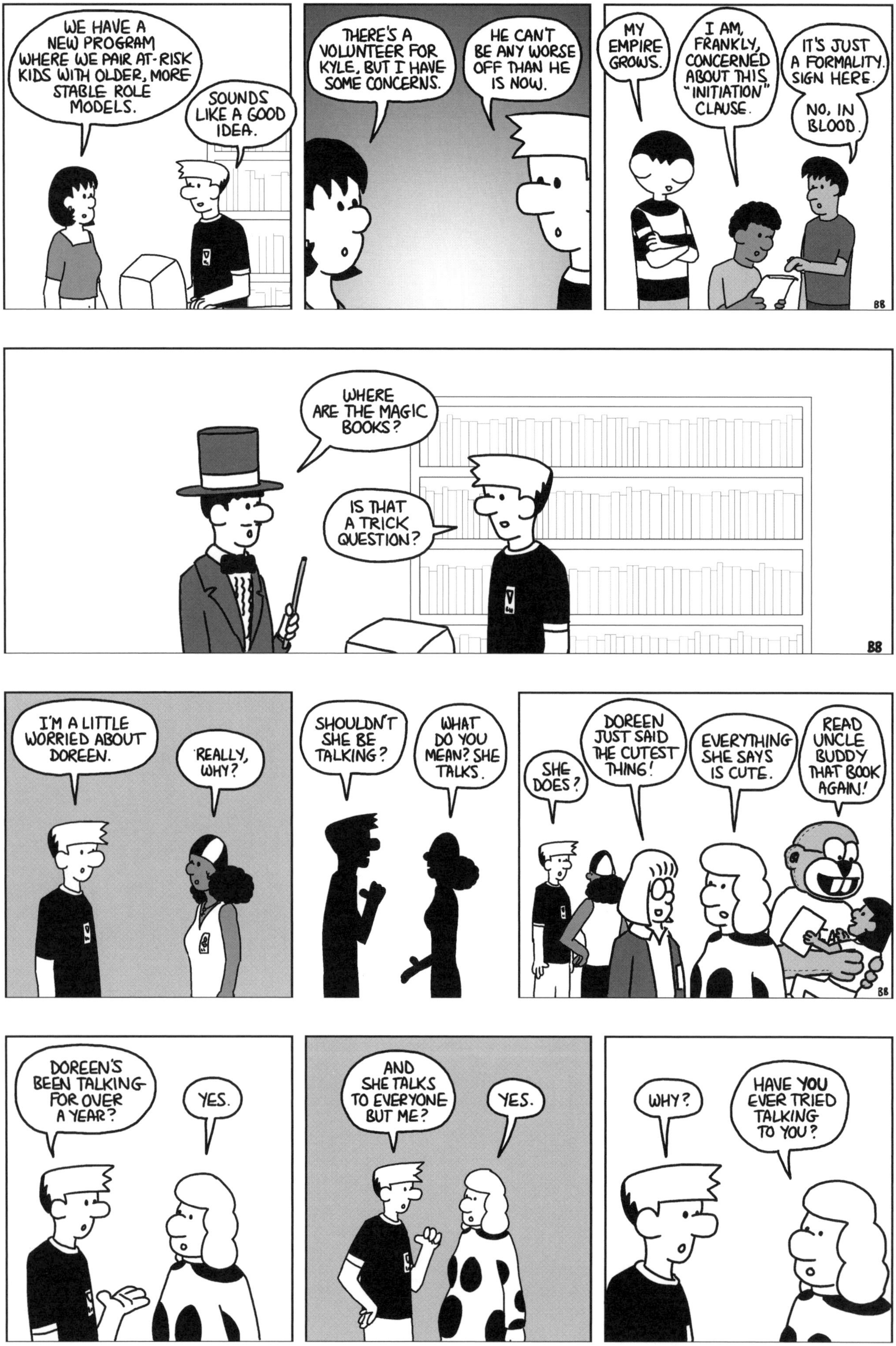
WE HAVE A NEW PROGRAM WHERE WE PAIR AT-RISK KIDS WITH OLDER, MORE STABLE ROLE MODELS.
SOUNDS LIKE A GOOD IDEA.
THERE'S A VOLUNTEER FOR KYLE, BUT I HAVE SOME CONCERNS.
HE CAN'T BE ANY WORSE OFF THAN HE IS NOW.
MY EMPIRE GROWS.
I AM, FRANKLY, CONCERNED ABOUT THIS "INITIATION" CLAUSE.
IT'S JUST A FORMALITY. SIGN HERE.
NO, IN BLOOD.
BB
WHERE ARE THE MAGIC BOOKS?
IS THAT A TRICK QUESTION?
BB
I'M A LITTLE WORRIED ABOUT DOREEN.
REALLY, WHY?
SHOULDN'T SHE BE TALKING?
WHAT DO YOU MEAN? SHE TALKS.
SHE DOES?
DOREEN JUST SAID THE CUTEST THING!
EVERYTHING SHE SAYS IS CUTE.
READ UNCLE BUDDY THAT BOOK AGAIN!
BB
DOREEN'S BEEN TALKING FOR OVER A YEAR?
YES.
AND SHE TALKS TO EVERYONE BUT ME?
YES.
WHY?
HAVE YOU EVER TRIED TALKING TO YOU?

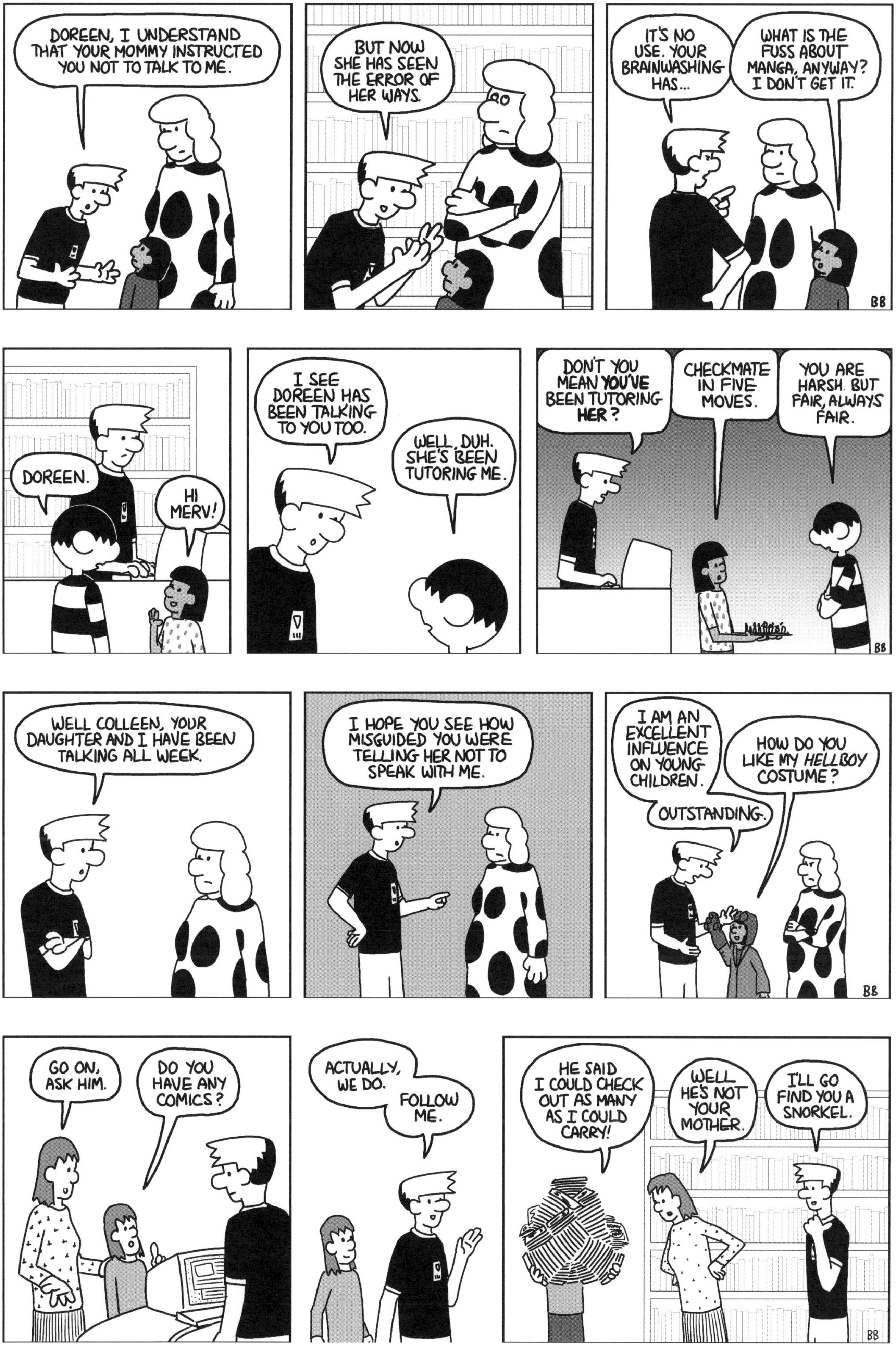
DOREEN, I UNDERSTAND THAT YOUR MOMMY INSTRUCTED YOU NOT TO TALK TO ME.
BUT NOW SHE HAS SEEN THE ERROR OF HER WAYS.
IT'S NO USE. YOUR BRAINWASHING HAS...
WHAT IS THE FUSS ABOUT MANGA, ANYWAY? I DON'T GET IT.
BB
DOREEN.
HI MERV!
I SEE DOREEN HAS BEEN TALKING TO YOU TOO.
WELL, DUH. SHE'S BEEN TUTORING ME.
DON'T YOU MEAN YOU'VE BEEN TUTORING HER?
CHECKMATE IN FIVE MOVES.
YOU ARE HARSH. BUT FAIR, ALWAYS FAIR.
BB
WELL COLLEEN, YOUR DAUGHTER AND I HAVE BEEN TALKING ALL WEEK.
I HOPE YOU SEE HOW MISGUIDED YOU WERE TELLING HER NOT TO SPEAK WITH ME.
I AM AN EXCELLENT INFLUENCE ON YOUNG CHILDREN.
OUTSTANDING.
HOW DO YOU LIKE MY HELLBOY COSTUME?
BB
GO ON, ASK HIM.
DO YOU HAVE ANY COMICS?
ACTUALLY, WE DO.
FOLLOW ME.
HE SAID I COULD CHECK OUT AS MANY AS I COULD CARRY!
WELL HE'S NOT YOUR MOTHER.
I'LL GO FIND YOU A SNORKEL.
BB

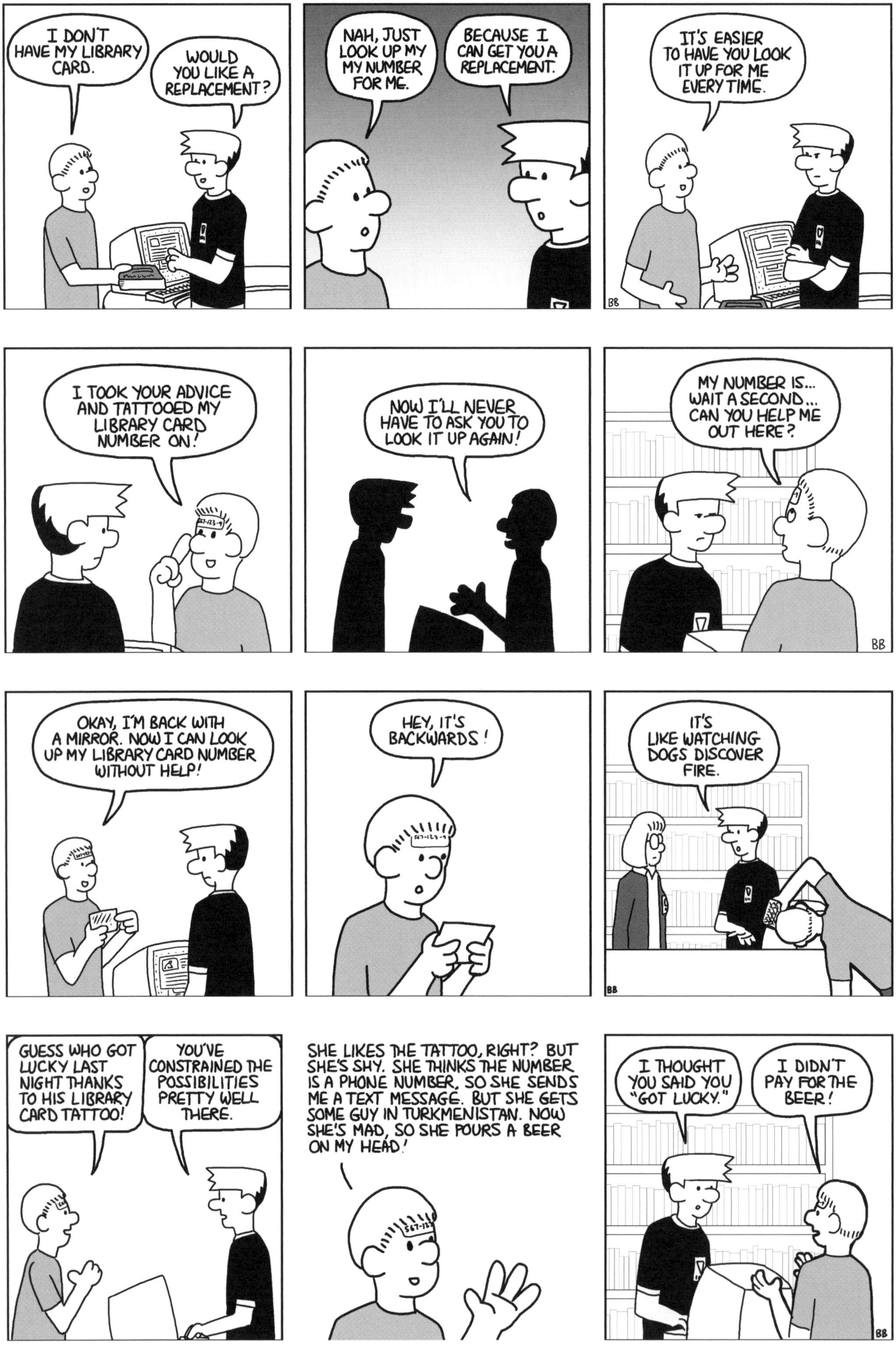
I DON'T HAVE MY LIBRARY CARD.
WOULD YOU LIKE A REPLACEMENT?
NAH, JUST LOOK UP MY MY NUMBER FOR ME.
BECAUSE I CAN GET YOU A REPLACEMENT.
IT'S EASIER TO HAVE YOU LOOK IT UP FOR ME EVERY TIME.
BB
I TOOK YOUR ADVICE AND TATTOOED MY LIBRARY CARD NUMBER ON!
NOW I'LL NEVER HAVE TO ASK YOU TO LOOK IT UP AGAIN!
MY NUMBER IS... WAIT A SECOND... CAN YOU HELP ME OUT HERE?
BB
OKAY, I'M BACK WITH A MIRROR. NOW I CAN LOOK UP MY LIBRARY CARD NUMBER WITHOUT HELP!
HEY, IT'S BACKWARDS!
IT'S LIKE WATCHING DOGS DISCOVER FIRE.
BB
GUESS WHO GOT LUCKY LAST NIGHT THANKS TO HIS LIBRARY CARD TATTOO!
YOU'VE CONSTRAINED THE POSSIBILITIES PRETTY WELL THERE.
SHE LIKES THE TATTOO, RIGHT? BUT SHE'S SHY. SHE THINKS THE NUMBER IS A PHONE NUMBER, SO SHE SENDS ME A TEXT MESSAGE. BUT SHE GETS SOME GUY IN TURKMENISTAN. NOW SHE'S MAD, SO SHE POURS A BEER ON MY HEAD!
I THOUGHT YOU SAID YOU "GOT LUCKY."
I DIDN'T PAY FOR THE BEER!
BB

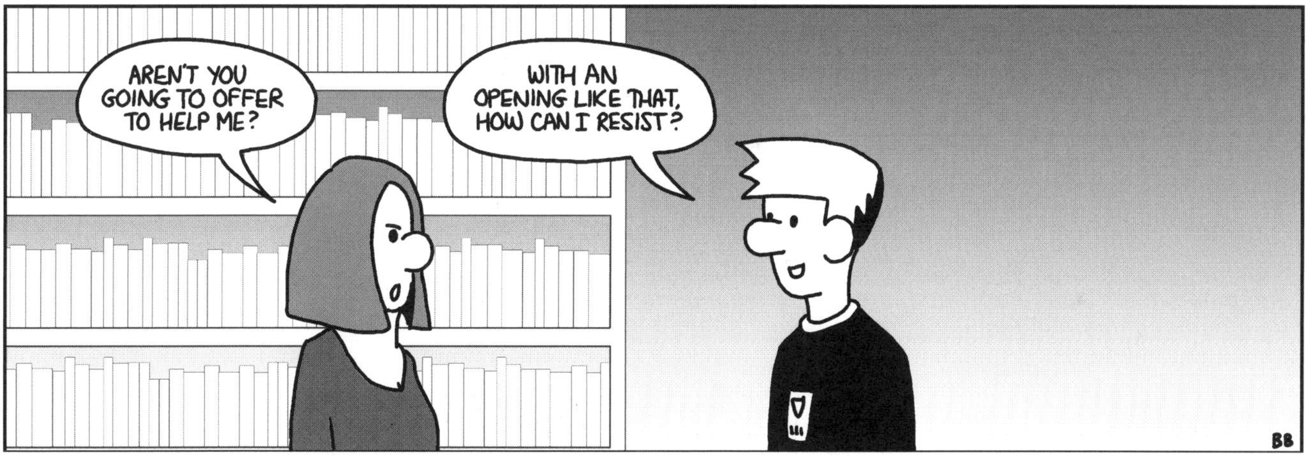
AREN'T YOU GOING TO OFFER TO HELP ME?
WITH AN OPENING LIKE THAT, HOW CAN I RESIST?
BB

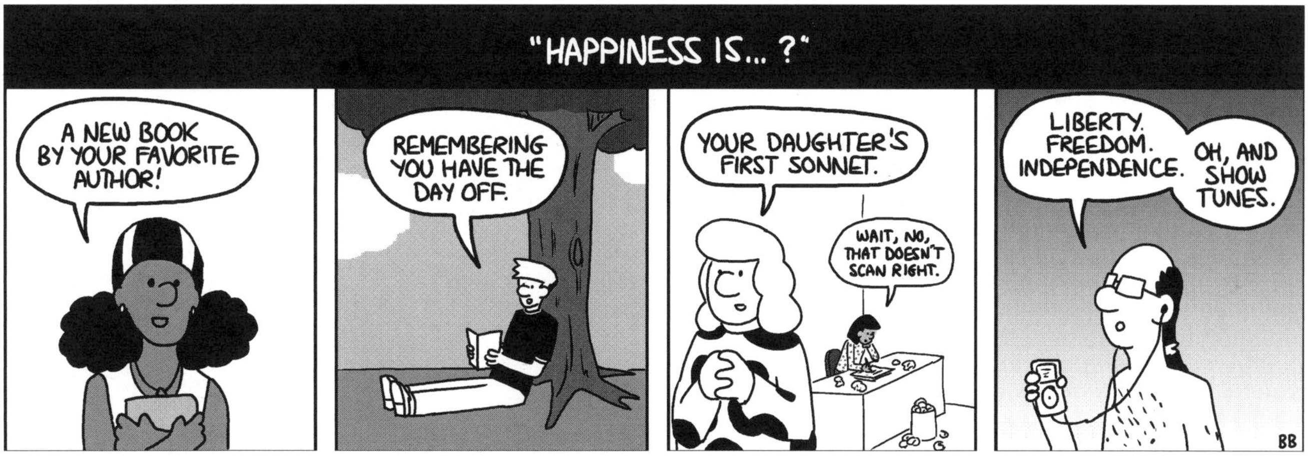
"HAPPINESS IS... ?"
A NEW BOOK BY YOUR FAVORITE AUTHOR!
REMEMBERING YOU HAVE THE DAY OFF.
YOUR DAUGHTER'S FIRST SONNET.
WAIT, NO, THAT DOESN'T SCAN RIGHT.
LIBERTY. FREEDOM. INDEPENDENCE.
OH, AND SHOW TUNES.
BB

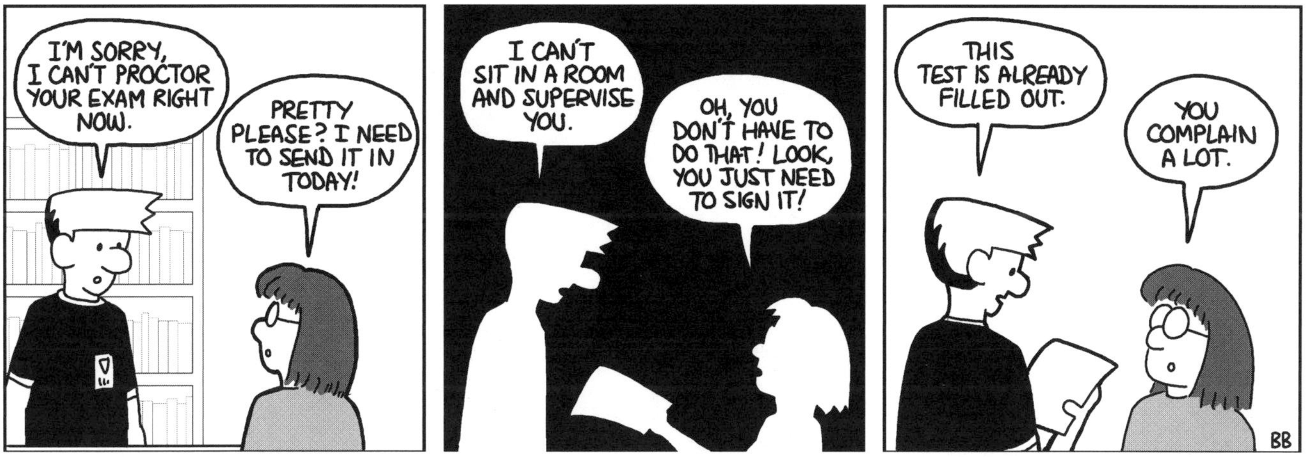
I'M SORRY, I CAN'T PROCTOR YOUR EXAM RIGHT NOW.
PRETTY PLEASE? I NEED TO SEND IT IN TODAY!
I CAN'T SIT IN A ROOM AND SUPERVISE YOU.
OH, YOU DON'T HAVE TO DO THAT! LOOK, YOU JUST NEED TO SIGN IT!
THIS TEST IS ALREADY FILLED OUT.
YOU COMPLAIN A LOT.
BB

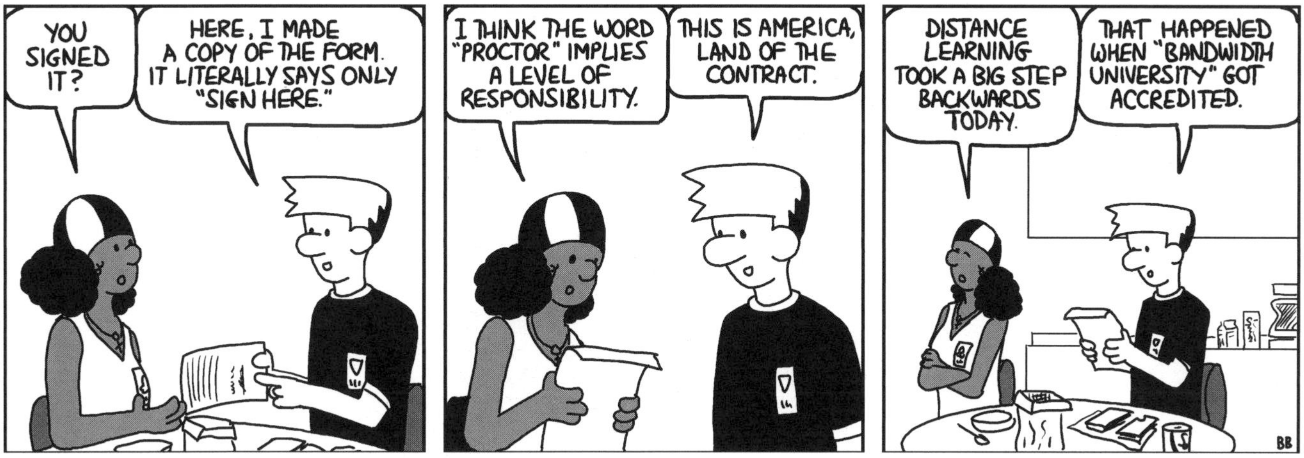
YOU SIGNED IT?
HERE, I MADE A COPY OF THE FORM. IT LITERALLY SAYS ONLY "SIGN HERE."
I THINK THE WORD "PROCTOR" IMPLIES A LEVEL OF RESPONSIBILITY.
THIS IS AMERICA, LAND OF THE CONTRACT.
DISTANCE LEARNING TOOK A BIG STEP BACKWARDS TODAY.
THAT HAPPENED WHEN "BANDWIDTH UNIVERSITY" GOT ACCREDITED.
BB

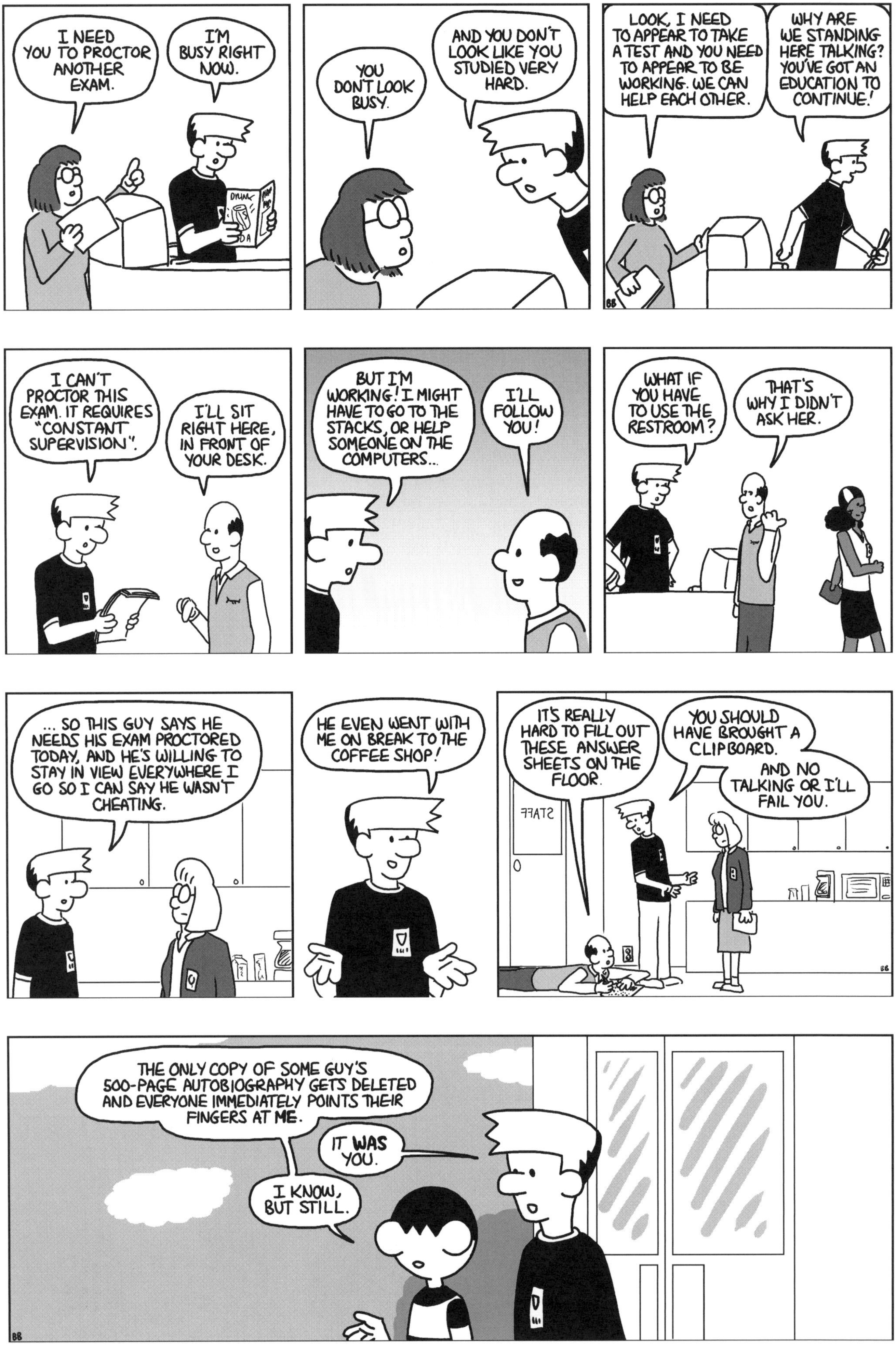
I NEED YOU TO PROCTOR ANOTHER EXAM.
I'M BUSY RIGHT NOW.
YOU DON'T LOOK BUSY.
AND YOU DON'T LOOK LIKE YOU STUDIED VERY HARD.
LOOK, I NEED TO APPEAR TO TAKE A TEST AND YOU NEED TO APPEAR TO BE WORKING. WE CAN HELP EACH OTHER.
WHY ARE WE STANDING HERE TALKING? YOU'VE GOT AN EDUCATION TO CONTINUE!
I CAN'T PROCTOR THIS EXAM. IT REQUIRES "CONSTANT SUPERVISION".
I'LL SIT RIGHT HERE, IN FRONT OF YOUR DESK.
BUT I'M WORKING! I MIGHT HAVE TO GO TO THE STACKS, OR HELP SOMEONE ON THE COMPUTERS...
I'LL FOLLOW YOU!
WHAT IF YOU HAVE TO USE THE RESTROOM?
THAT'S WHY I DIDN'T ASK HER.
... SO THIS GUY SAYS HE NEEDS HIS EXAM PROCTORED TODAY, AND HE'S WILLING TO STAY IN VIEW EVERYWHERE I GO SO I CAN SAY HE WASN'T CHEATING.
HE EVEN WENT WITH ME ON BREAK TO THE COFFEE SHOP!
IT'S REALLY HARD TO FILL OUT THESE ANSWER SHEETS ON THE FLOOR.
YOU SHOULD HAVE BROUGHT A CLIPBOARD.
AND NO TALKING OR I'LL FAIL YOU.
THE ONLY COPY OF SOME GUY'S 500-PAGE AUTOBIOGRAPHY GETS DELETED AND EVERYONE IMMEDIATELY POINTS THEIR FINGERS AT ME.
IT WAS YOU.
I KNOW, BUT STILL.

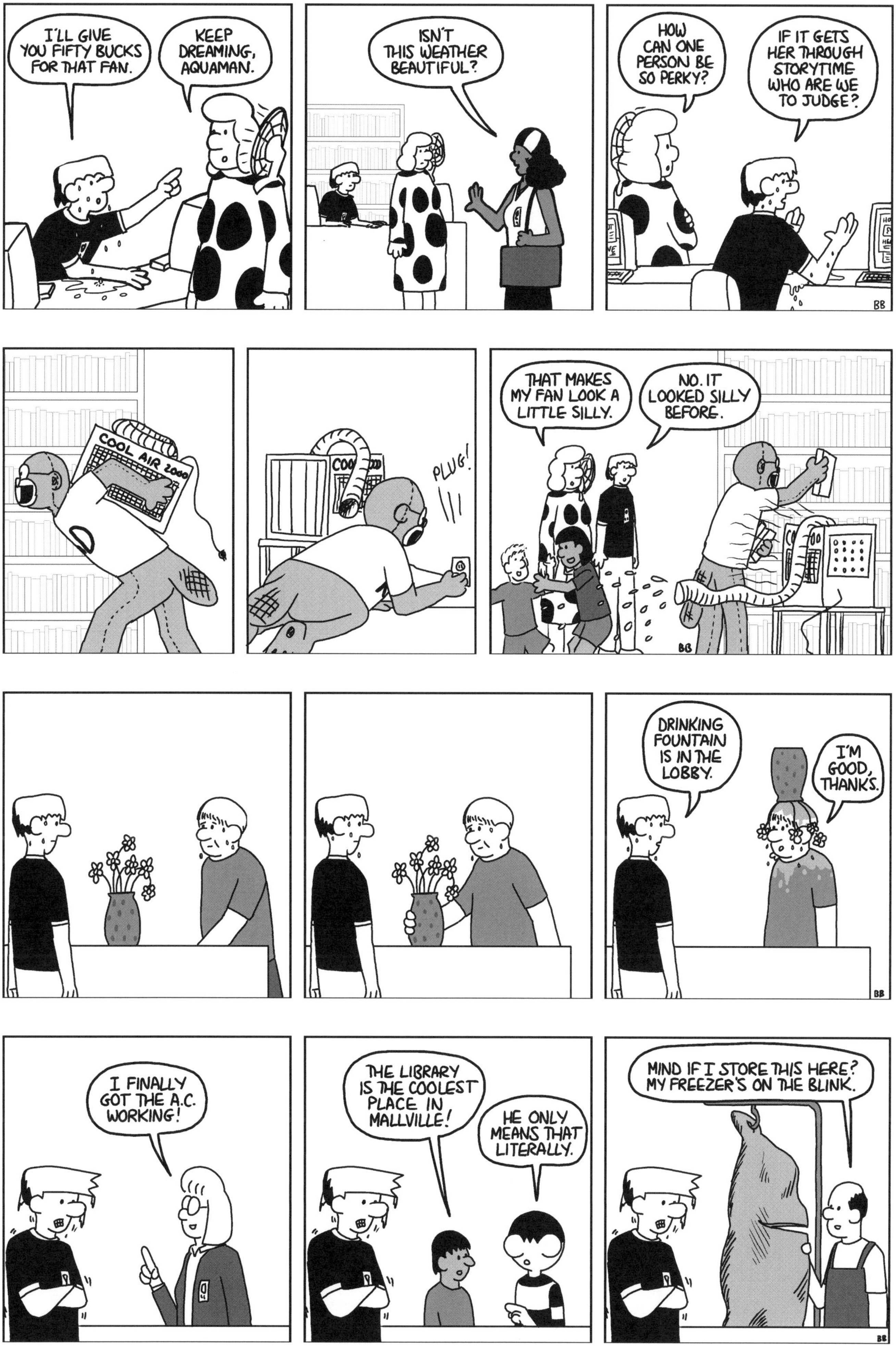
I'LL GIVE YOU FIFTY BUCKS FOR THAT FAN.
KEEP DREAMING, AQUAMAN.
ISN'T THIS WEATHER BEAUTIFUL?
HOW CAN ONE PERSON BE SO PERKY?
IF IT GETS HER THROUGH STORYTIME WHO ARE WE TO JUDGE?
BB
COOL AIR 2000
PLUG!
THAT MAKES MY FAN LOOK A LITTLE SILLY.
NO. IT LOOKED SILLY BEFORE.
BB
DRINKING FOUNTAIN IS IN THE LOBBY.
I'M GOOD, THANKS.
BB
I FINALLY GOT THE A.C. WORKING!
THE LIBRARY IS THE COOLEST PLACE IN MALLVILLE!
HE ONLY MEANS THAT LITERALLY.
MIND IF I STORE THIS HERE? MY FREEZER'S ON THE BLINK.
BB

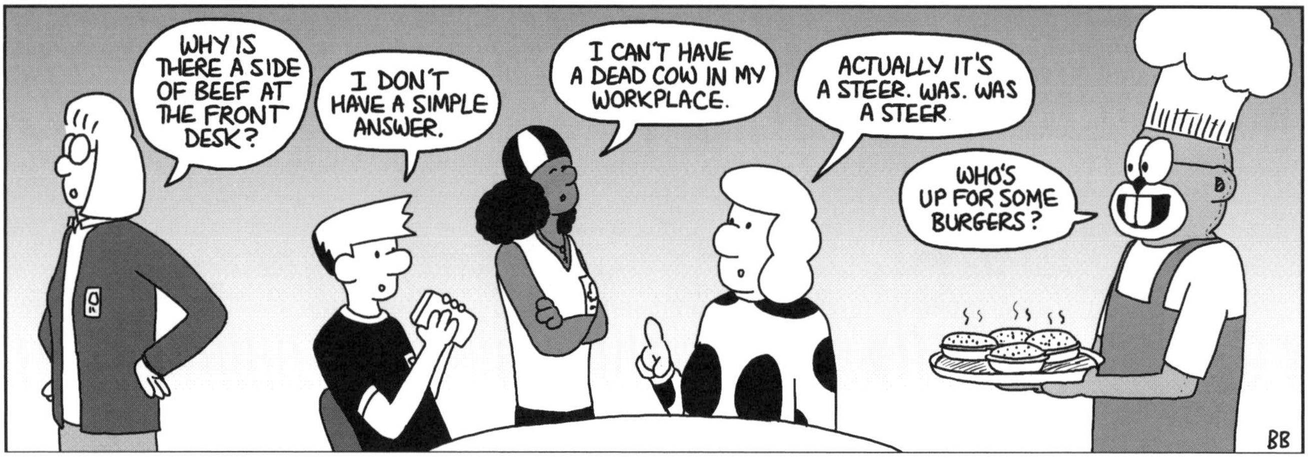
WHY IS THERE A SIDE OF BEEF AT THE FRONT DESK?
I DON'T HAVE A SIMPLE ANSWER.
I CAN'T HAVE A DEAD COW IN MY WORKPLACE.
ACTUALLY IT'S A STEER. WAS. WAS A STEER.
WHO'S UP FOR SOME BURGERS?
BB

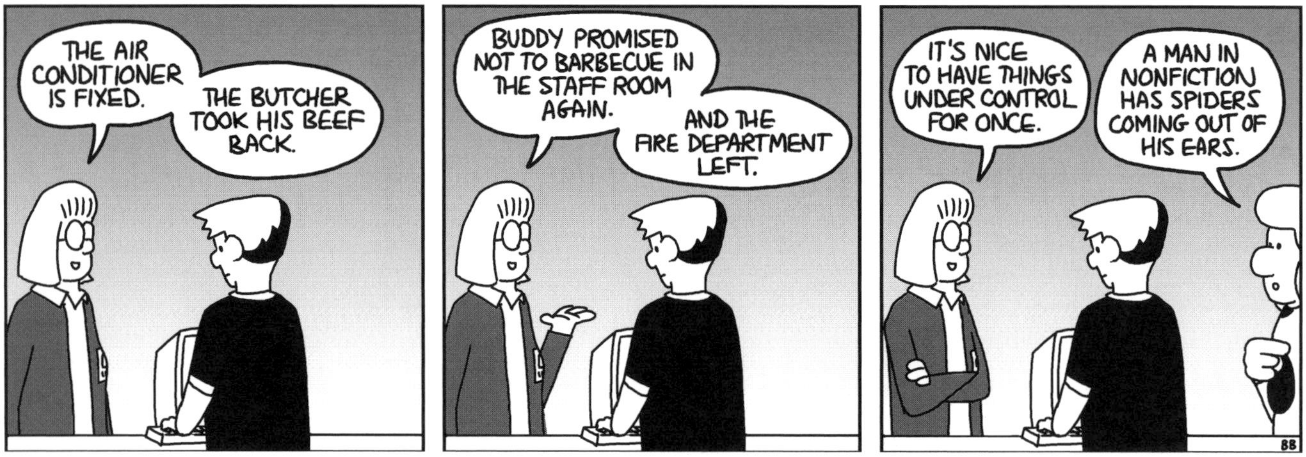
THE AIR CONDITIONER IS FIXED.
THE BUTCHER TOOK HIS BEEF BACK.
BUDDY PROMISED NOT TO BARBECUE IN THE STAFF ROOM AGAIN.
AND THE FIRE DEPARTMENT LEFT.
IT'S NICE TO HAVE THINGS UNDER CONTROL FOR ONCE.
A MAN IN NONFICTION HAS SPIDERS COMING OUT OF HIS EARS.
BB

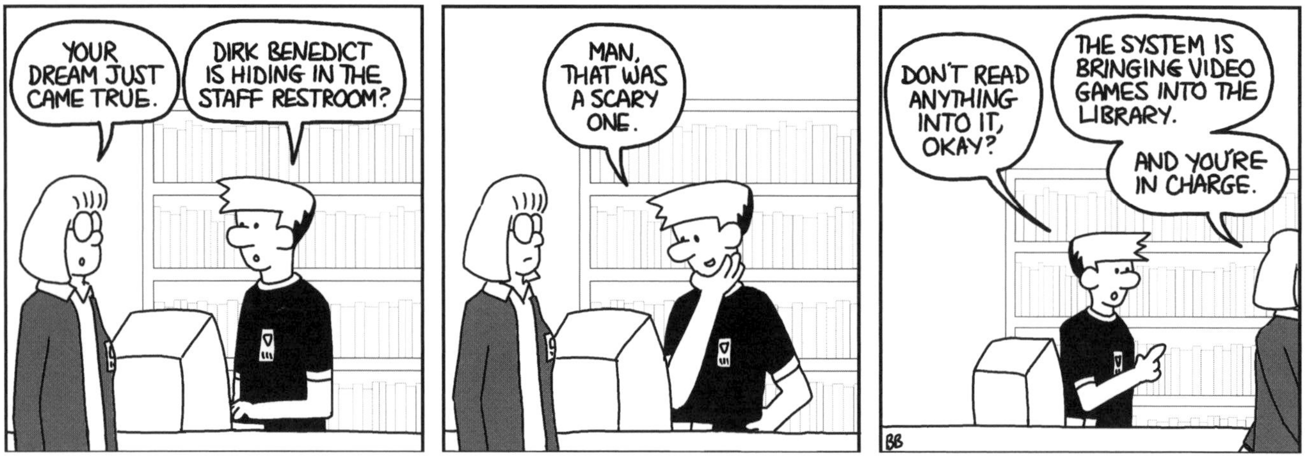
YOUR DREAM JUST CAME TRUE.
DIRK BENEDICT IS HIDING IN THE STAFF RESTROOM?
MAN, THAT WAS A SCARY ONE.
DON'T READ ANYTHING INTO IT, OKAY?
THE SYSTEM IS BRINGING VIDEO GAMES INTO THE LIBRARY.
AND YOU'RE IN CHARGE.
BB

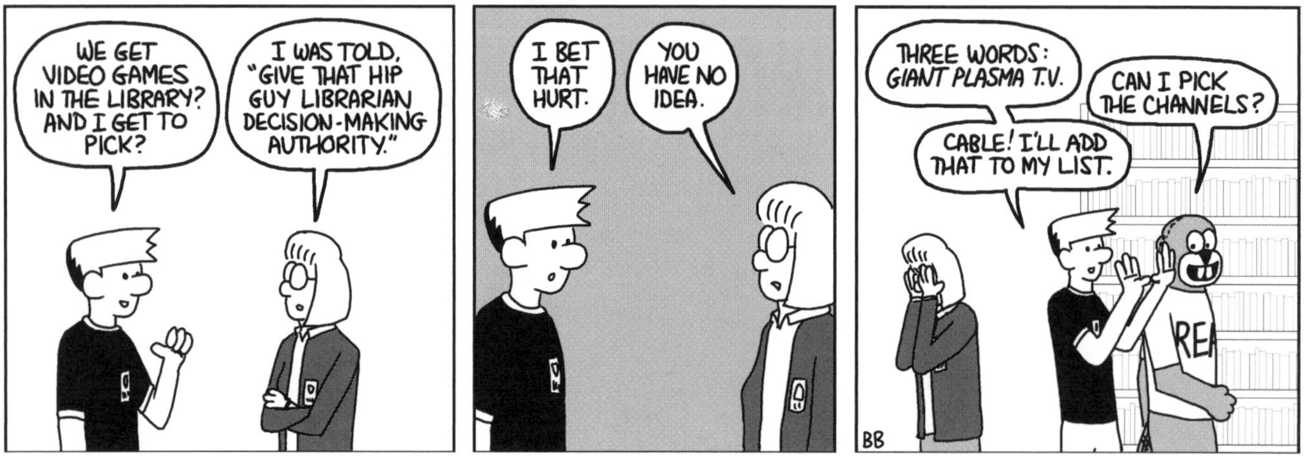
WE GET VIDEO GAMES IN THE LIBRARY? AND I GET TO PICK?
I WAS TOLD, "GIVE THAT HIP GUY LIBRARIAN DECISION-MAKING AUTHORITY."
I BET THAT HURT.
YOU HAVE NO IDEA.
THREE WORDS: GIANT PLASMA T.V.
CAN I PICK THE CHANNELS?
CABLE! I'LL ADD THAT TO MY LIST.
REA
BB

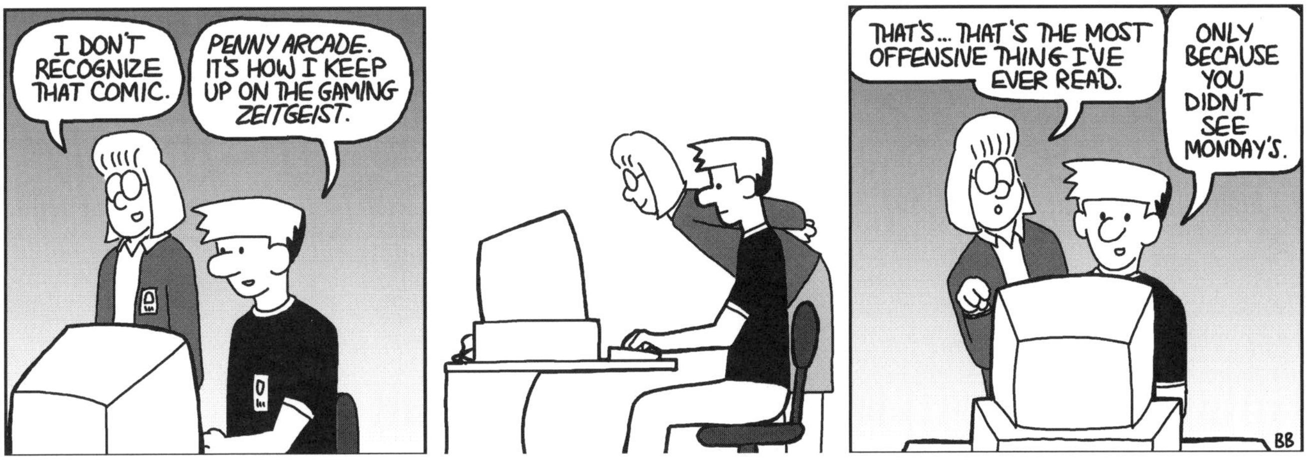
I DON'T RECOGNIZE THAT COMIC.
PENNY ARCADE. IT'S HOW I KEEP UP ON THE GAMING ZEITGEIST.
THAT'S... THAT'S THE MOST OFFENSIVE THING I'VE EVER READ.
ONLY BECAUSE YOU DIDN'T SEE MONDAY'S.
BB

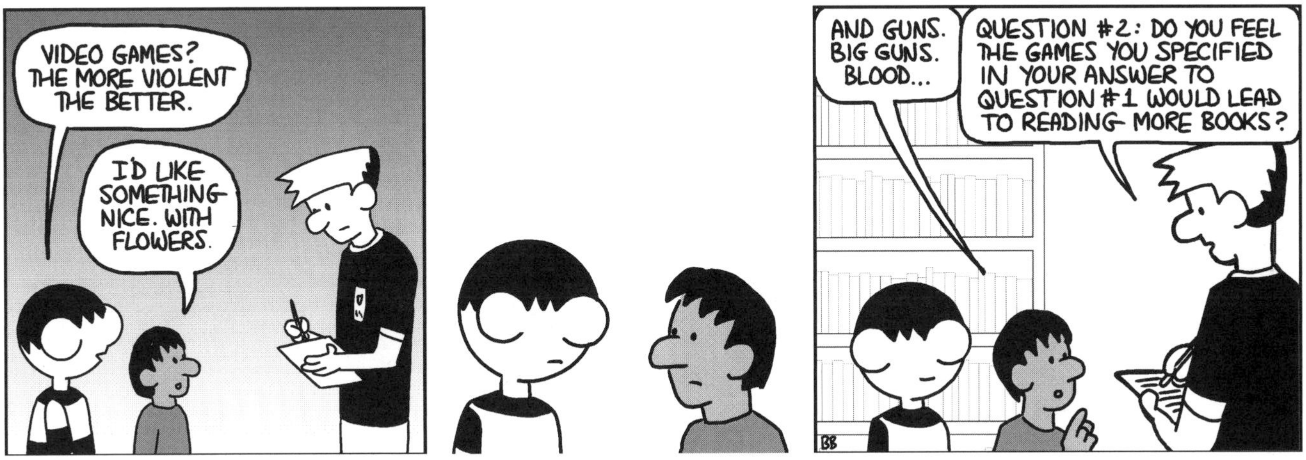
VIDEO GAMES? THE MORE VIOLENT THE BETTER.
I'D LIKE SOMETHING NICE. WITH FLOWERS.
AND GUNS. BIG GUNS. BLOOD...
QUESTION #2: DO YOU FEEL THE GAMES YOU SPECIFIED IN YOUR ANSWER TO QUESTION #1 WOULD LEAD TO READING MORE BOOKS?
BB

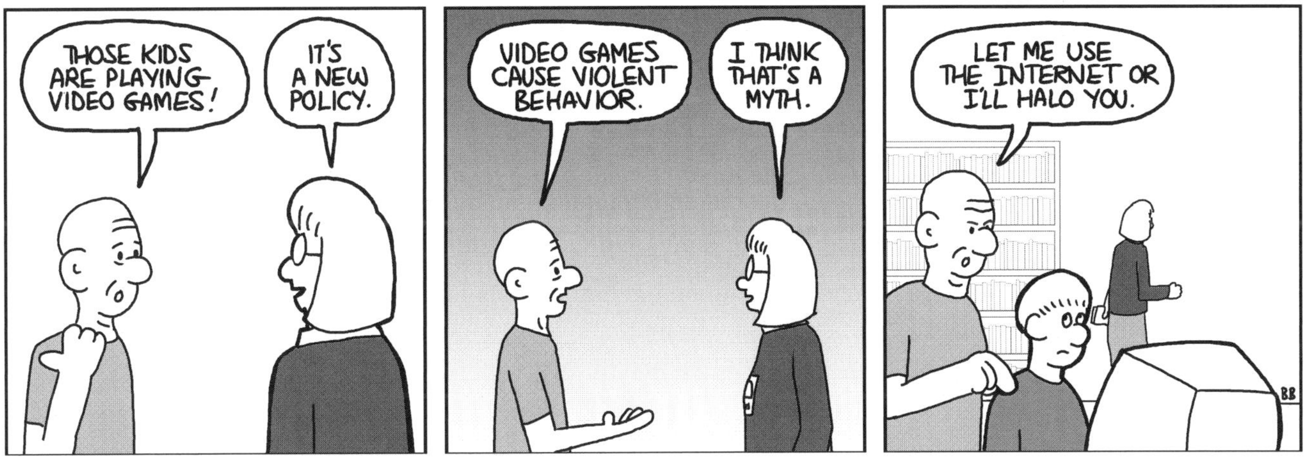
THOSE KIDS ARE PLAYING VIDEO GAMES!
IT'S A NEW POLICY.
VIDEO GAMES CAUSE VIOLENT BEHAVIOR.
I THINK THAT'S A MYTH.
LET ME USE THE INTERNET OR I'LL HALO YOU.
BB

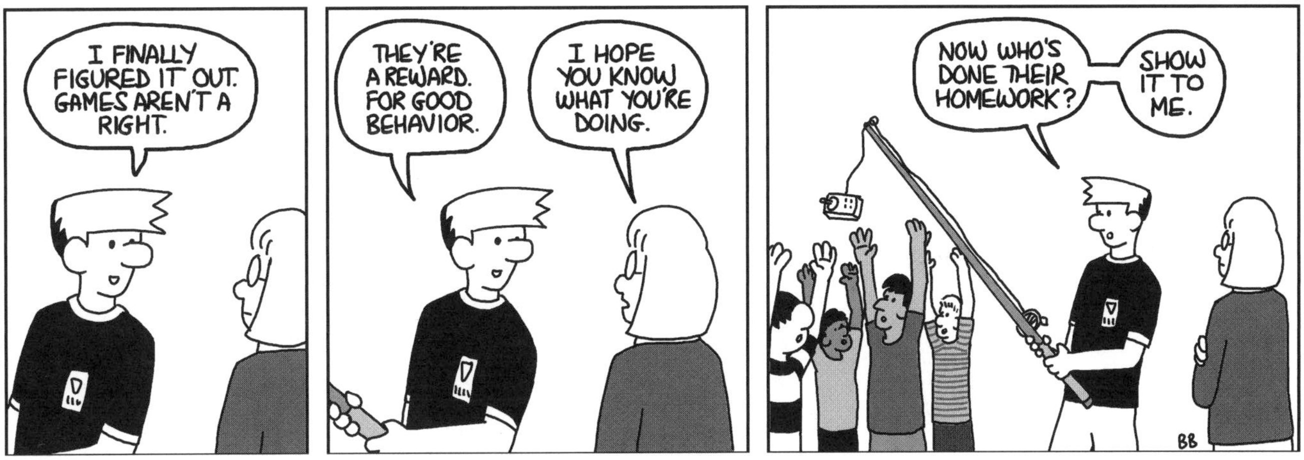
I FINALLY FIGURED IT OUT. GAMES AREN'T A RIGHT.
THEY'RE A REWARD. FOR GOOD BEHAVIOR.
I HOPE YOU KNOW WHAT YOU'RE DOING.
NOW WHO'S DONE THEIR HOMEWORK?
SHOW IT TO ME.
BB

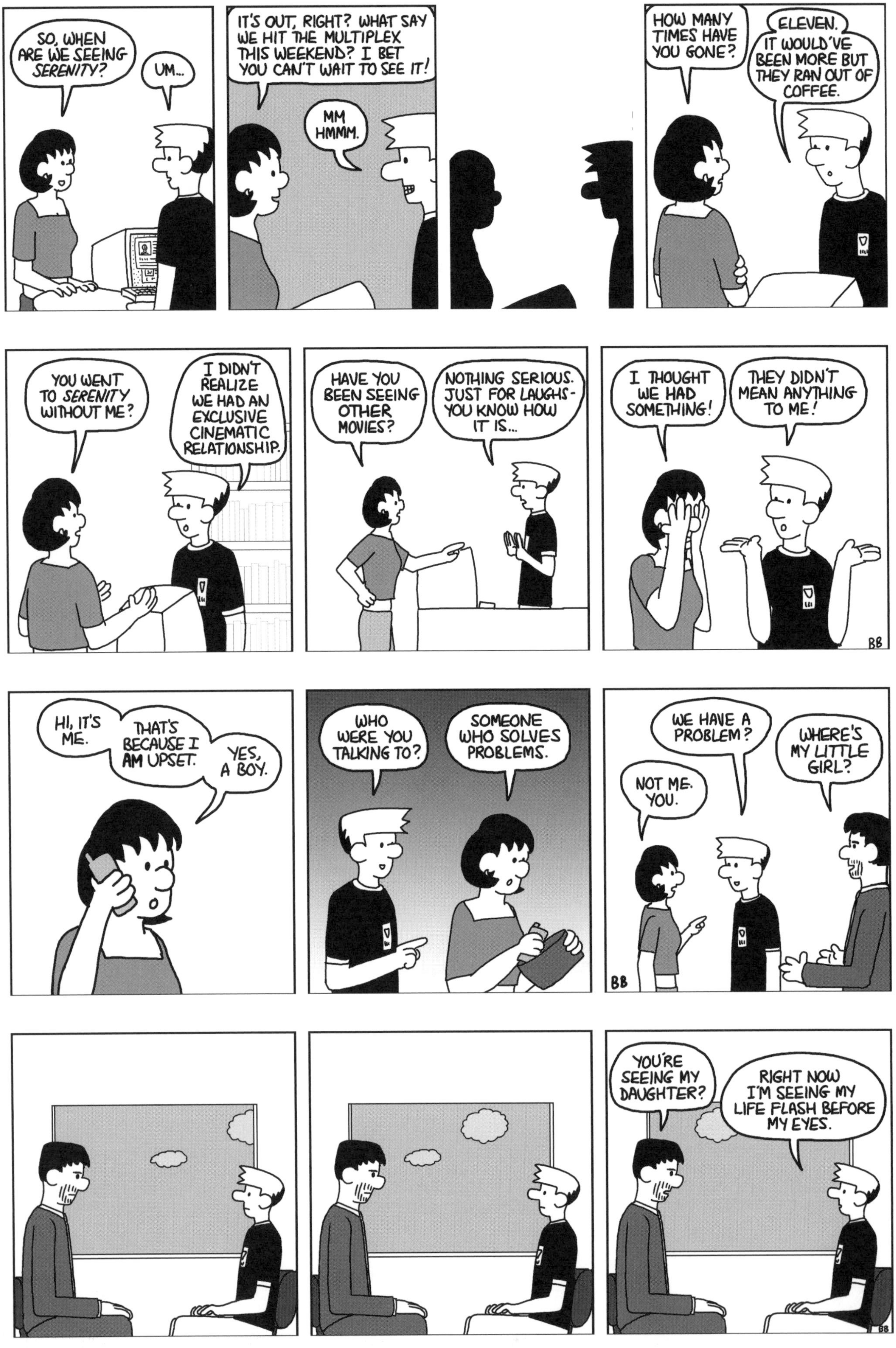
SO, WHEN ARE WE SEEING SERENITY?
UM...
IT'S OUT, RIGHT? WHAT SAY WE HIT THE MULTIPLEX THIS WEEKEND? I BET YOU CAN'T WAIT TO SEE IT!
MM HMMM.
HOW MANY TIMES HAVE YOU GONE?
ELEVEN. IT WOULD'VE BEEN MORE BUT THEY RAN OUT OF COFFEE.
YOU WENT TO SERENITY WITHOUT ME?
I DIDN'T REALIZE WE HAD AN EXCLUSIVE CINEMATIC RELATIONSHIP.
HAVE YOU BEEN SEEING OTHER MOVIES?
NOTHING SERIOUS. JUST FOR LAUGHS - YOU KNOW HOW IT IS...
I THOUGHT WE HAD SOMETHING!
THEY DIDN'T MEAN ANYTHING TO ME!
BB
HI, IT'S ME.
THAT'S BECAUSE I AM UPSET.
YES, A BOY.
WHO WERE YOU TALKING TO?
SOMEONE WHO SOLVES PROBLEMS.
WE HAVE A PROBLEM?
NOT ME. YOU.
WHERE'S MY LITTLE GIRL?
BB
YOU'RE SEEING MY DAUGHTER?
RIGHT NOW I'M SEEING MY LIFE FLASH BEFORE MY EYES.
BB

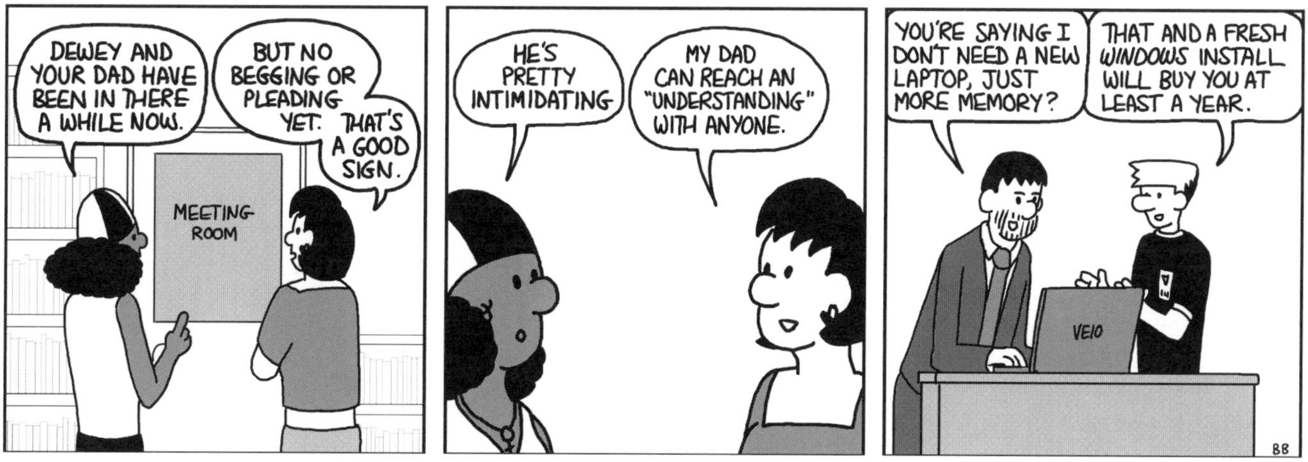
DEWEY AND YOUR DAD HAVE BEEN IN THERE A WHILE NOW.
BUT NO BEGGING OR PLEADING YET.
THAT'S A GOOD SIGN.
MEETING ROOM
HE'S PRETTY INTIMIDATING.
MY DAD CAN REACH AN "UNDERSTANDING" WITH ANYONE.
YOU'RE SAYING I DON'T NEED A NEW LAPTOP, JUST MORE MEMORY?
THAT AND A FRESH *WINDOWS* INSTALL WILL BUY YOU AT LEAST A YEAR.
VEIO
BB

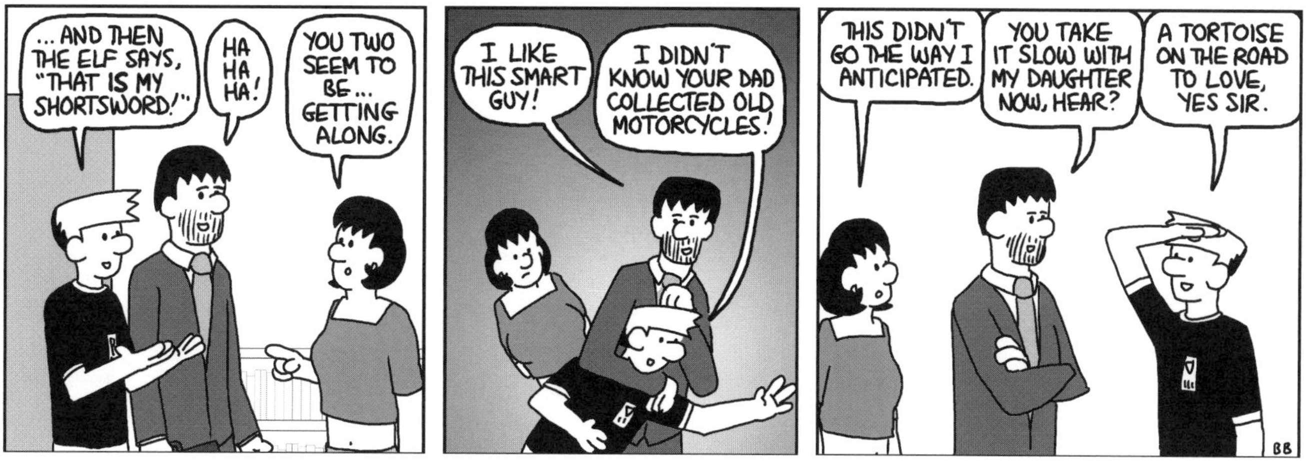
...AND THEN THE ELF SAYS, "THAT IS MY SHORTSWORD!"
HA HA HA!
YOU TWO SEEM TO BE... GETTING ALONG.
I LIKE THIS SMART GUY!
I DIDN'T KNOW YOUR DAD COLLECTED OLD MOTORCYCLES!
THIS DIDN'T GO THE WAY I ANTICIPATED.
YOU TAKE IT SLOW WITH MY DAUGHTER NOW, HEAR?
A TORTOISE ON THE ROAD TO LOVE, YES SIR.
BB

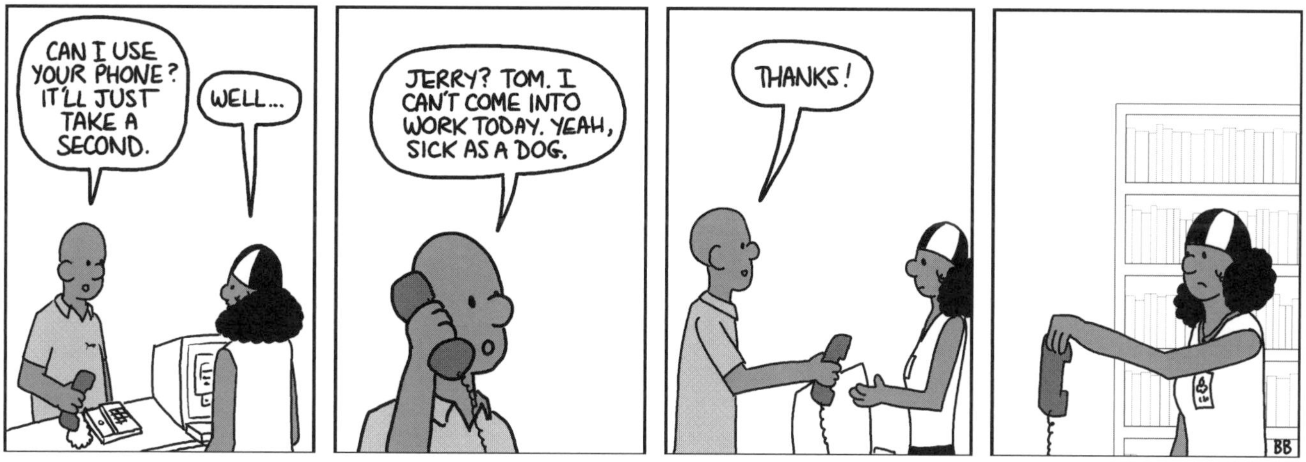
CAN I USE YOUR PHONE? IT'LL JUST TAKE A SECOND.
WELL...
JERRY? TOM. I CAN'T COME INTO WORK TODAY. YEAH, SICK AS A DOG.
THANKS!
BB

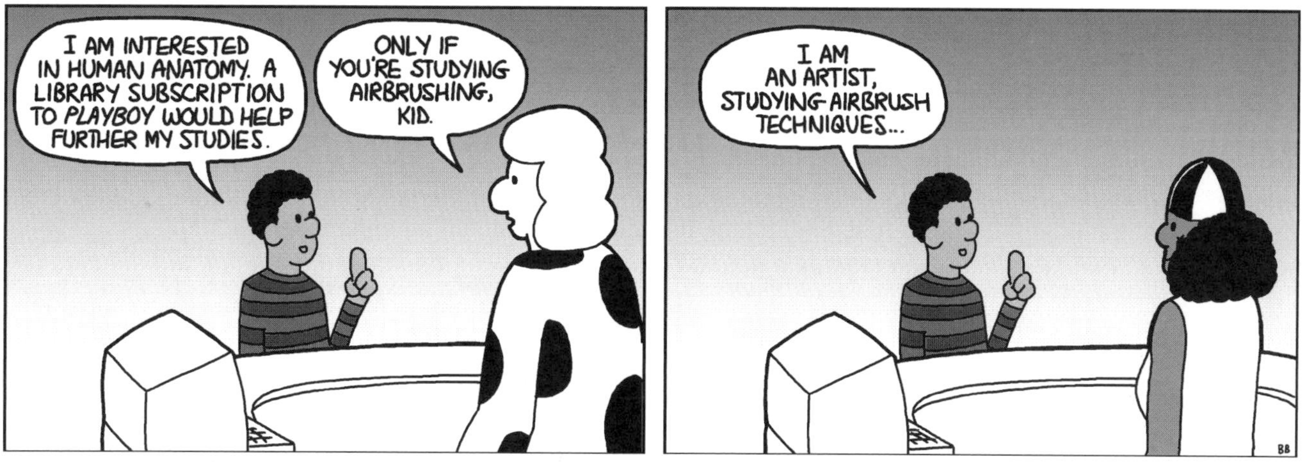
I AM INTERESTED IN HUMAN ANATOMY. A LIBRARY SUBSCRIPTION TO *PLAYBOY* WOULD HELP FURTHER MY STUDIES.
ONLY IF YOU'RE STUDYING AIRBRUSHING, KID.
I AM AN ARTIST, STUDYING AIRBRUSH TECHNIQUES...
BB

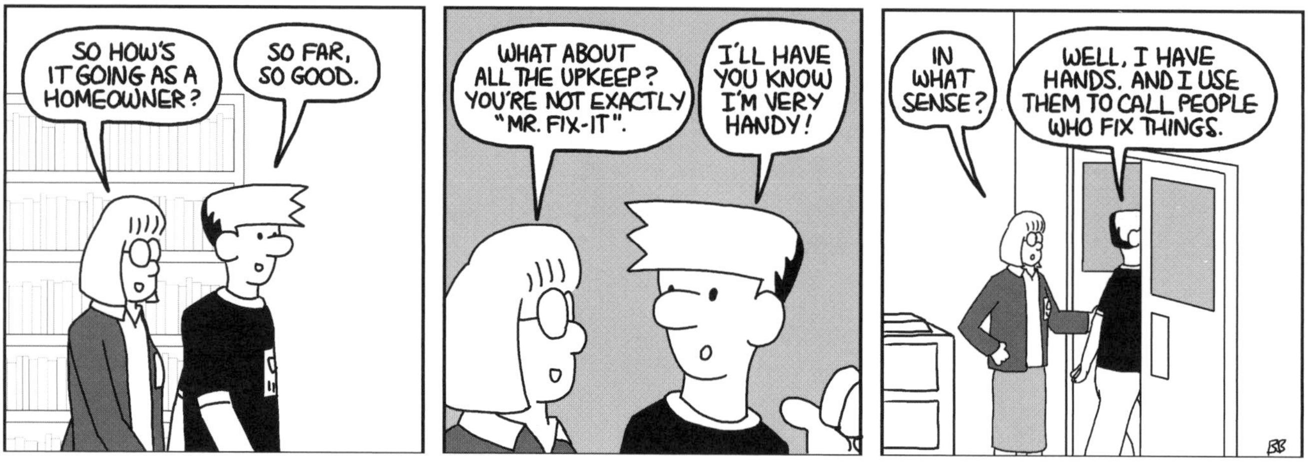
SO HOW'S IT GOING AS A HOMEOWNER?
SO FAR, SO GOOD.
WHAT ABOUT ALL THE UPKEEP? YOU'RE NOT EXACTLY "MR. FIX-IT".
I'LL HAVE YOU KNOW I'M VERY HANDY!
IN WHAT SENSE?
WELL, I HAVE HANDS. AND I USE THEM TO CALL PEOPLE WHO FIX THINGS.

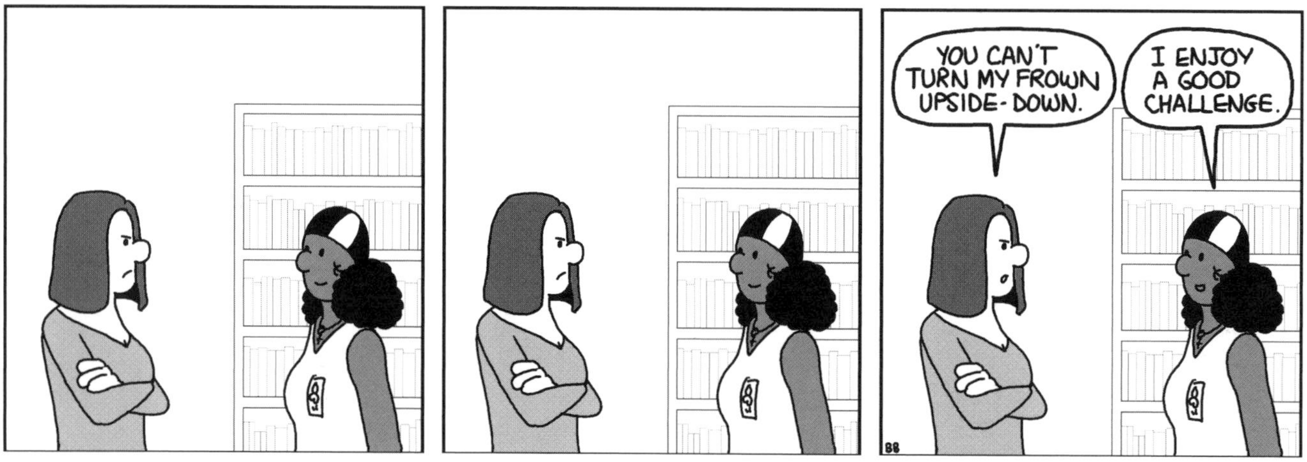
YOU CAN'T TURN MY FROWN UPSIDE-DOWN.
I ENJOY A GOOD CHALLENGE.

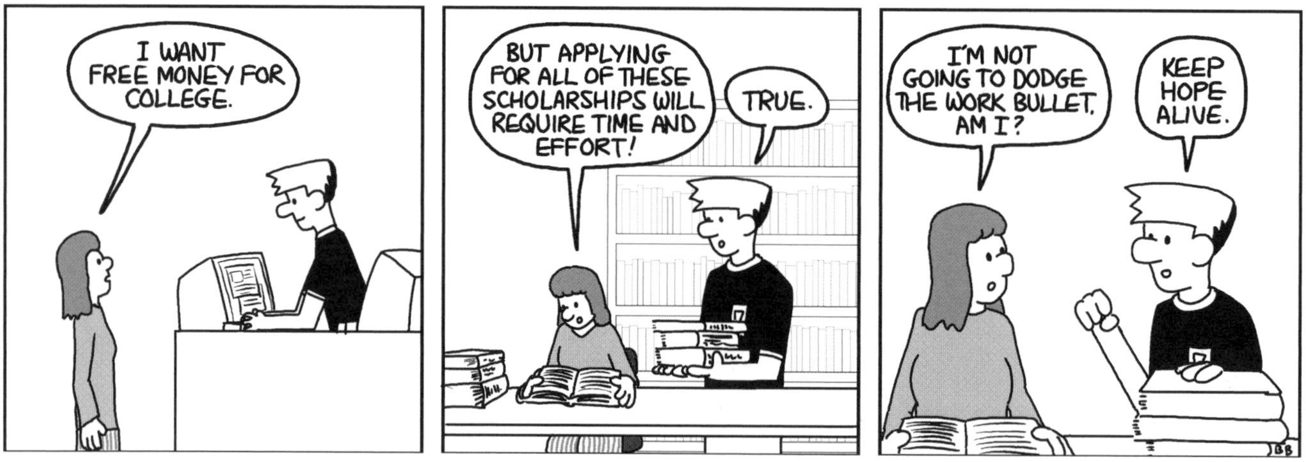
I WANT FREE MONEY FOR COLLEGE.
BUT APPLYING FOR ALL OF THESE SCHOLARSHIPS WILL REQUIRE TIME AND EFFORT!
TRUE.
I'M NOT GOING TO DODGE THE WORK BULLET, AM I?
KEEP HOPE ALIVE.

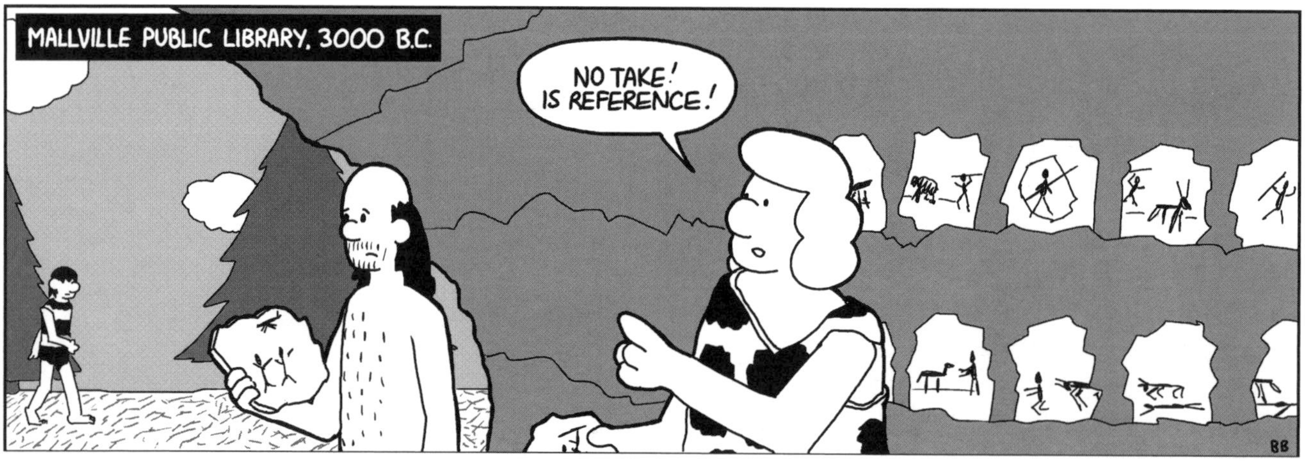
MALLVILLE PUBLIC LIBRARY, 3000 B.C.
NO TAKE! IS REFERENCE!

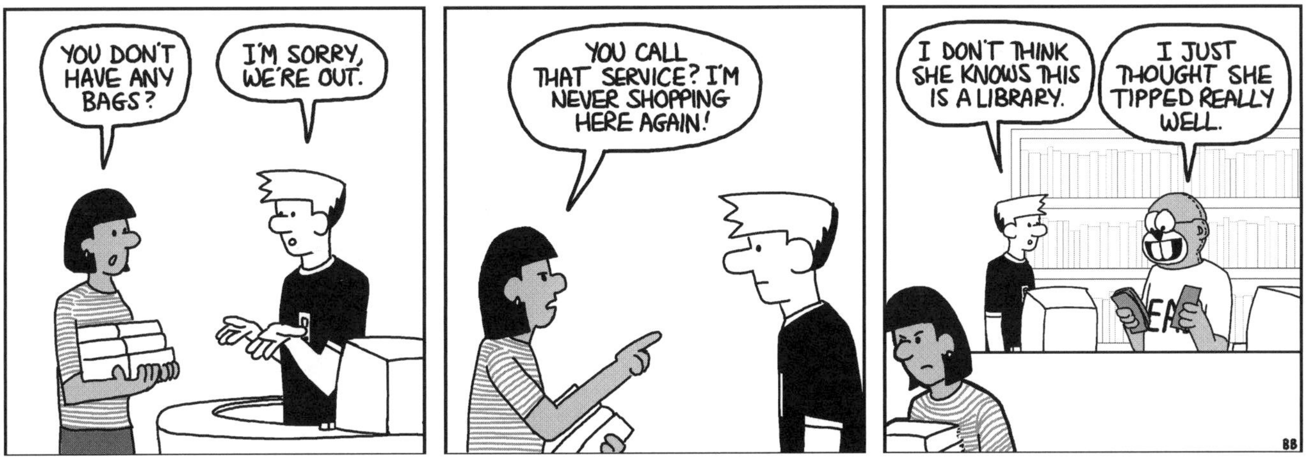
YOU DON'T HAVE ANY BAGS?
I'M SORRY, WE'RE OUT.
YOU CALL THAT SERVICE? I'M NEVER SHOPPING HERE AGAIN!
I DON'T THINK SHE KNOWS THIS IS A LIBRARY.
I JUST THOUGHT SHE TIPPED REALLY WELL.
BB

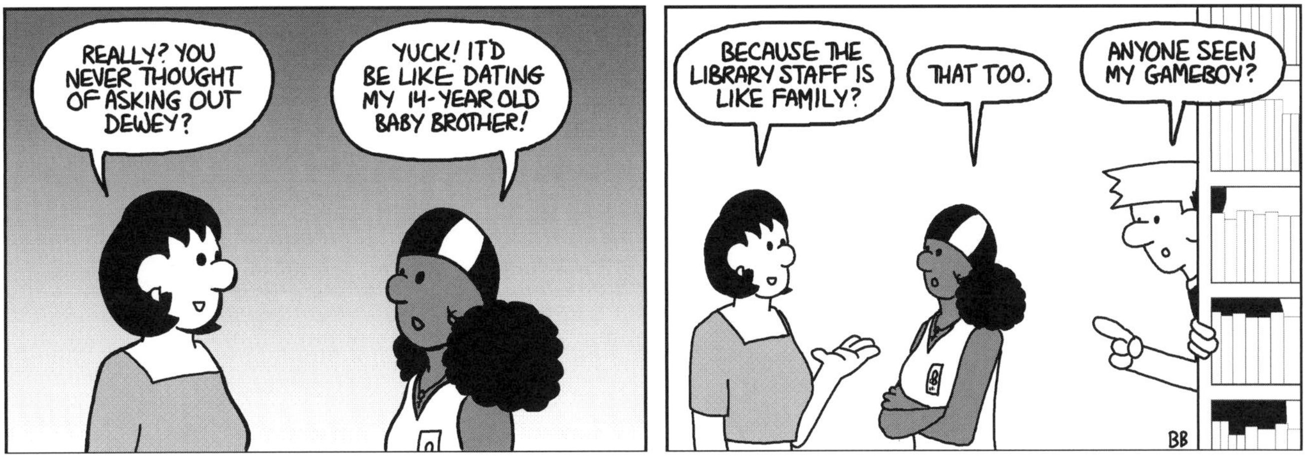
REALLY? YOU NEVER THOUGHT OF ASKING OUT DEWEY?
YUCK! IT'D BE LIKE DATING MY 14-YEAR OLD BABY BROTHER!
BECAUSE THE LIBRARY STAFF IS LIKE FAMILY?
THAT TOO.
ANYONE SEEN MY GAMEBOY?
BB

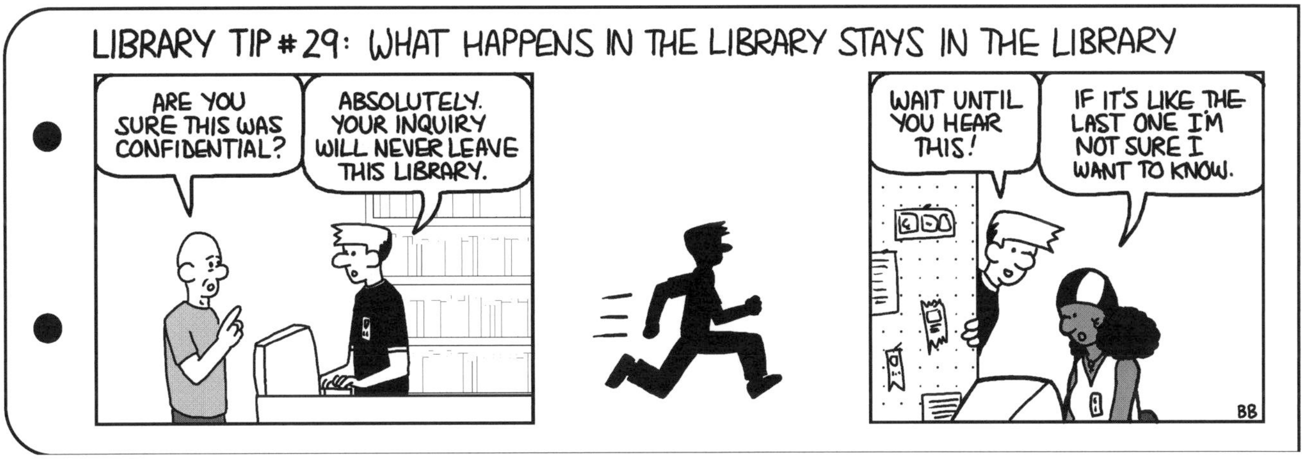
LIBRARY TIP # 29: WHAT HAPPENS IN THE LIBRARY STAYS IN THE LIBRARY
ARE YOU SURE THIS WAS CONFIDENTIAL?
ABSOLUTELY. YOUR INQUIRY WILL NEVER LEAVE THIS LIBRARY.
WAIT UNTIL YOU HEAR THIS!
IF IT'S LIKE THE LAST ONE I'M NOT SURE I WANT TO KNOW.
BB

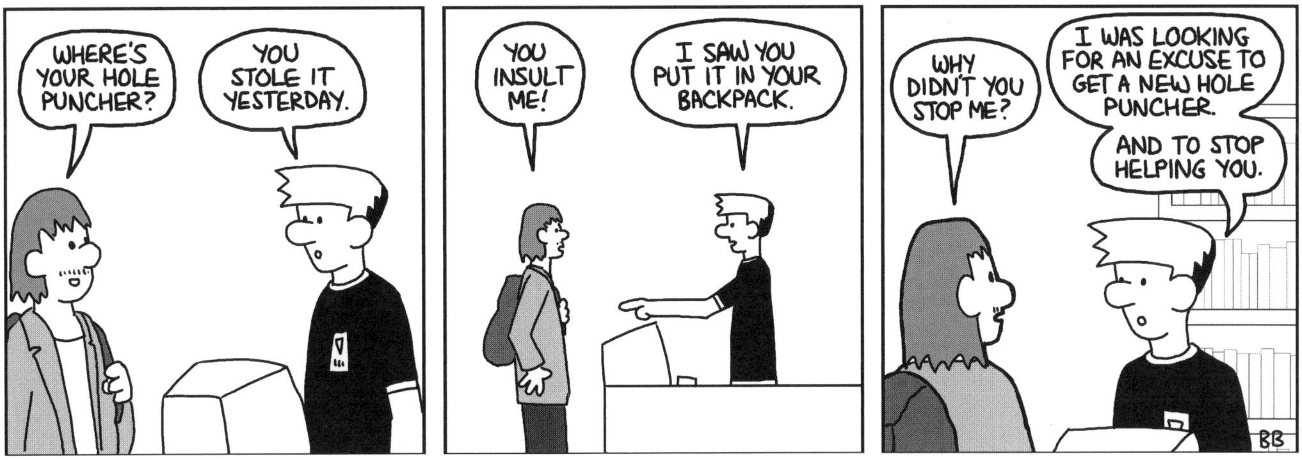
WHERE'S YOUR HOLE PUNCHER?
YOU STOLE IT YESTERDAY.
YOU INSULT ME!
I SAW YOU PUT IT IN YOUR BACKPACK.
WHY DIDN'T YOU STOP ME?
I WAS LOOKING FOR AN EXCUSE TO GET A NEW HOLE PUNCHER.
AND TO STOP HELPING YOU.
BB

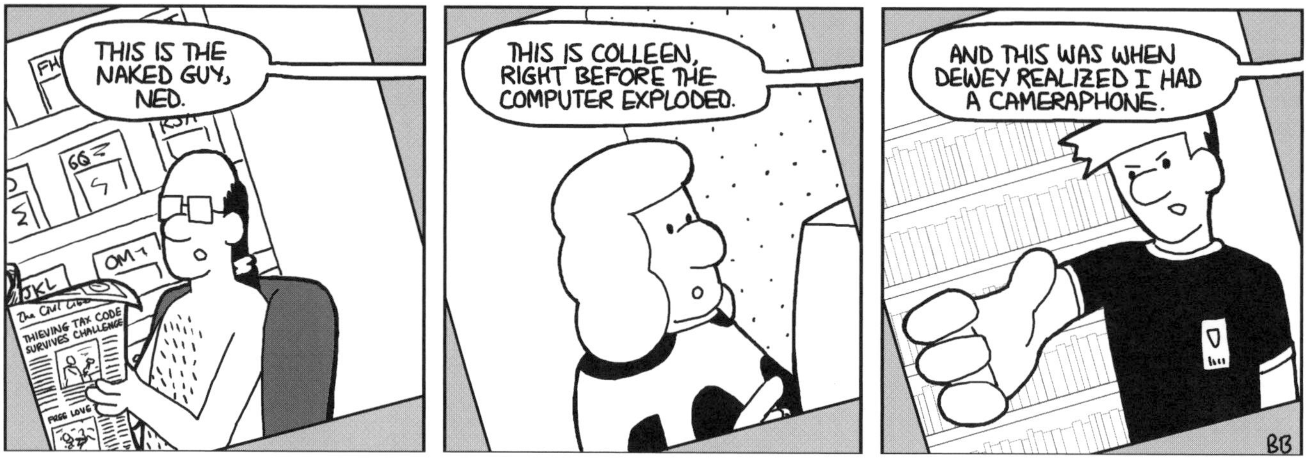
THIS IS THE NAKED GUY, NED.
THIEVING TAX CODE SURVIVES CHALLENGE
THIS IS COLLEEN, RIGHT BEFORE THE COMPUTER EXPLODED.
AND THIS WAS WHEN DEWEY REALIZED I HAD A CAMERAPHONE.
BB

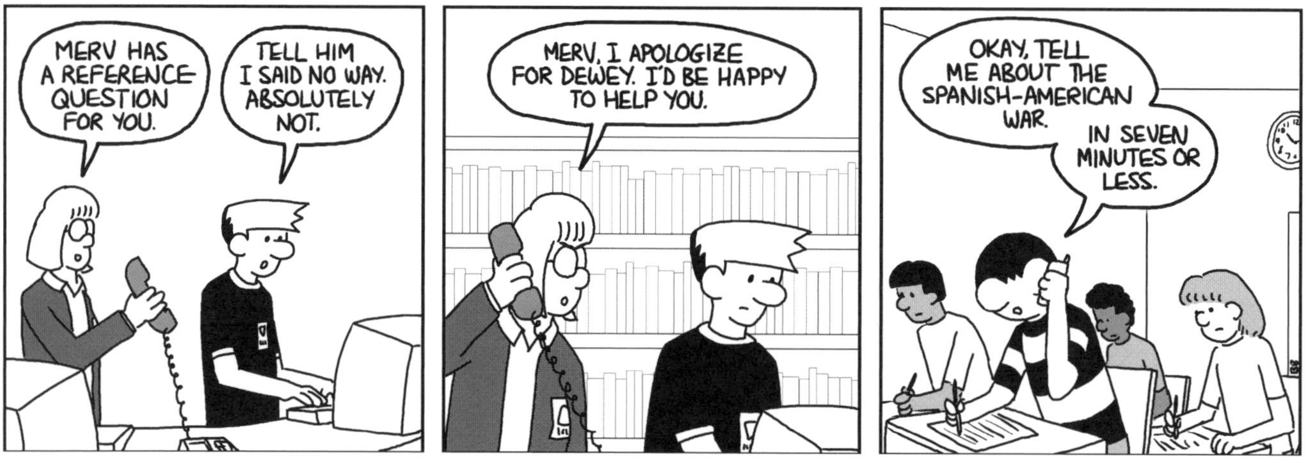
MERV HAS A REFERENCE QUESTION FOR YOU.
TELL HIM I SAID NO WAY. ABSOLUTELY NOT.
MERV, I APOLOGIZE FOR DEWEY. I'D BE HAPPY TO HELP YOU.
OKAY, TELL ME ABOUT THE SPANISH-AMERICAN WAR.
IN SEVEN MINUTES OR LESS.

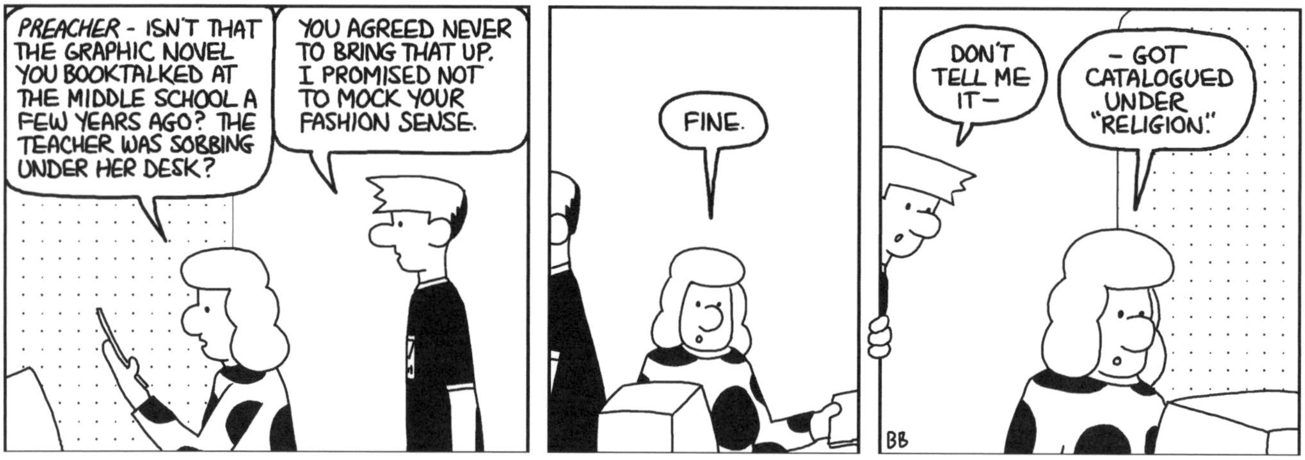
PREACHER - ISN'T THAT THE GRAPHIC NOVEL YOU BOOKTALKED AT THE MIDDLE SCHOOL A FEW YEARS AGO? THE TEACHER WAS SOBBING UNDER HER DESK?
YOU AGREED NEVER TO BRING THAT UP. I PROMISED NOT TO MOCK YOUR FASHION SENSE.
FINE.
DON'T TELL ME IT—
– GOT CATALOGUED UNDER "RELIGION."
BB

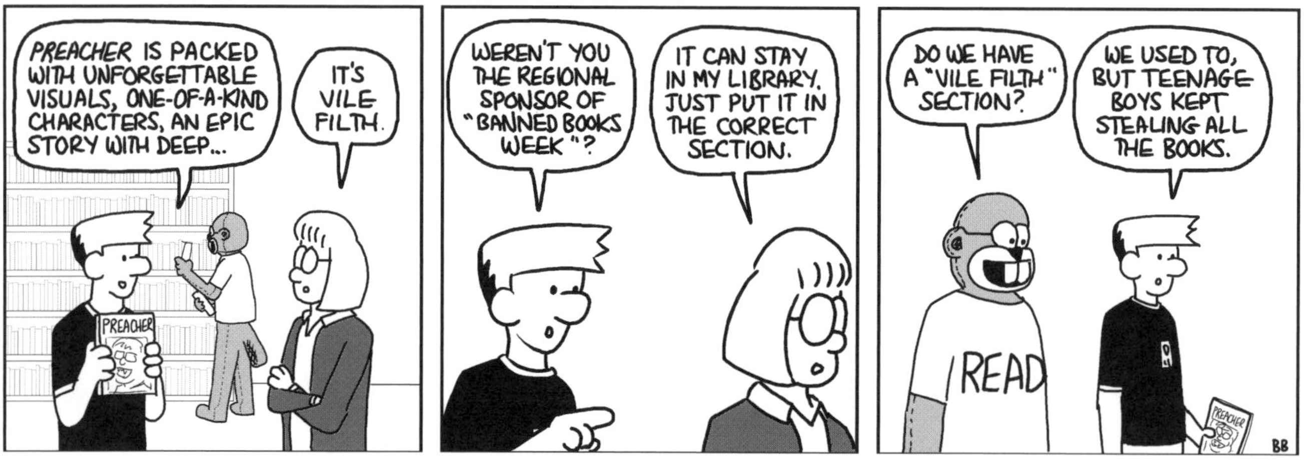
PREACHER IS PACKED WITH UNFORGETTABLE VISUALS, ONE-OF-A-KIND CHARACTERS, AN EPIC STORY WITH DEEP...
IT'S VILE FILTH.
PREACHER
WEREN'T YOU THE REGIONAL SPONSOR OF "BANNED BOOKS WEEK"?
IT CAN STAY IN MY LIBRARY. JUST PUT IT IN THE CORRECT SECTION.
DO WE HAVE A "VILE FILTH" SECTION?
WE USED TO, BUT TEENAGE BOYS KEPT STEALING ALL THE BOOKS.
READ
PREACHER
BB

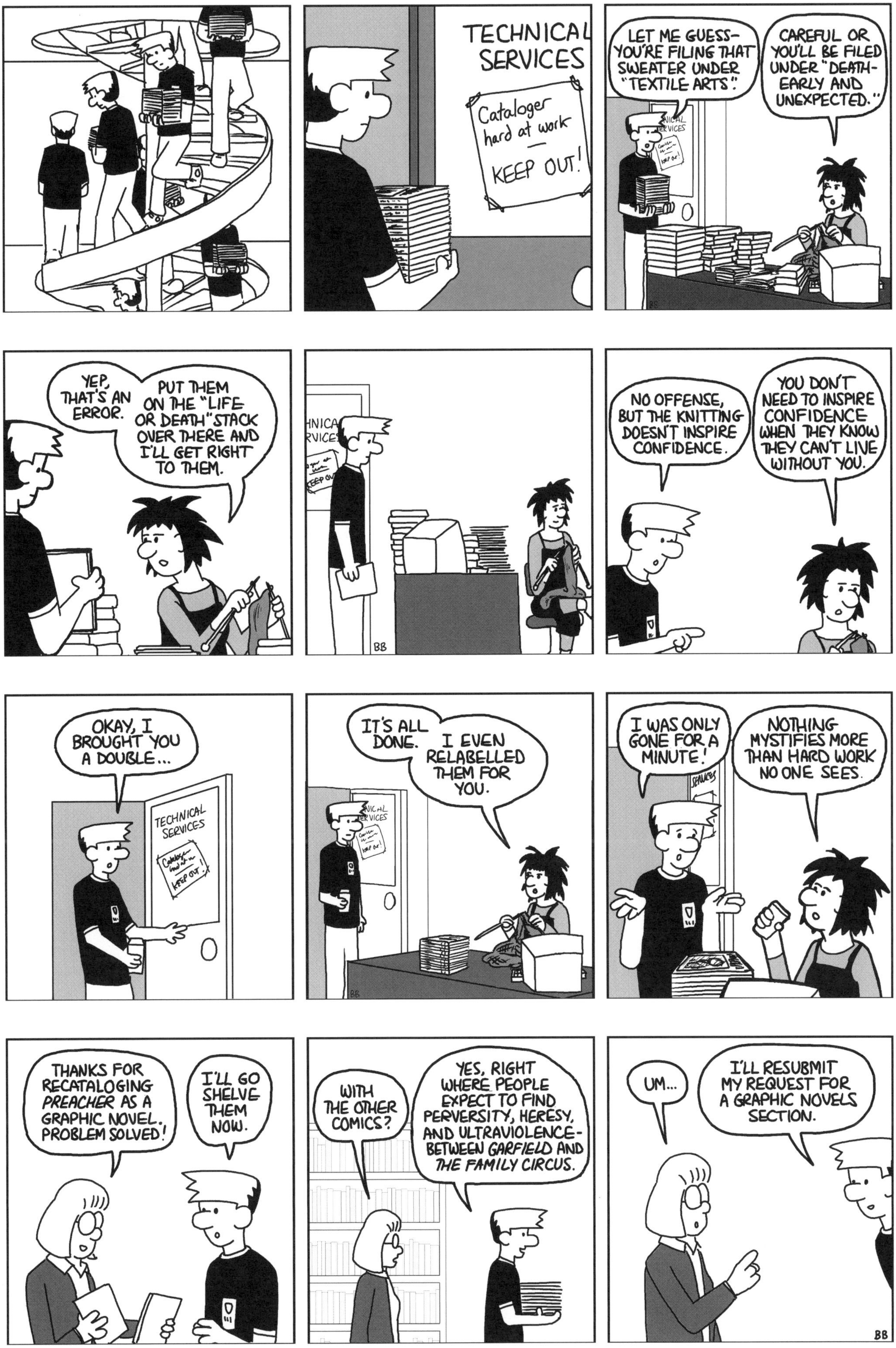
TECHNICAL SERVICES
Cataloger hard at work — KEEP OUT!
LET ME GUESS— YOU'RE FILING THAT SWEATER UNDER "TEXTILE ARTS".
CAREFUL OR YOU'LL BE FILED UNDER "DEATH-EARLY AND UNEXPECTED."
YEP, THAT'S AN ERROR.
PUT THEM ON THE "LIFE OR DEATH" STACK OVER THERE AND I'LL GET RIGHT TO THEM.
NO OFFENSE, BUT THE KNITTING DOESN'T INSPIRE CONFIDENCE.
YOU DON'T NEED TO INSPIRE CONFIDENCE WHEN THEY KNOW THEY CAN'T LIVE WITHOUT YOU.
OKAY, I BROUGHT YOU A DOUBLE...
TECHNICAL SERVICES
IT'S ALL DONE.
I EVEN RELABELLED THEM FOR YOU.
I WAS ONLY GONE FOR A MINUTE!
NOTHING MYSTIFIES MORE THAN HARD WORK NO ONE SEES.
THANKS FOR RECATALOGING *PREACHER* AS A GRAPHIC NOVEL. PROBLEM SOLVED!
I'LL GO SHELVE THEM NOW.
WITH THE OTHER COMICS?
YES, RIGHT WHERE PEOPLE EXPECT TO FIND PERVERSITY, HERESY, AND ULTRAVIOLENCE- BETWEEN *GARFIELD* AND *THE FAMILY CIRCUS*.
UM...
I'LL RESUBMIT MY REQUEST FOR A GRAPHIC NOVELS SECTION.

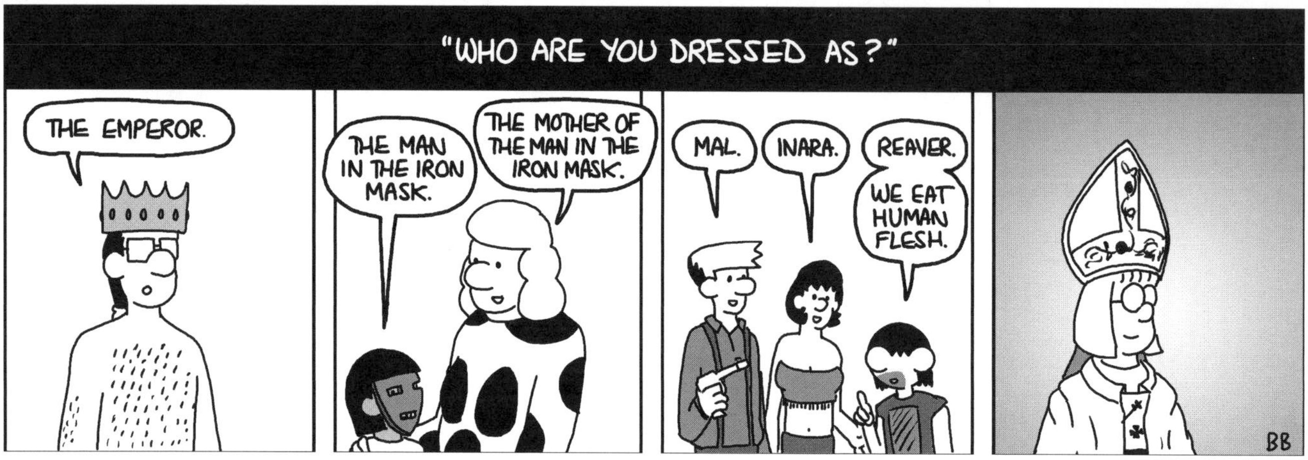
"WHO ARE YOU DRESSED AS?"
THE EMPEROR.
THE MAN IN THE IRON MASK.
THE MOTHER OF THE MAN IN THE IRON MASK.
MAL.
INARA.
REAVER.
WE EAT HUMAN FLESH.
BB

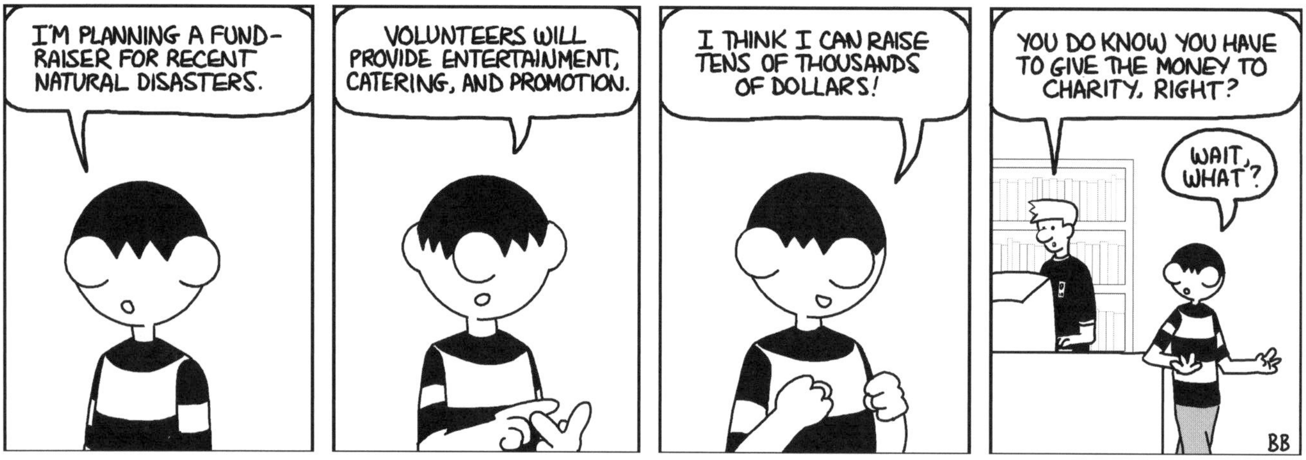
I'M PLANNING A FUND-RAISER FOR RECENT NATURAL DISASTERS.
VOLUNTEERS WILL PROVIDE ENTERTAINMENT, CATERING, AND PROMOTION.
I THINK I CAN RAISE TENS OF THOUSANDS OF DOLLARS!
YOU DO KNOW YOU HAVE TO GIVE THE MONEY TO CHARITY, RIGHT?
WAIT, WHAT?
BB

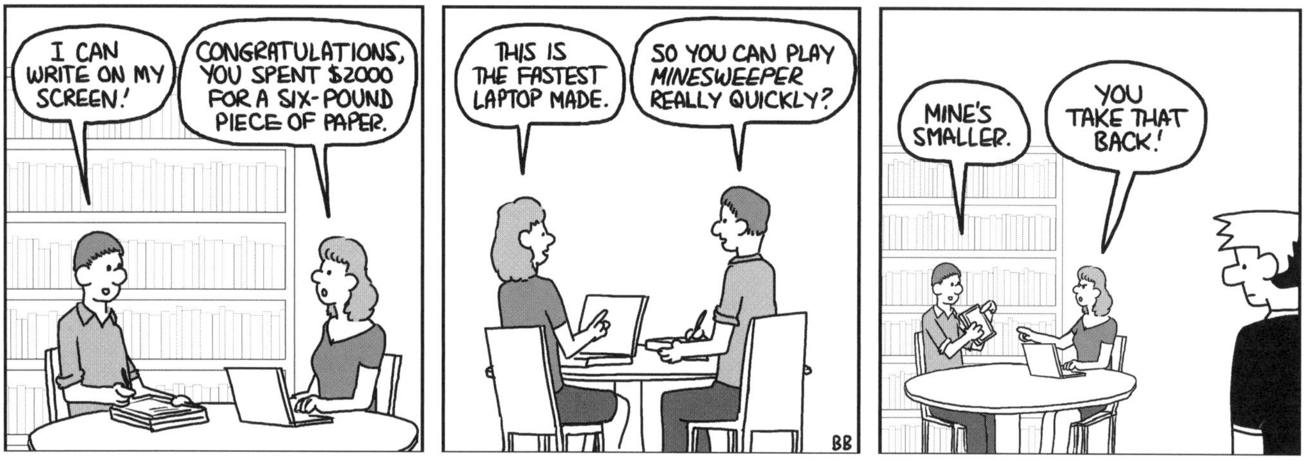
I CAN WRITE ON MY SCREEN!
CONGRATULATIONS, YOU SPENT $2000 FOR A SIX-POUND PIECE OF PAPER.
THIS IS THE FASTEST LAPTOP MADE.
SO YOU CAN PLAY *MINESWEEPER* REALLY QUICKLY?
BB
MINE'S SMALLER.
YOU TAKE THAT BACK!

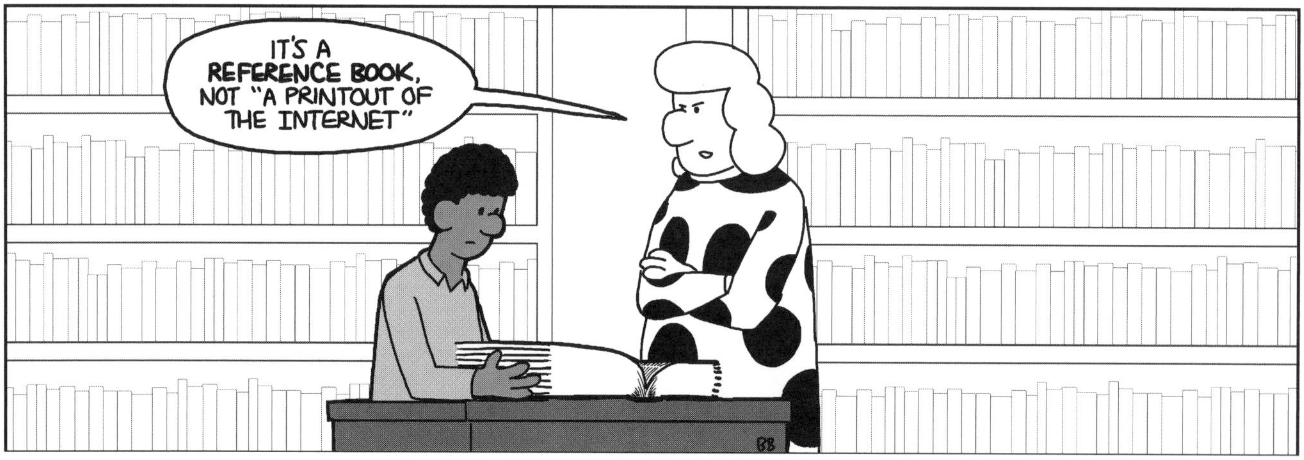
IT'S A **REFERENCE BOOK**, NOT "A PRINTOUT OF THE INTERNET"
BB

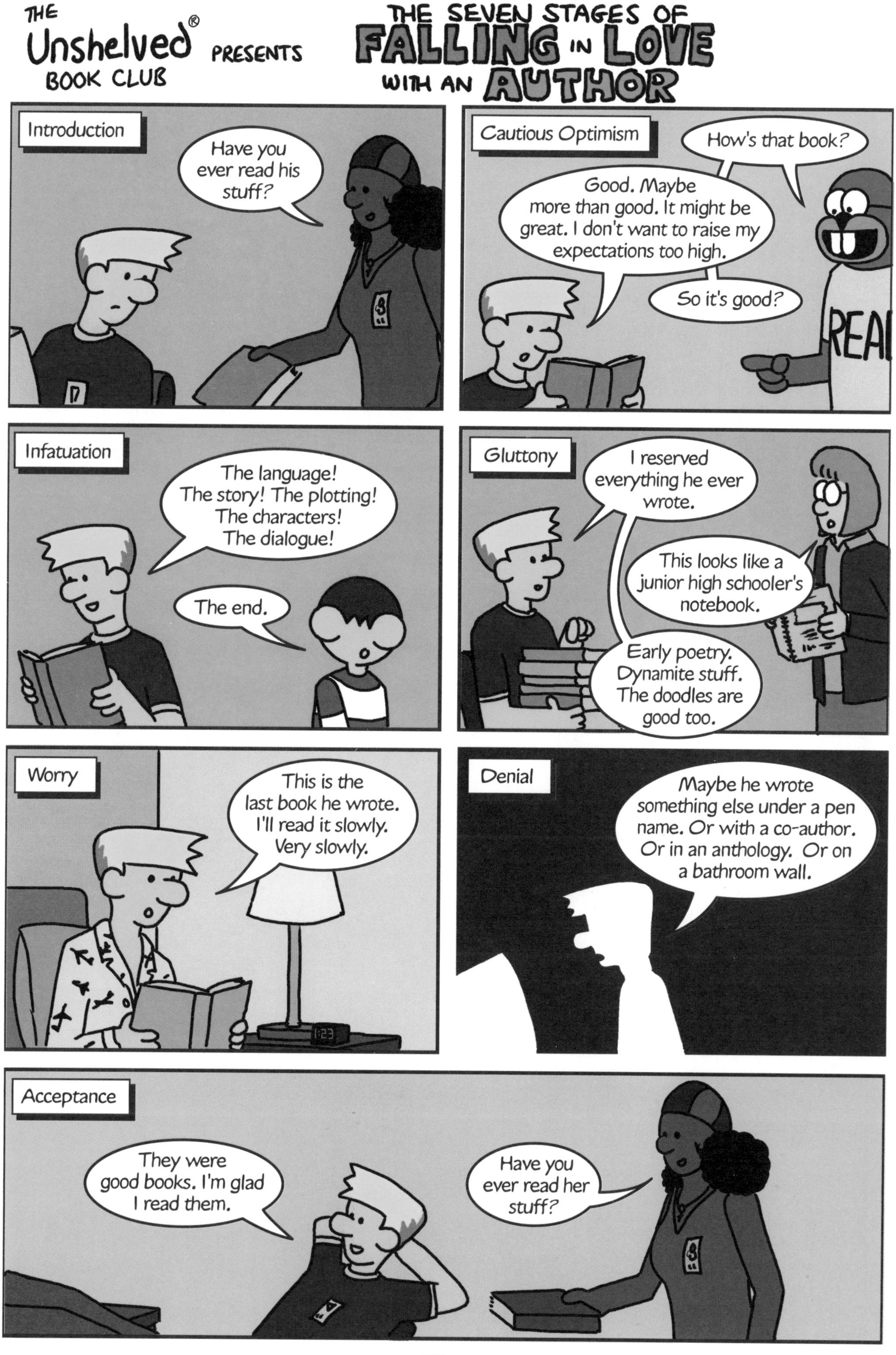

THE Unshelved® BOOK CLUB PRESENTS
THE SEVEN STAGES OF FALLING IN LOVE WITH AN AUTHOR
Introduction
Have you ever read his stuff?
Cautious Optimism
How's that book?
Good. Maybe more than good. It might be great. I don't want to raise my expectations too high.
So it's good?
READ
Infatuation
The language! The story! The plotting! The characters! The dialogue!
The end.
Gluttony
I reserved everything he ever wrote.
This looks like a junior high schooler's notebook.
Early poetry. Dynamite stuff. The doodles are good too.
Worry
This is the last book he wrote. I'll read it slowly. Very slowly.
1:23
Denial
Maybe he wrote something else under a pen name. Or with a co-author. Or in an anthology. Or on a bathroom wall.
Acceptance
They were good books. I'm glad I read them.
Have you ever read her stuff?

THE Unshelved® BOOK CLUB PRESENTS ENDER'S GAME

BY ORSON SCOTT CARD

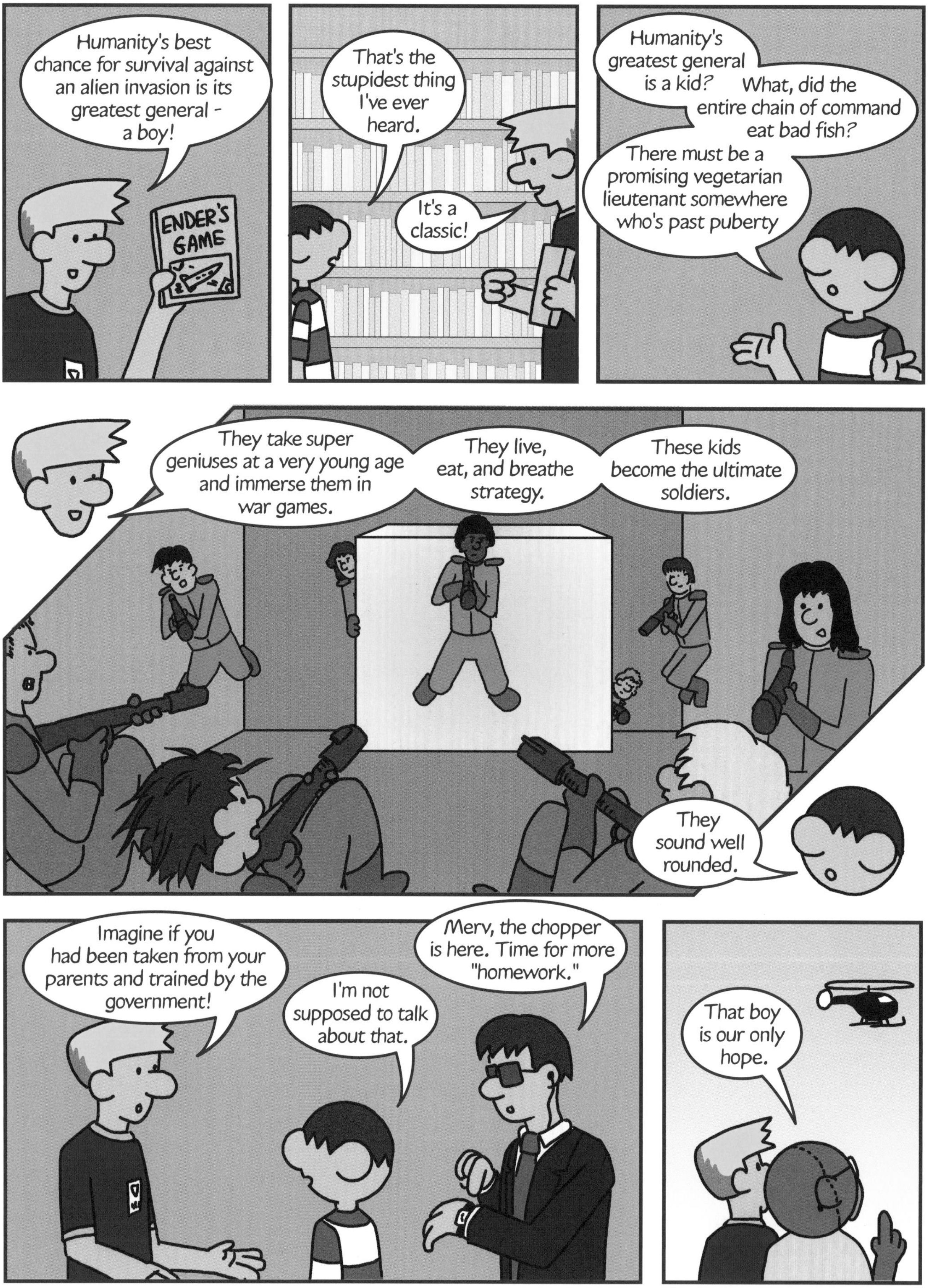

Humanity's best chance for survival against an alien invasion is its greatest general - a boy!
ENDER'S GAME
That's the stupidest thing I've ever heard.
It's a classic!
Humanity's greatest general is a kid?
What, did the entire chain of command eat bad fish?
There must be a promising vegetarian lieutenant somewhere who's past puberty
They take super geniuses at a very young age and immerse them in war games.
They live, eat, and breathe strategy.
These kids become the ultimate soldiers.
They sound well rounded.
Imagine if you had been taken from your parents and trained by the government!
I'm not supposed to talk about that.
Merv, the chopper is here. Time for more "homework."
That boy is our only hope.

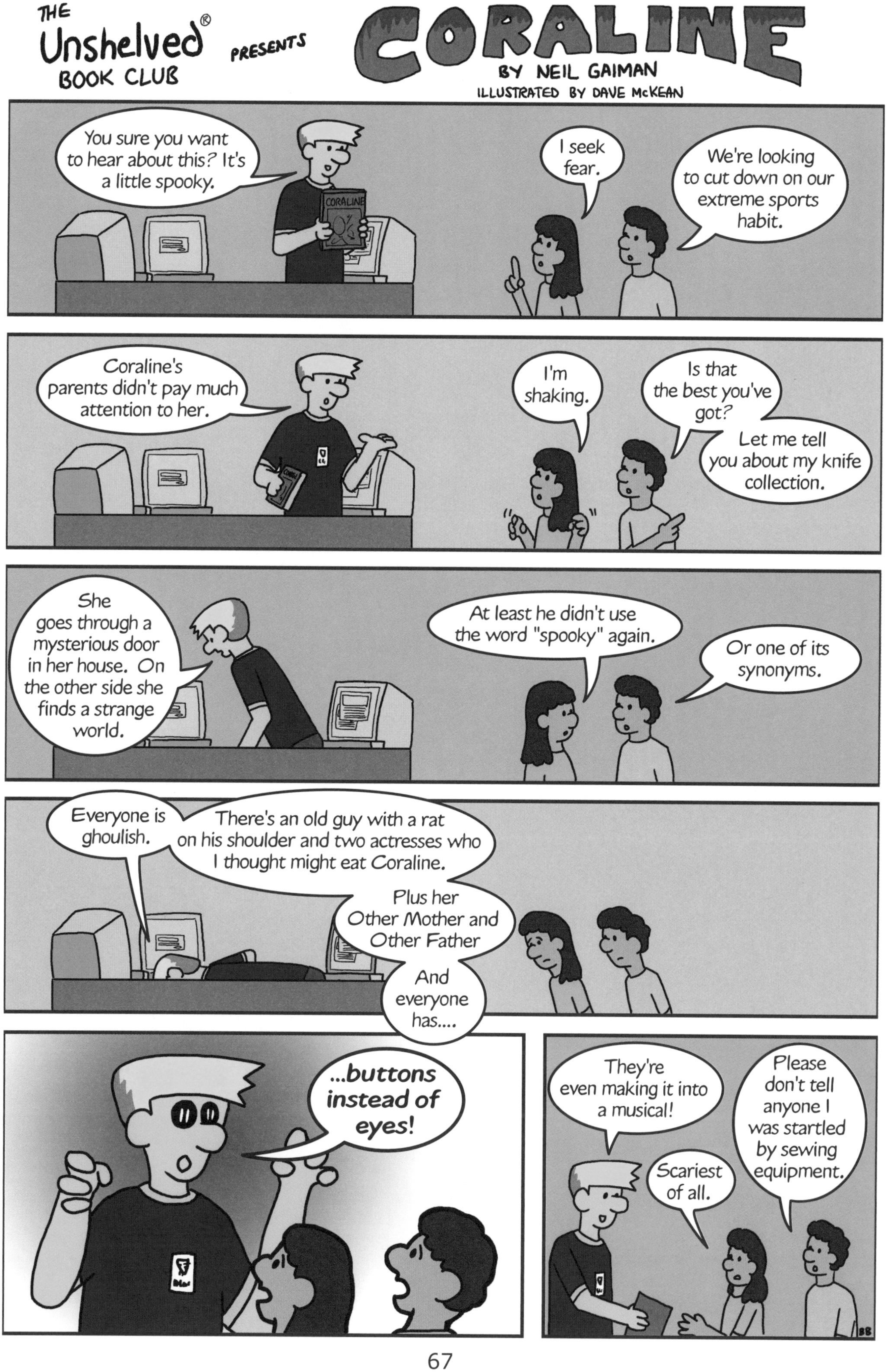
THE Unshelved® BOOK CLUB PRESENTS
CORALINE
BY NEIL GAIMAN
ILLUSTRATED BY DAVE McKEAN
You sure you want to hear about this? It's a little spooky.
CORALINE
I seek fear.
We're looking to cut down on our extreme sports habit.
Coraline's parents didn't pay much attention to her.
I'm shaking.
Is that the best you've got?
Let me tell you about my knife collection.
She goes through a mysterious door in her house. On the other side she finds a strange world.
At least he didn't use the word "spooky" again.
Or one of its synonyms.
Everyone is ghoulish.
There's an old guy with a rat on his shoulder and two actresses who I thought might eat Coraline.
Plus her Other Mother and Other Father
And everyone has....
...buttons instead of eyes!
They're even making it into a musical!
Scariest of all.
Please don't tell anyone I was startled by sewing equipment.

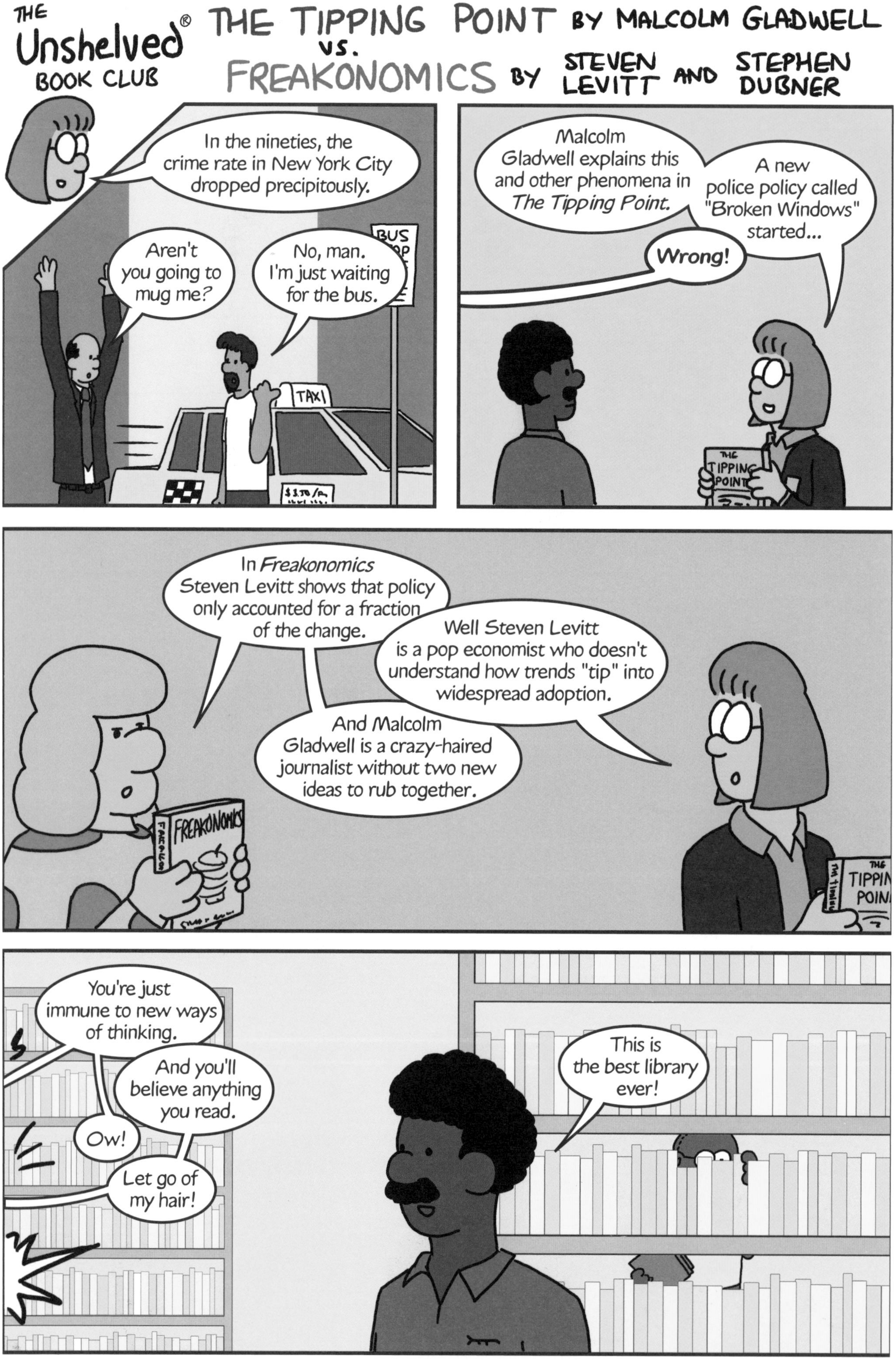
THE Unshelved® BOOK CLUB
THE TIPPING POINT BY MALCOLM GLADWELL
VS.
FREAKONOMICS BY STEVEN LEVITT AND STEPHEN DUBNER
In the nineties, the crime rate in New York City dropped precipitously.
Aren't you going to mug me?
No, man. I'm just waiting for the bus.
BUS
TAXI
Malcolm Gladwell explains this and other phenomena in The Tipping Point.
A new police policy called "Broken Windows" started...
Wrong!
THE TIPPING POINT
In Freakonomics Steven Levitt shows that policy only accounted for a fraction of the change.
Well Steven Levitt is a pop economist who doesn't understand how trends "tip" into widespread adoption.
And Malcolm Gladwell is a crazy-haired journalist without two new ideas to rub together.
FREAKONOMICS
You're just immune to new ways of thinking.
And you'll believe anything you read.
Ow!
Let go of my hair!
This is the best library ever!

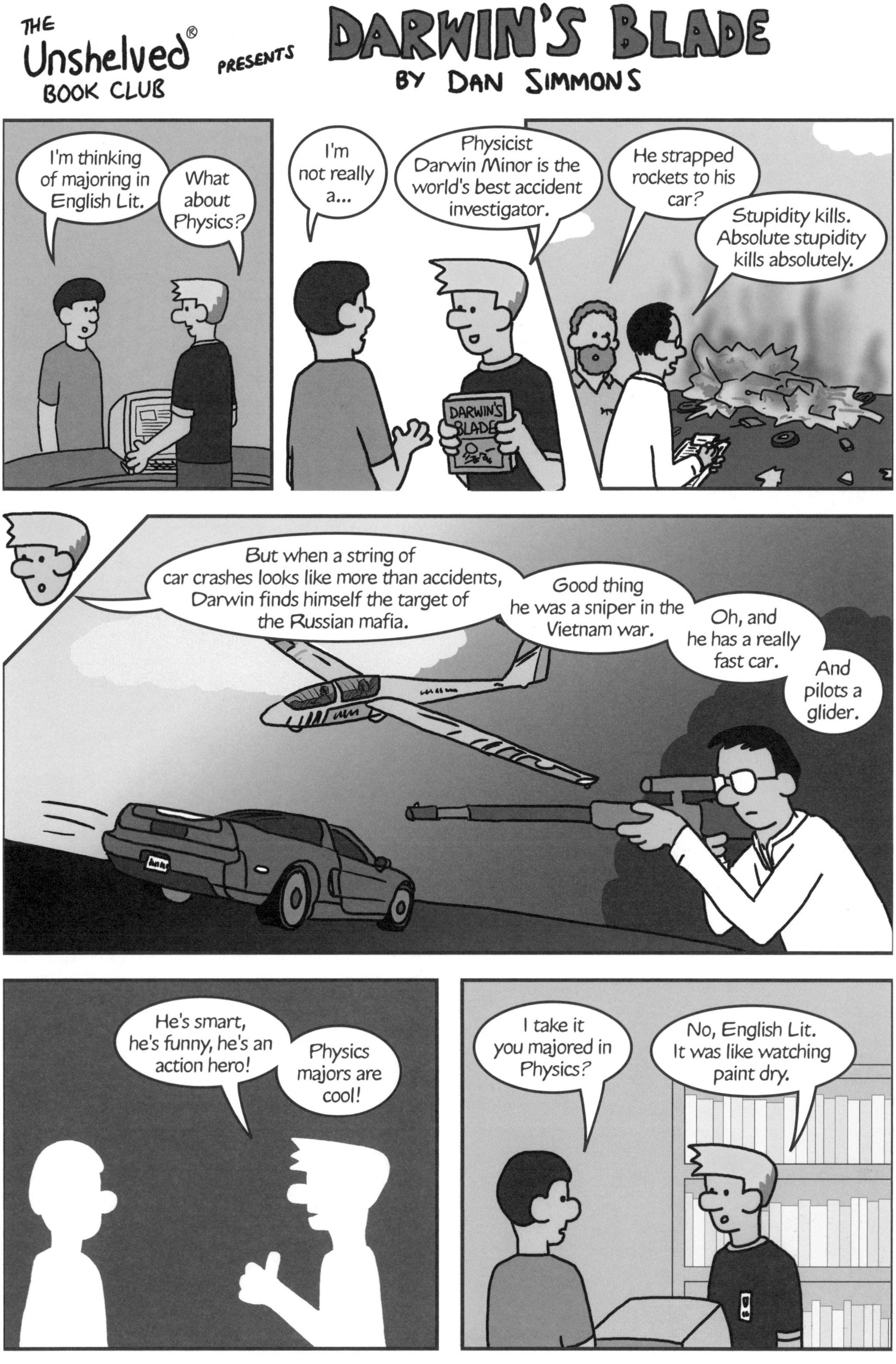
THE Unshelved® BOOK CLUB PRESENTS
DARWIN'S BLADE
BY DAN SIMMONS
I'm thinking of majoring in English Lit.
What about Physics?
I'm not really a...
Physicist Darwin Minor is the world's best accident investigator.
He strapped rockets to his car?
Stupidity kills. Absolute stupidity kills absolutely.
DARWIN'S BLADE
But when a string of car crashes looks like more than accidents, Darwin finds himself the target of the Russian mafia.
Good thing he was a sniper in the Vietnam war.
Oh, and he has a really fast car.
And pilots a glider.
He's smart, he's funny, he's an action hero!
Physics majors are cool!
I take it you majored in Physics?
No, English Lit. It was like watching paint dry.

THE Unshelved® BOOK CLUB PRESENTS

A Wizard of Earthsea

BY URSULA K. LEGUIN

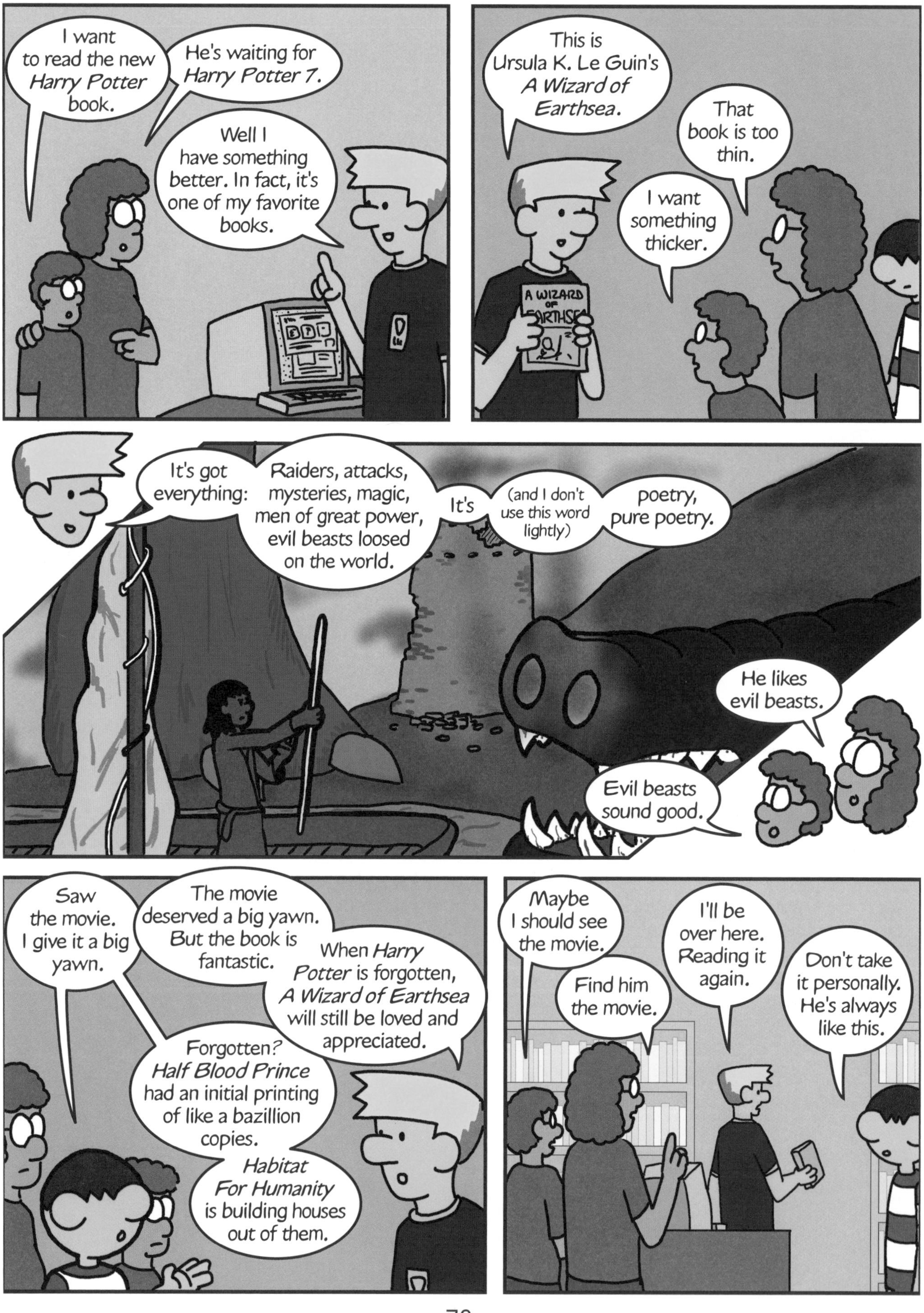
I want to read the new *Harry Potter* book.
He's waiting for *Harry Potter 7*.
Well I have something better. In fact, it's one of my favorite books.
This is Ursula K. Le Guin's *A Wizard of Earthsea*.
A WIZARD OF EARTHSEA
That book is too thin.
I want something thicker.
It's got everything:
Raiders, attacks, mysteries, magic, men of great power, evil beasts loosed on the world.
It's
(and I don't use this word lightly)
poetry, pure poetry.
He likes evil beasts.
Evil beasts sound good.
Saw the movie. I give it a big yawn.
The movie deserved a big yawn. But the book is fantastic.
When *Harry Potter* is forgotten, *A Wizard of Earthsea* will still be loved and appreciated.
Forgotten? *Half Blood Prince* had an initial printing of like a bazillion copies.
Habitat For Humanity is building houses out of them.
Maybe I should see the movie.
Find him the movie.
I'll be over here. Reading it again.
Don't take it personally. He's always like this.

The Unshelved® Book Club presents

Getting Things Done

by David Allen

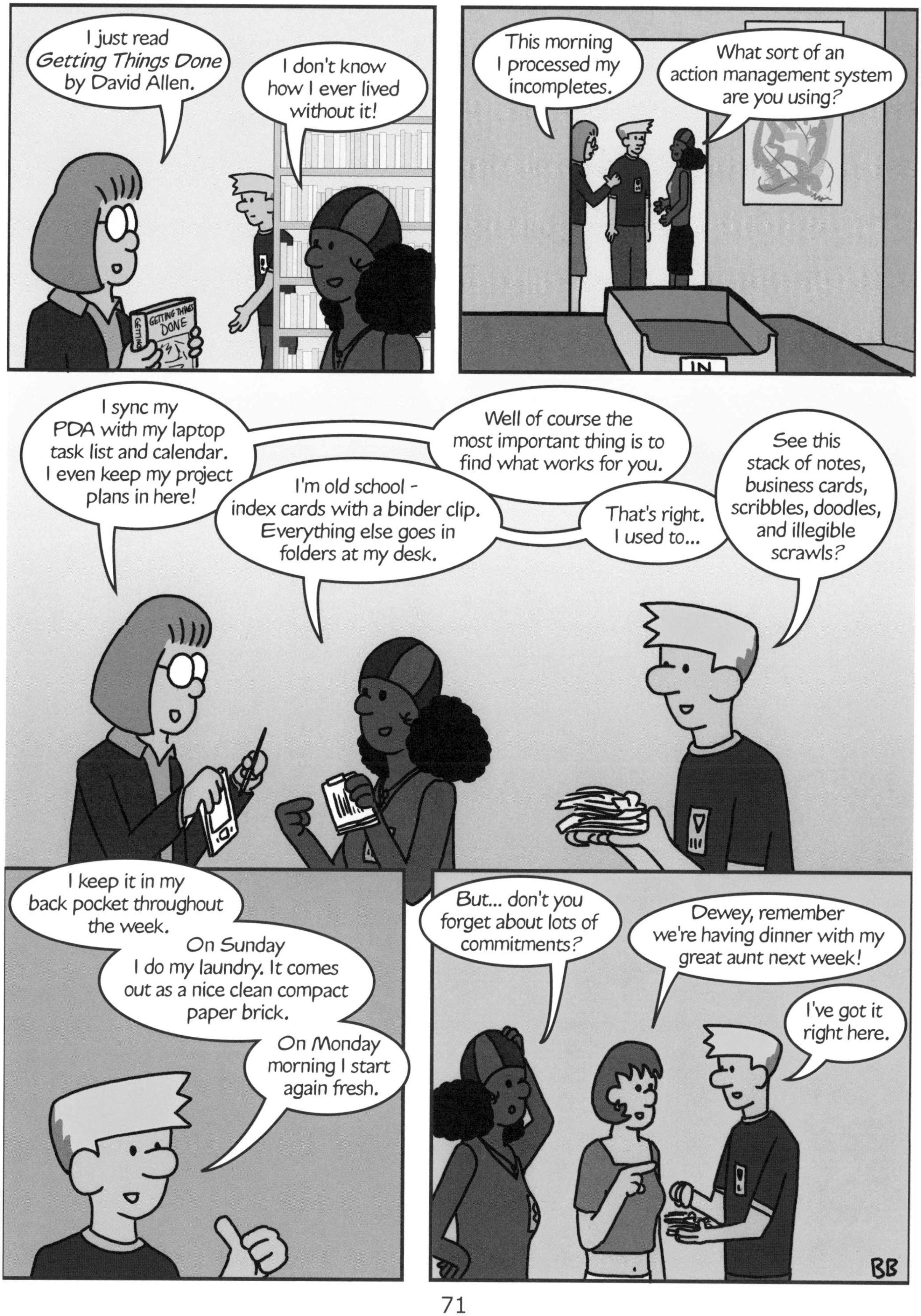
I just read *Getting Things Done* by David Allen.
I don't know how I ever lived without it!
GETTING THINGS DONE
This morning I processed my incompletes.
What sort of an action management system are you using?
IN
I sync my PDA with my laptop task list and calendar. I even keep my project plans in here!
Well of course the most important thing is to find what works for you.
I'm old school - index cards with a binder clip. Everything else goes in folders at my desk.
That's right. I used to...
See this stack of notes, business cards, scribbles, doodles, and illegible scrawls?
I keep it in my back pocket throughout the week.
On Sunday I do my laundry. It comes out as a nice clean compact paper brick.
On Monday morning I start again fresh.
But... don't you forget about lots of commitments?
Dewey, remember we're having dinner with my great aunt next week!
I've got it right here.
BB

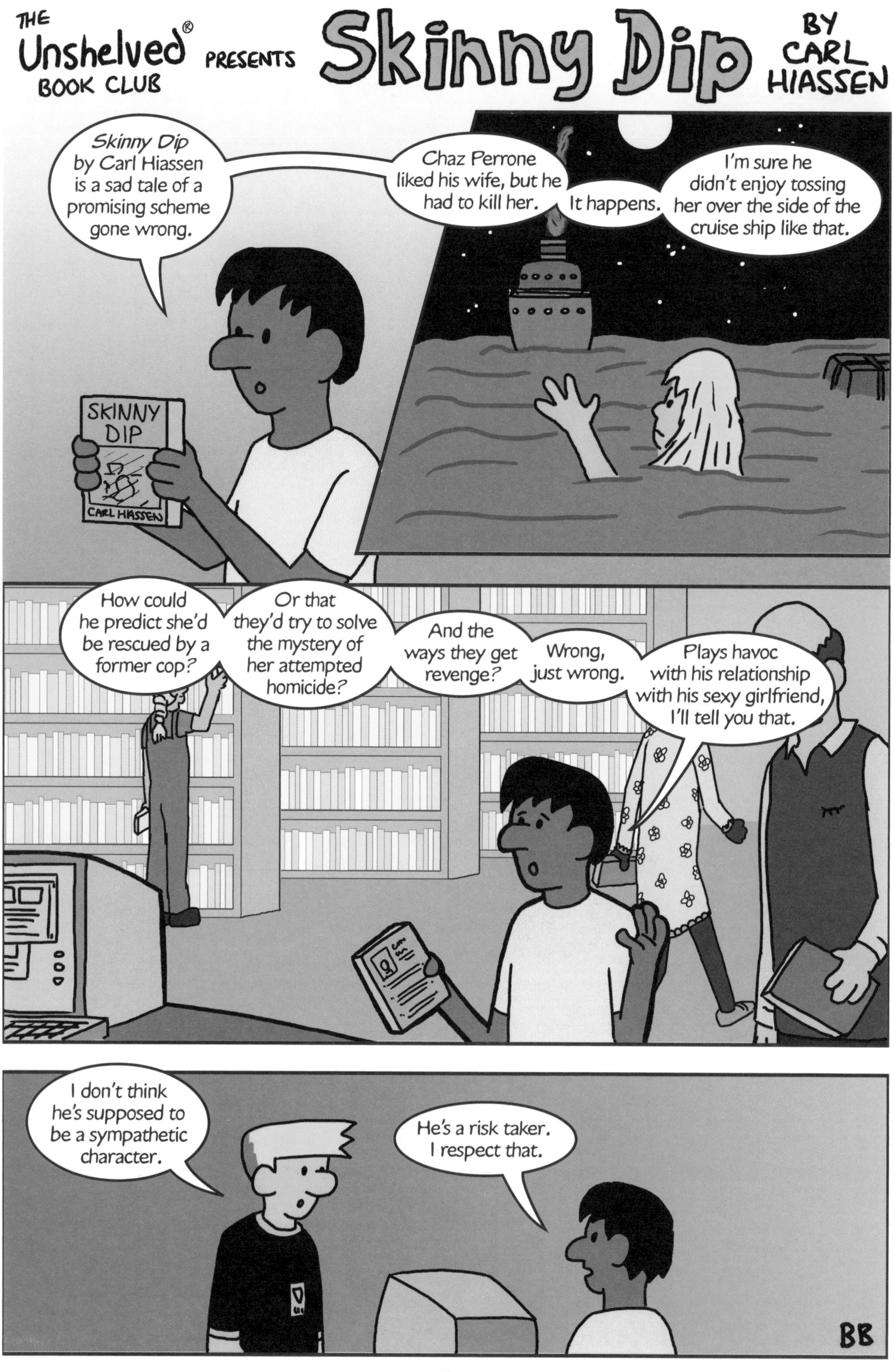
THE Unshelved® BOOK CLUB PRESENTS Skinny Dip BY CARL HIASSEN
Skinny Dip by Carl Hiassen is a sad tale of a promising scheme gone wrong.
SKINNY DIP
CARL HIASSEN
Chaz Perrone liked his wife, but he had to kill her.
It happens.
I'm sure he didn't enjoy tossing her over the side of the cruise ship like that.
How could he predict she'd be rescued by a former cop?
Or that they'd try to solve the mystery of her attempted homicide?
And the ways they get revenge?
Wrong, just wrong.
Plays havoc with his relationship with his sexy girlfriend, I'll tell you that.
I don't think he's supposed to be a sympathetic character.
He's a risk taker. I respect that.
BB

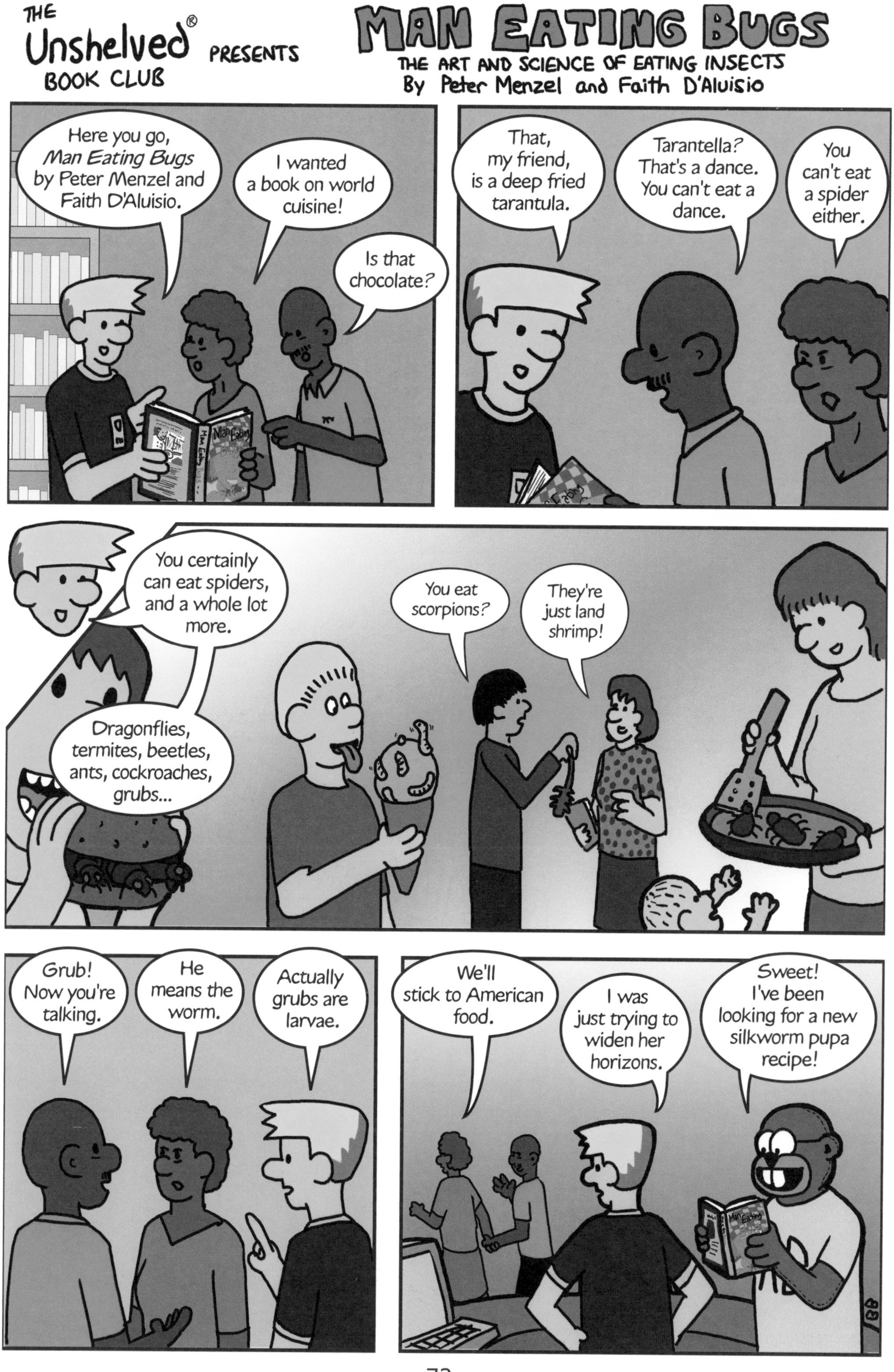
THE Unshelved® BOOK CLUB PRESENTS
MAN EATING BUGS
THE ART AND SCIENCE OF EATING INSECTS
By Peter Menzel and Faith D'Aluisio
Here you go, *Man Eating Bugs* by Peter Menzel and Faith D'Aluisio.
I wanted a book on world cuisine!
Is that chocolate?
That, my friend, is a deep fried tarantula.
Tarantella? That's a dance. You can't eat a dance.
You can't eat a spider either.
You certainly can eat spiders, and a whole lot more.
Dragonflies, termites, beetles, ants, cockroaches, grubs...
You eat scorpions?
They're just land shrimp!
Grub! Now you're talking.
He means the worm.
Actually grubs are larvae.
We'll stick to American food.
I was just trying to widen her horizons.
Sweet! I've been looking for a new silkworm pupa recipe!

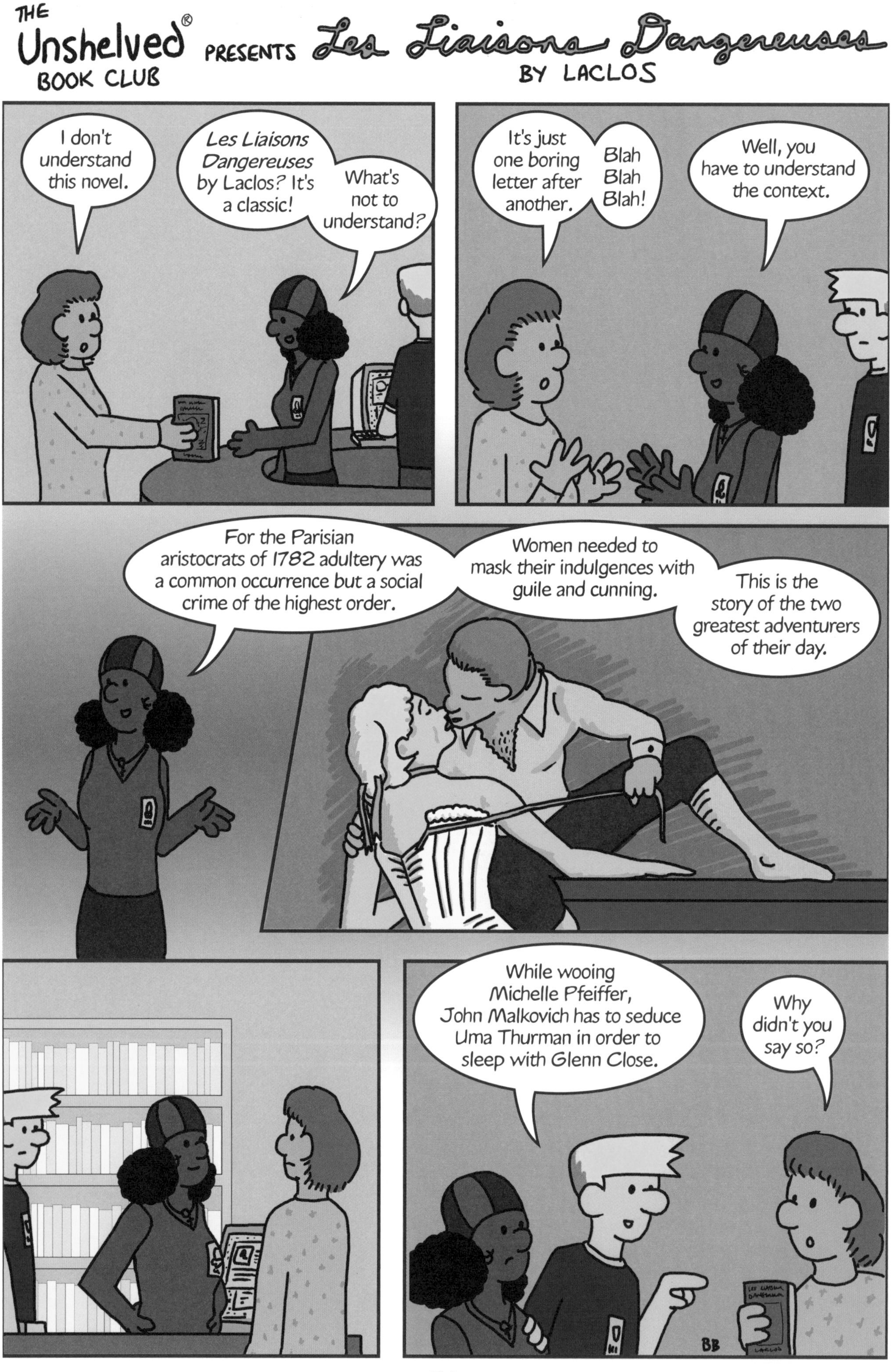
THE Unshelved® BOOK CLUB PRESENTS Les Liaisons Dangereuses BY LACLOS
I don't understand this novel.
Les Liaisons Dangereuses by Laclos? It's a classic!
What's not to understand?
It's just one boring letter after another.
Blah Blah Blah!
Well, you have to understand the context.
For the Parisian aristocrats of 1782 adultery was a common occurrence but a social crime of the highest order.
Women needed to mask their indulgences with guile and cunning.
This is the story of the two greatest adventurers of their day.
While wooing Michelle Pfeiffer, John Malkovich has to seduce Uma Thurman in order to sleep with Glenn Close.
Why didn't you say so?
BB

THE Unshelved® BOOK CLUB PRESENTS

The Tale of Despereaux

Being the Story of a Mouse, a Princess, Some Soup and a Spool of Thread

By Kate DiCamillo, illustrated by Timothy Basil Ering

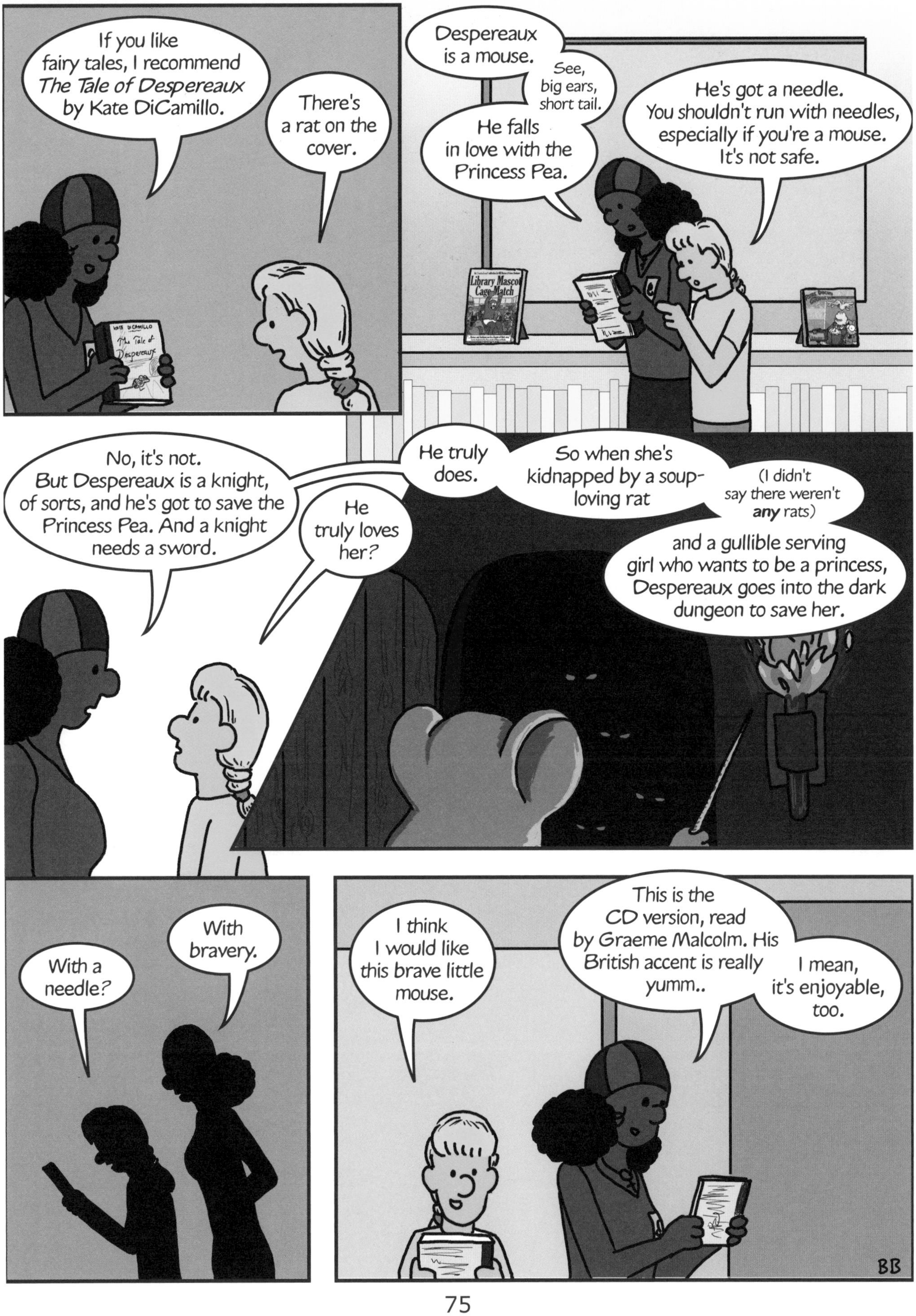

If you like fairy tales, I recommend *The Tale of Despereaux* by Kate DiCamillo.
There's a rat on the cover.
Despereaux is a mouse.
See, big ears, short tail.
He falls in love with the Princess Pea.
He's got a needle. You shouldn't run with needles, especially if you're a mouse. It's not safe.
Library Mascot Cage Match
No, it's not. But Despereaux is a knight, of sorts, and he's got to save the Princess Pea. And a knight needs a sword.
He truly loves her?
He truly does.
So when she's kidnapped by a soup-loving rat
(I didn't say there weren't **any** rats)
and a gullible serving girl who wants to be a princess, Despereaux goes into the dark dungeon to save her.
With a needle?
With bravery.
I think I would like this brave little mouse.
This is the CD version, read by Graeme Malcolm. His British accent is really yumm..
I mean, it's enjoyable, too.
BB

The Unshelved® Book Club presents Ringworld by Larry Niven

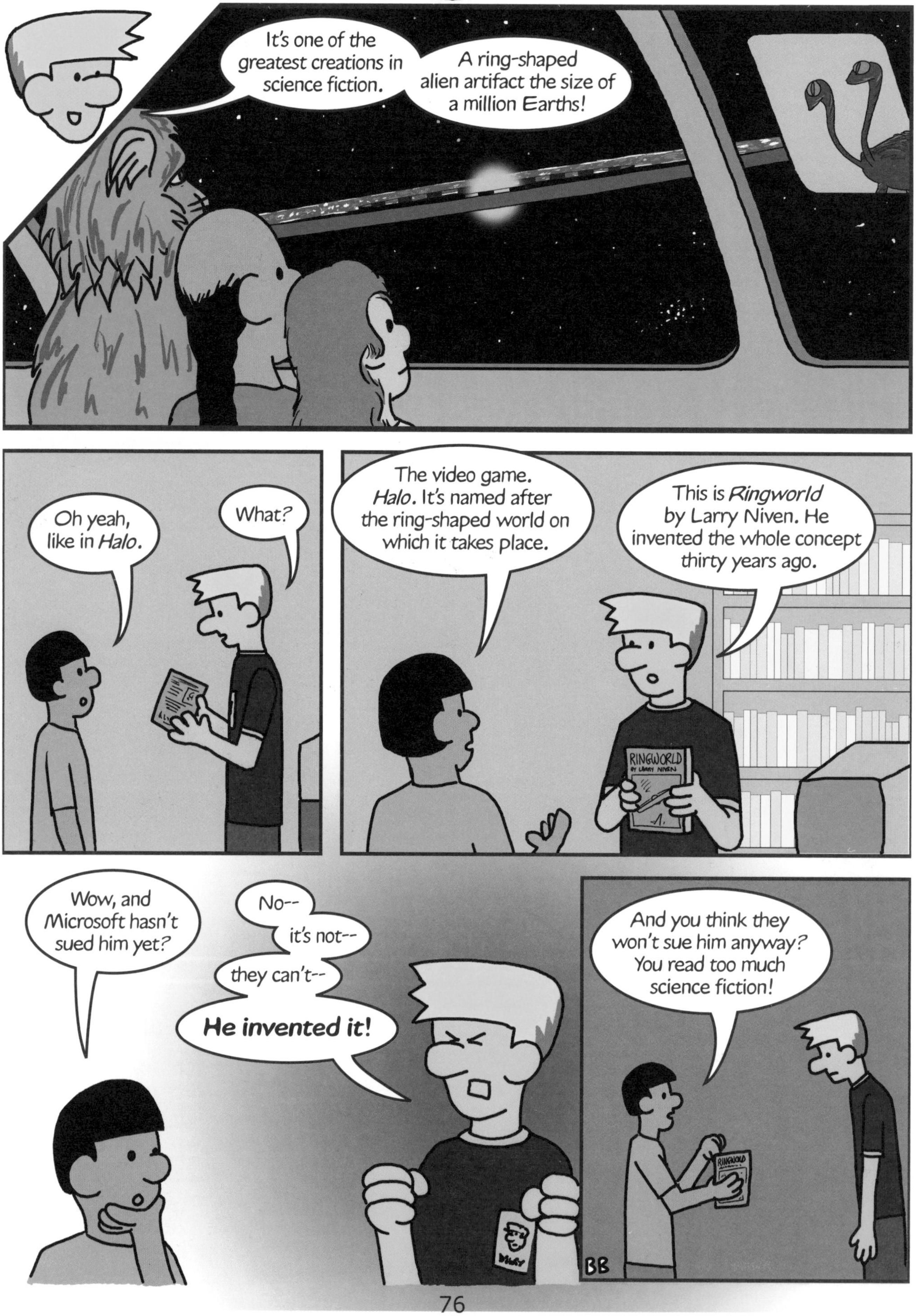
It's one of the greatest creations in science fiction.
A ring-shaped alien artifact the size of a million Earths!
Oh yeah, like in *Halo*.
What?
The video game. *Halo*. It's named after the ring-shaped world on which it takes place.
This is *Ringworld* by Larry Niven. He invented the whole concept thirty years ago.
RINGWORLD
BY LARRY NIVEN
Wow, and Microsoft hasn't sued him yet?
No--
it's not--
they can't--
He invented it!
And you think they won't sue him anyway? You read too much science fiction!
BB

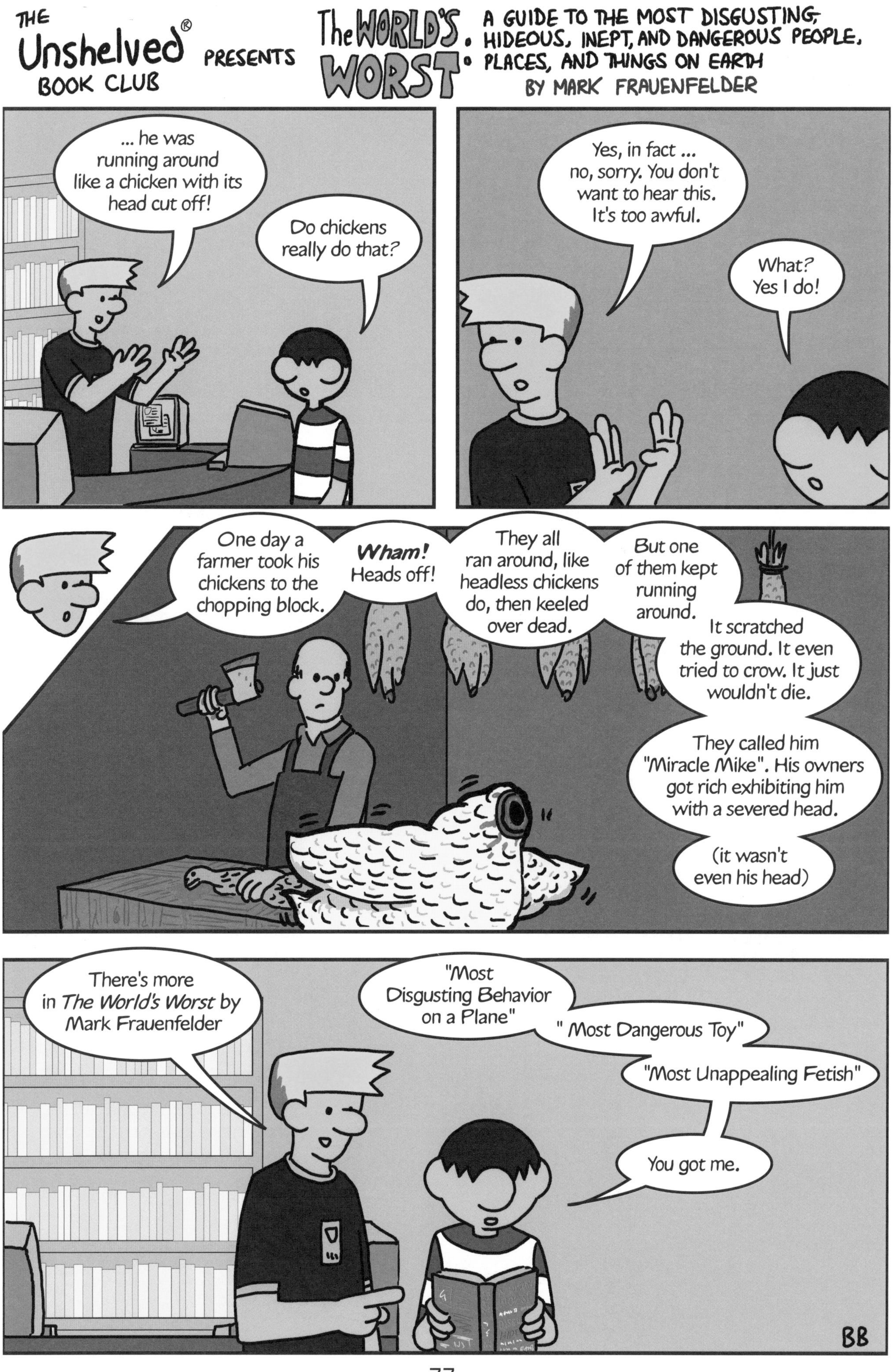
THE Unshelved® BOOK CLUB PRESENTS
The WORLD'S WORST
A GUIDE TO THE MOST DISGUSTING, HIDEOUS, INEPT, AND DANGEROUS PEOPLE, PLACES, AND THINGS ON EARTH
BY MARK FRAUENFELDER
... he was running around like a chicken with its head cut off!
Do chickens really do that?
Yes, in fact ... no, sorry. You don't want to hear this. It's too awful.
What? Yes I do!
One day a farmer took his chickens to the chopping block.
Wham! Heads off!
They all ran around, like headless chickens do, then keeled over dead.
But one of them kept running around.
It scratched the ground. It even tried to crow. It just wouldn't die.
They called him "Miracle Mike". His owners got rich exhibiting him with a severed head.
(it wasn't even his head)
There's more in The World's Worst by Mark Frauenfelder
"Most Disgusting Behavior on a Plane"
" Most Dangerous Toy"
"Most Unappealing Fetish"
You got me.
BB

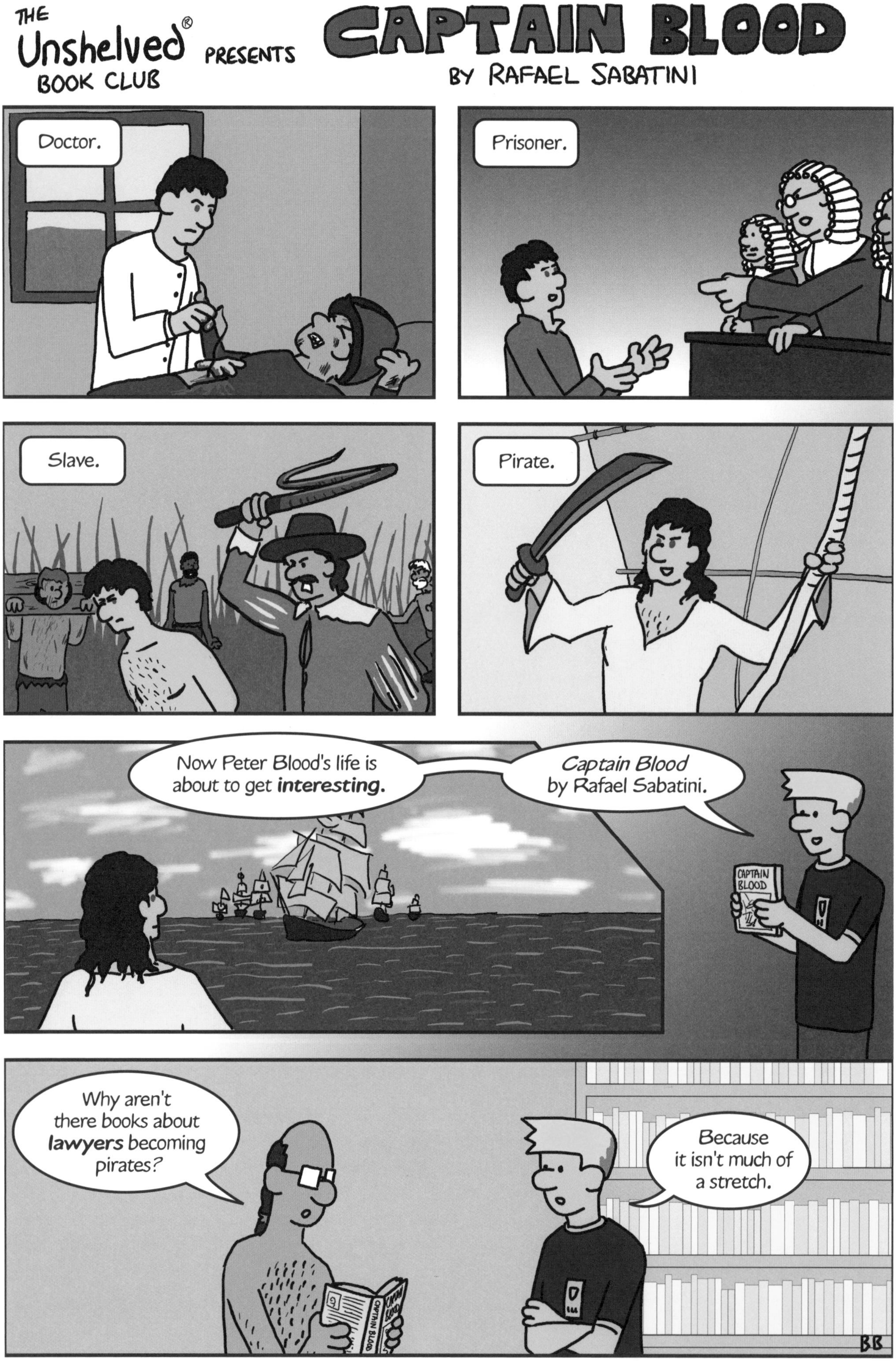
THE Unshelved® BOOK CLUB PRESENTS
CAPTAIN BLOOD
BY RAFAEL SABATINI
Doctor.
Prisoner.
Slave.
Pirate.
Now Peter Blood's life is about to get **interesting.**
Captain Blood by Rafael Sabatini.
CAPTAIN BLOOD
Why aren't there books about **lawyers** becoming pirates?
Because it isn't much of a stretch.
CAPTAIN BLOOD
BB

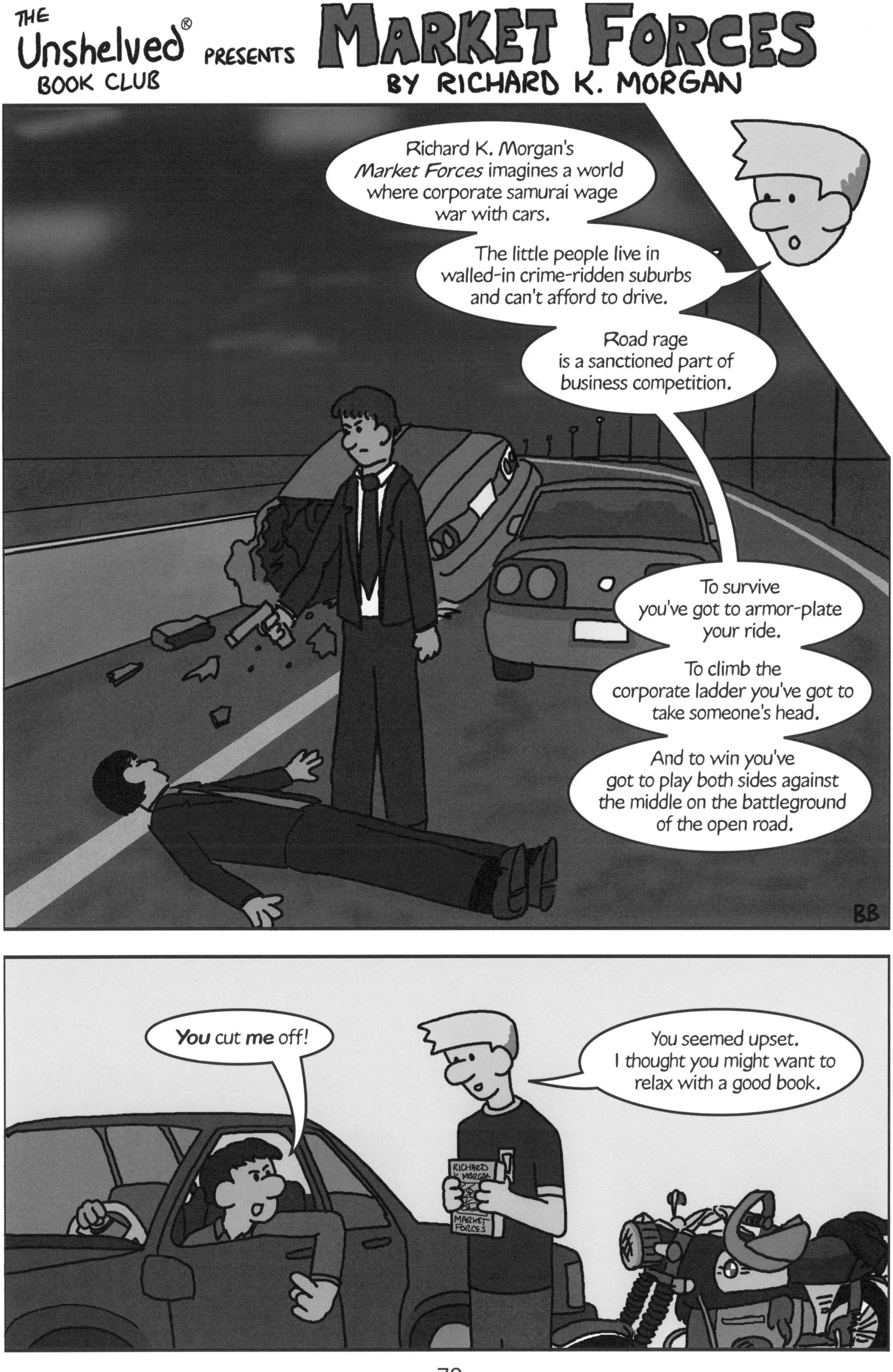
THE Unshelved® BOOK CLUB PRESENTS
MARKET FORCES
BY RICHARD K. MORGAN
Richard K. Morgan's *Market Forces* imagines a world where corporate samurai wage war with cars.
The little people live in walled-in crime-ridden suburbs and can't afford to drive.
Road rage is a sanctioned part of business competition.
To survive you've got to armor-plate your ride.
To climb the corporate ladder you've got to take someone's head.
And to win you've got to play both sides against the middle on the battleground of the open road.
BB
You cut **me** off!
You seemed upset. I thought you might want to relax with a good book.
RICHARD K. MORGAN MARKET FORCES

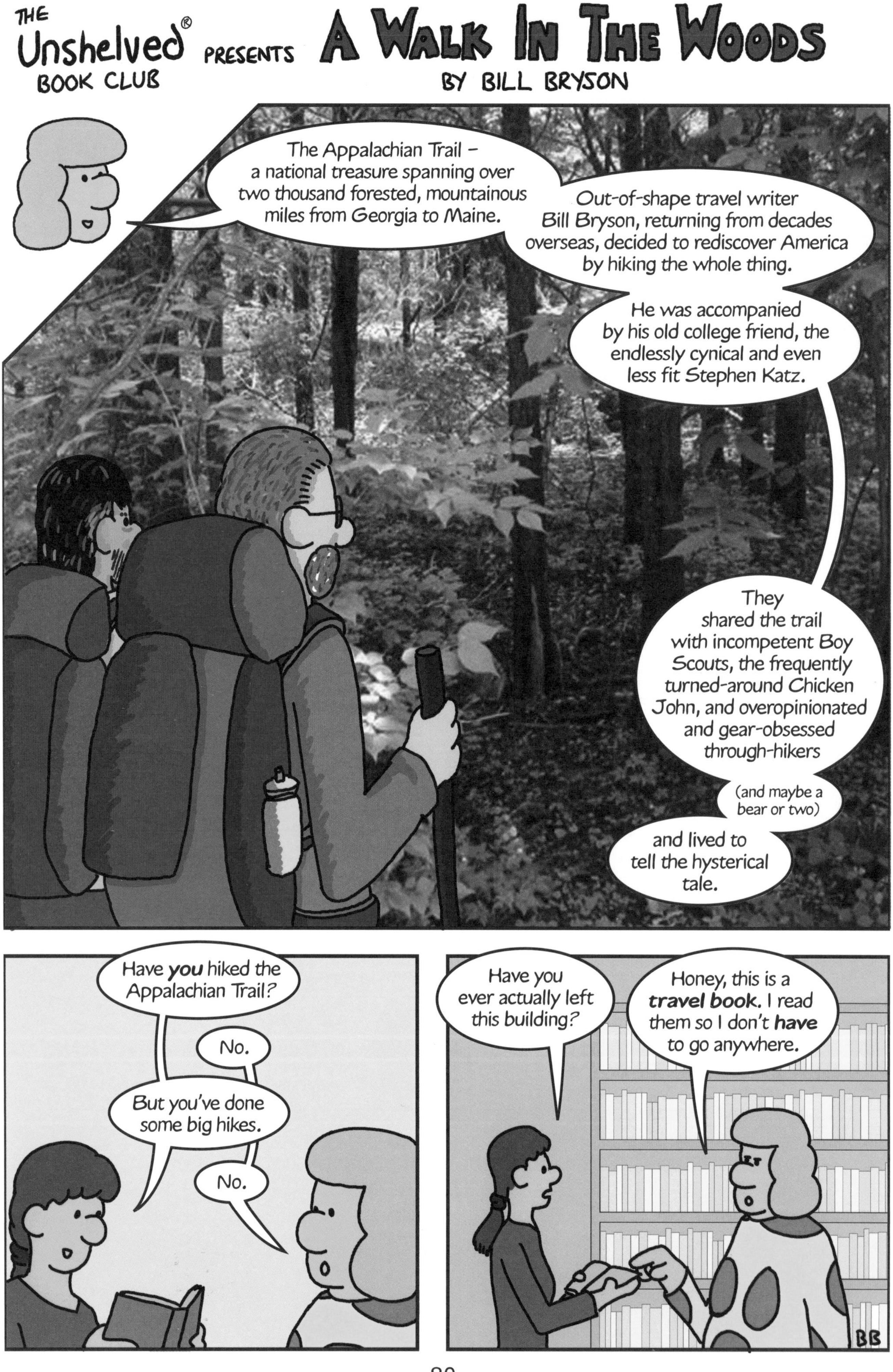
THE Unshelved® BOOK CLUB PRESENTS A WALK IN THE WOODS
BY BILL BRYSON
The Appalachian Trail – a national treasure spanning over two thousand forested, mountainous miles from Georgia to Maine.
Out-of-shape travel writer Bill Bryson, returning from decades overseas, decided to rediscover America by hiking the whole thing.
He was accompanied by his old college friend, the endlessly cynical and even less fit Stephen Katz.
They shared the trail with incompetent Boy Scouts, the frequently turned-around Chicken John, and overopinionated and gear-obsessed through-hikers
(and maybe a bear or two)
and lived to tell the hysterical tale.
Have you hiked the Appalachian Trail?
No.
But you've done some big hikes.
No.
Have you ever actually left this building?
Honey, this is a travel book. I read them so I don't have to go anywhere.
BB

THE Unshelved® BOOK CLUB PRESENTS

Bucking THE Sarge

BY CHRISTOPHER PAUL CURTIS

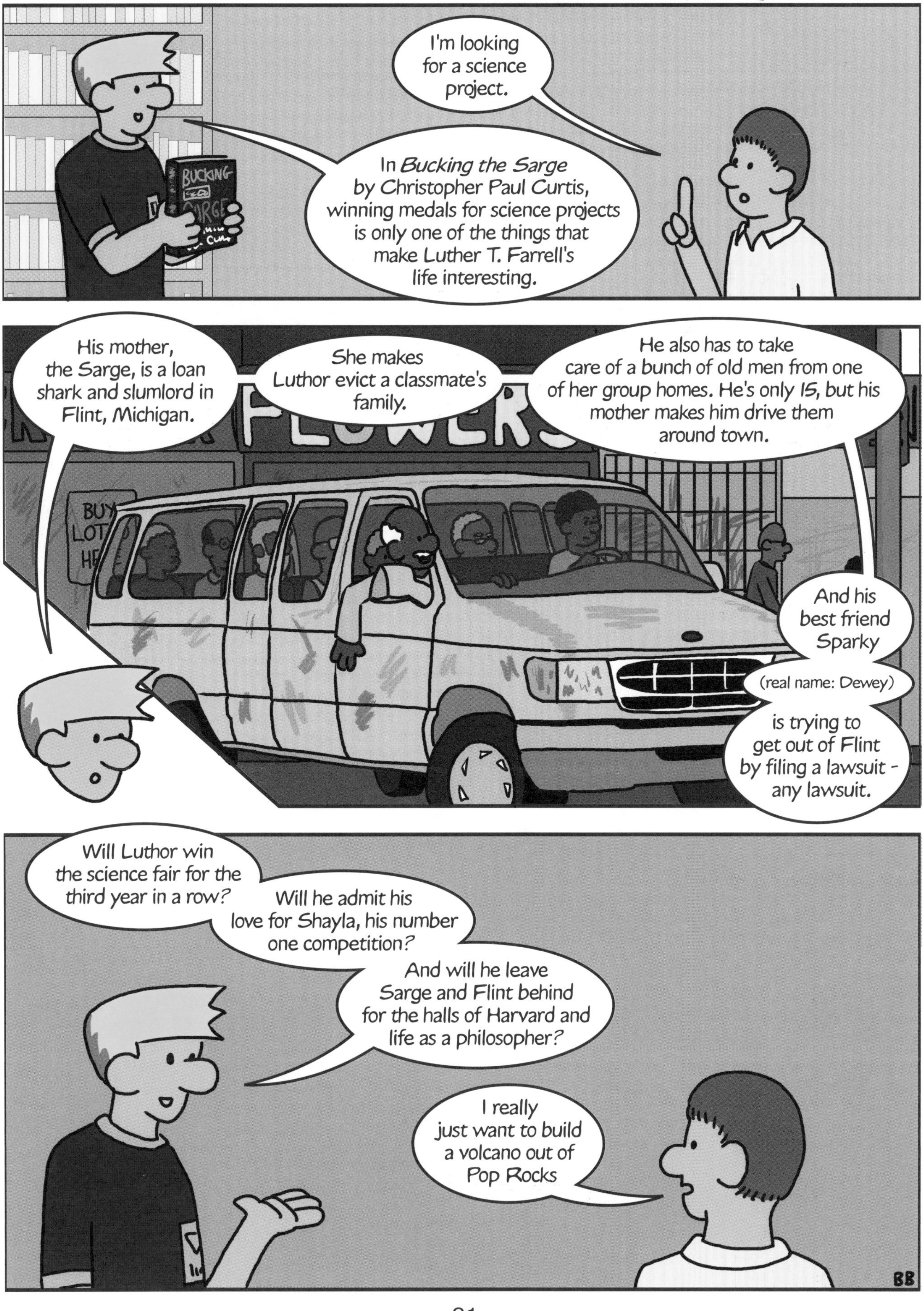
I'm looking for a science project.
In *Bucking the Sarge* by Christopher Paul Curtis, winning medals for science projects is only one of the things that make Luther T. Farrell's life interesting.
FLOWERS
His mother, the Sarge, is a loan shark and slumlord in Flint, Michigan.
She makes Luthor evict a classmate's family.
He also has to take care of a bunch of old men from one of her group homes. He's only 15, but his mother makes him drive them around town.
And his best friend Sparky
(real name: Dewey)
is trying to get out of Flint by filing a lawsuit - any lawsuit.
Will Luthor win the science fair for the third year in a row?
Will he admit his love for Shayla, his number one competition?
And will he leave Sarge and Flint behind for the halls of Harvard and life as a philosopher?
I really just want to build a volcano out of Pop Rocks
BB

The Unshelved® Book Club presents

Farmer Boy

by Laura Ingalls Wilder

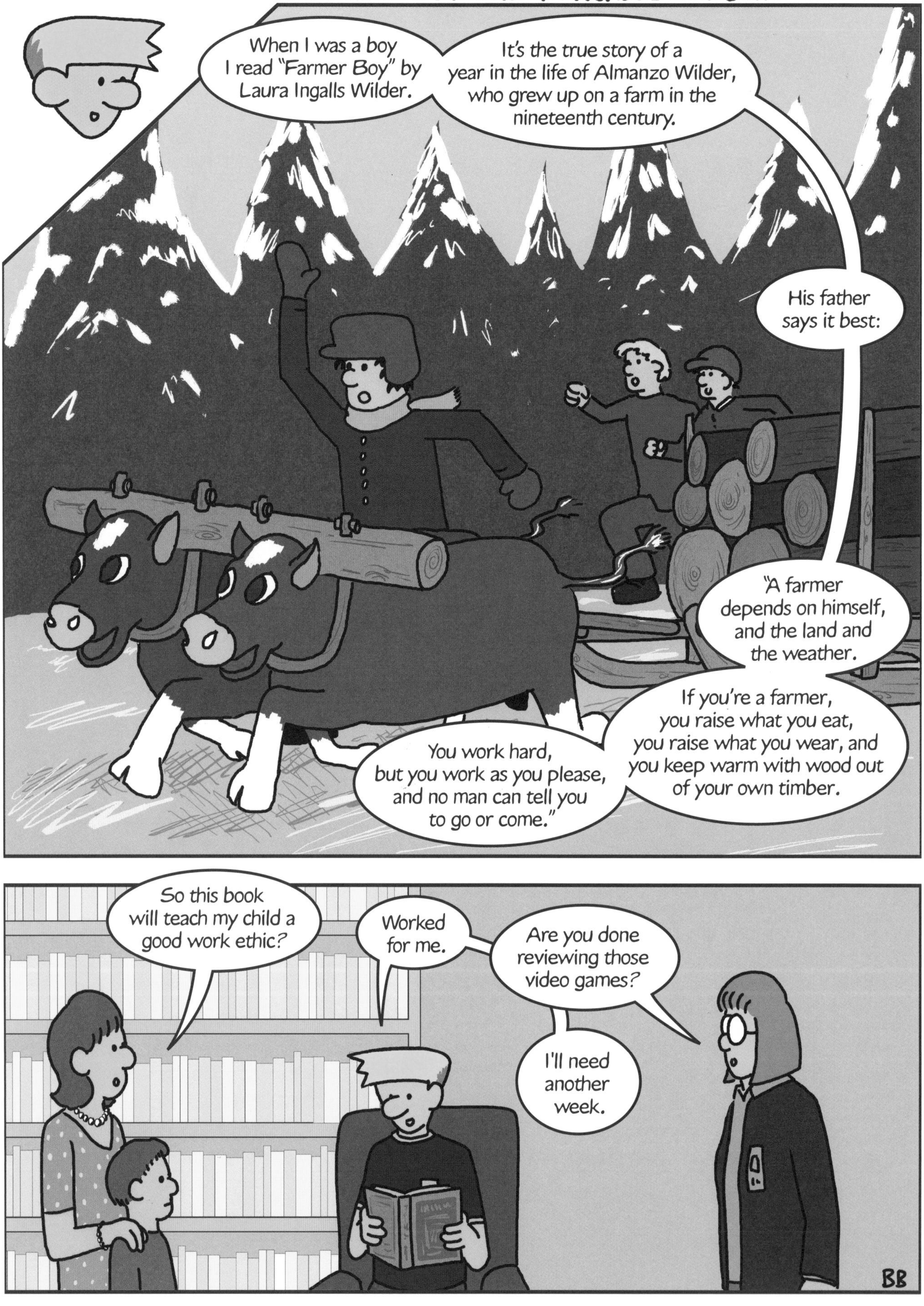

When I was a boy I read "Farmer Boy" by Laura Ingalls Wilder.
It's the true story of a year in the life of Almanzo Wilder, who grew up on a farm in the nineteenth century.
His father says it best:
"A farmer depends on himself, and the land and the weather.
If you're a farmer, you raise what you eat, you raise what you wear, and you keep warm with wood out of your own timber.
You work hard, but you work as you please, and no man can tell you to go or come."
So this book will teach my child a good work ethic?
Worked for me.
Are you done reviewing those video games?
I'll need another week.
BB

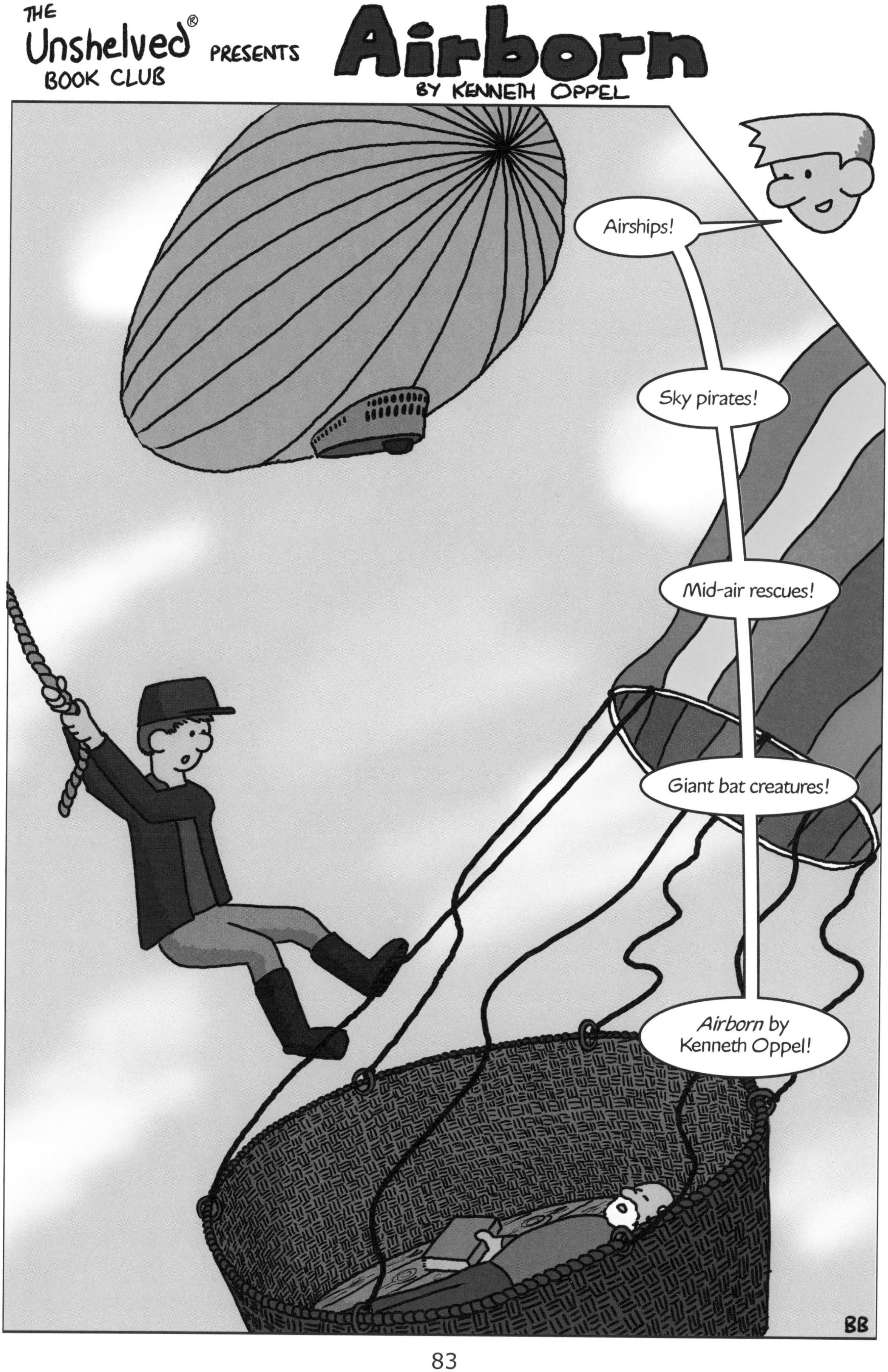

THE
Unshelved®
BOOK CLUB
PRESENTS
Airborn
BY KENNETH OPPEL
Airships!
Sky pirates!
Mid-air rescues!
Giant bat creatures!
Airborn by Kenneth Oppel!
BB

THE Unshelved® BOOK CLUB PRESENTS

Inside Job

BY CONNIE WILLIS

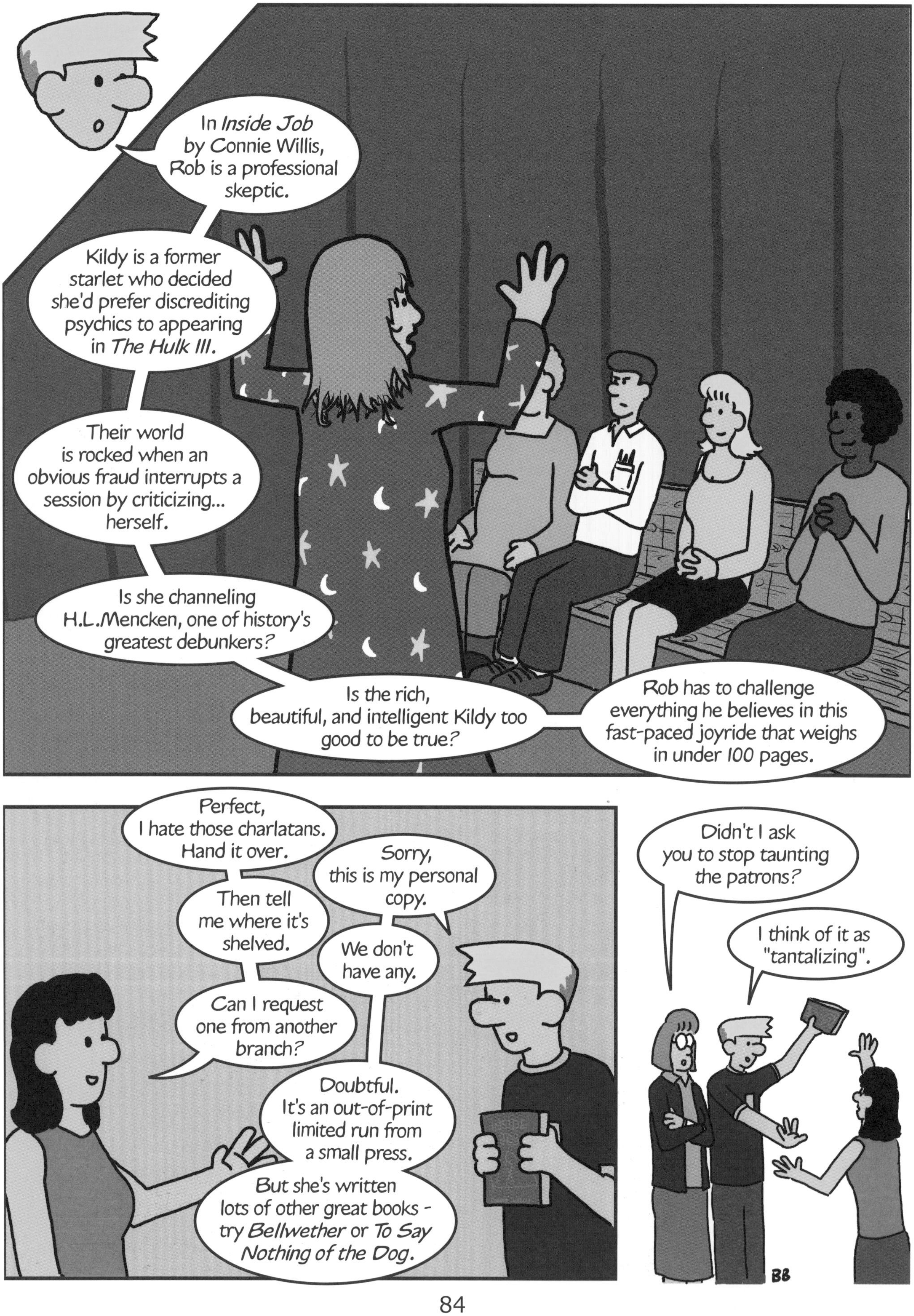

In *Inside Job* by Connie Willis, Rob is a professional skeptic.
Kildy is a former starlet who decided she'd prefer discrediting psychics to appearing in *The Hulk III*.
Their world is rocked when an obvious fraud interrupts a session by criticizing... herself.
Is she channeling H.L.Mencken, one of history's greatest debunkers?
Is the rich, beautiful, and intelligent Kildy too good to be true?
Rob has to challenge everything he believes in this fast-paced joyride that weighs in under 100 pages.
Perfect, I hate those charlatans. Hand it over.
Sorry, this is my personal copy.
Then tell me where it's shelved.
We don't have any.
Can I request one from another branch?
Doubtful. It's an out-of-print limited run from a small press.
But she's written lots of other great books - try *Bellwether* or *To Say Nothing of the Dog*.
Didn't I ask you to stop taunting the patrons?
I think of it as "tantalizing".
BB

THE Unshelved® BOOK CLUB PRESENTS **King of the Mild Frontier**

an ill-advised autobiography by

CHRIS CRUTCHER

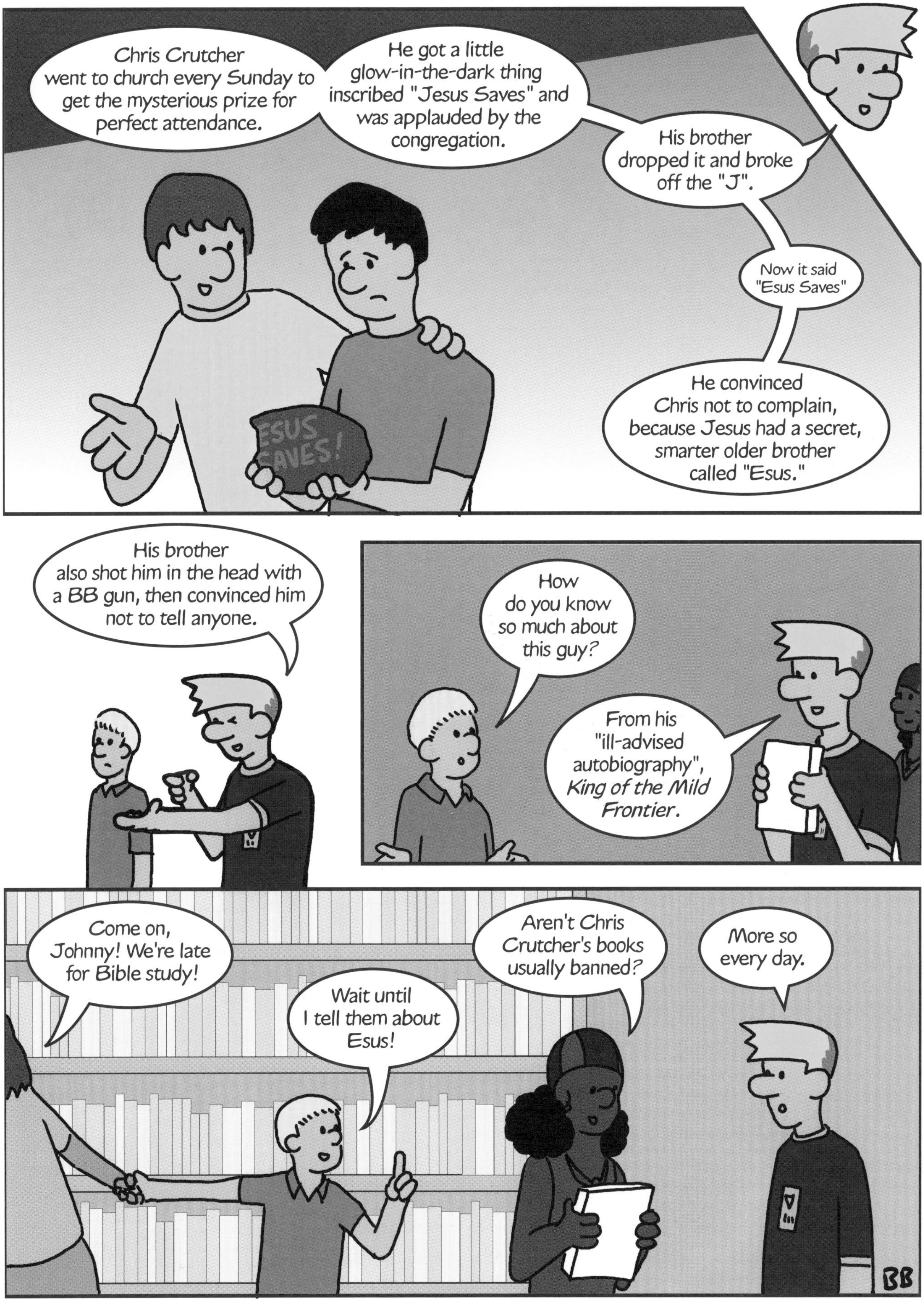

Chris Crutcher went to church every Sunday to get the mysterious prize for perfect attendance.
He got a little glow-in-the-dark thing inscribed "Jesus Saves" and was applauded by the congregation.
His brother dropped it and broke off the "J".
Now it said "Esus Saves"
He convinced Chris not to complain, because Jesus had a secret, smarter older brother called "Esus."
ESUS SAVES!
His brother also shot him in the head with a BB gun, then convinced him not to tell anyone.
How do you know so much about this guy?
From his "ill-advised autobiography", *King of the Mild Frontier*.
Come on, Johnny! We're late for Bible study!
Wait until I tell them about Esus!
Aren't Chris Crutcher's books usually banned?
More so every day.
BB

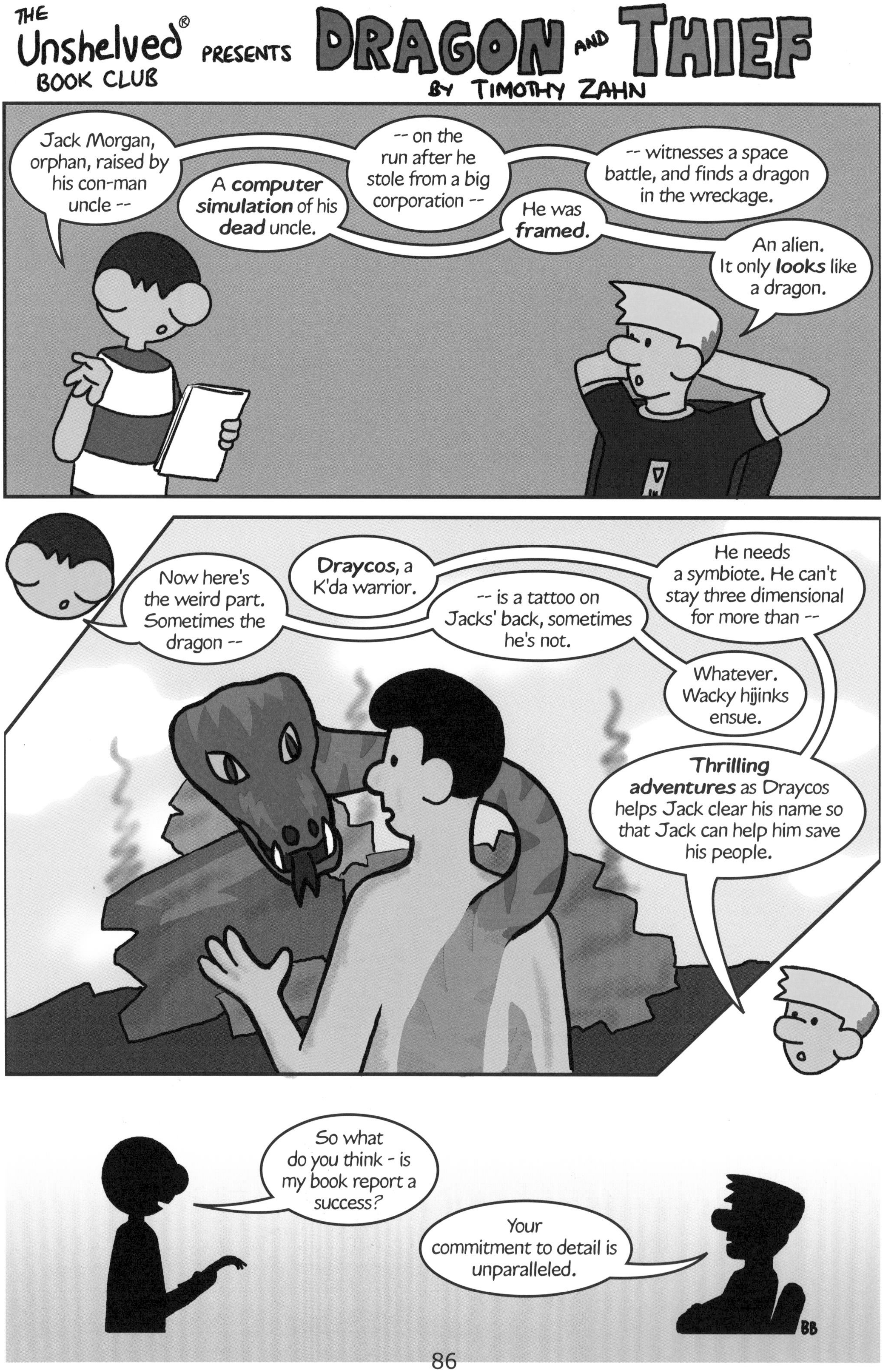
THE Unshelved® BOOK CLUB PRESENTS DRAGON AND THIEF BY TIMOTHY ZAHN
Jack Morgan, orphan, raised by his con-man uncle --
A **computer simulation** of his **dead** uncle.
-- on the run after he stole from a big corporation --
He was **framed.**
-- witnesses a space battle, and finds a dragon in the wreckage.
An alien. It only **looks** like a dragon.
Now here's the weird part. Sometimes the dragon --
Draycos, a K'da warrior.
-- is a tattoo on Jacks' back, sometimes he's not.
He needs a symbiote. He can't stay three dimensional for more than --
Whatever. Wacky hijinks ensue.
Thrilling adventures as Draycos helps Jack clear his name so that Jack can help him save his people.
So what do you think - is my book report a success?
Your commitment to detail is unparalleled.
BB

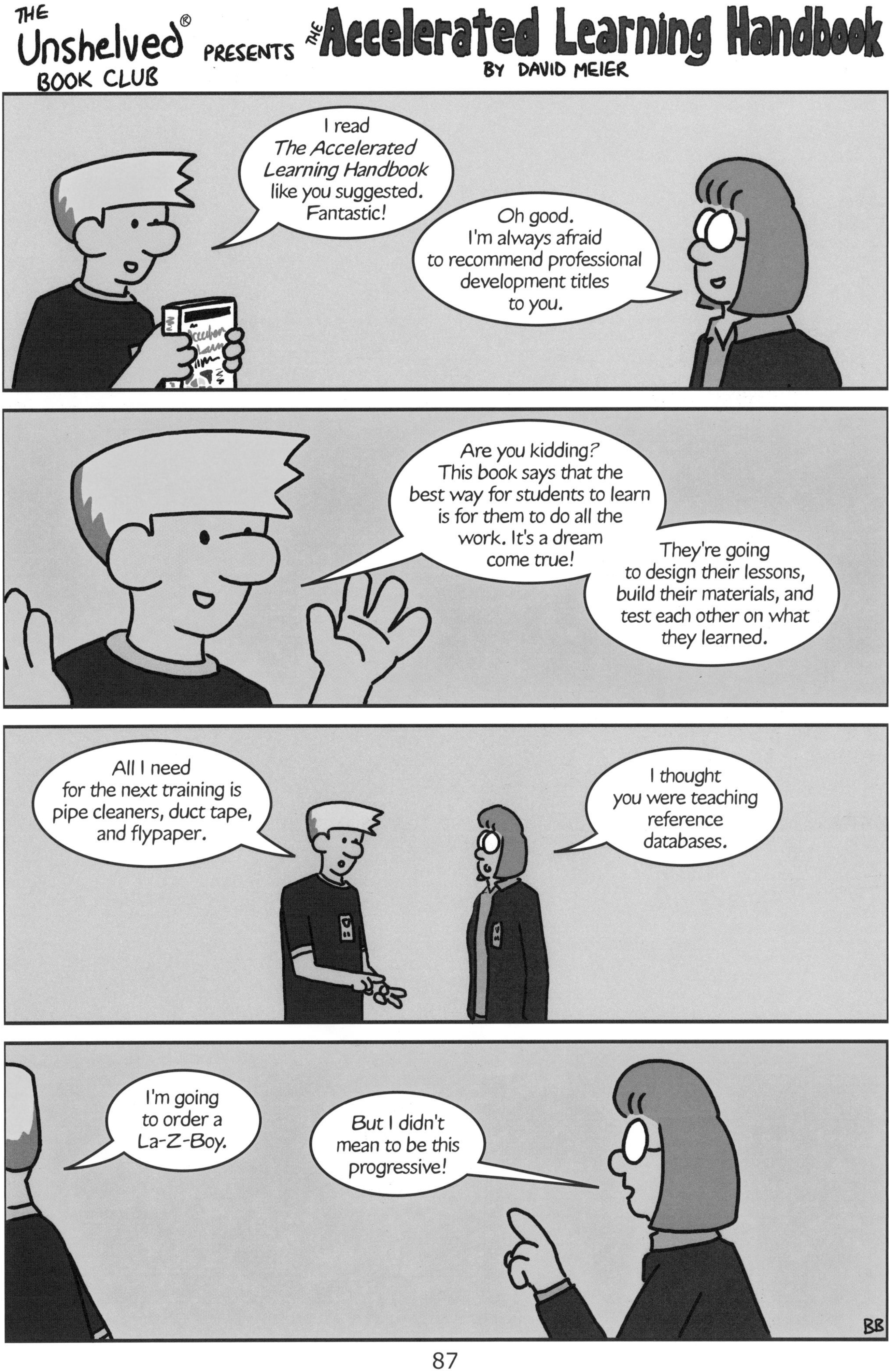
THE Unshelved® BOOK CLUB
PRESENTS
THE Accelerated Learning Handbook
BY DAVID MEIER
I read *The Accelerated Learning Handbook* like you suggested. Fantastic!
Oh good. I'm always afraid to recommend professional development titles to you.
Are you kidding? This book says that the best way for students to learn is for them to do all the work. It's a dream come true!
They're going to design their lessons, build their materials, and test each other on what they learned.
All I need for the next training is pipe cleaners, duct tape, and flypaper.
I thought you were teaching reference databases.
I'm going to order a La-Z-Boy.
But I didn't mean to be this progressive!
BB

THE Unshelved® BOOK CLUB PRESENTS

ONE DAY IN THE LIFE OF IVAN DENISOVICH

BY ALEXANDER SOLZHENITSYN

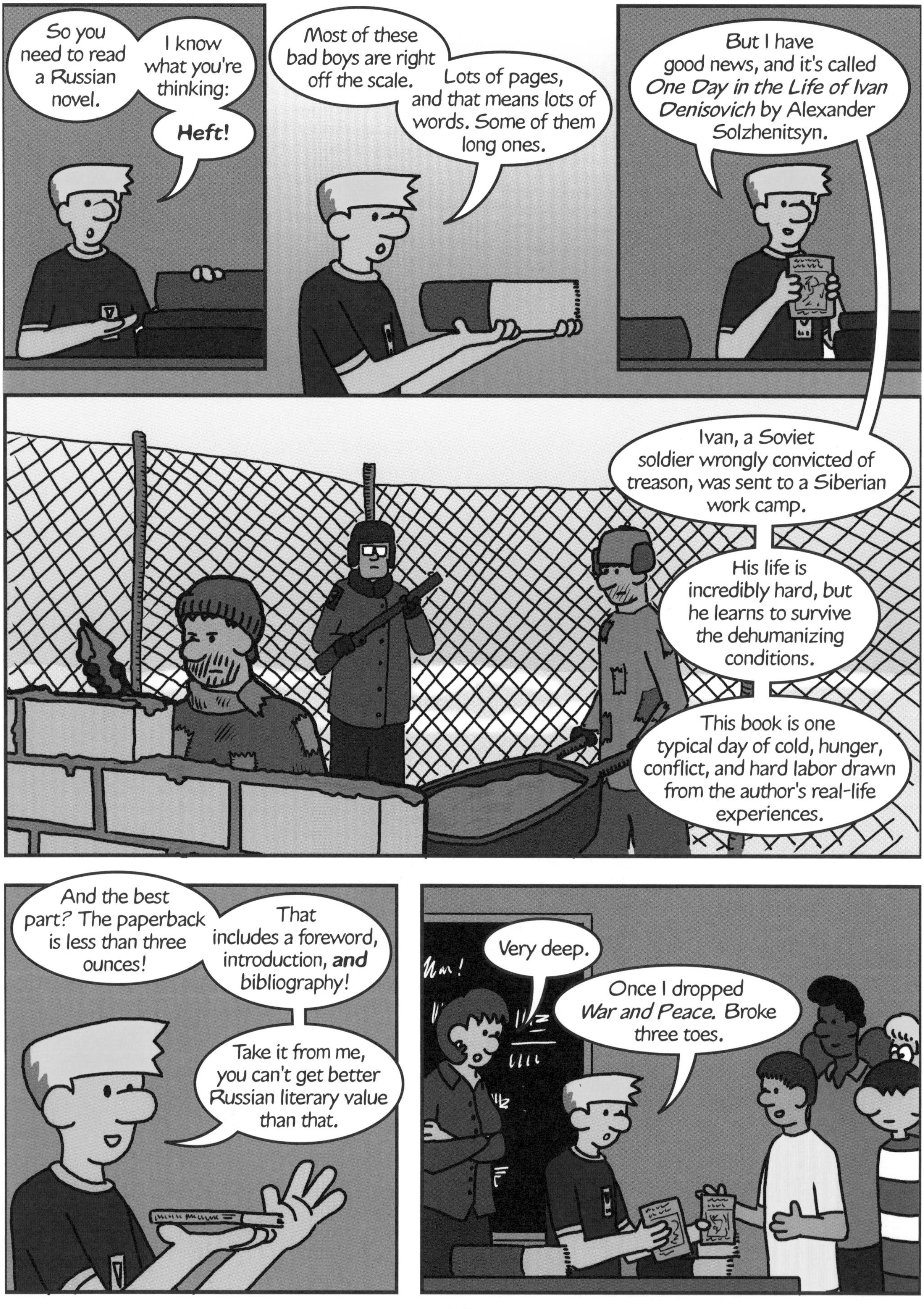

So you need to read a Russian novel.
I know what you're thinking:
Heft!
Most of these bad boys are right off the scale.
Lots of pages, and that means lots of words. Some of them long ones.
But I have good news, and it's called *One Day in the Life of Ivan Denisovich* by Alexander Solzhenitsyn.
Ivan, a Soviet soldier wrongly convicted of treason, was sent to a Siberian work camp.
His life is incredibly hard, but he learns to survive the dehumanizing conditions.
This book is one typical day of cold, hunger, conflict, and hard labor drawn from the author's real-life experiences.
And the best part? The paperback is less than three ounces!
That includes a foreword, introduction, **and** bibliography!
Take it from me, you can't get better Russian literary value than that.
Very deep.
Once I dropped *War and Peace.* Broke three toes.

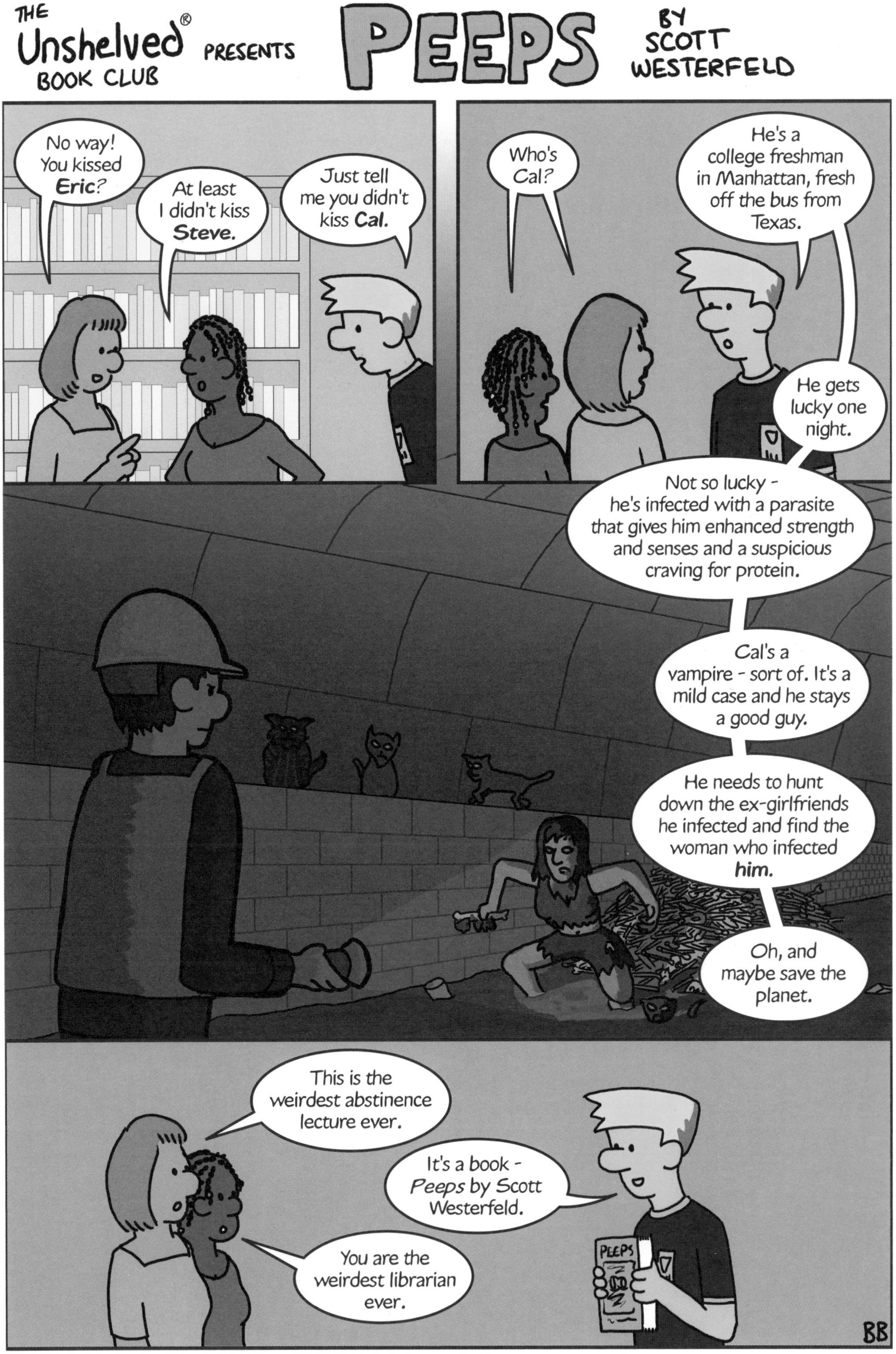
THE Unshelved® BOOK CLUB PRESENTS
PEEPS
BY SCOTT WESTERFELD
No way! You kissed **Eric**?
At least I didn't kiss **Steve.**
Just tell me you didn't kiss **Cal.**
Who's Cal?
He's a college freshman in Manhattan, fresh off the bus from Texas.
He gets lucky one night.
Not so lucky - he's infected with a parasite that gives him enhanced strength and senses and a suspicious craving for protein.
Cal's a vampire - sort of. It's a mild case and he stays a good guy.
He needs to hunt down the ex-girlfriends he infected and find the woman who infected **him.**
Oh, and maybe save the planet.
This is the weirdest abstinence lecture ever.
It's a book - *Peeps* by Scott Westerfeld.
You are the weirdest librarian ever.
PEEPS
BB

THE Unshelved® BOOK CLUB PRESENTS

STARTIDE RISING

BY DAVID BRIN

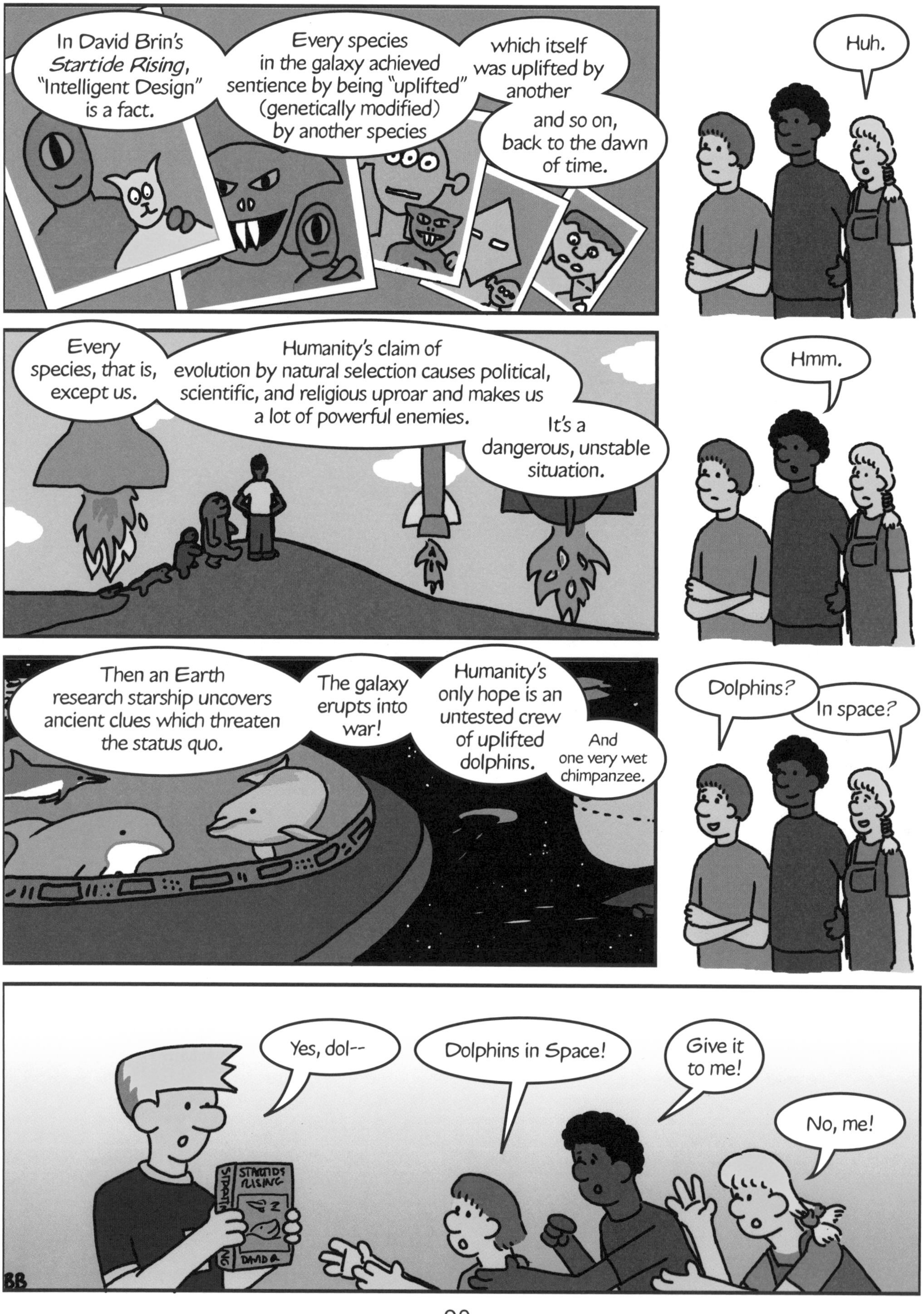

In David Brin's *Startide Rising*, "Intelligent Design" is a fact.
Every species in the galaxy achieved sentience by being "uplifted" (genetically modified) by another species
which itself was uplifted by another
and so on, back to the dawn of time.
Huh.
Every species, that is, except us.
Humanity's claim of evolution by natural selection causes political, scientific, and religious uproar and makes us a lot of powerful enemies.
It's a dangerous, unstable situation.
Hmm.
Then an Earth research starship uncovers ancient clues which threaten the status quo.
The galaxy erupts into war!
Humanity's only hope is an untested crew of uplifted dolphins.
And one very wet chimpanzee.
Dolphins?
In space?
Yes, dol--
Dolphins in Space!
Give it to me!
No, me!

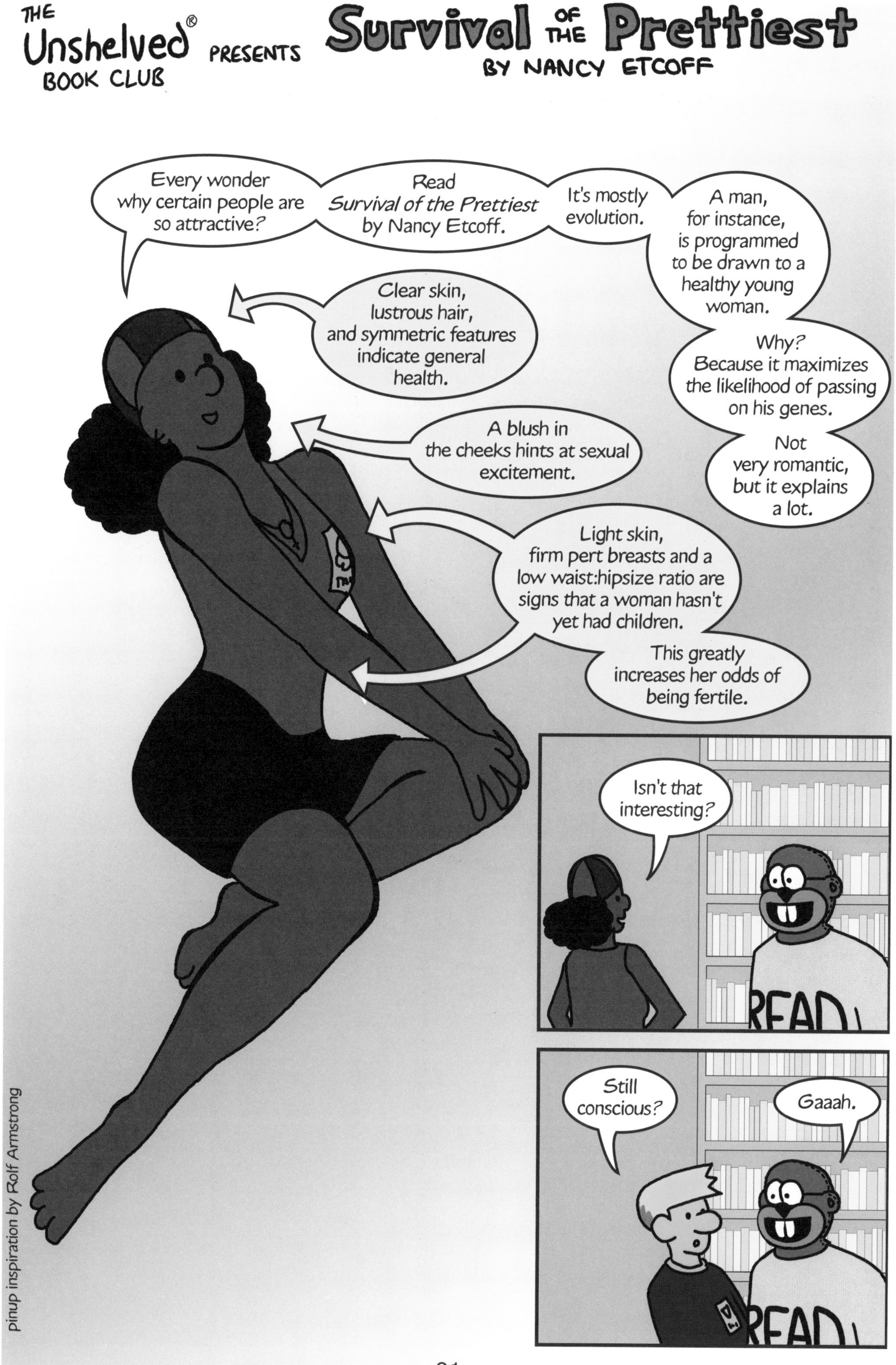
THE Unshelved® BOOK CLUB PRESENTS
Survival OF THE Prettiest
BY NANCY ETCOFF
Every wonder why certain people are so attractive?
Read *Survival of the Prettiest* by Nancy Etcoff.
It's mostly evolution.
A man, for instance, is programmed to be drawn to a healthy young woman.
Why? Because it maximizes the likelihood of passing on his genes.
Not very romantic, but it explains a lot.
Clear skin, lustrous hair, and symmetric features indicate general health.
A blush in the cheeks hints at sexual excitement.
Light skin, firm pert breasts and a low waist:hipsize ratio are signs that a woman hasn't yet had children.
This greatly increases her odds of being fertile.
Isn't that interesting?
Still conscious?
Gaaah.
pinup inspiration by Rolf Armstrong

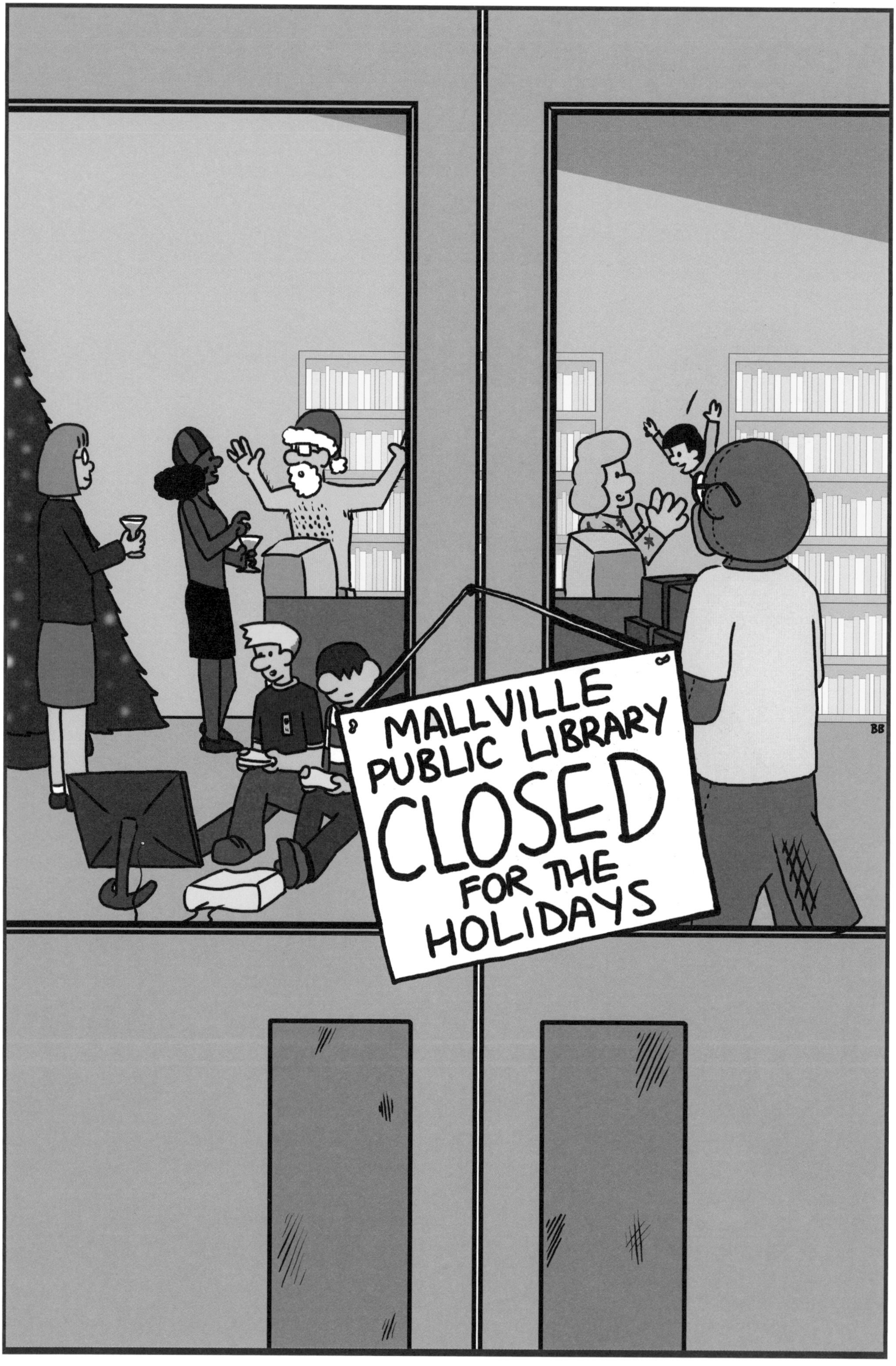
MALLVILLE
PUBLIC LIBRARY
CLOSED
FOR THE
HOLIDAYS
BB

BIZMAR Unshelved™

by Bill Barnes and Gene Ambaum

The first time we exhibited at San Diego's storied Comic Con we had the honor of sharing the Small Press area with Tod Parkhill of Young American Comics. Tod is the mad genius behind the BIZMAR Experiment. Its unholy challenge: to create a comic featuring a **B**unny, an **I**nsect, a **Z**ombie, a **M**onkey, an **A**lien, and a **R**obot. That we'd eventually create an *Unshelved* BIZMAR was destiny. Thanks to Barb "Foo Foo" Treen and the Foofettes for the idea.

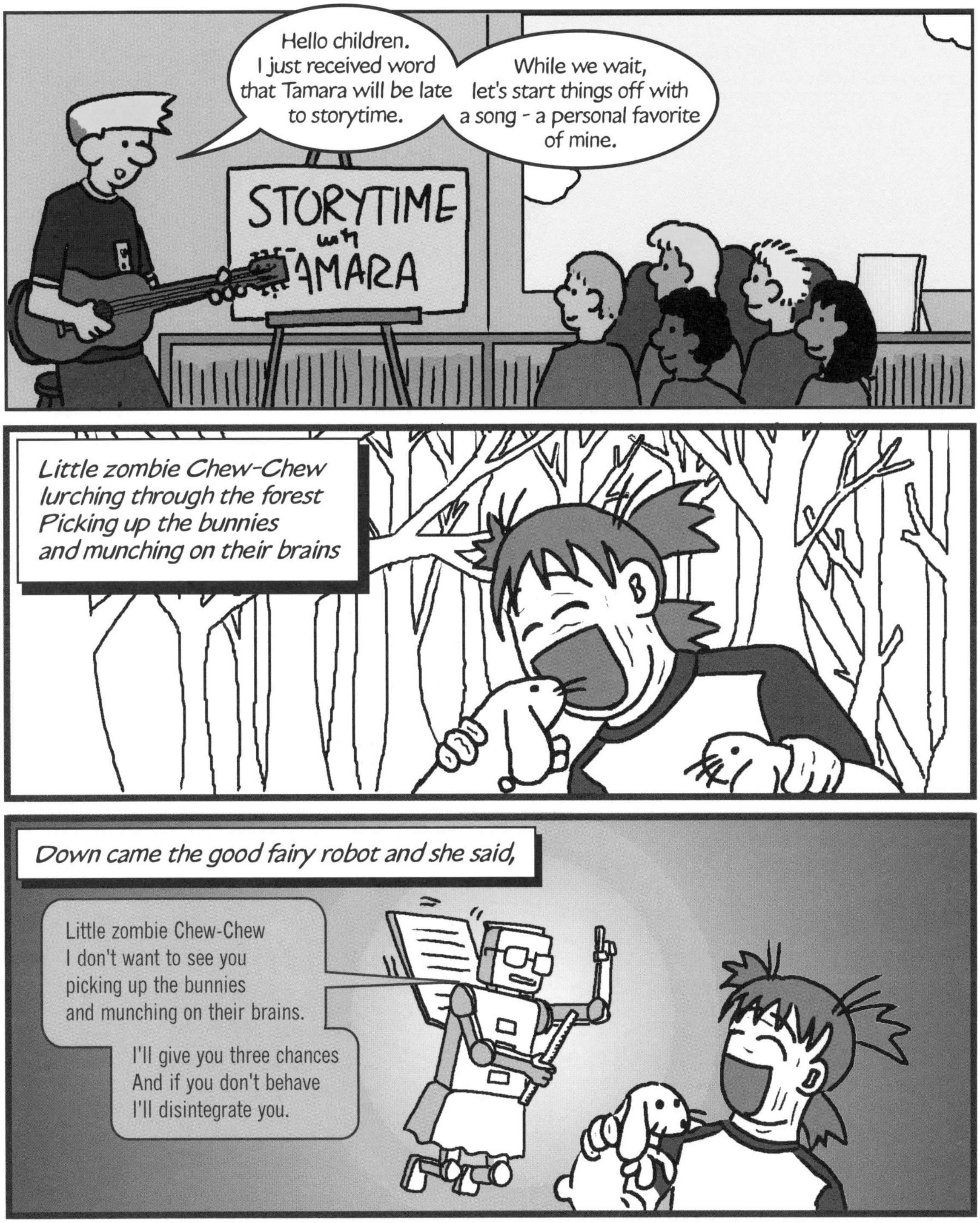

Hello children. I just received word that Tamara will be late to storytime.
While we wait, let's start things off with a song - a personal favorite of mine.
STORYTIME with TAMARA
Little zombie Chew-Chew lurching through the forest Picking up the bunnies and munching on their brains
Down came the good fairy robot and she said,
Little zombie Chew-Chew I don't want to see you picking up the bunnies and munching on their brains.
I'll give you three chances And if you don't behave I'll disintegrate you.

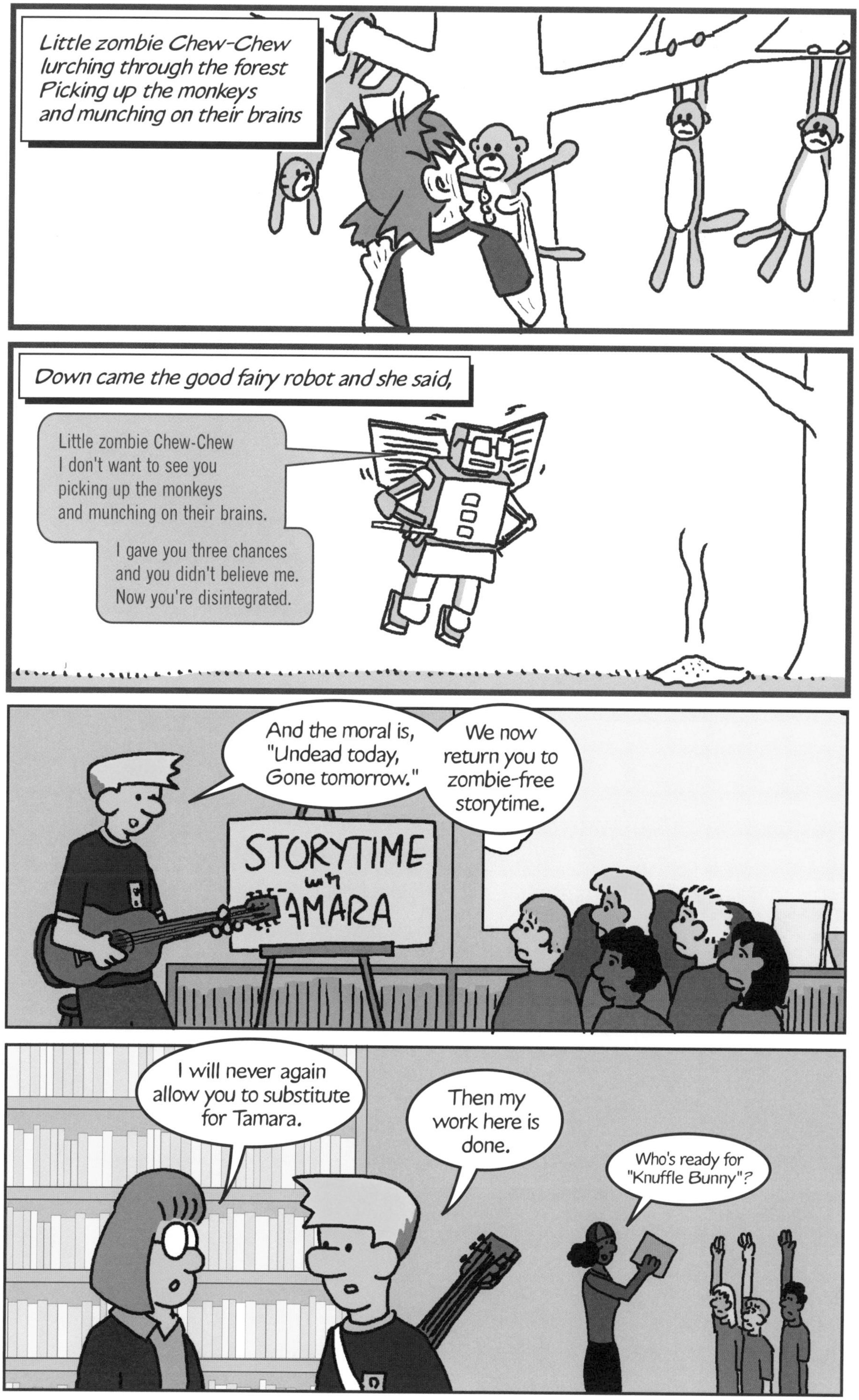
Little zombie Chew-Chew
lurching through the forest
Picking up the monkeys
and munching on their brains
Down came the good fairy robot and she said,
Little zombie Chew-Chew
I don't want to see you
picking up the monkeys
and munching on their brains.
I gave you three chances
and you didn't believe me.
Now you're disintegrated.
And the moral is, "Undead today, Gone tomorrow."
We now return you to zombie-free storytime.
STORYTIME with TAMARA
I will never again allow you to substitute for Tamara.
Then my work here is done.
Who's ready for "Knuffle Bunny"?

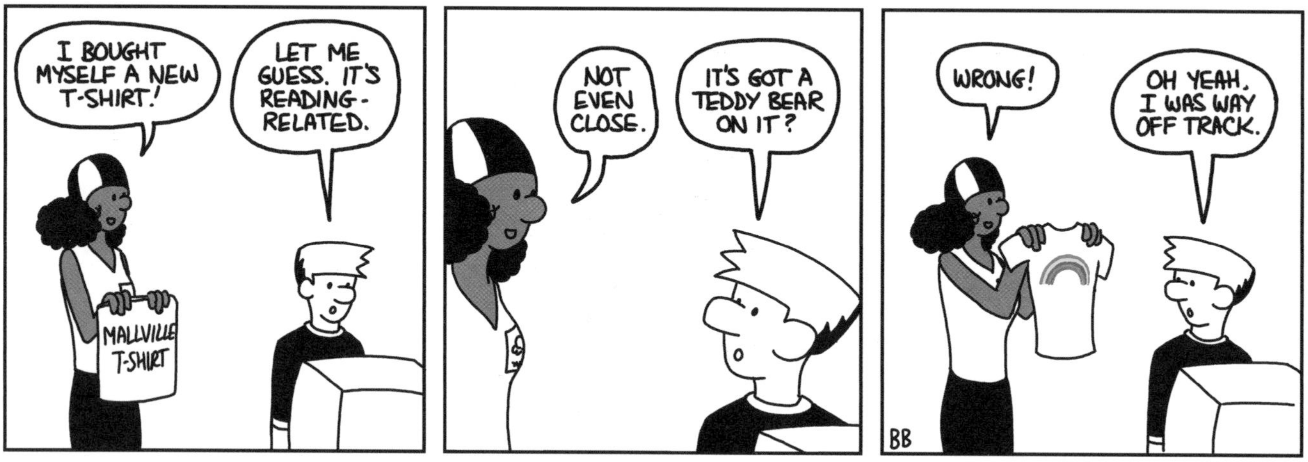
I BOUGHT MYSELF A NEW T-SHIRT!
LET ME GUESS. IT'S READING-RELATED.
MALLVILLE T-SHIRT
NOT EVEN CLOSE.
IT'S GOT A TEDDY BEAR ON IT?
WRONG!
OH YEAH. I WAS WAY OFF TRACK.
BB

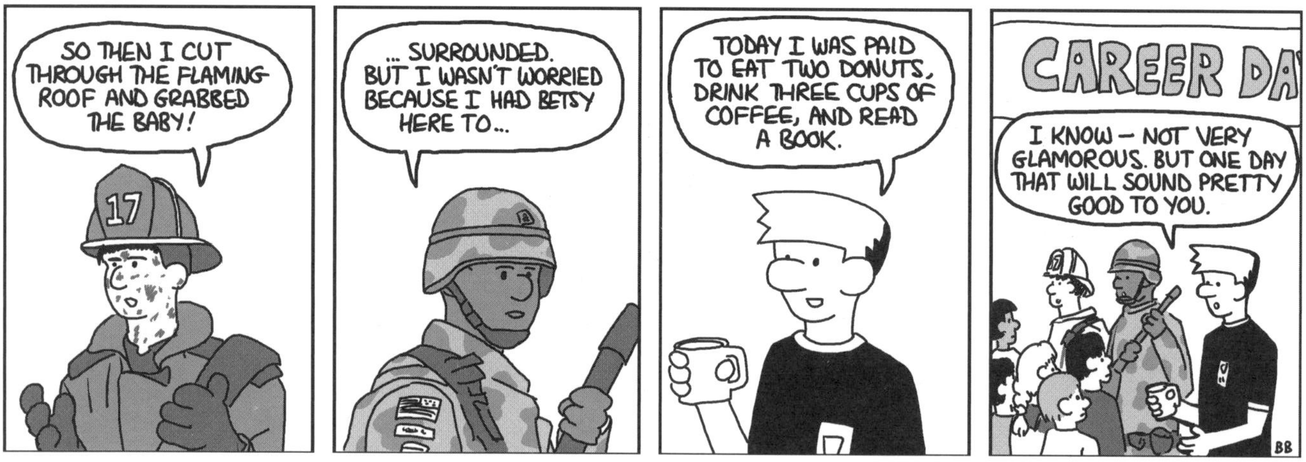
SO THEN I CUT THROUGH THE FLAMING ROOF AND GRABBED THE BABY!
17
... SURROUNDED. BUT I WASN'T WORRIED BECAUSE I HAD BETSY HERE TO...
TODAY I WAS PAID TO EAT TWO DONUTS, DRINK THREE CUPS OF COFFEE, AND READ A BOOK.
CAREER DA
I KNOW – NOT VERY GLAMOROUS. BUT ONE DAY THAT WILL SOUND PRETTY GOOD TO YOU.
BB

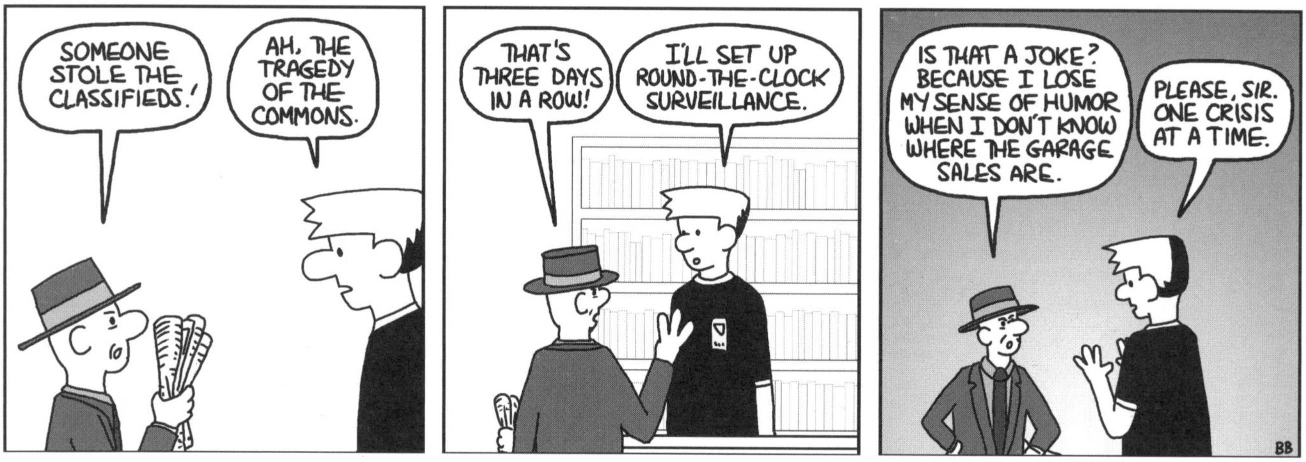
SOMEONE STOLE THE CLASSIFIEDS!
AH, THE TRAGEDY OF THE COMMONS.
THAT'S THREE DAYS IN A ROW!
I'LL SET UP ROUND-THE-CLOCK SURVEILLANCE.
IS THAT A JOKE? BECAUSE I LOSE MY SENSE OF HUMOR WHEN I DON'T KNOW WHERE THE GARAGE SALES ARE.
PLEASE, SIR. ONE CRISIS AT A TIME.
BB

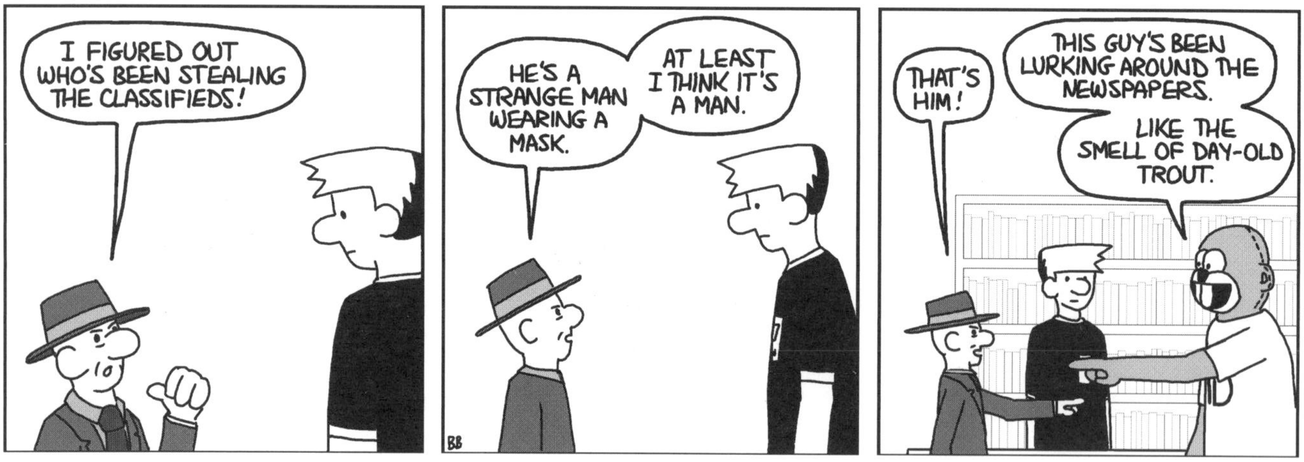
I FIGURED OUT WHO'S BEEN STEALING THE CLASSIFIEDS!
HE'S A STRANGE MAN WEARING A MASK.
AT LEAST I THINK IT'S A MAN.
BB
THAT'S HIM!
THIS GUY'S BEEN LURKING AROUND THE NEWSPAPERS.
LIKE THE SMELL OF DAY-OLD TROUT.

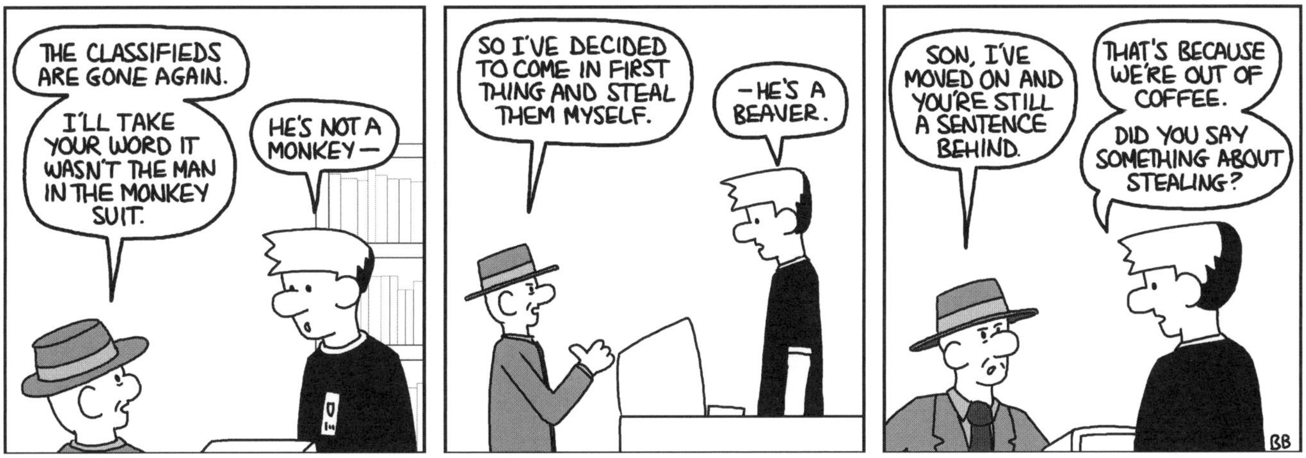
THE CLASSIFIEDS ARE GONE AGAIN.
I'LL TAKE YOUR WORD IT WASN'T THE MAN IN THE MONKEY SUIT.
HE'S NOT A MONKEY—
SO I'VE DECIDED TO COME IN FIRST THING AND STEAL THEM MYSELF.
—HE'S A BEAVER.
SON, I'VE MOVED ON AND YOU'RE STILL A SENTENCE BEHIND.
THAT'S BECAUSE WE'RE OUT OF COFFEE.
DID YOU SAY SOMETHING ABOUT STEALING?
BB

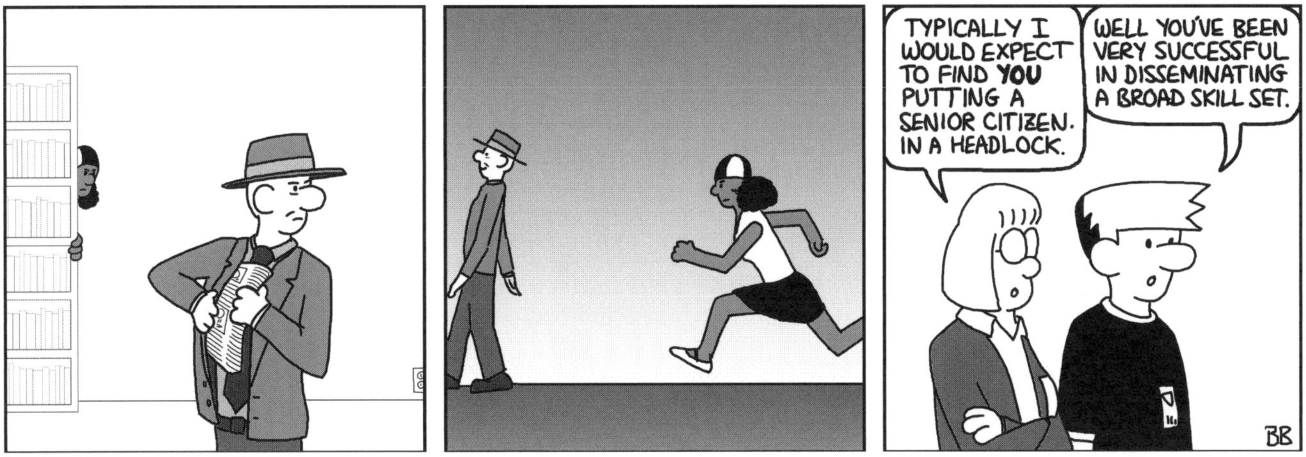
TYPICALLY I WOULD EXPECT TO FIND **YOU** PUTTING A SENIOR CITIZEN IN A HEADLOCK.
WELL YOU'VE BEEN VERY SUCCESSFUL IN DISSEMINATING A BROAD SKILL SET.
BB

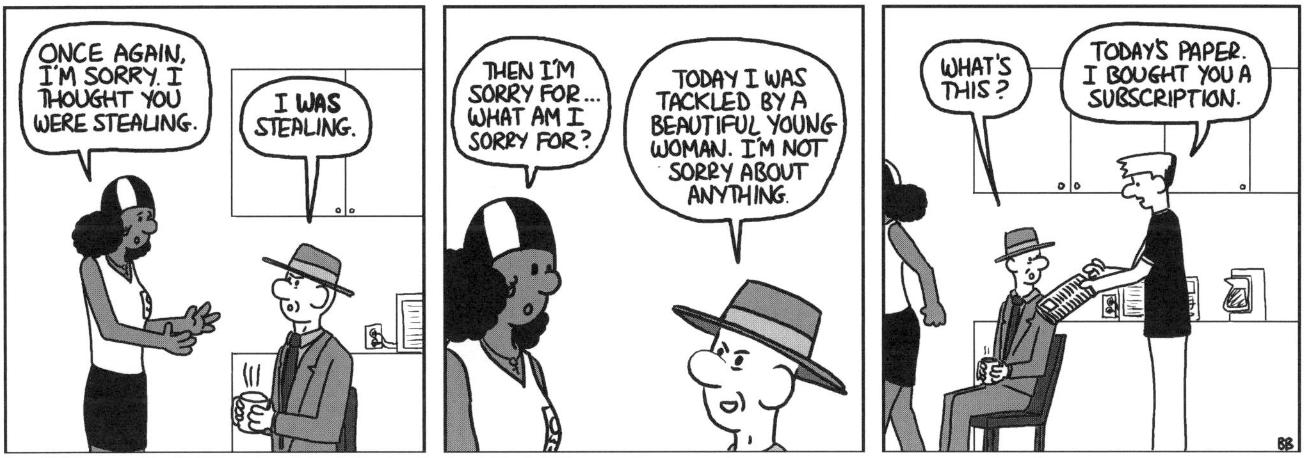
ONCE AGAIN, I'M SORRY. I THOUGHT YOU WERE STEALING.
I **WAS** STEALING.
THEN I'M SORRY FOR... WHAT AM I SORRY FOR?
TODAY I WAS TACKLED BY A BEAUTIFUL YOUNG WOMAN. I'M NOT SORRY ABOUT ANYTHING.
WHAT'S THIS?
TODAY'S PAPER. I BOUGHT YOU A SUBSCRIPTION.
BB

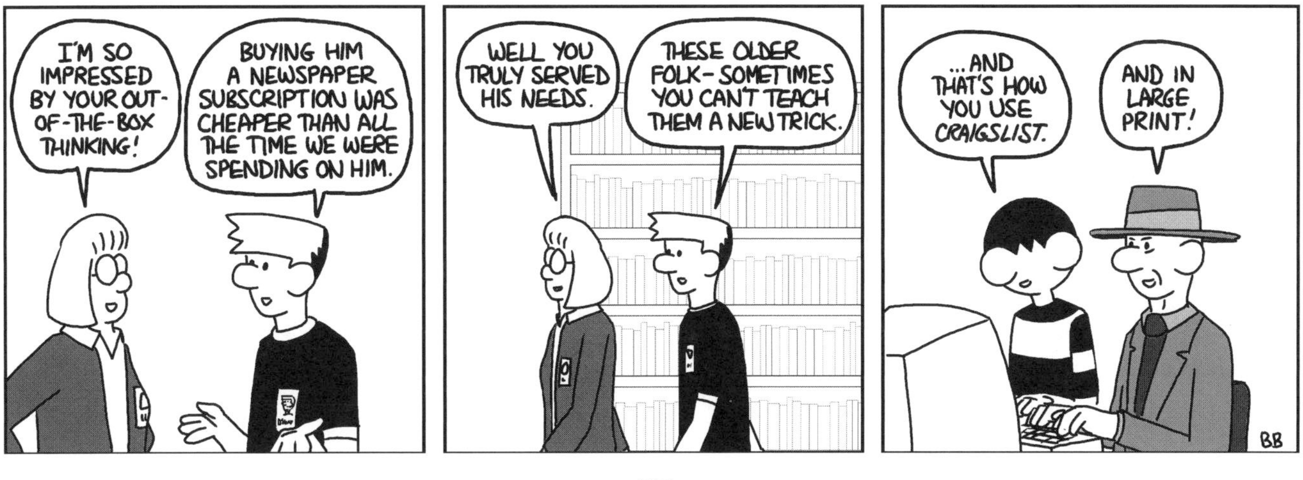
I'M SO IMPRESSED BY YOUR OUT-OF-THE-BOX THINKING!
BUYING HIM A NEWSPAPER SUBSCRIPTION WAS CHEAPER THAN ALL THE TIME WE WERE SPENDING ON HIM.
WELL YOU TRULY SERVED HIS NEEDS.
THESE OLDER FOLK—SOMETIMES YOU CAN'T TEACH THEM A NEW TRICK.
...AND THAT'S HOW YOU USE *CRAIGSLIST*.
AND IN LARGE PRINT!
BB

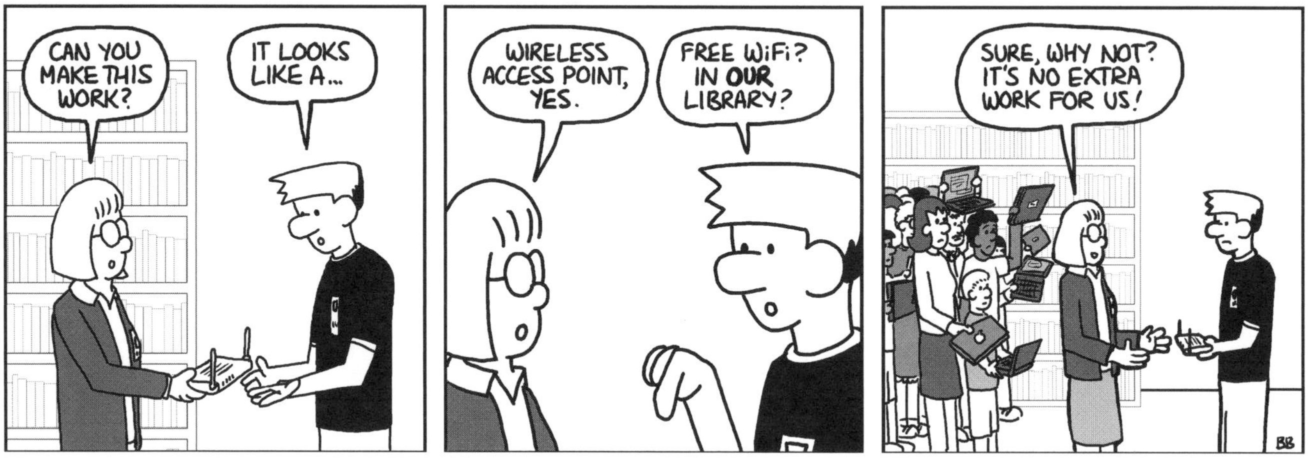
CAN YOU MAKE THIS WORK?
IT LOOKS LIKE A...
WIRELESS ACCESS POINT, YES.
FREE WiFi? IN **OUR** LIBRARY?
SURE, WHY NOT? IT'S NO EXTRA WORK FOR US!
BB

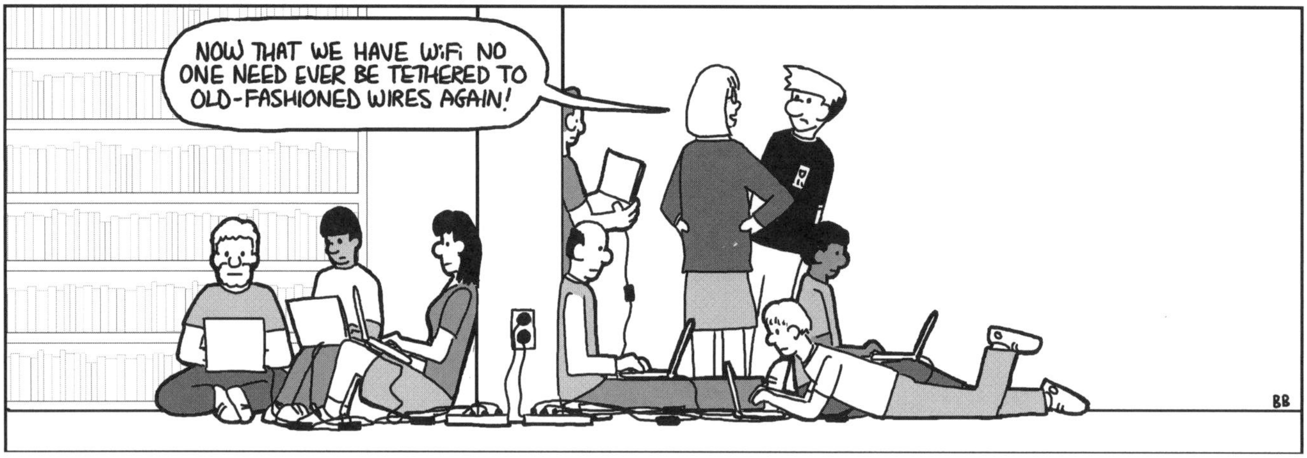
NOW THAT WE HAVE WiFi NO ONE NEED EVER BE TETHERED TO OLD-FASHIONED WIRES AGAIN!
BB

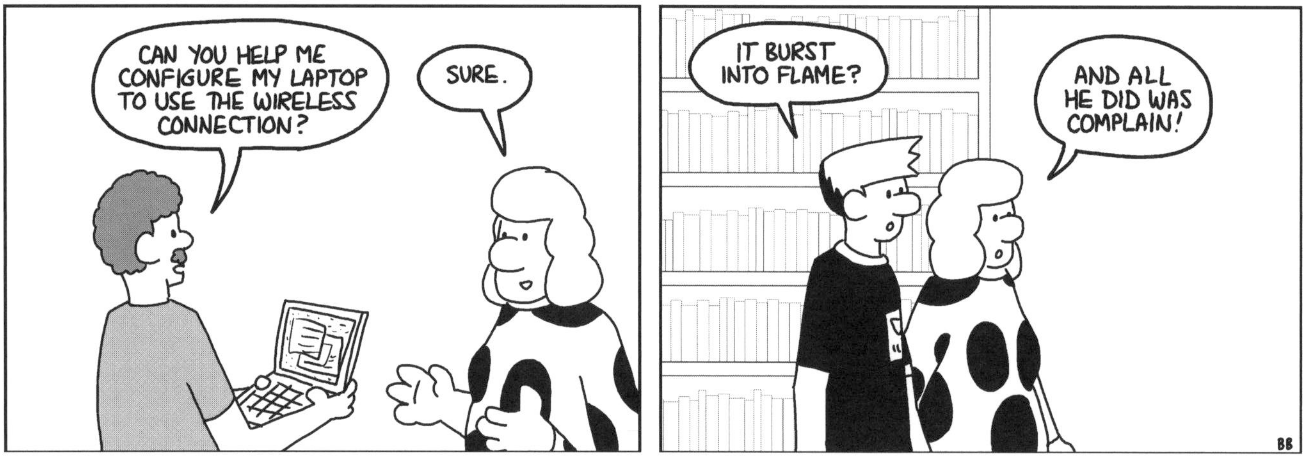
CAN YOU HELP ME CONFIGURE MY LAPTOP TO USE THE WIRELESS CONNECTION?
SURE.
IT BURST INTO FLAME?
AND ALL HE DID WAS COMPLAIN!
BB

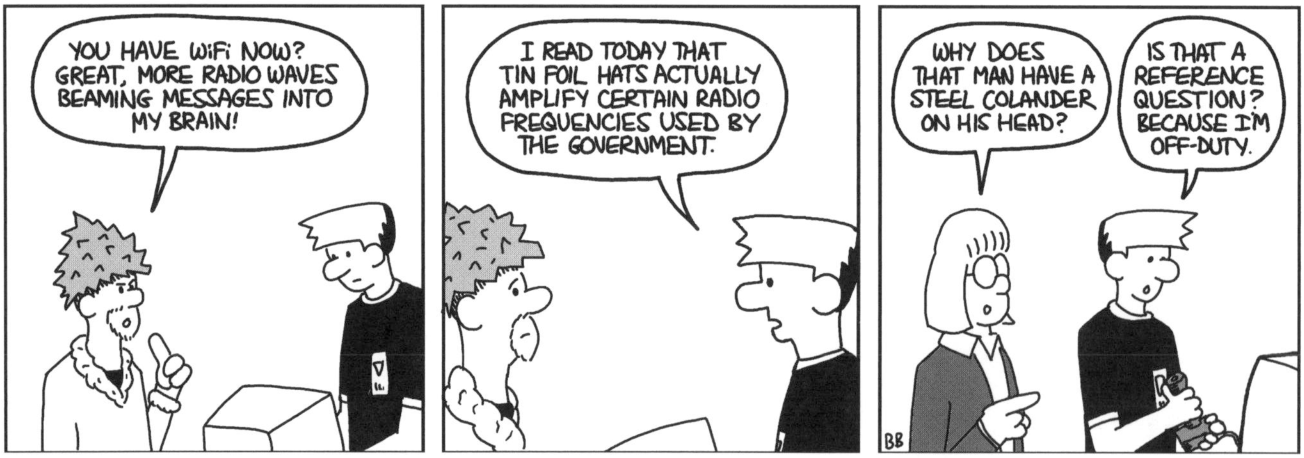
YOU HAVE WiFi NOW? GREAT, MORE RADIO WAVES BEAMING MESSAGES INTO MY BRAIN!
I READ TODAY THAT TIN FOIL HATS ACTUALLY AMPLIFY CERTAIN RADIO FREQUENCIES USED BY THE GOVERNMENT.
WHY DOES THAT MAN HAVE A STEEL COLANDER ON HIS HEAD?
IS THAT A REFERENCE QUESTION? BECAUSE I'M OFF-DUTY.
BB

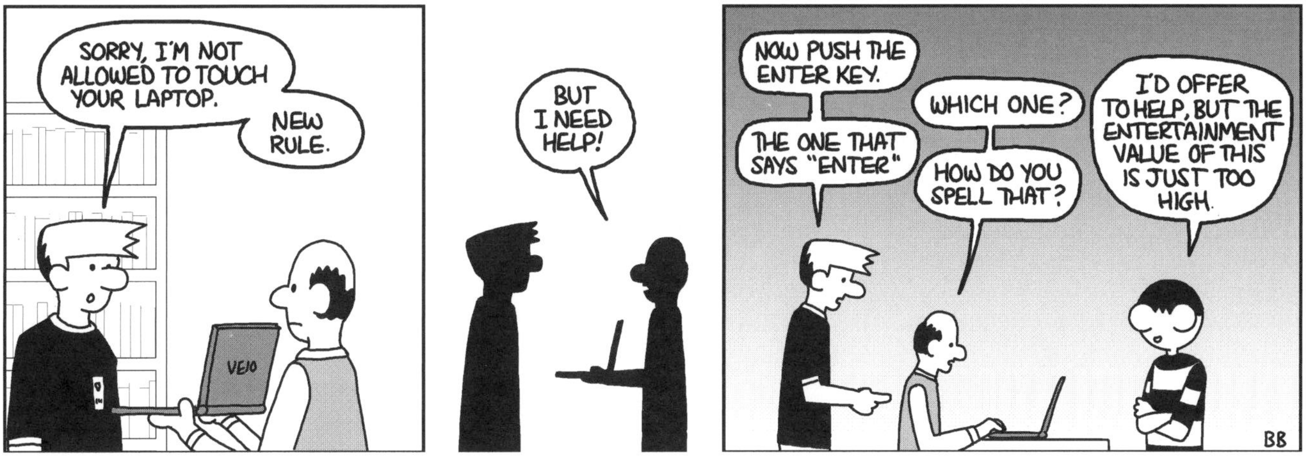
SORRY, I'M NOT ALLOWED TO TOUCH YOUR LAPTOP.
NEW RULE.
VEJO
BUT I NEED HELP!
NOW PUSH THE ENTER KEY.
WHICH ONE?
THE ONE THAT SAYS "ENTER"
HOW DO YOU SPELL THAT?
I'D OFFER TO HELP, BUT THE ENTERTAINMENT VALUE OF THIS IS JUST TOO HIGH.
BB

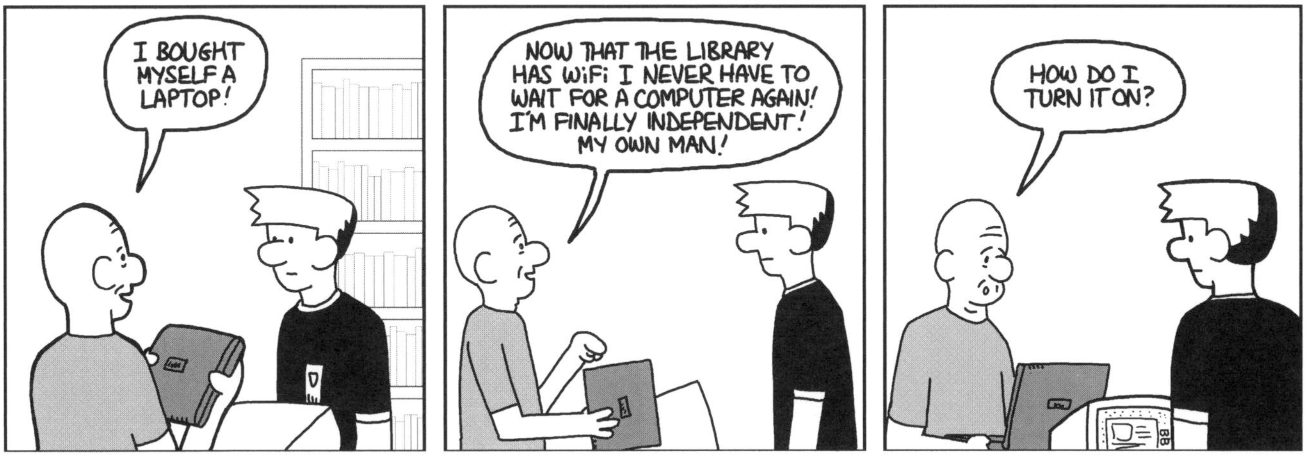
I BOUGHT MYSELF A LAPTOP!
NOW THAT THE LIBRARY HAS WiFi I NEVER HAVE TO WAIT FOR A COMPUTER AGAIN! I'M FINALLY INDEPENDENT! MY OWN MAN!
HOW DO I TURN IT ON?
BB

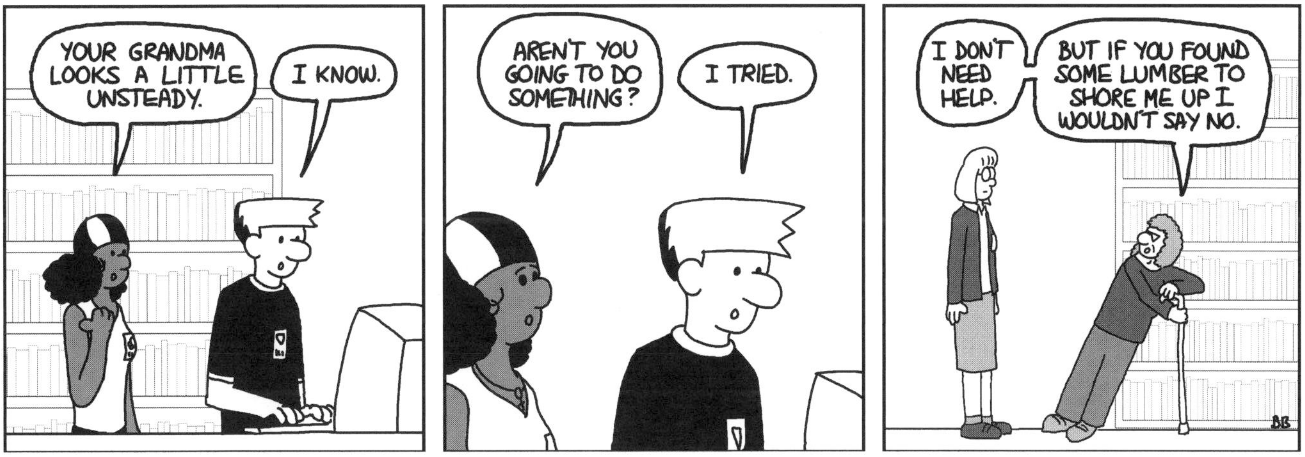
YOUR GRANDMA LOOKS A LITTLE UNSTEADY.
I KNOW.
AREN'T YOU GOING TO DO SOMETHING?
I TRIED.
I DON'T NEED HELP.
BUT IF YOU FOUND SOME LUMBER TO SHORE ME UP I WOULDN'T SAY NO.
BB

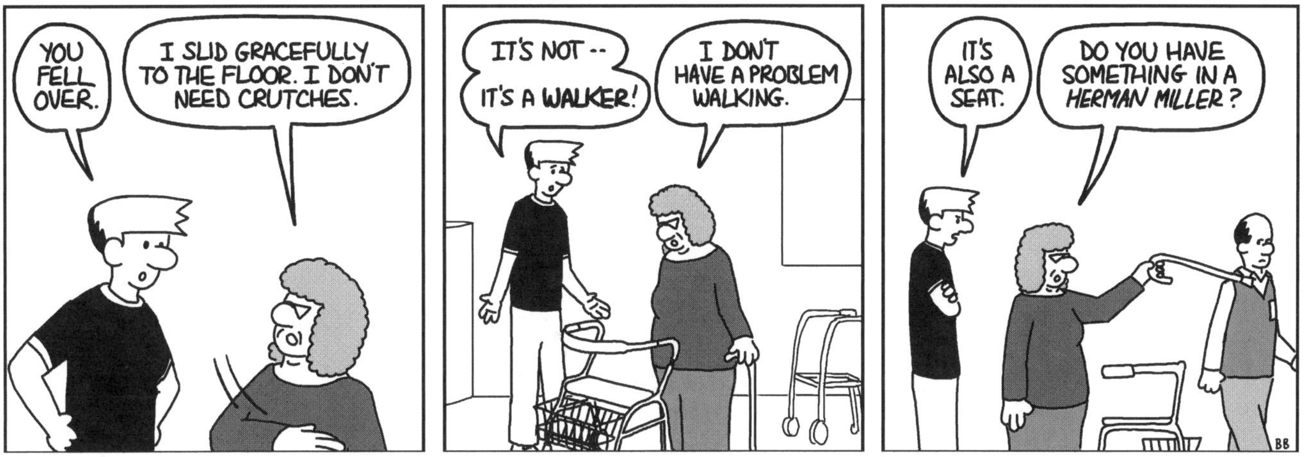
YOU FELL OVER.
I SLID GRACEFULLY TO THE FLOOR. I DON'T NEED CRUTCHES.
IT'S NOT --
IT'S A WALKER!
I DON'T HAVE A PROBLEM WALKING.
IT'S ALSO A SEAT.
DO YOU HAVE SOMETHING IN A HERMAN MILLER?
BB

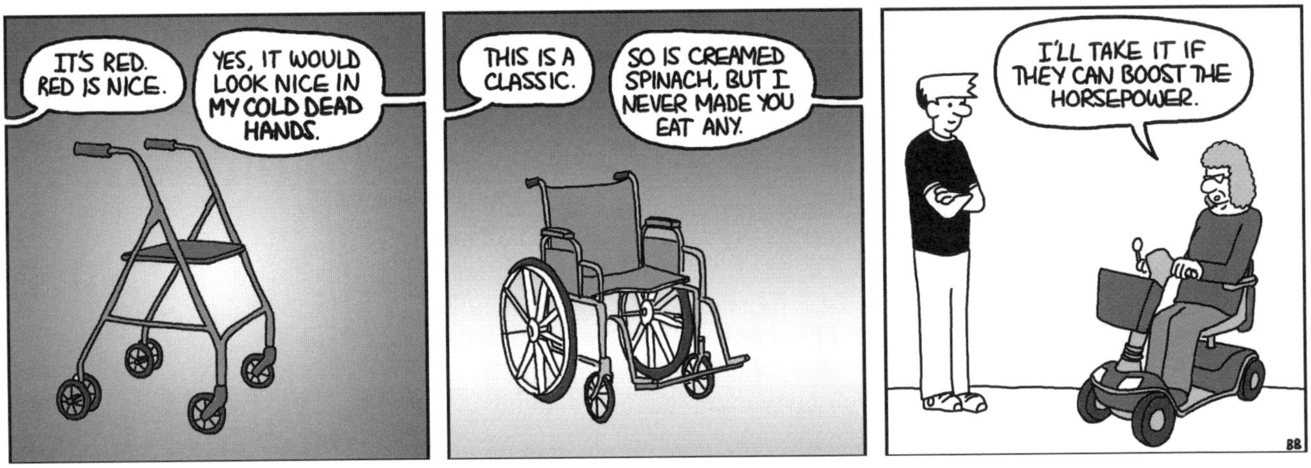
IT'S RED. RED IS NICE.
YES, IT WOULD LOOK NICE IN MY COLD DEAD HANDS.
THIS IS A CLASSIC.
SO IS CREAMED SPINACH, BUT I NEVER MADE YOU EAT ANY.
I'LL TAKE IT IF THEY CAN BOOST THE HORSEPOWER.
BB

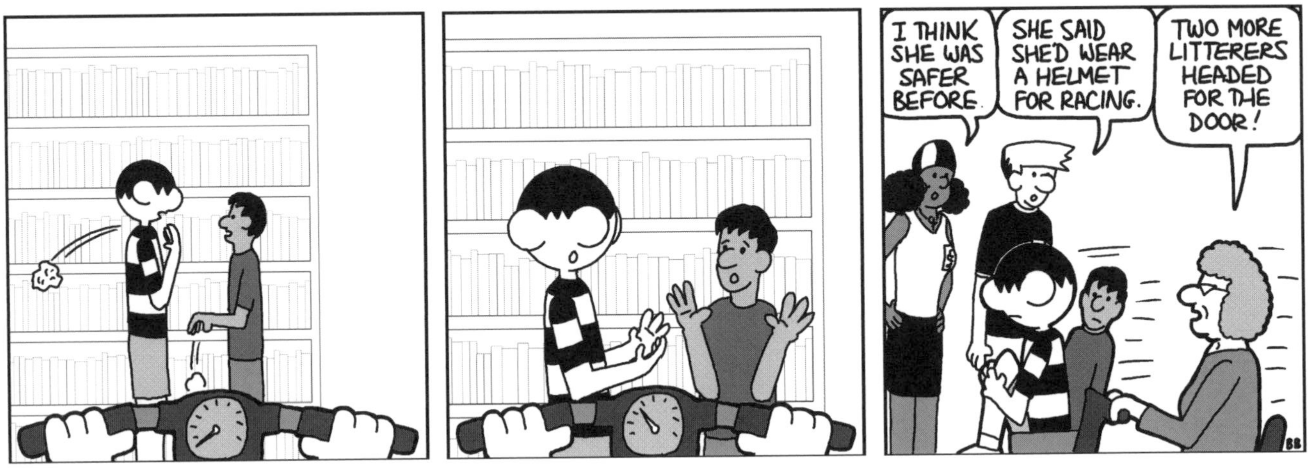
I THINK SHE WAS SAFER BEFORE.
SHE SAID SHE'D WEAR A HELMET FOR RACING.
TWO MORE LITTERERS HEADED FOR THE DOOR!
BB

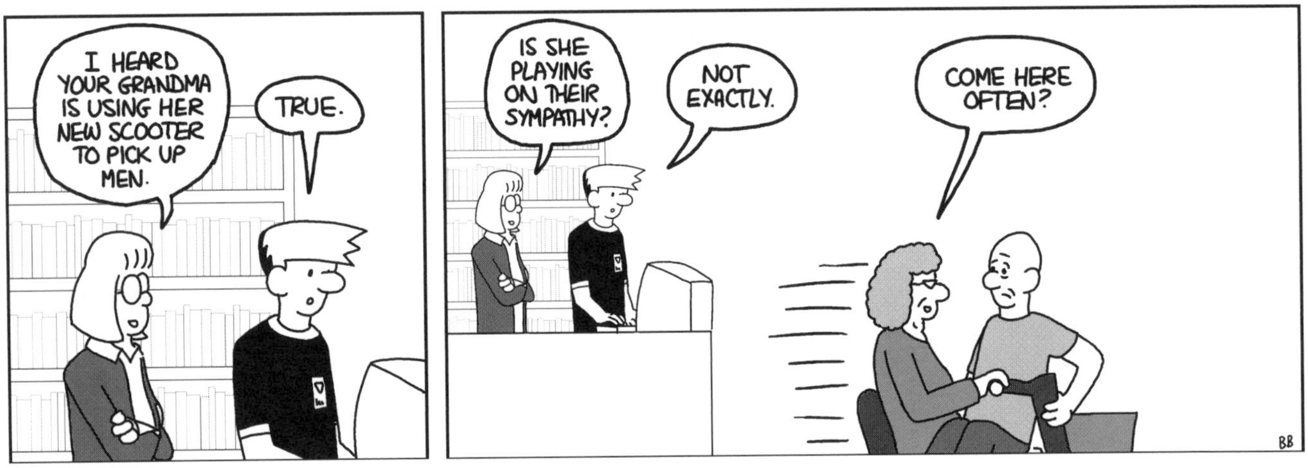
I HEARD YOUR GRANDMA IS USING HER NEW SCOOTER TO PICK UP MEN.
TRUE.
IS SHE PLAYING ON THEIR SYMPATHY?
NOT EXACTLY.
COME HERE OFTEN?
BB

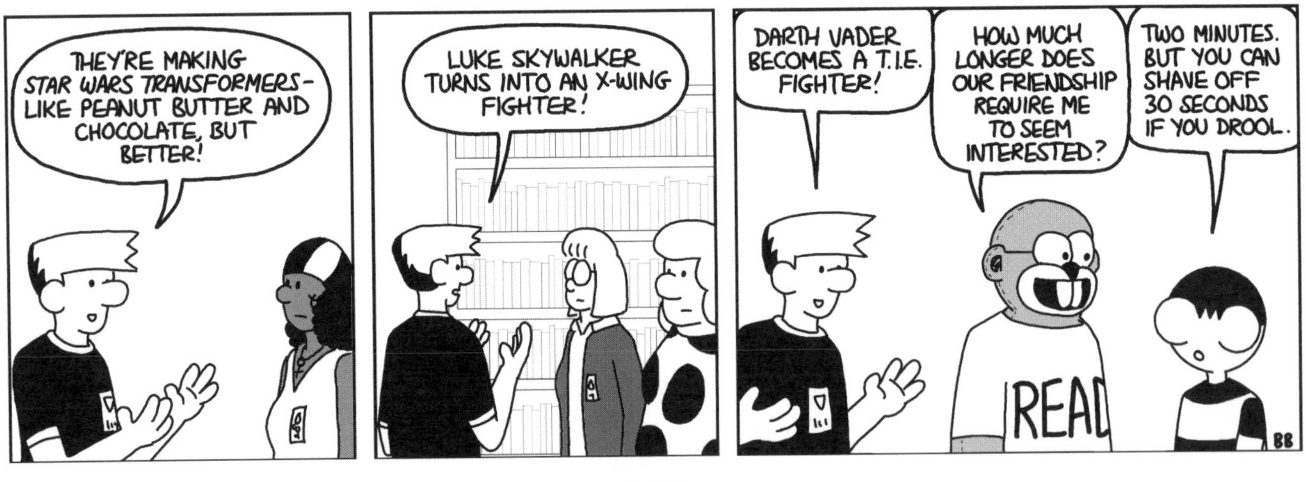
THEY'RE MAKING *STAR WARS TRANSFORMERS*- LIKE PEANUT BUTTER AND CHOCOLATE, BUT BETTER!
LUKE SKYWALKER TURNS INTO AN X-WING FIGHTER!
DARTH VADER BECOMES A T.I.E. FIGHTER!
HOW MUCH LONGER DOES OUR FRIENDSHIP REQUIRE ME TO SEEM INTERESTED?
TWO MINUTES. BUT YOU CAN SHAVE OFF 30 SECONDS IF YOU DROOL.
READ
BB

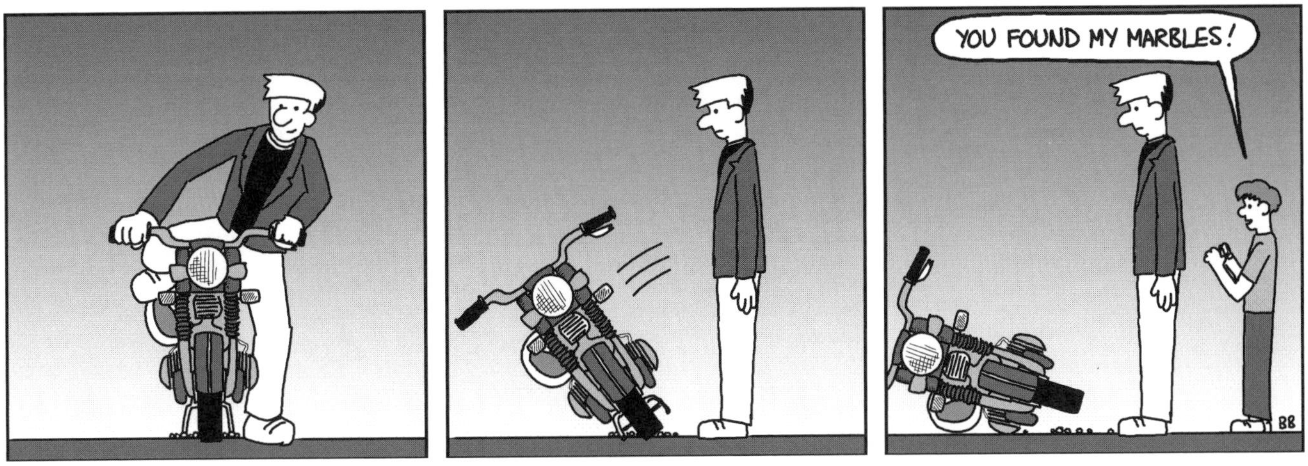
YOU FOUND MY MARBLES!
BB

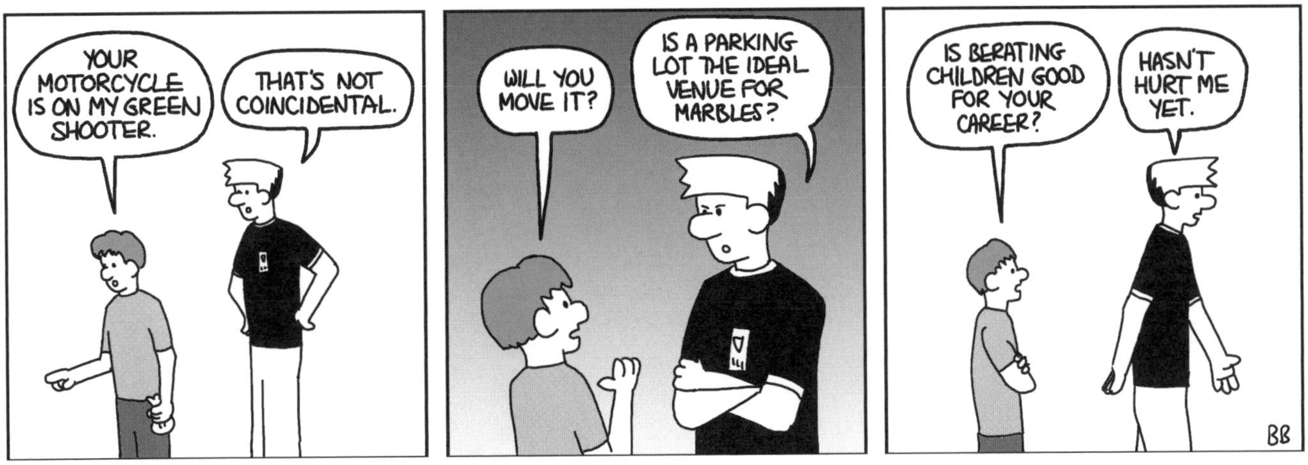
YOUR MOTORCYCLE IS ON MY GREEN SHOOTER.
THAT'S NOT COINCIDENTAL.
WILL YOU MOVE IT?
IS A PARKING LOT THE IDEAL VENUE FOR MARBLES?
IS BERATING CHILDREN GOOD FOR YOUR CAREER?
HASN'T HURT ME YET.
BB

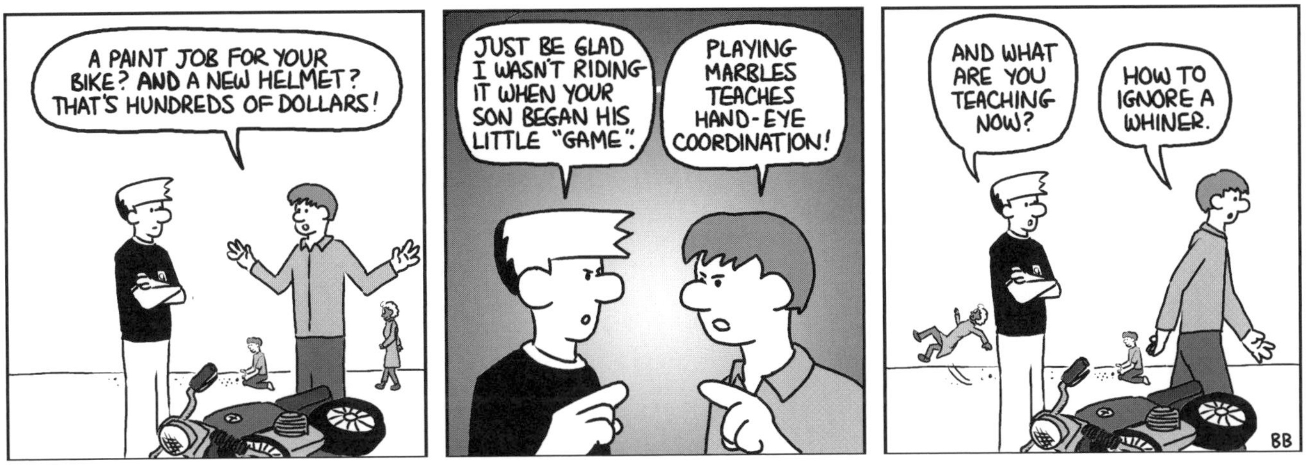
A PAINT JOB FOR YOUR BIKE? AND A NEW HELMET? THAT'S HUNDREDS OF DOLLARS!
JUST BE GLAD I WASN'T RIDING IT WHEN YOUR SON BEGAN HIS LITTLE "GAME".
PLAYING MARBLES TEACHES HAND-EYE COORDINATION!
AND WHAT ARE YOU TEACHING NOW?
HOW TO IGNORE A WHINER.
BB

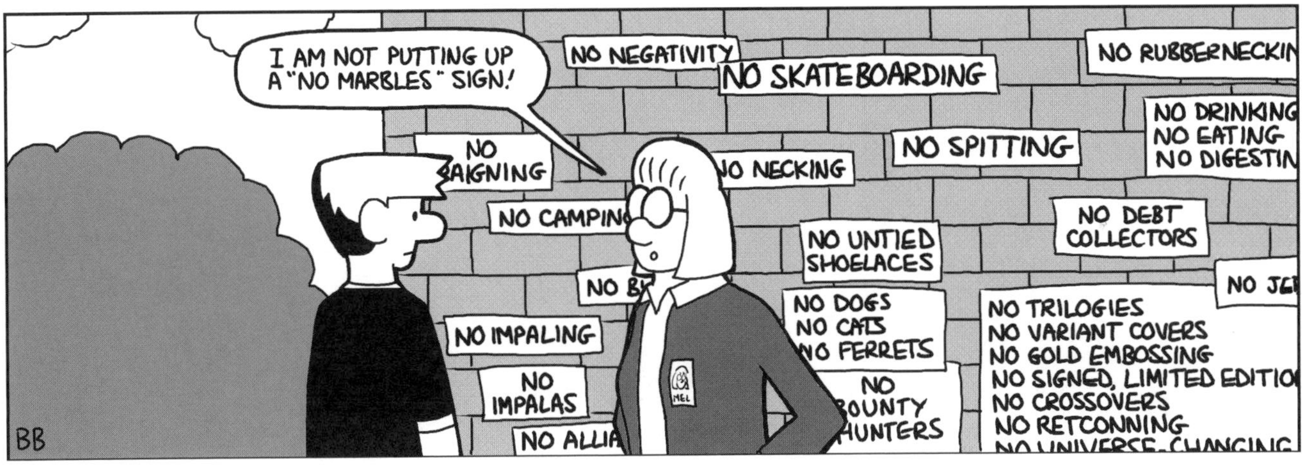
I AM NOT PUTTING UP A "NO MARBLES" SIGN!
NO NEGATIVITY
NO SKATEBOARDING
NO SPITTING
NO CAMPING
NO UNTIED SHOELACES
NO DEBT COLLECTORS
NO DOGS
NO CATS
NO IMPALING
NO IMPALAS
NO TRILOGIES
NO VARIANT COVERS
NO GOLD EMBOSSING
NO CROSSOVERS
NO RETCONNING
BB

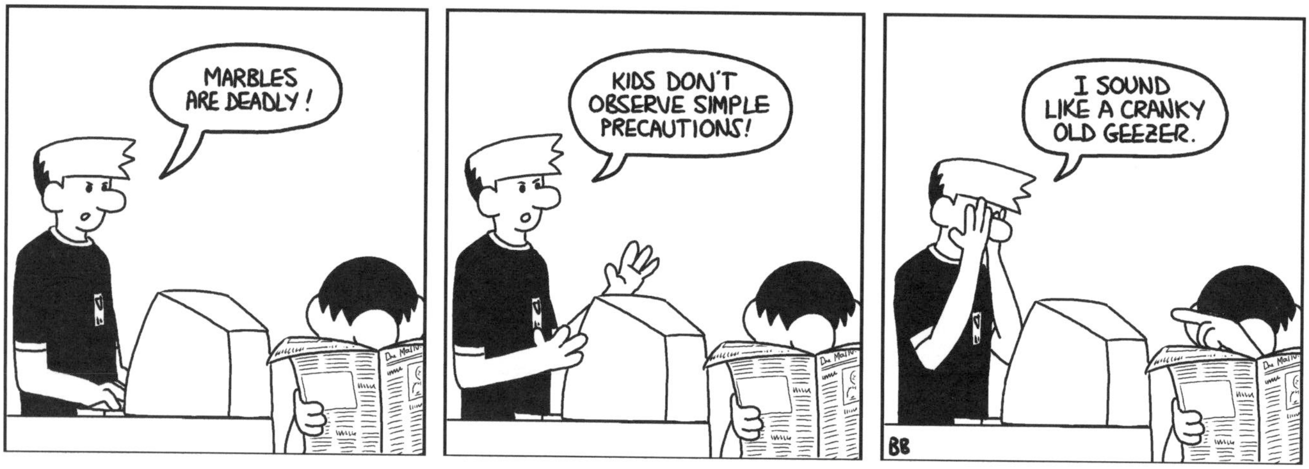
MARBLES ARE DEADLY!
KIDS DON'T OBSERVE SIMPLE PRECAUTIONS!
I SOUND LIKE A CRANKY OLD GEEZER.
BB

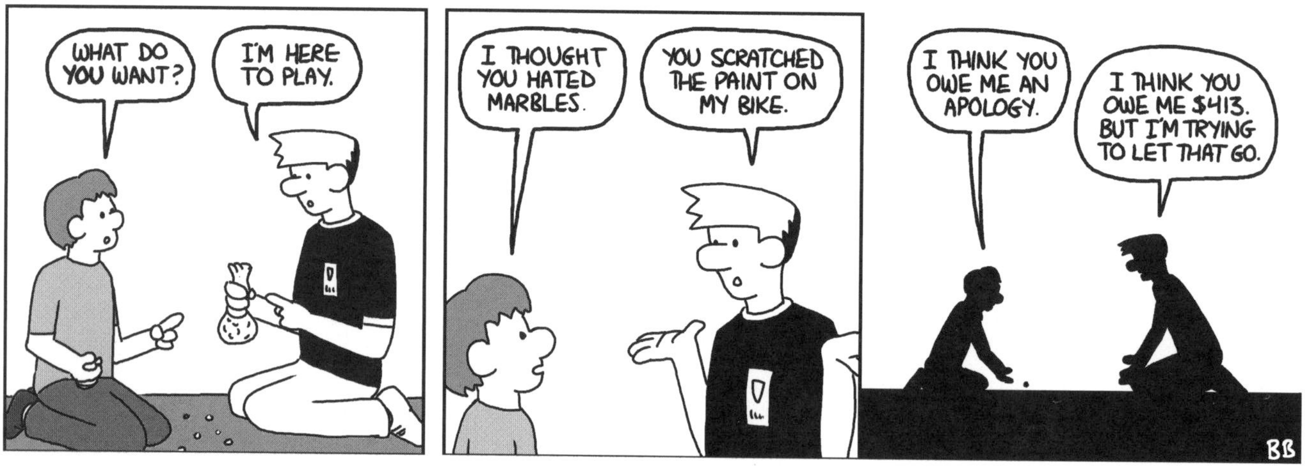
WHAT DO YOU WANT?
I'M HERE TO PLAY.
I THOUGHT YOU HATED MARBLES.
YOU SCRATCHED THE PAINT ON MY BIKE.
I THINK YOU OWE ME AN APOLOGY.
I THINK YOU OWE ME $413. BUT I'M TRYING TO LET THAT GO.
BB

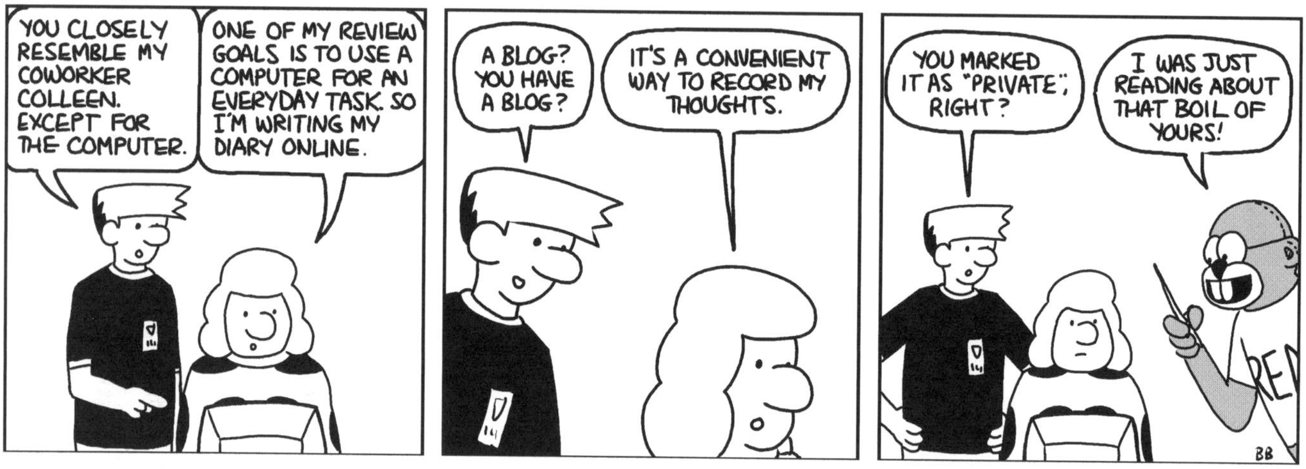
YOU CLOSELY RESEMBLE MY COWORKER COLLEEN. EXCEPT FOR THE COMPUTER.
ONE OF MY REVIEW GOALS IS TO USE A COMPUTER FOR AN EVERYDAY TASK. SO I'M WRITING MY DIARY ONLINE.
A BLOG? YOU HAVE A BLOG?
IT'S A CONVENIENT WAY TO RECORD MY THOUGHTS.
YOU MARKED IT AS "PRIVATE", RIGHT?
I WAS JUST READING ABOUT THAT BOIL OF YOURS!
BB

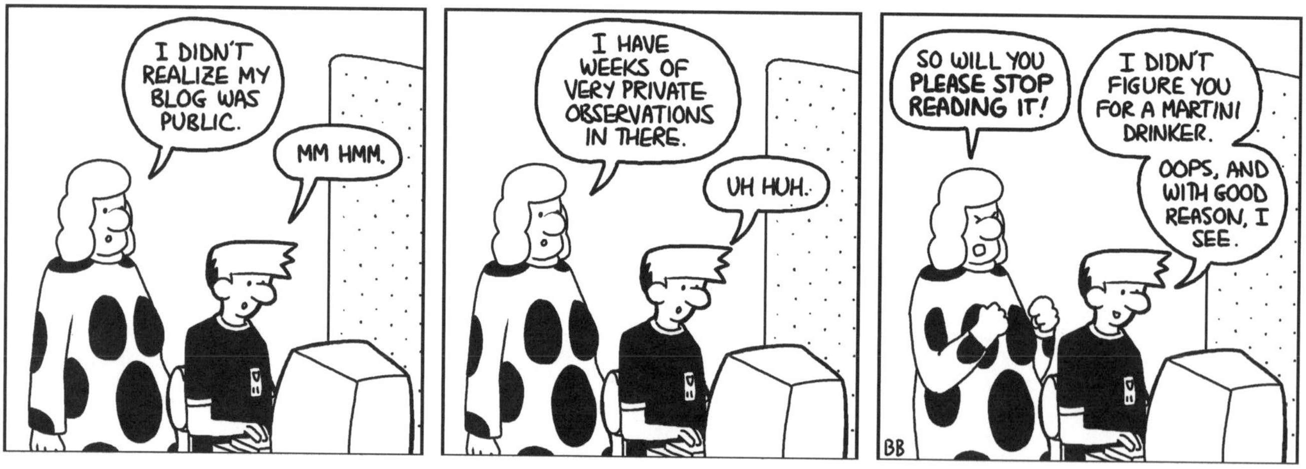
I DIDN'T REALIZE MY BLOG WAS PUBLIC.
MM HMM.
I HAVE WEEKS OF VERY PRIVATE OBSERVATIONS IN THERE.
UH HUH.
SO WILL YOU PLEASE STOP READING IT!
I DIDN'T FIGURE YOU FOR A MARTINI DRINKER.
OOPS, AND WITH GOOD REASON, I SEE.
BB

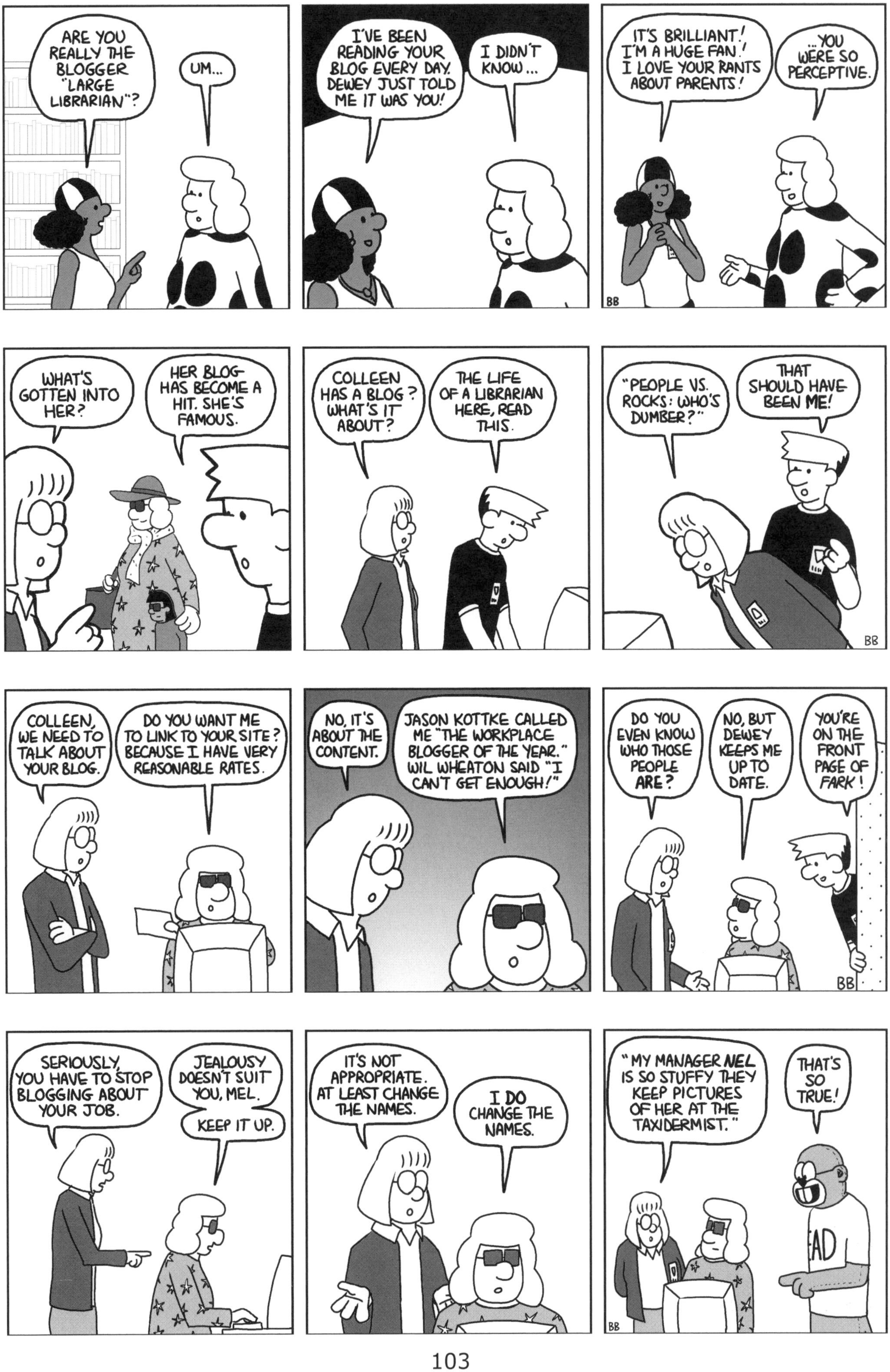

ARE YOU REALLY THE BLOGGER "LARGE LIBRARIAN"?
UM...
I'VE BEEN READING YOUR BLOG EVERY DAY. DEWEY JUST TOLD ME IT WAS YOU!
I DIDN'T KNOW...
IT'S BRILLIANT! I'M A HUGE FAN! I LOVE YOUR RANTS ABOUT PARENTS!
...YOU WERE SO PERCEPTIVE.
BB
WHAT'S GOTTEN INTO HER?
HER BLOG HAS BECOME A HIT. SHE'S FAMOUS.
COLLEEN HAS A BLOG? WHAT'S IT ABOUT?
THE LIFE OF A LIBRARIAN HERE, READ THIS.
"PEOPLE VS. ROCKS: WHO'S DUMBER?"
THAT SHOULD HAVE BEEN **ME**!
BB
COLLEEN, WE NEED TO TALK ABOUT YOUR BLOG.
DO YOU WANT ME TO LINK TO YOUR SITE? BECAUSE I HAVE VERY REASONABLE RATES.
NO, IT'S ABOUT THE CONTENT.
JASON KOTTKE CALLED ME "THE WORKPLACE BLOGGER OF THE YEAR." WIL WHEATON SAID "I CAN'T GET ENOUGH!"
DO YOU EVEN KNOW WHO THOSE PEOPLE **ARE**?
NO, BUT DEWEY KEEPS ME UP TO DATE.
YOU'RE ON THE FRONT PAGE OF *FARK*!
BB
SERIOUSLY, YOU HAVE TO STOP BLOGGING ABOUT YOUR JOB.
JEALOUSY DOESN'T SUIT YOU, MEL.
KEEP IT UP.
IT'S NOT APPROPRIATE. AT LEAST CHANGE THE NAMES.
I **DO** CHANGE THE NAMES.
"MY MANAGER **NEL** IS SO STUFFY THEY KEEP PICTURES OF HER AT THE TAXIDERMIST."
THAT'S SO TRUE!
BB

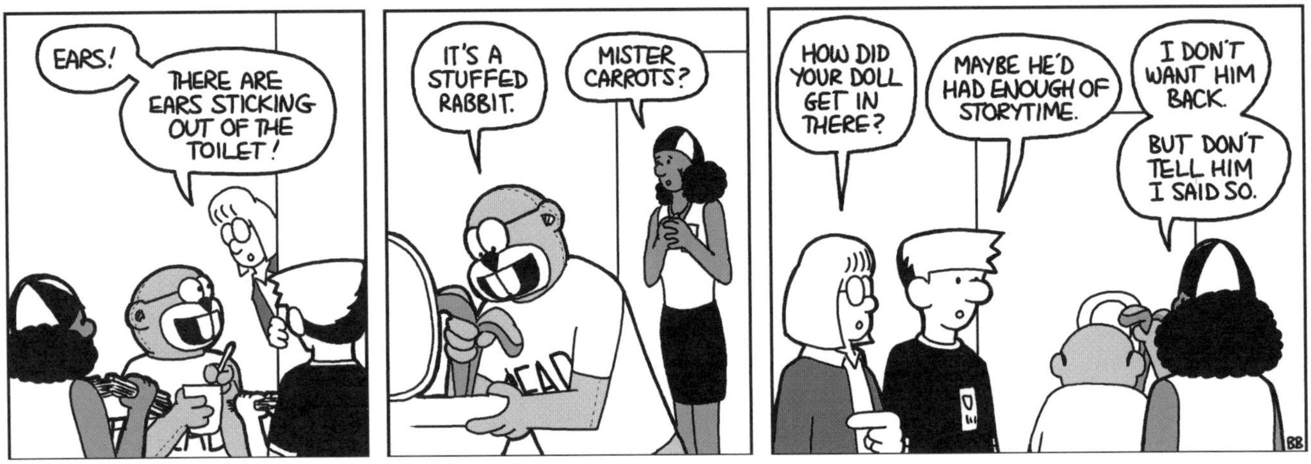
EARS!
THERE ARE EARS STICKING OUT OF THE TOILET!
IT'S A STUFFED RABBIT.
MISTER CARROTS?
HOW DID YOUR DOLL GET IN THERE?
MAYBE HE'D HAD ENOUGH OF STORYTIME.
I DON'T WANT HIM BACK.
BUT DON'T TELL HIM I SAID SO.
BB

As a birthday present to Gene, Bill finally relented and ran a week's worth of bathroom humor.

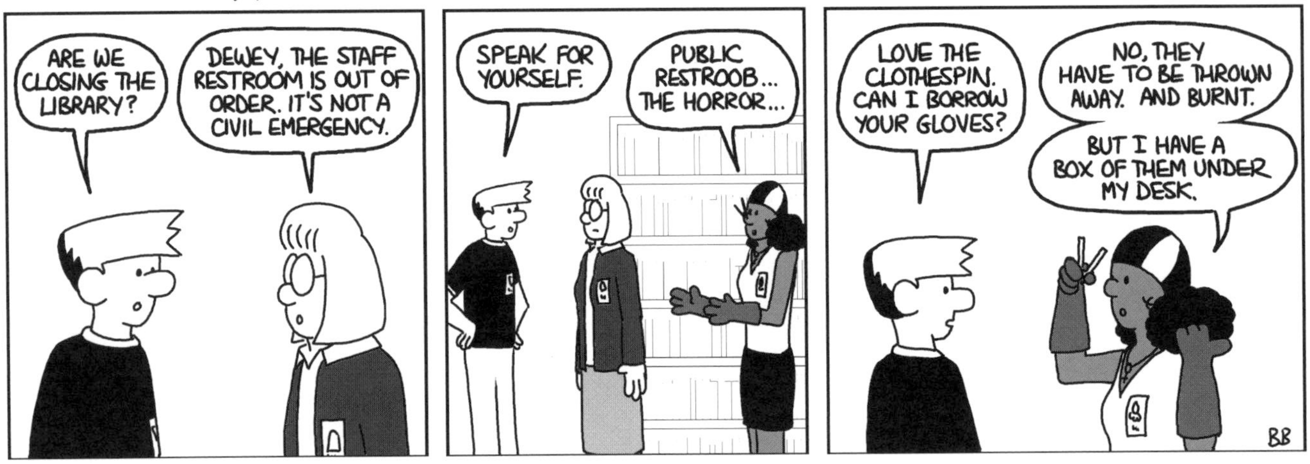
ARE WE CLOSING THE LIBRARY?
DEWEY, THE STAFF RESTROOM IS OUT OF ORDER. IT'S NOT A CIVIL EMERGENCY.
SPEAK FOR YOURSELF.
PUBLIC RESTROOB... THE HORROR...
LOVE THE CLOTHESPIN. CAN I BORROW YOUR GLOVES?
NO, THEY HAVE TO BE THROWN AWAY. AND BURNT.
BUT I HAVE A BOX OF THEM UNDER MY DESK.
BB

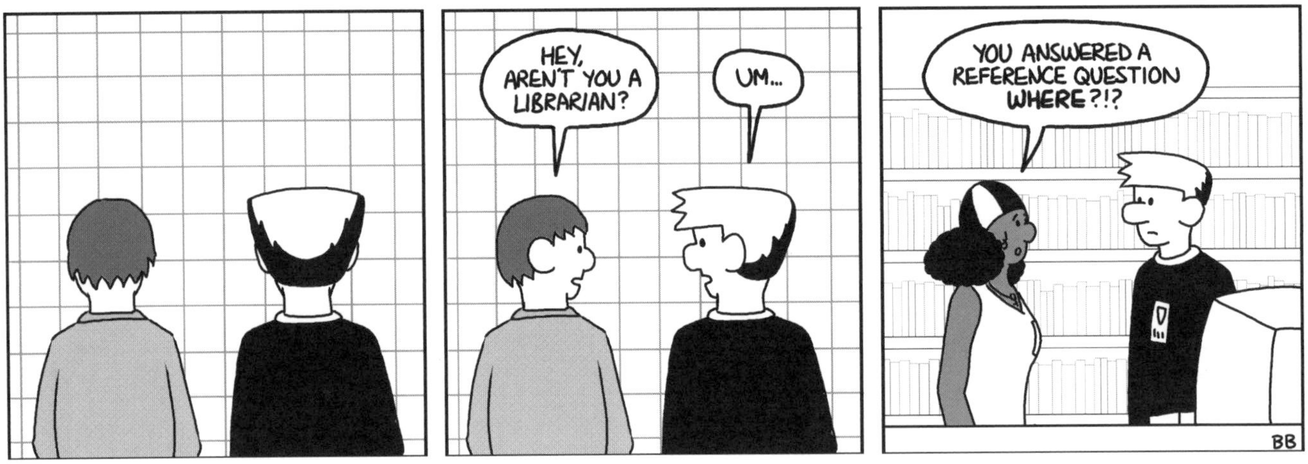
HEY, AREN'T YOU A LIBRARIAN?
UM...
YOU ANSWERED A REFERENCE QUESTION **WHERE**?!?
BB

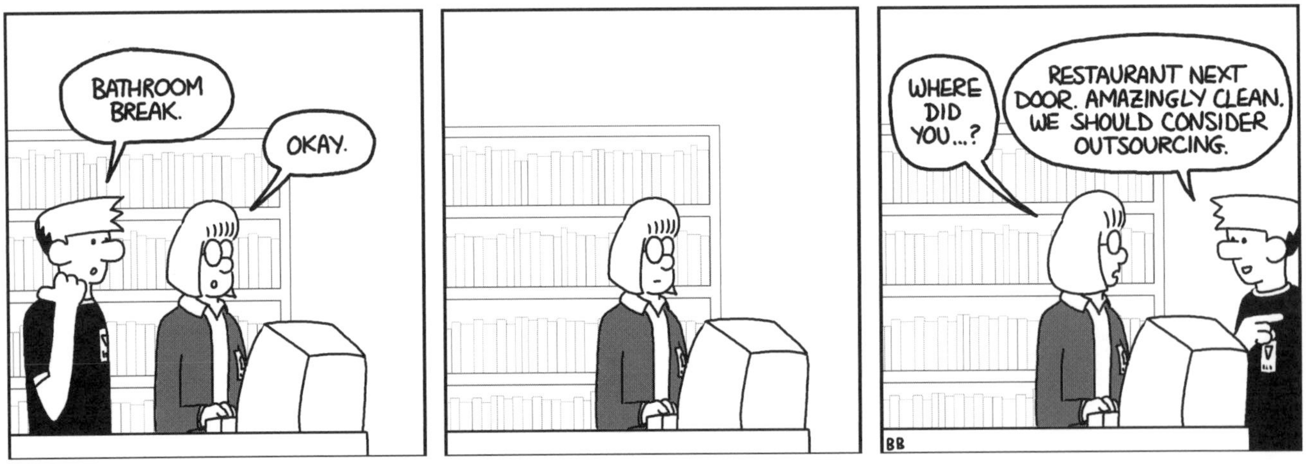
BATHROOM BREAK.
OKAY.
WHERE DID YOU...?
RESTAURANT NEXT DOOR. AMAZINGLY CLEAN. WE SHOULD CONSIDER OUTSOURCING.
BB

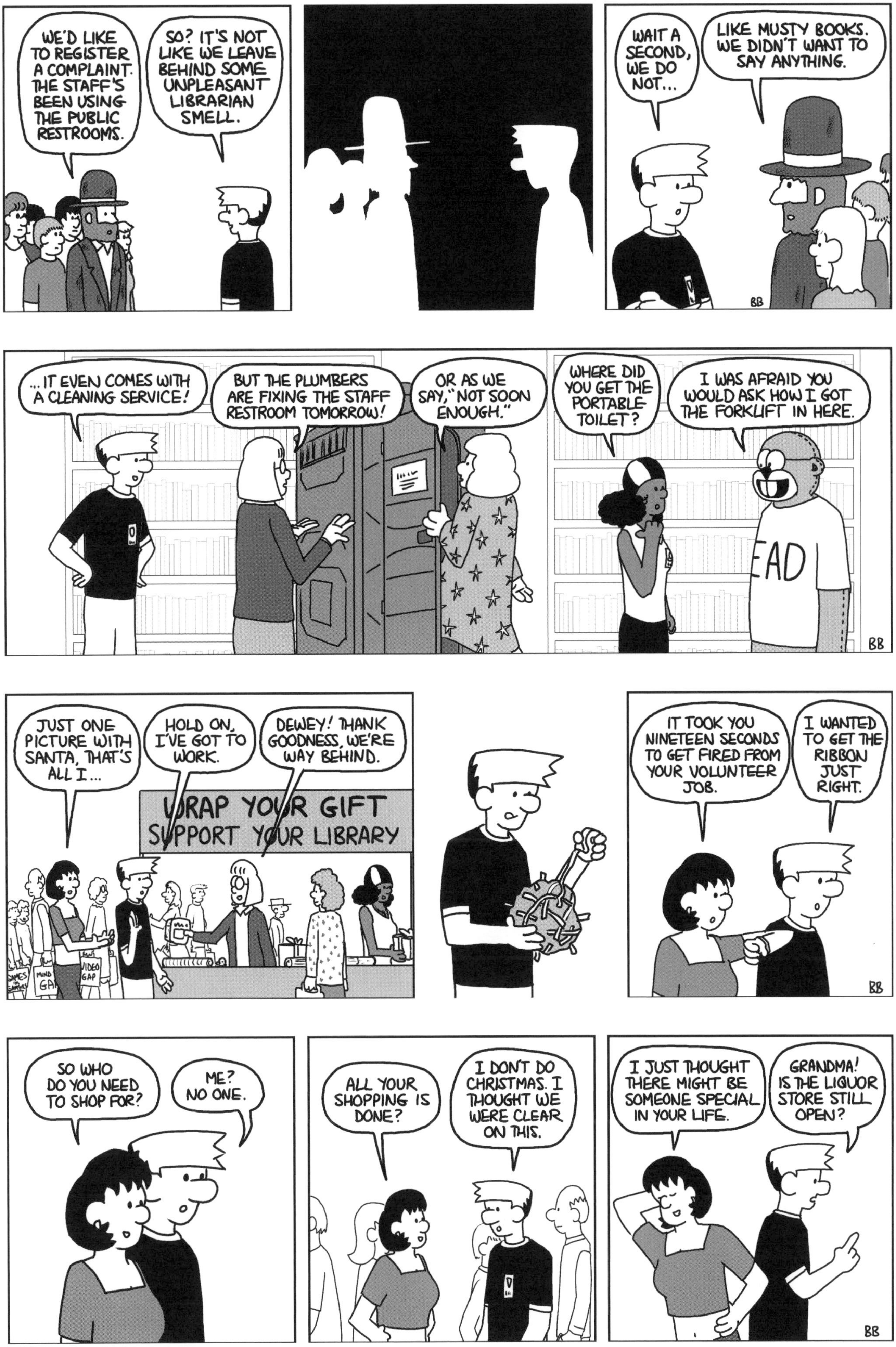
WE'D LIKE TO REGISTER A COMPLAINT. THE STAFF'S BEEN USING THE PUBLIC RESTROOMS.
SO? IT'S NOT LIKE WE LEAVE BEHIND SOME UNPLEASANT LIBRARIAN SMELL.
WAIT A SECOND, WE DO NOT...
LIKE MUSTY BOOKS. WE DIDN'T WANT TO SAY ANYTHING.
...IT EVEN COMES WITH A CLEANING SERVICE!
BUT THE PLUMBERS ARE FIXING THE STAFF RESTROOM TOMORROW!
OR AS WE SAY, "NOT SOON ENOUGH."
WHERE DID YOU GET THE PORTABLE TOILET?
I WAS AFRAID YOU WOULD ASK HOW I GOT THE FORKLIFT IN HERE.
JUST ONE PICTURE WITH SANTA, THAT'S ALL I...
HOLD ON, I'VE GOT TO WORK.
DEWEY! THANK GOODNESS, WE'RE WAY BEHIND.
WRAP YOUR GIFT
SUPPORT YOUR LIBRARY
IT TOOK YOU NINETEEN SECONDS TO GET FIRED FROM YOUR VOLUNTEER JOB.
I WANTED TO GET THE RIBBON JUST RIGHT.
SO WHO DO YOU NEED TO SHOP FOR?
ME? NO ONE.
ALL YOUR SHOPPING IS DONE?
I DON'T DO CHRISTMAS. I THOUGHT WE WERE CLEAR ON THIS.
I JUST THOUGHT THERE MIGHT BE SOMEONE SPECIAL IN YOUR LIFE.
GRANDMA! IS THE LIQUOR STORE STILL OPEN?

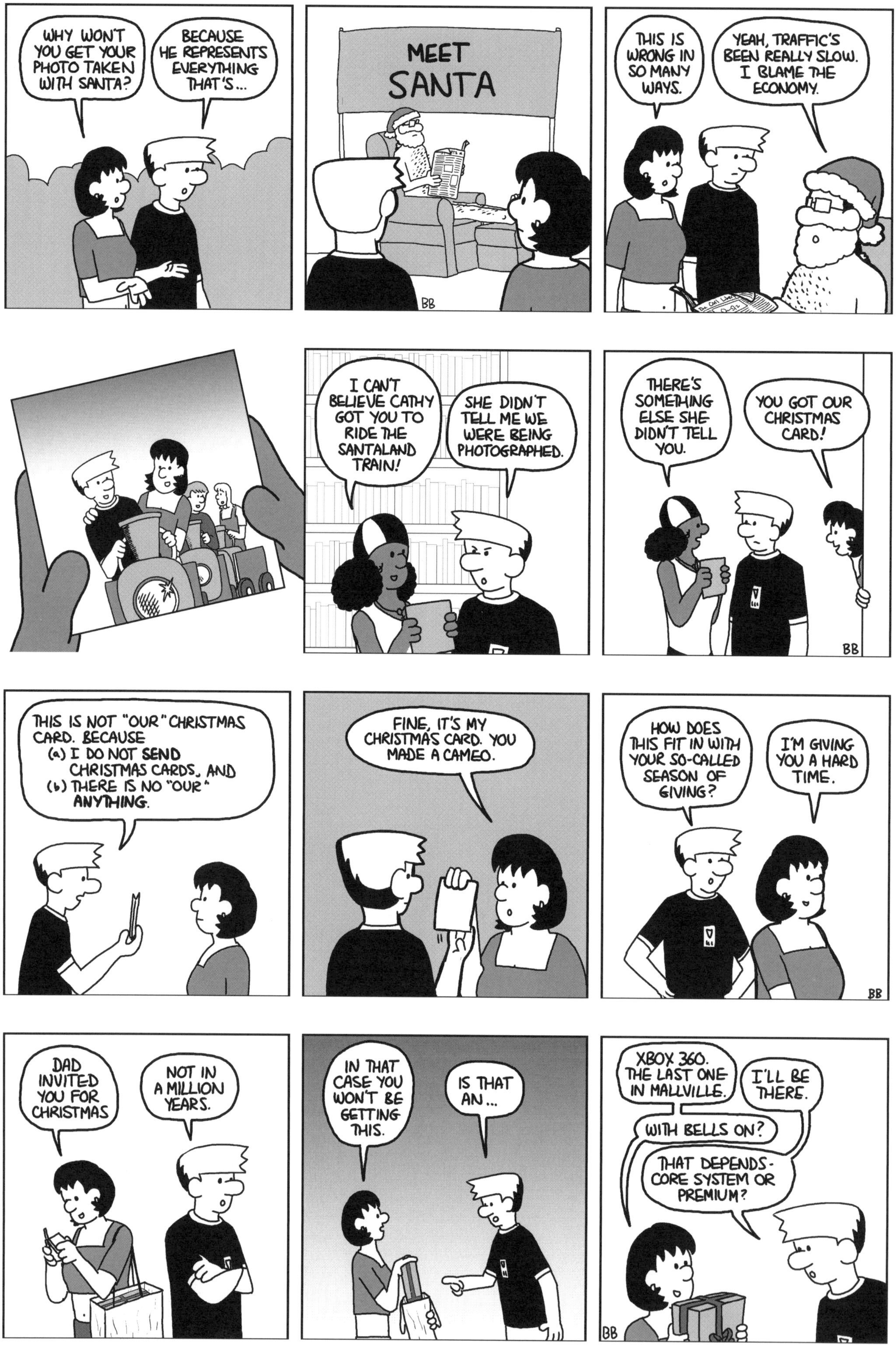
WHY WON'T YOU GET YOUR PHOTO TAKEN WITH SANTA?
BECAUSE HE REPRESENTS EVERYTHING THAT'S...
MEET SANTA
THIS IS WRONG IN SO MANY WAYS.
YEAH, TRAFFIC'S BEEN REALLY SLOW. I BLAME THE ECONOMY.
I CAN'T BELIEVE CATHY GOT YOU TO RIDE THE SANTALAND TRAIN!
SHE DIDN'T TELL ME WE WERE BEING PHOTOGRAPHED.
THERE'S SOMETHING ELSE SHE DIDN'T TELL YOU.
YOU GOT OUR CHRISTMAS CARD!
THIS IS NOT "OUR" CHRISTMAS CARD. BECAUSE (a) I DO NOT SEND CHRISTMAS CARDS, AND (b) THERE IS NO "OUR" ANYTHING.
FINE, IT'S MY CHRISTMAS CARD. YOU MADE A CAMEO.
HOW DOES THIS FIT IN WITH YOUR SO-CALLED SEASON OF GIVING?
I'M GIVING YOU A HARD TIME.
DAD INVITED YOU FOR CHRISTMAS
NOT IN A MILLION YEARS.
IN THAT CASE YOU WON'T BE GETTING THIS.
IS THAT AN...
XBOX 360. THE LAST ONE IN MALLVILLE.
I'LL BE THERE.
WITH BELLS ON?
THAT DEPENDS- CORE SYSTEM OR PREMIUM?

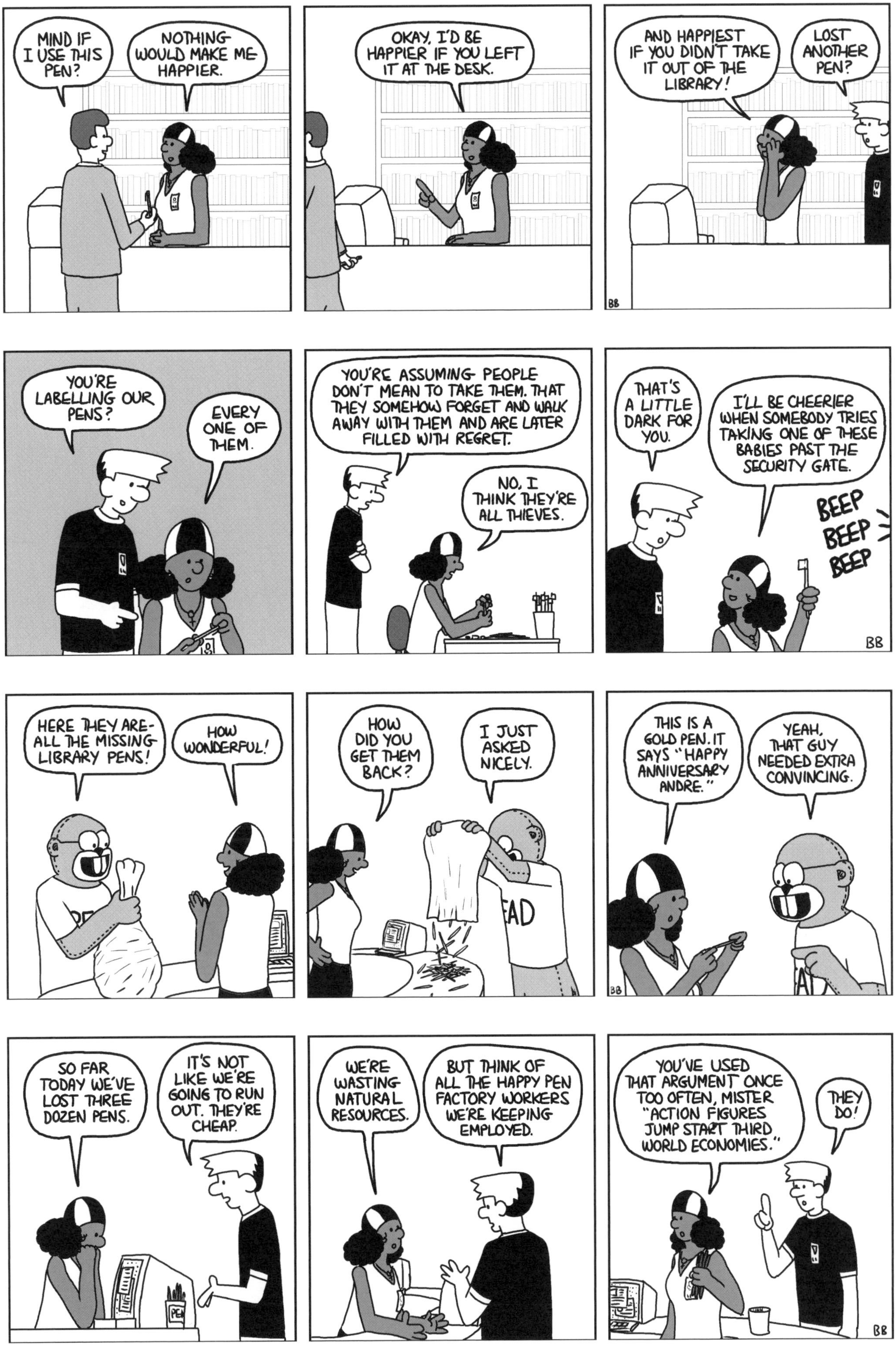
MIND IF I USE THIS PEN?
NOTHING WOULD MAKE ME HAPPIER.
OKAY, I'D BE HAPPIER IF YOU LEFT IT AT THE DESK.
AND HAPPIEST IF YOU DIDN'T TAKE IT OUT OF THE LIBRARY!
LOST ANOTHER PEN?
BB
YOU'RE LABELLING OUR PENS?
EVERY ONE OF THEM.
YOU'RE ASSUMING PEOPLE DON'T MEAN TO TAKE THEM. THAT THEY SOMEHOW FORGET AND WALK AWAY WITH THEM AND ARE LATER FILLED WITH REGRET.
NO, I THINK THEY'RE ALL THIEVES.
THAT'S A LITTLE DARK FOR YOU.
I'LL BE CHEERIER WHEN SOMEBODY TRIES TAKING ONE OF THESE BABIES PAST THE SECURITY GATE.
BEEP BEEP BEEP
BB
HERE THEY ARE- ALL THE MISSING LIBRARY PENS!
HOW WONDERFUL!
HOW DID YOU GET THEM BACK?
I JUST ASKED NICELY.
THIS IS A GOLD PEN. IT SAYS "HAPPY ANNIVERSARY ANDRE."
YEAH, THAT GUY NEEDED EXTRA CONVINCING.
BB
SO FAR TODAY WE'VE LOST THREE DOZEN PENS.
IT'S NOT LIKE WE'RE GOING TO RUN OUT. THEY'RE CHEAP.
PEN
WE'RE WASTING NATURAL RESOURCES.
BUT THINK OF ALL THE HAPPY PEN FACTORY WORKERS WE'RE KEEPING EMPLOYED.
YOU'VE USED THAT ARGUMENT ONCE TOO OFTEN, MISTER "ACTION FIGURES JUMP START THIRD WORLD ECONOMIES."
THEY DO!
BB

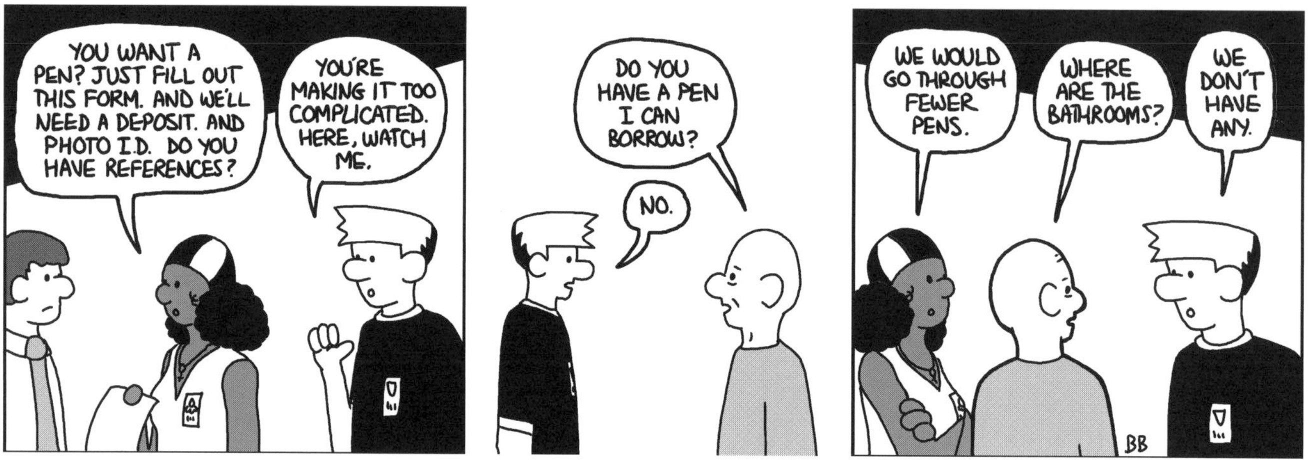
YOU WANT A PEN? JUST FILL OUT THIS FORM. AND WE'LL NEED A DEPOSIT. AND PHOTO I.D. DO YOU HAVE REFERENCES?
YOU'RE MAKING IT TOO COMPLICATED. HERE, WATCH ME.
DO YOU HAVE A PEN I CAN BORROW?
NO.
WE WOULD GO THROUGH FEWER PENS.
WHERE ARE THE BATHROOMS?
WE DON'T HAVE ANY.
BB

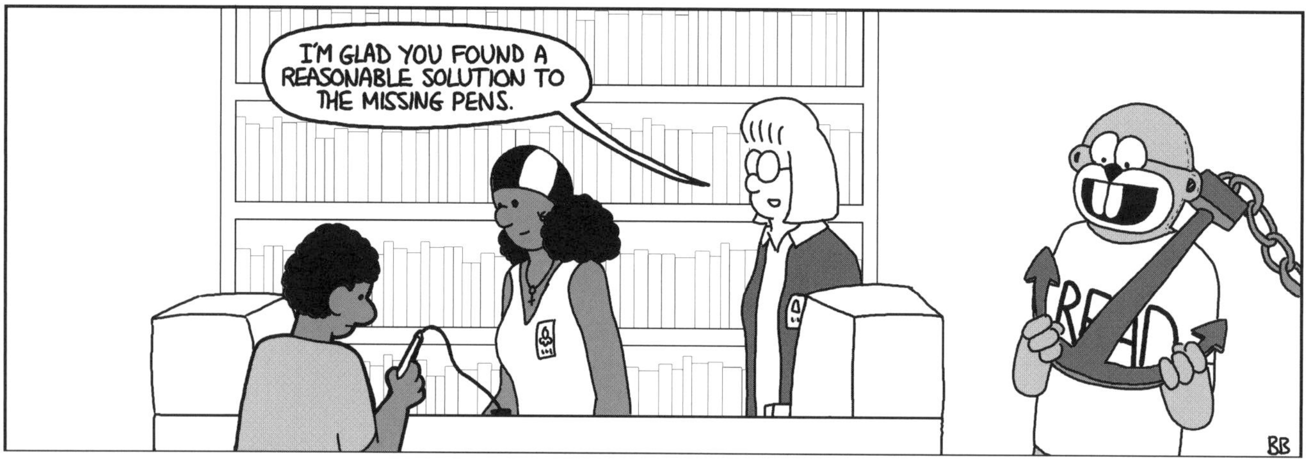
I'M GLAD YOU FOUND A REASONABLE SOLUTION TO THE MISSING PENS.
READ
BB

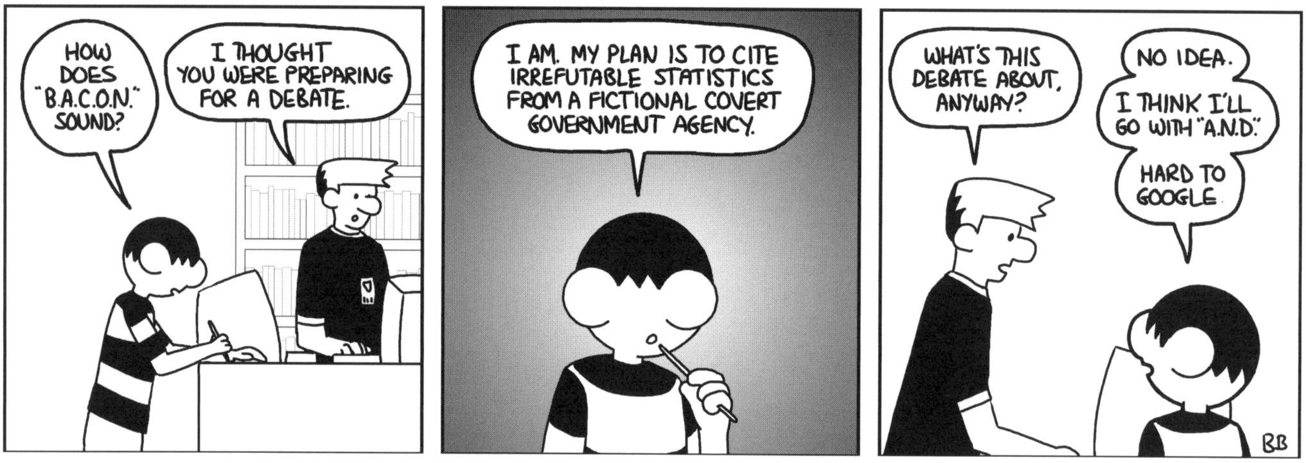
HOW DOES "B.A.C.O.N." SOUND?
I THOUGHT YOU WERE PREPARING FOR A DEBATE.
I AM. MY PLAN IS TO CITE IRREFUTABLE STATISTICS FROM A FICTIONAL COVERT GOVERNMENT AGENCY.
WHAT'S THIS DEBATE ABOUT, ANYWAY?
NO IDEA.
I THINK I'LL GO WITH "A.N.D."
HARD TO GOOGLE.
BB

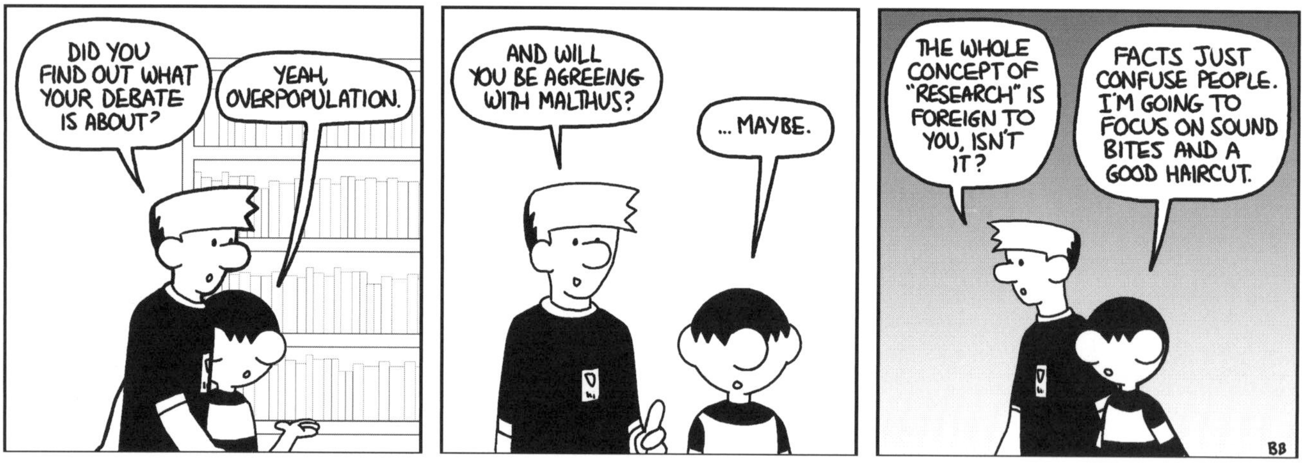
DID YOU FIND OUT WHAT YOUR DEBATE IS ABOUT?
YEAH, OVERPOPULATION.
AND WILL YOU BE AGREEING WITH MALTHUS?
... MAYBE.
THE WHOLE CONCEPT OF "RESEARCH" IS FOREIGN TO YOU, ISN'T IT?
FACTS JUST CONFUSE PEOPLE. I'M GOING TO FOCUS ON SOUND BITES AND A GOOD HAIRCUT.
BB

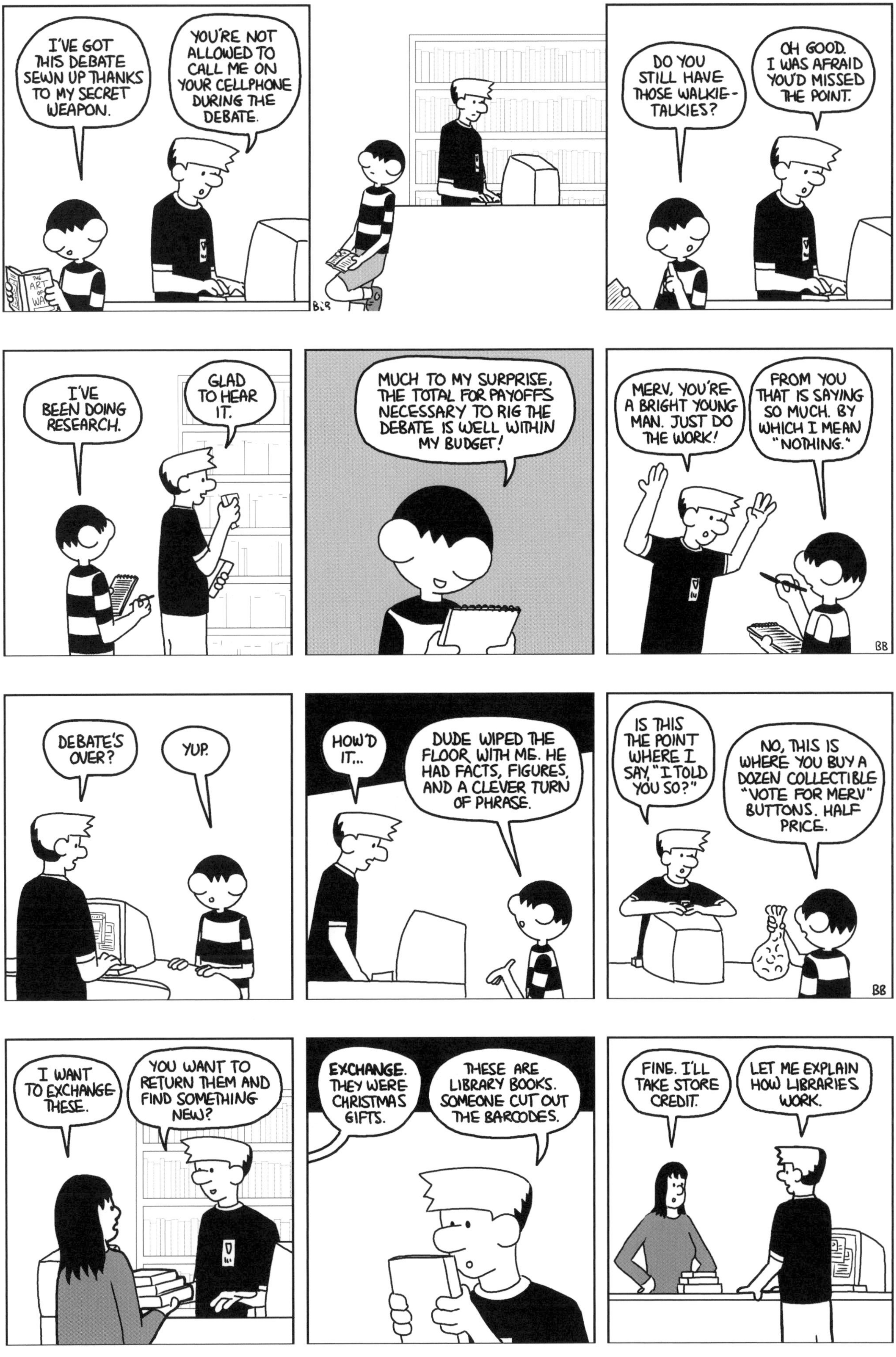
I'VE GOT THIS DEBATE SEWN UP THANKS TO MY SECRET WEAPON.
YOU'RE NOT ALLOWED TO CALL ME ON YOUR CELLPHONE DURING THE DEBATE.
DO YOU STILL HAVE THOSE WALKIE-TALKIES?
OH GOOD. I WAS AFRAID YOU'D MISSED THE POINT.
I'VE BEEN DOING RESEARCH.
GLAD TO HEAR IT.
MUCH TO MY SURPRISE, THE TOTAL FOR PAYOFFS NECESSARY TO RIG THE DEBATE IS WELL WITHIN MY BUDGET!
MERV, YOU'RE A BRIGHT YOUNG MAN. JUST DO THE WORK!
FROM YOU THAT IS SAYING SO MUCH. BY WHICH I MEAN "NOTHING."
DEBATE'S OVER?
YUP.
HOW'D IT...
DUDE WIPED THE FLOOR WITH ME. HE HAD FACTS, FIGURES, AND A CLEVER TURN OF PHRASE.
IS THIS THE POINT WHERE I SAY, "I TOLD YOU SO?"
NO, THIS IS WHERE YOU BUY A DOZEN COLLECTIBLE "VOTE FOR MERV" BUTTONS. HALF PRICE.
I WANT TO EXCHANGE THESE.
YOU WANT TO RETURN THEM AND FIND SOMETHING NEW?
EXCHANGE. THEY WERE CHRISTMAS GIFTS.
THESE ARE LIBRARY BOOKS. SOMEONE CUT OUT THE BARCODES.
FINE. I'LL TAKE STORE CREDIT.
LET ME EXPLAIN HOW LIBRARIES WORK.

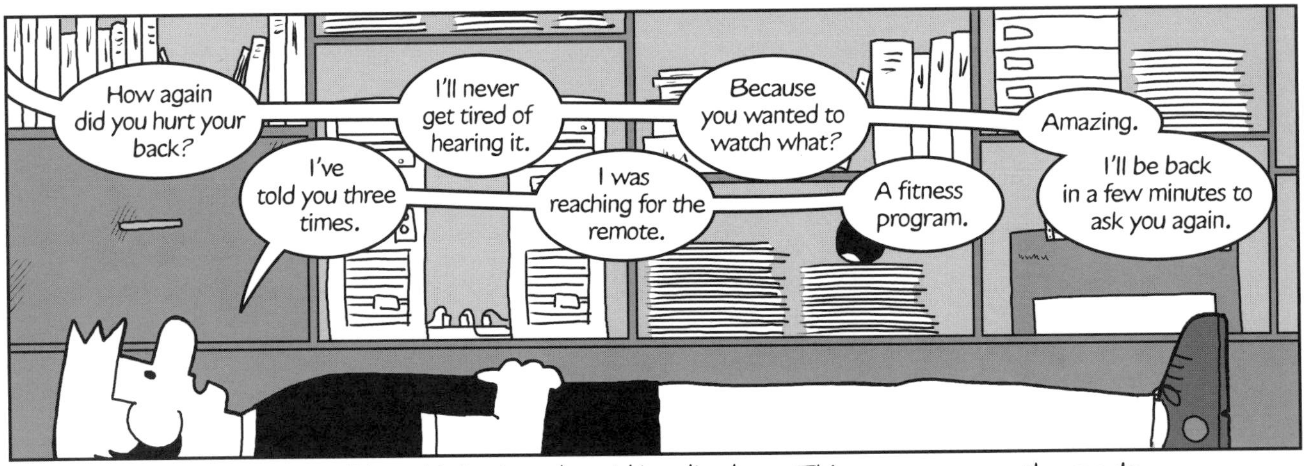
How again did you hurt your back?
I've told you three times.
I'll never get tired of hearing it.
I was reaching for the remote.
Because you wanted to watch what?
A fitness program.
Amazing.
I'll be back in a few minutes to ask you again.

Late in 2005 Bill hurt his back and could hardly draw. This sequence was the result.

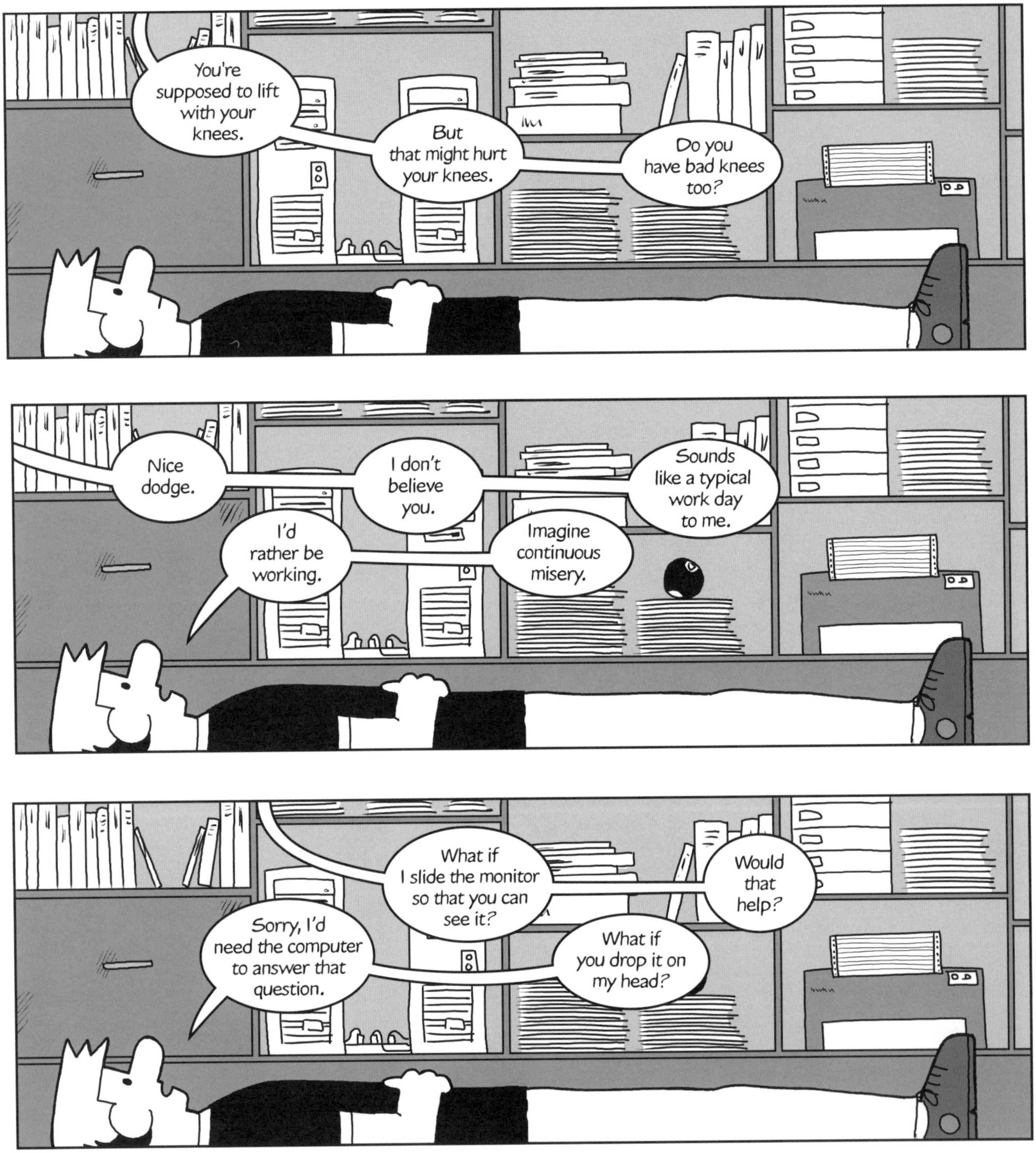
You're supposed to lift with your knees.
But that might hurt your knees.
Do you have bad knees too?
Nice dodge.
I'd rather be working.
I don't believe you.
Imagine continuous misery.
Sounds like a typical work day to me.
What if I slide the monitor so that you can see it?
Would that help?
Sorry, I'd need the computer to answer that question.
What if you drop it on my head?

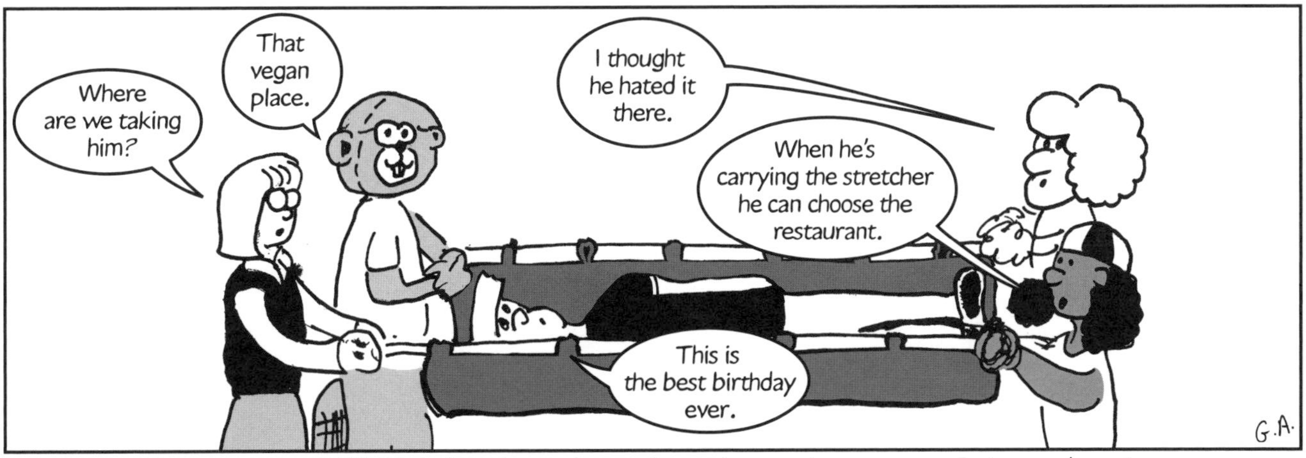
Where are we taking him?
That vegan place.
I thought he hated it there.
When he's carrying the stretcher he can choose the restaurant.
This is the best birthday ever.
G.A.

Every year on Bill's birthday Gene draws the strip, causing mass confusion and panic.

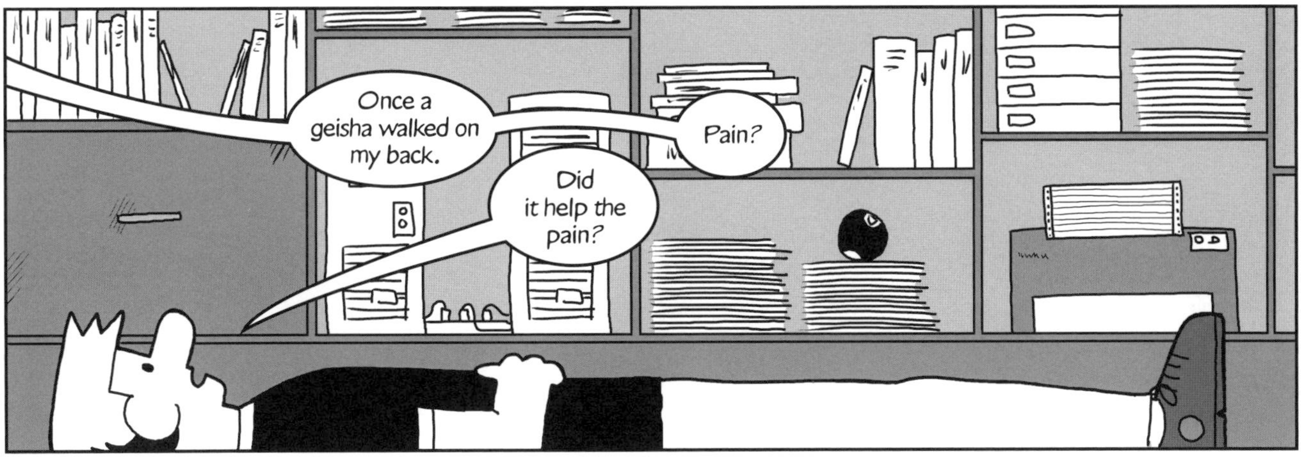
Once a geisha walked on my back.
Pain?
Did it help the pain?

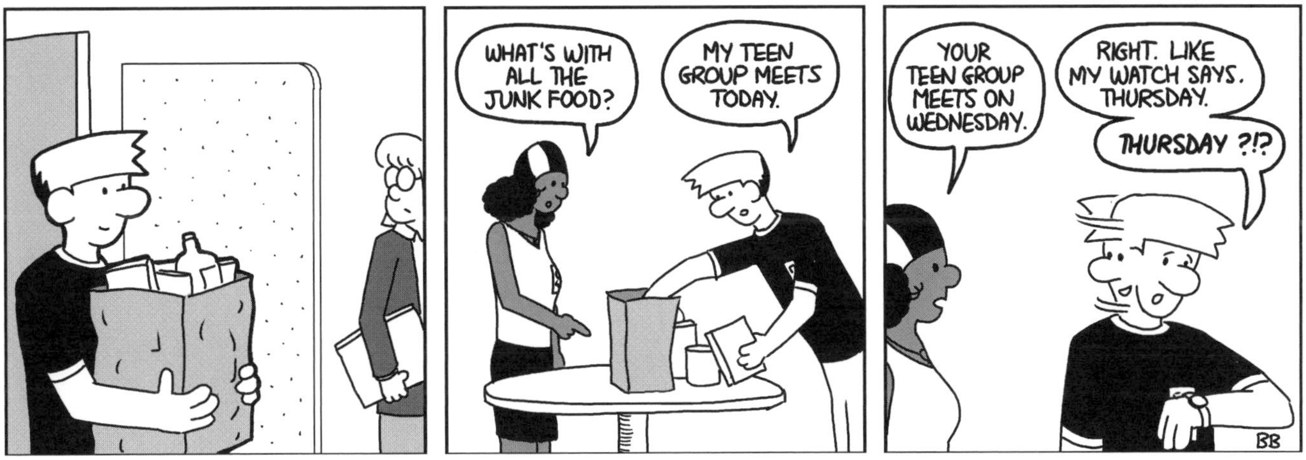
WHAT'S WITH ALL THE JUNK FOOD?
MY TEEN GROUP MEETS TODAY.
YOUR TEEN GROUP MEETS ON WEDNESDAY.
RIGHT. LIKE MY WATCH SAYS. THURSDAY.
THURSDAY ?!?
BB

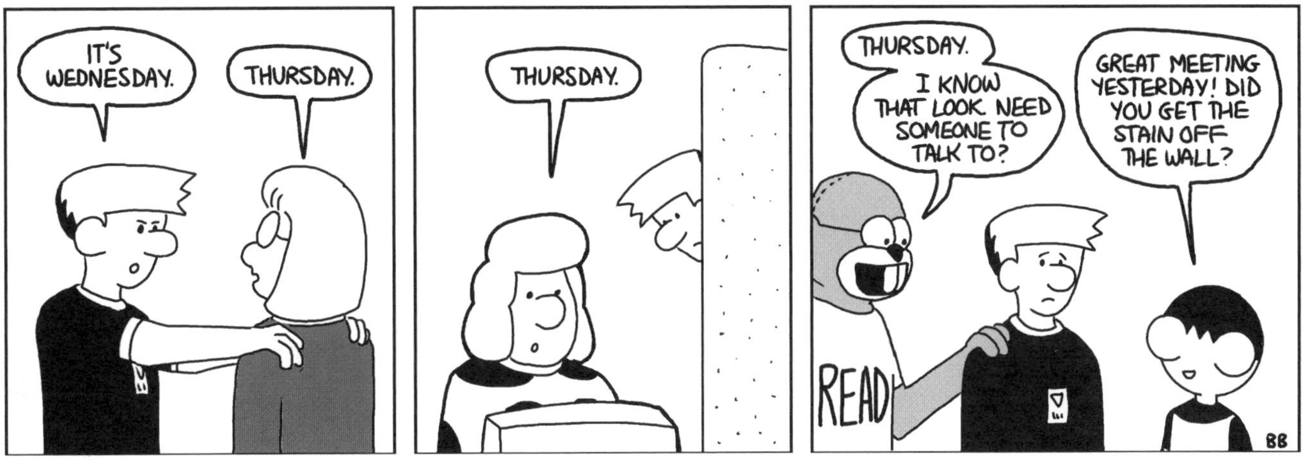
IT'S WEDNESDAY.
THURSDAY.
THURSDAY.
THURSDAY.
I KNOW THAT LOOK. NEED SOMEONE TO TALK TO?
GREAT MEETING YESTERDAY! DID YOU GET THE STAIN OFF THE WALL?
READ
BB

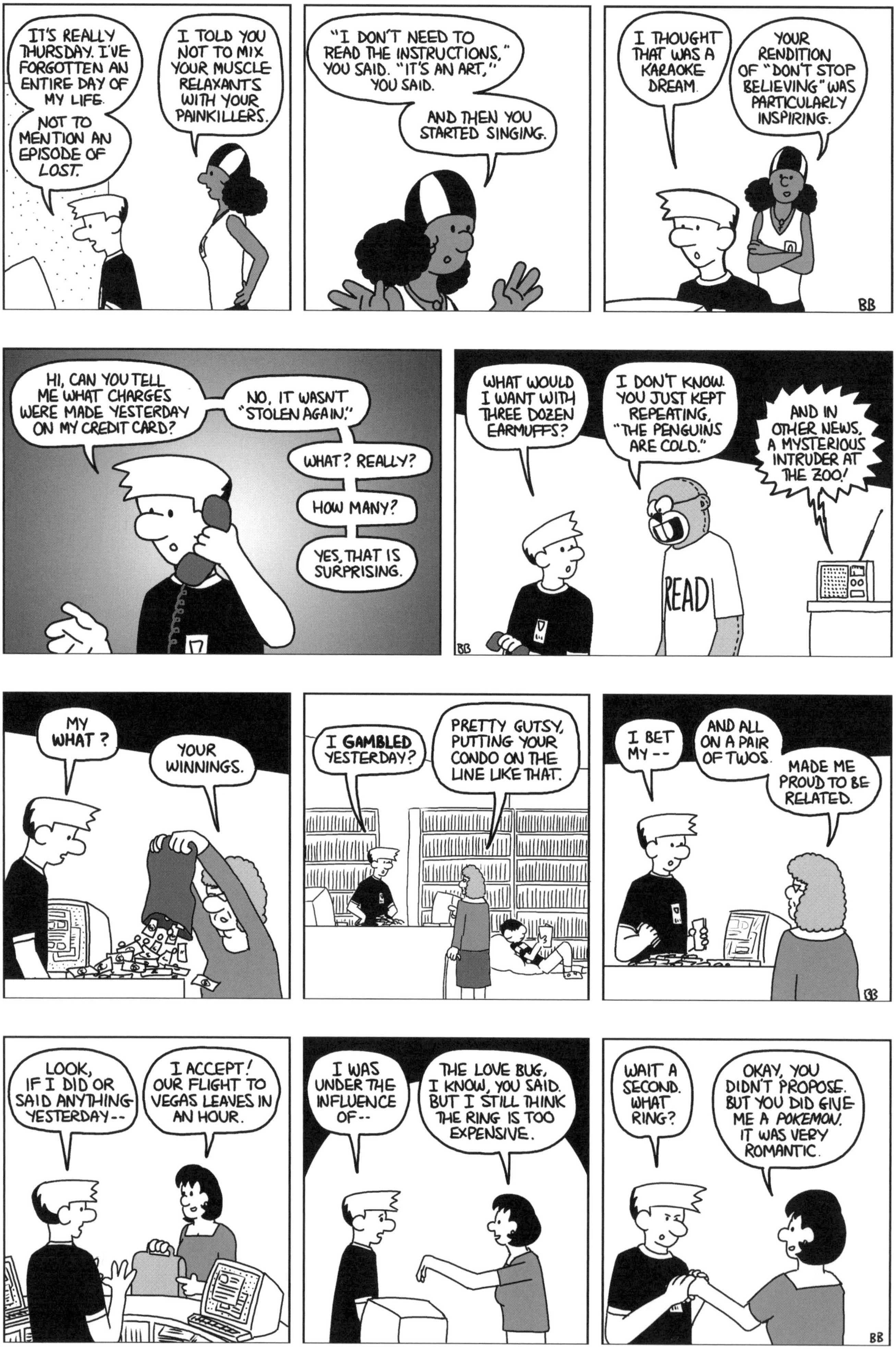

IT'S REALLY THURSDAY. I'VE FORGOTTEN AN ENTIRE DAY OF MY LIFE.
NOT TO MENTION AN EPISODE OF *LOST*.
I TOLD YOU NOT TO MIX YOUR MUSCLE RELAXANTS WITH YOUR PAINKILLERS.
"I DON'T NEED TO READ THE INSTRUCTIONS," YOU SAID. "IT'S AN ART," YOU SAID.
AND THEN YOU STARTED SINGING.
I THOUGHT THAT WAS A KARAOKE DREAM.
YOUR RENDITION OF "DON'T STOP BELIEVING" WAS PARTICULARLY INSPIRING.
BB
HI, CAN YOU TELL ME WHAT CHARGES WERE MADE YESTERDAY ON MY CREDIT CARD?
NO, IT WASN'T "STOLEN AGAIN."
WHAT? REALLY?
HOW MANY?
YES, THAT IS SURPRISING.
WHAT WOULD I WANT WITH THREE DOZEN EARMUFFS?
I DON'T KNOW. YOU JUST KEPT REPEATING, "THE PENGUINS ARE COLD."
AND IN OTHER NEWS, A MYSTERIOUS INTRUDER AT THE ZOO!
READ
BB
MY **WHAT**?
YOUR WINNINGS.
I **GAMBLED** YESTERDAY?
PRETTY GUTSY, PUTTING YOUR CONDO ON THE LINE LIKE THAT.
I BET MY --
AND ALL ON A PAIR OF TWOS.
MADE ME PROUD TO BE RELATED.
BB
LOOK, IF I DID OR SAID ANYTHING YESTERDAY--
I ACCEPT! OUR FLIGHT TO VEGAS LEAVES IN AN HOUR.
I WAS UNDER THE INFLUENCE OF--
THE LOVE BUG, I KNOW, YOU SAID. BUT I STILL THINK THE RING IS TOO EXPENSIVE.
WAIT A SECOND. WHAT RING?
OKAY, YOU DIDN'T PROPOSE. BUT YOU DID GIVE ME A *POKEMON*. IT WAS VERY ROMANTIC.
BB

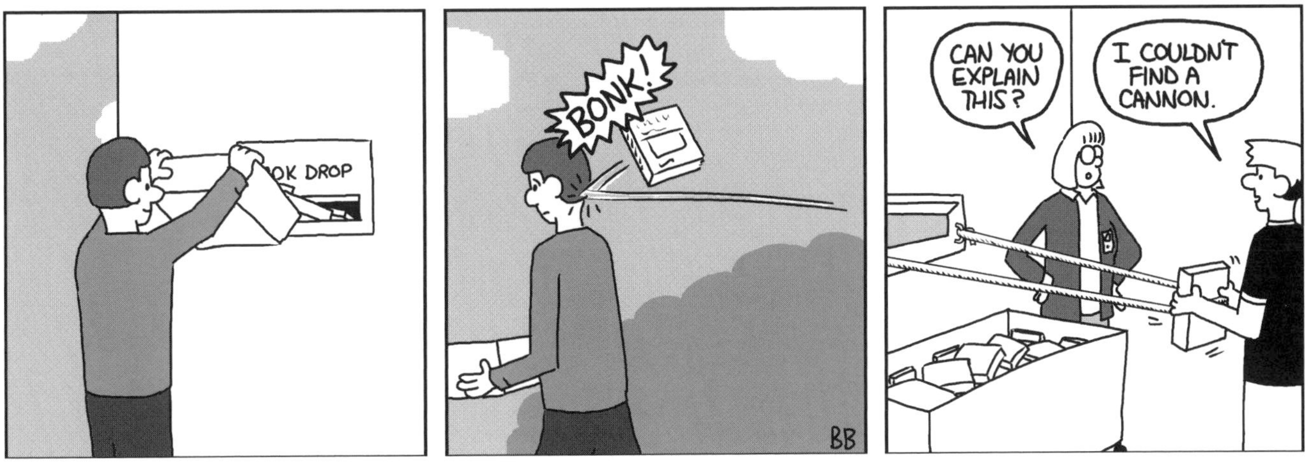
BONK!
CAN YOU EXPLAIN THIS?
I COULDN'T FIND A CANNON.

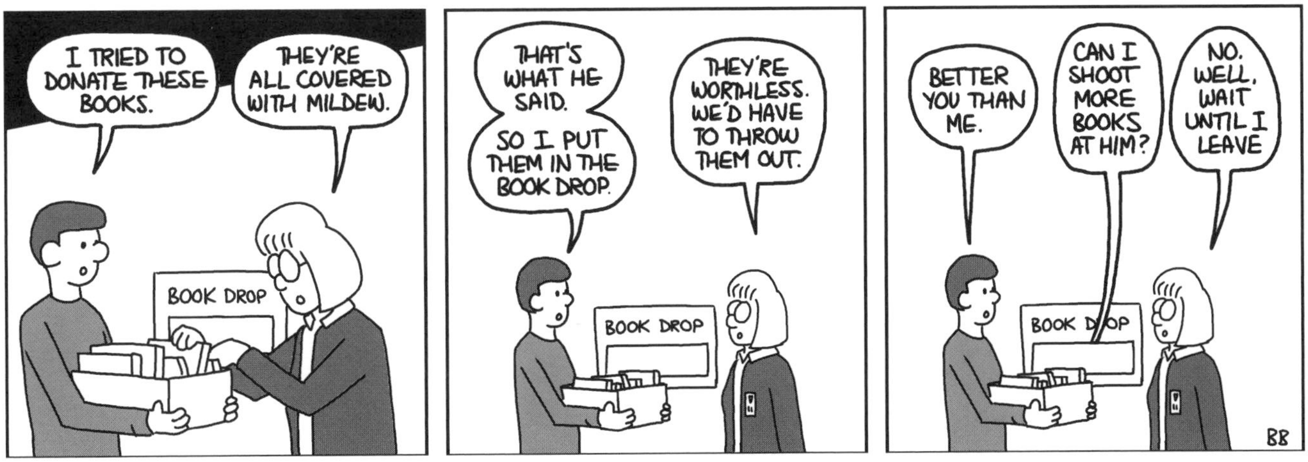
I TRIED TO DONATE THESE BOOKS.
THEY'RE ALL COVERED WITH MILDEW.
BOOK DROP
THAT'S WHAT HE SAID.
SO I PUT THEM IN THE BOOK DROP.
THEY'RE WORTHLESS. WE'D HAVE TO THROW THEM OUT.
BOOK DROP
BETTER YOU THAN ME.
CAN I SHOOT MORE BOOKS AT HIM?
NO. WELL, WAIT UNTIL I LEAVE

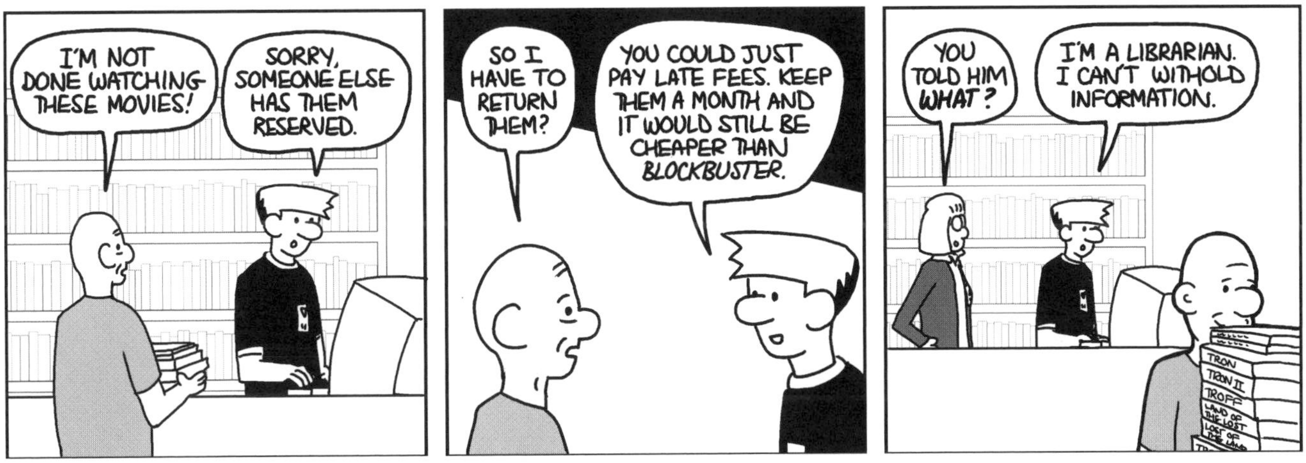
I'M NOT DONE WATCHING THESE MOVIES!
SORRY, SOMEONE ELSE HAS THEM RESERVED.
SO I HAVE TO RETURN THEM?
YOU COULD JUST PAY LATE FEES. KEEP THEM A MONTH AND IT WOULD STILL BE CHEAPER THAN *BLOCKBUSTER*.
YOU TOLD HIM *WHAT?*
I'M A LIBRARIAN. I CAN'T WITHOLD INFORMATION.
TRON
TRON II
TROFF

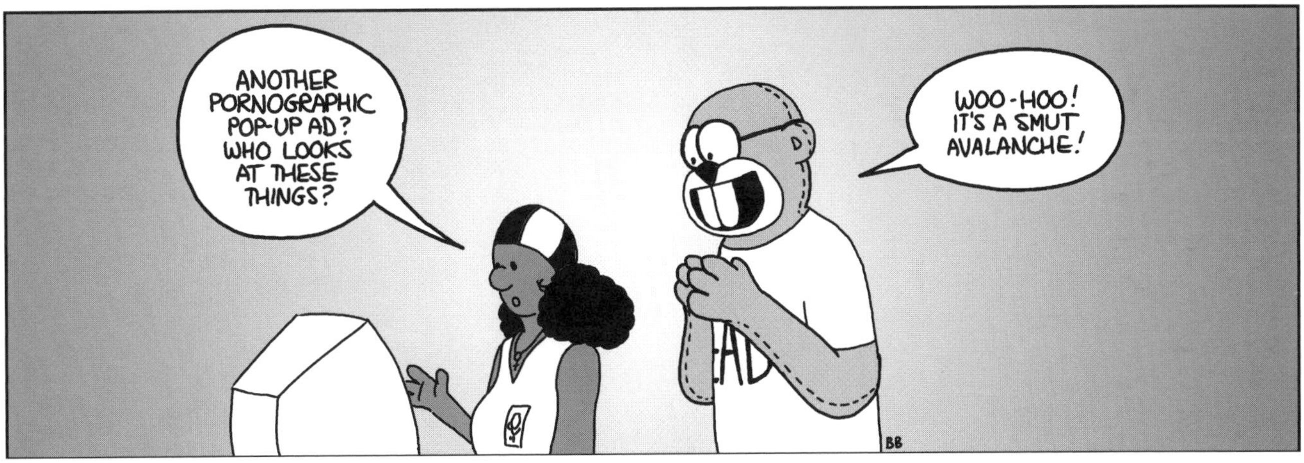
ANOTHER PORNOGRAPHIC POP-UP AD? WHO LOOKS AT THESE THINGS?
WOO-HOO! IT'S A SMUT AVALANCHE!

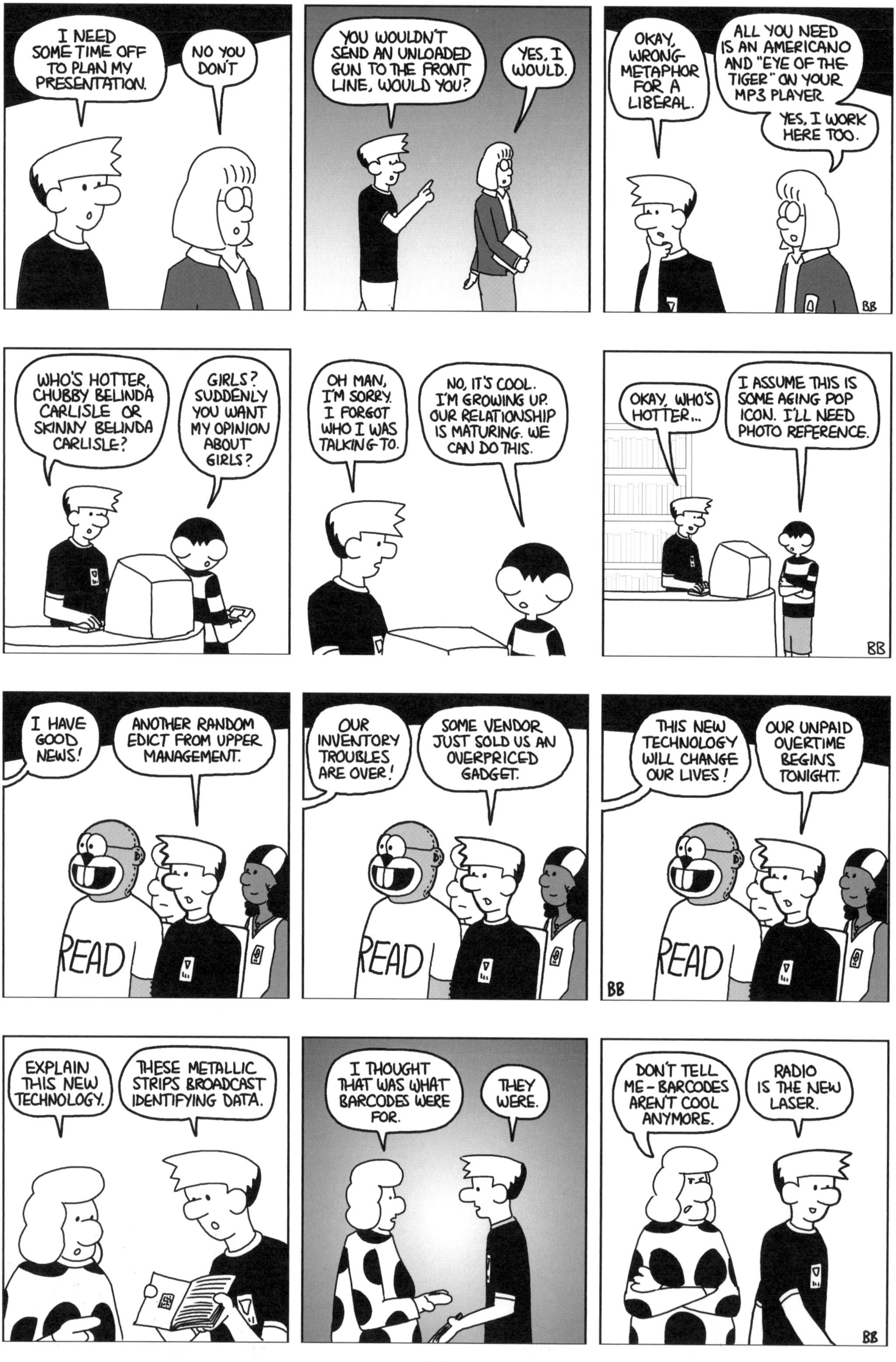
I NEED SOME TIME OFF TO PLAN MY PRESENTATION.
NO YOU DON'T
YOU WOULDN'T SEND AN UNLOADED GUN TO THE FRONT LINE, WOULD YOU?
YES, I WOULD.
OKAY, WRONG METAPHOR FOR A LIBERAL.
ALL YOU NEED IS AN AMERICANO AND "EYE OF THE TIGER" ON YOUR MP3 PLAYER.
YES, I WORK HERE TOO.
BB
WHO'S HOTTER, CHUBBY BELINDA CARLISLE OR SKINNY BELINDA CARLISLE?
GIRLS? SUDDENLY YOU WANT MY OPINION ABOUT GIRLS?
OH MAN, I'M SORRY. I FORGOT WHO I WAS TALKING TO.
NO, IT'S COOL. I'M GROWING UP. OUR RELATIONSHIP IS MATURING. WE CAN DO THIS.
OKAY, WHO'S HOTTER...
I ASSUME THIS IS SOME AGING POP ICON. I'LL NEED PHOTO REFERENCE.
BB
I HAVE GOOD NEWS!
ANOTHER RANDOM EDICT FROM UPPER MANAGEMENT.
READ
OUR INVENTORY TROUBLES ARE OVER!
SOME VENDOR JUST SOLD US AN OVERPRICED GADGET.
READ
THIS NEW TECHNOLOGY WILL CHANGE OUR LIVES!
OUR UNPAID OVERTIME BEGINS TONIGHT.
READ
BB
EXPLAIN THIS NEW TECHNOLOGY.
THESE METALLIC STRIPS BROADCAST IDENTIFYING DATA.
I THOUGHT THAT WAS WHAT BARCODES WERE FOR.
THEY WERE.
DON'T TELL ME - BARCODES AREN'T COOL ANYMORE.
RADIO IS THE NEW LASER.
BB

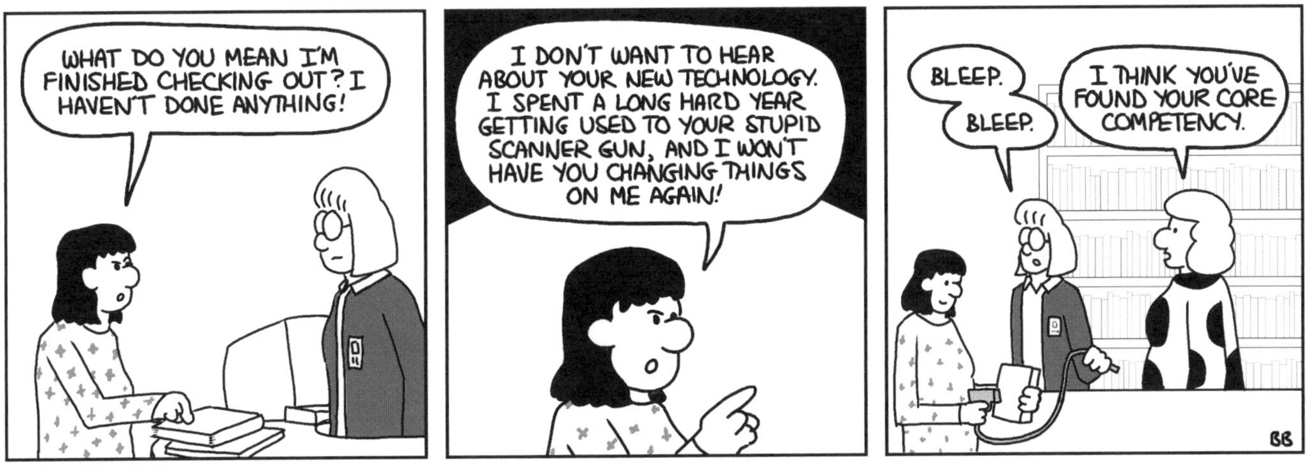
WHAT DO YOU MEAN I'M FINISHED CHECKING OUT? I HAVEN'T DONE ANYTHING!
I DON'T WANT TO HEAR ABOUT YOUR NEW TECHNOLOGY. I SPENT A LONG HARD YEAR GETTING USED TO YOUR STUPID SCANNER GUN, AND I WON'T HAVE YOU CHANGING THINGS ON ME AGAIN!
BLEEP.
BLEEP.
I THINK YOU'VE FOUND YOUR CORE COMPETENCY.
BB

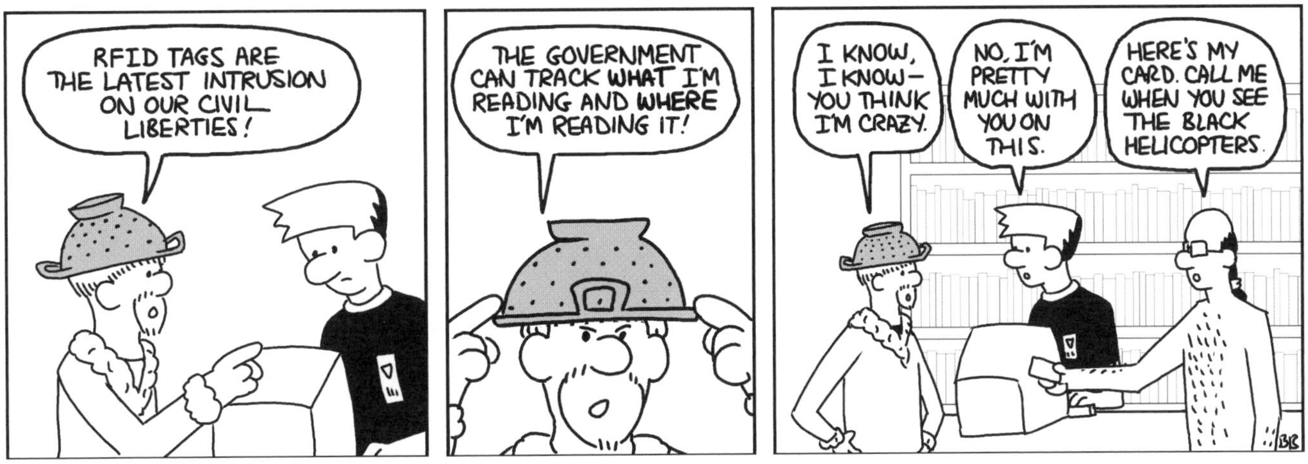
RFID TAGS ARE THE LATEST INTRUSION ON OUR CIVIL LIBERTIES!
THE GOVERNMENT CAN TRACK WHAT I'M READING AND WHERE I'M READING IT!
I KNOW, I KNOW— YOU THINK I'M CRAZY.
NO, I'M PRETTY MUCH WITH YOU ON THIS.
HERE'S MY CARD. CALL ME WHEN YOU SEE THE BLACK HELICOPTERS.
BB

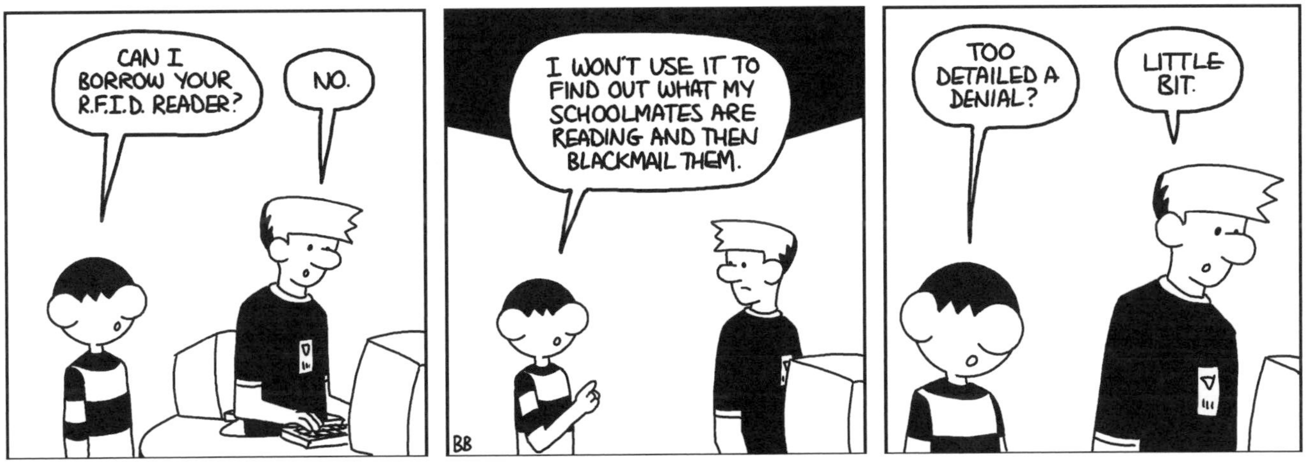
CAN I BORROW YOUR R.F.I.D. READER?
NO.
BB
I WON'T USE IT TO FIND OUT WHAT MY SCHOOLMATES ARE READING AND THEN BLACKMAIL THEM.
TOO DETAILED A DENIAL?
LITTLE BIT.

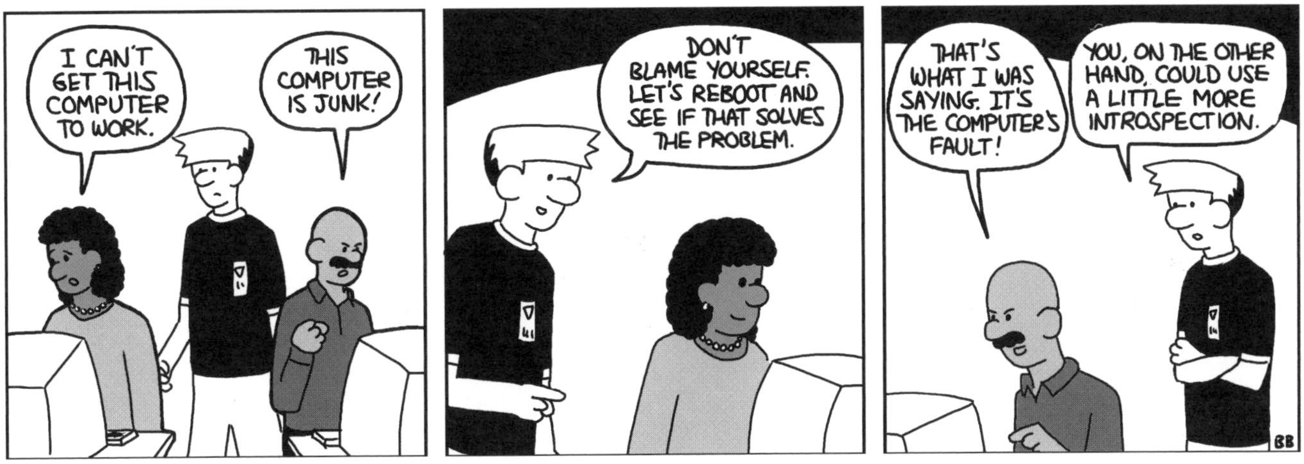
I CAN'T GET THIS COMPUTER TO WORK.
THIS COMPUTER IS JUNK!
DON'T BLAME YOURSELF. LET'S REBOOT AND SEE IF THAT SOLVES THE PROBLEM.
THAT'S WHAT I WAS SAYING: IT'S THE COMPUTER'S FAULT!
YOU, ON THE OTHER HAND, COULD USE A LITTLE MORE INTROSPECTION.
BB

Unshelved Guest Strips

When we began *Unshelved* in February of 2002 we didn't think of it as a "webcomic." We published it on our website because we didn't have any other options - we thought we were developing a comic strip for newspaper syndication, and we wanted the feedback of a live audience. But the post-bubble economy meant that newspapers, already stingy about buying new comics, became downright miserly. Meanwhile this whole Internet thing? Well it kinda caught on. Especially for comics. Unbounded by the tastes of syndicates, the fears of editors, and the constraints of the newspaper page, webcomics

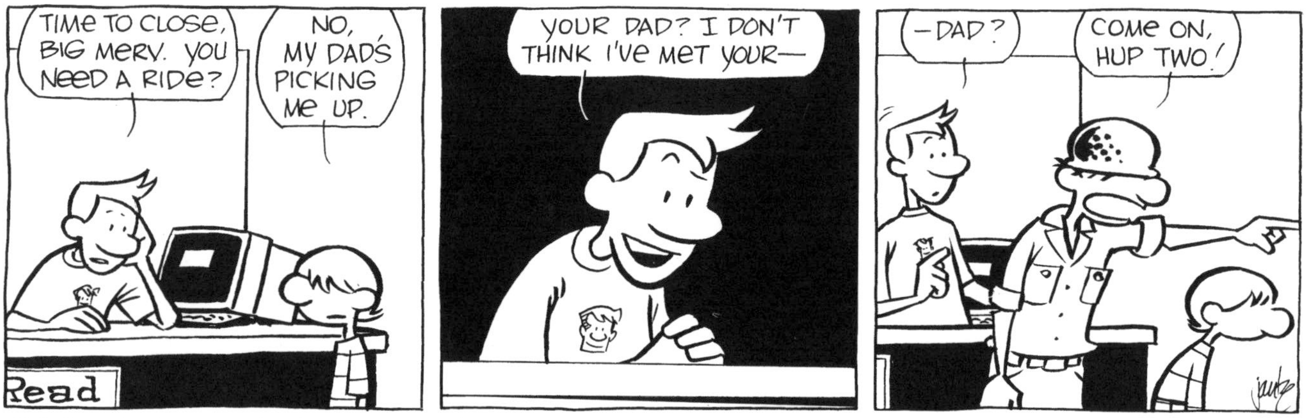

TIME TO CLOSE, BIG MERV. YOU NEED A RIDE?
NO, MY DAD'S PICKING ME UP.
Read
YOUR DAD? I DON'T THINK I'VE MET YOUR—
—DAD?
COME ON, HUP TWO!

Michael Jantze is the creator of *The Norm* (www.thenorm.com), a beautifully crafted comic strip chronicling the life and insights of, well, a guy called Norm.

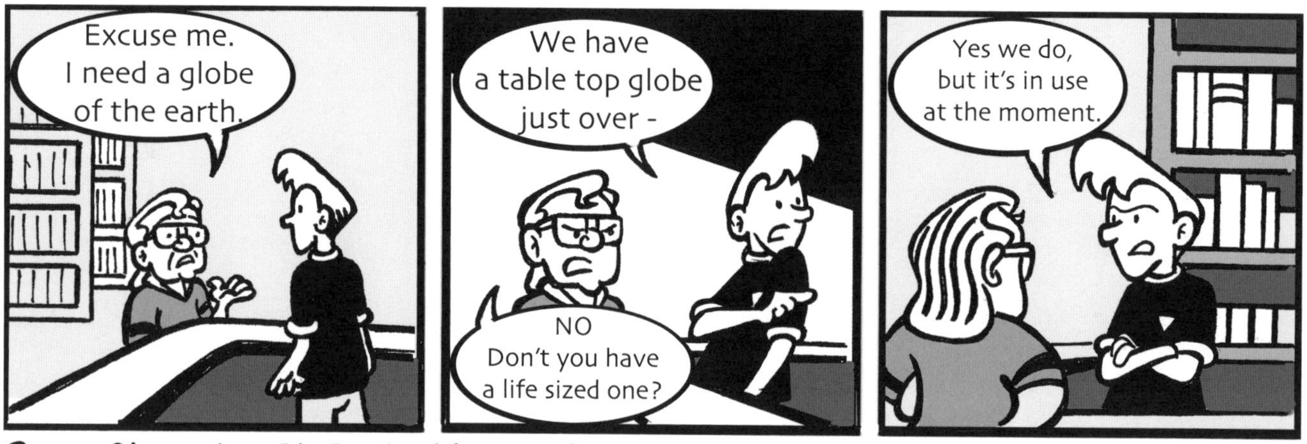

Excuse me. I need a globe of the earth.
We have a table top globe just over -
NO Don't you have a life sized one?
Yes we do, but it's in use at the moment.

Scott Alan makes *Oh Brother!* (www.ohbro.net), a warm semiautobiographical strip about three quirky siblings. He's also a many-times president of Cartoonists Northwest.

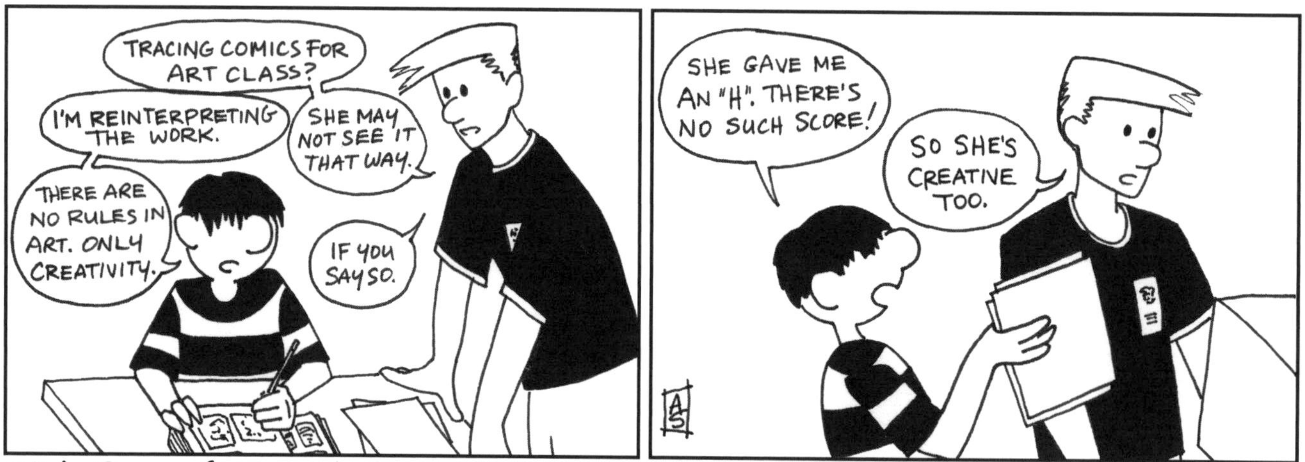

TRACING COMICS FOR ART CLASS?
I'M REINTERPRETING THE WORK.
SHE MAY NOT SEE IT THAT WAY.
THERE ARE NO RULES IN ART. ONLY CREATIVITY.
IF YOU SAY SO.
SHE GAVE ME AN "H". THERE'S NO SUCH SCORE!
SO SHE'S CREATIVE TOO.

Alida Saxon (www.alidasaxon.com) is a talented artist with the good taste to be a big fan of *Unshelved*. When Bill hurt his back she suggested a guest week - and here it is!

have become a profoundly fecund medium for creative expression where every strip can find its own unique audience.

Web cartoonists have a strange sort of community, and even the beginnings of tradition. One of these is the Guest Strip, where cartoonist A contributes a strip for cartoonist B. It's a fascinating way to see your favorite characters in a new light, and a great way to weasel out of a week's work. We asked some of our best cartooning buddies to render *Unshelved* in their image. Here is what they gave us.

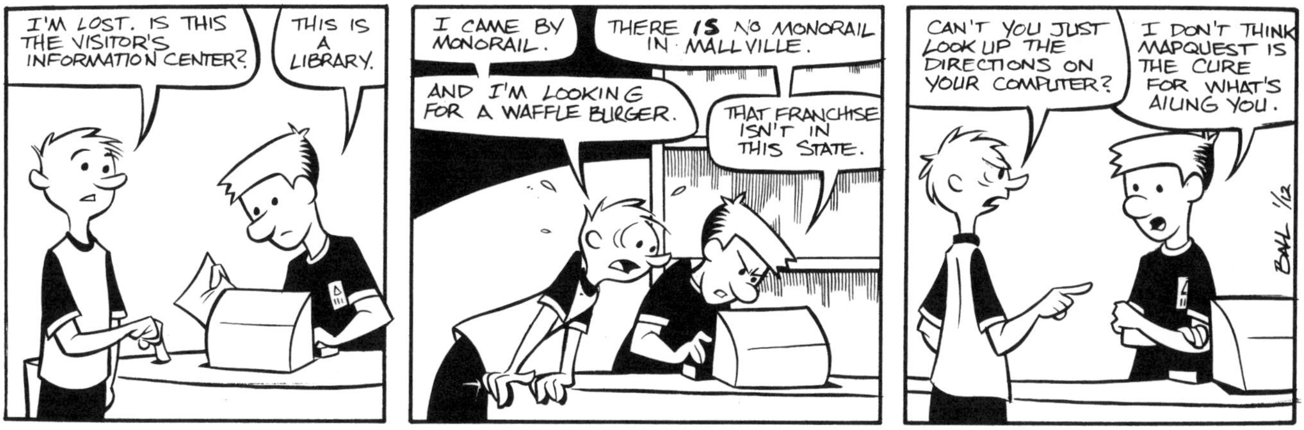
I'M LOST. IS THIS THE VISITOR'S INFORMATION CENTER?
THIS IS A LIBRARY.
I CAME BY MONORAIL.
THERE IS NO MONORAIL IN MALLVILLE.
AND I'M LOOKING FOR A WAFFLE BURGER.
THAT FRANCHISE ISN'T IN THIS STATE.
CAN'T YOU JUST LOOK UP THE DIRECTIONS ON YOUR COMPUTER?
I DON'T THINK MAPQUEST IS THE CURE FOR WHAT'S AILING YOU.
BALL

Scott and Georgia Ball are the overly talented husband-and-wife team behind *Scooter and Ferret* (www.scooterandferret.com).

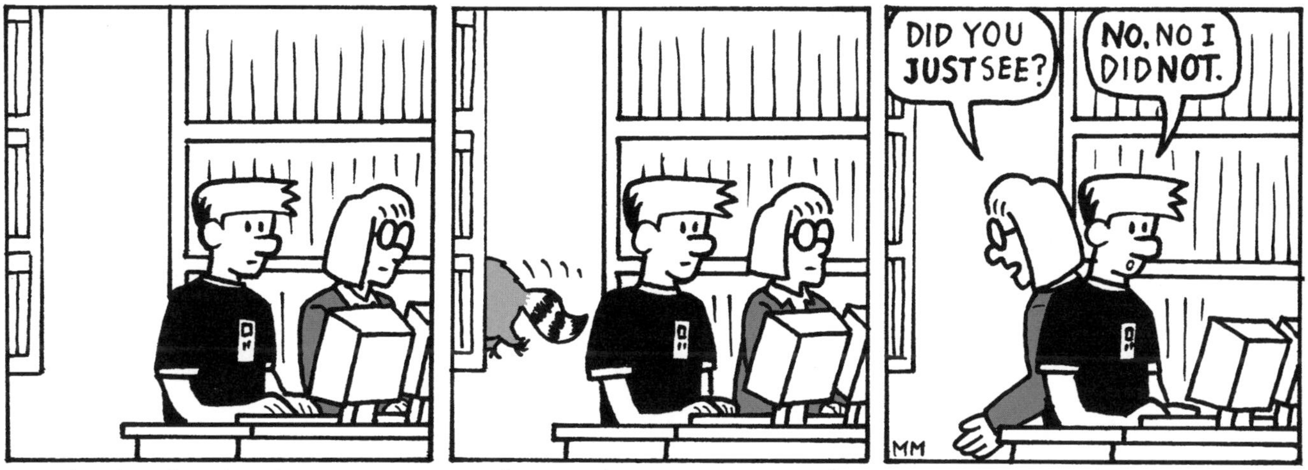
DID YOU JUST SEE?
NO. NO I DID NOT.
MM

Mark Monlux is *The Comic Critic* (www.thecomiccritic.com). He is also responsible for the sublime *StickMan* and the best online holiday cards ever.

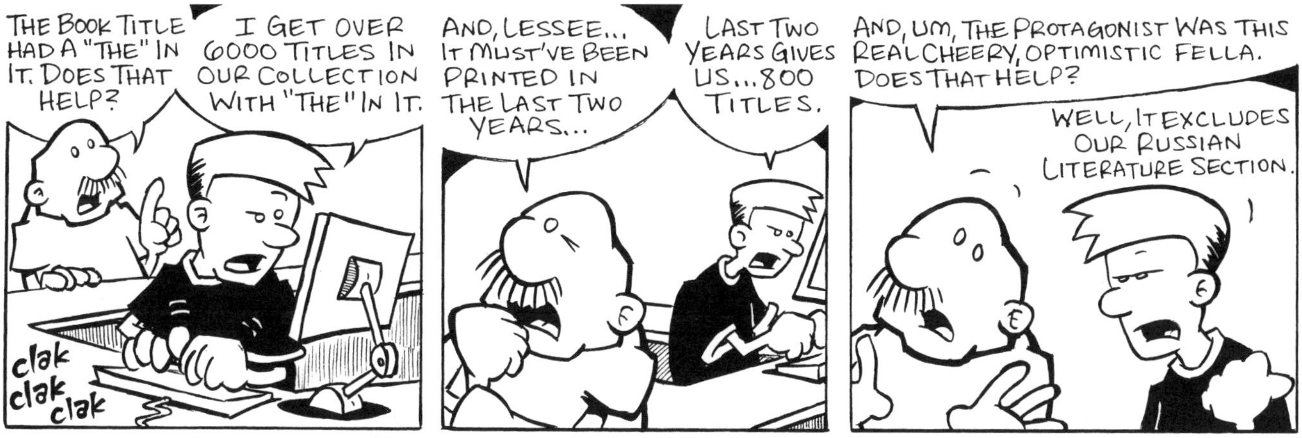
THE BOOK TITLE HAD A "THE" IN IT. DOES THAT HELP?
I GET OVER 6000 TITLES IN OUR COLLECTION WITH "THE" IN IT.
clak clak clak
AND, LESSEE... IT MUST'VE BEEN PRINTED IN THE LAST TWO YEARS...
LAST TWO YEARS GIVES US...800 TITLES.
AND, UM, THE PROTAGONIST WAS THIS REAL CHEERY, OPTIMISTIC FELLA. DOES THAT HELP?
WELL, IT EXCLUDES OUR RUSSIAN LITERATURE SECTION.

Dave Kellett makes *Sheldon* (www.sheldoncomics.com), the adventures of a boy billionaire, his grandpa (that's him above), and his talking duck. It's sweet, funny, and utterly random.

Conference Tips

If you've never been to a library conference you've never seen tens of thousands of librarians lugging around book bags full of free books, posters, pens, magnets, and any other schwag they can take home. You've also never seen an Elvis impersonator singing about the benefits of cataloging software, but that might be for the best. Read on and find out what else you're missing with these strips that we created for *CogNotes*, the daily newsletter of the American Library Association conferences.

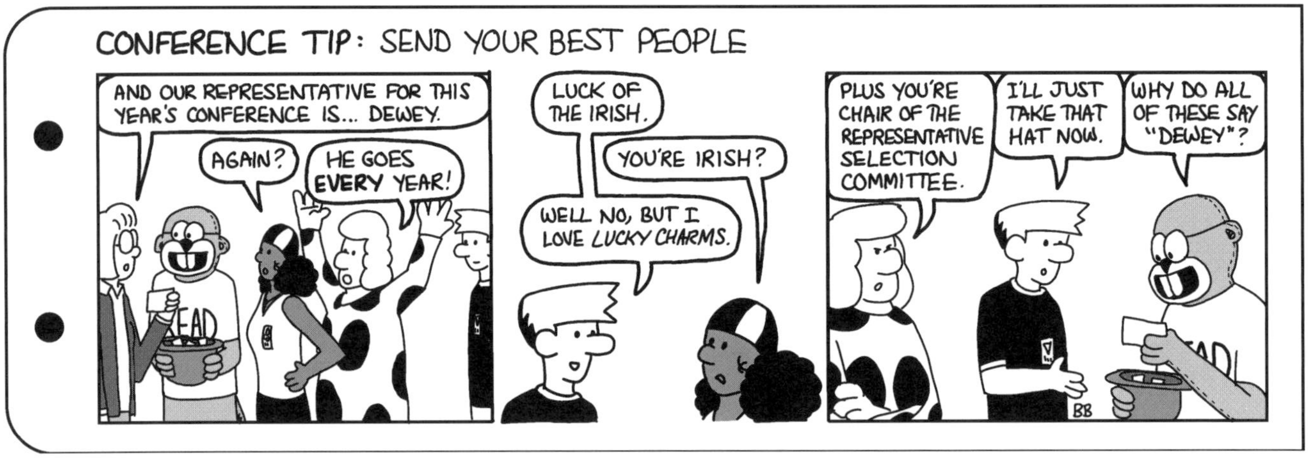
CONFERENCE TIP: SEND YOUR BEST PEOPLE
AND OUR REPRESENTATIVE FOR THIS YEAR'S CONFERENCE IS... DEWEY.
AGAIN?
HE GOES EVERY YEAR!
LUCK OF THE IRISH.
YOU'RE IRISH?
WELL NO, BUT I LOVE LUCKY CHARMS.
PLUS YOU'RE CHAIR OF THE REPRESENTATIVE SELECTION COMMITTEE.
I'LL JUST TAKE THAT HAT NOW.
WHY DO ALL OF THESE SAY "DEWEY"?
BB

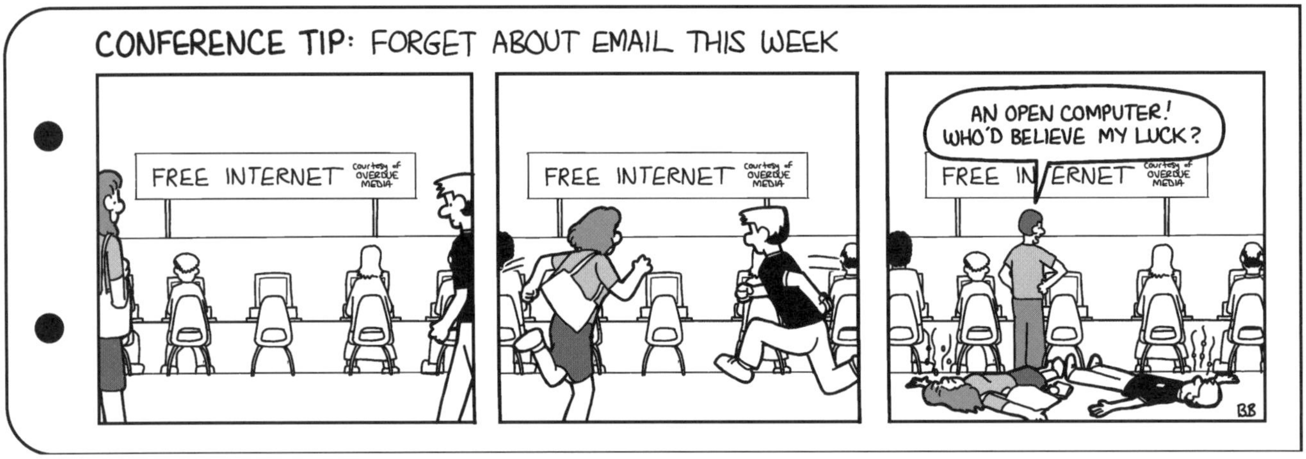
CONFERENCE TIP: FORGET ABOUT EMAIL THIS WEEK
FREE INTERNET
FREE INTERNET
AN OPEN COMPUTER! WHO'D BELIEVE MY LUCK?
BB

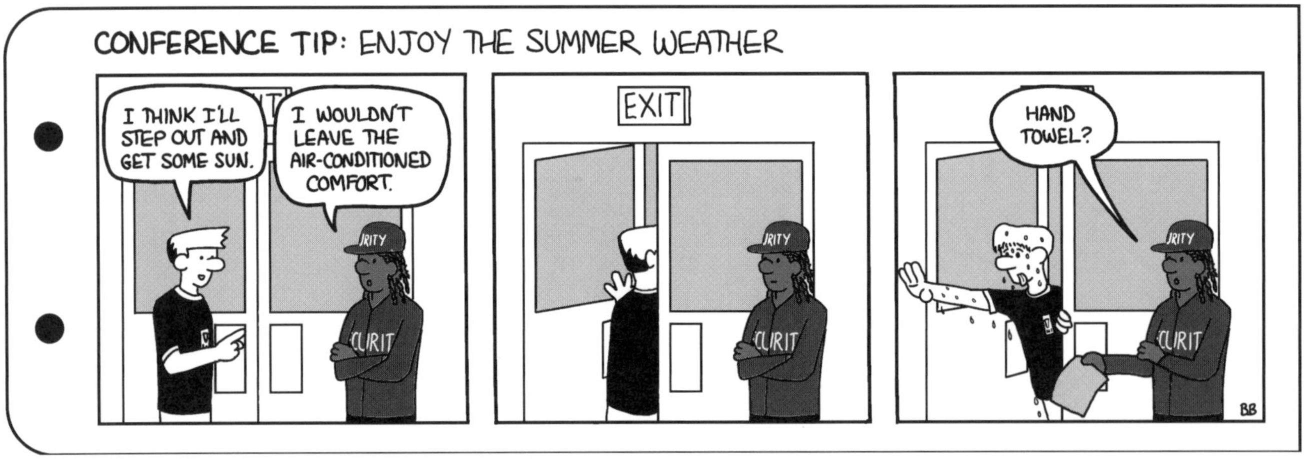
CONFERENCE TIP: ENJOY THE SUMMER WEATHER
I THINK I'LL STEP OUT AND GET SOME SUN.
I WOULDN'T LEAVE THE AIR-CONDITIONED COMFORT.
EXIT
HAND TOWEL?
BB

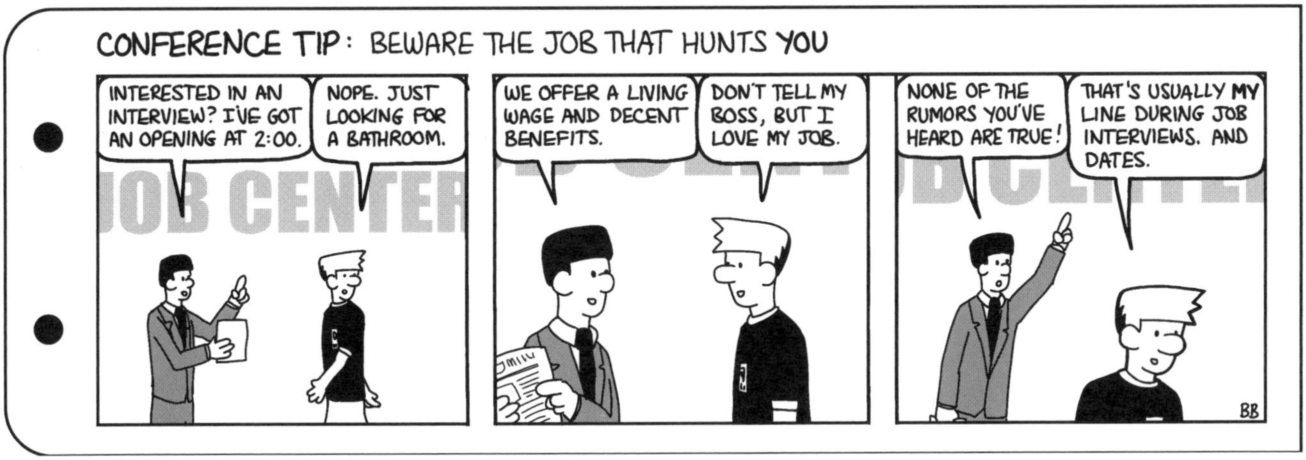
CONFERENCE TIP: BEWARE THE JOB THAT HUNTS YOU
INTERESTED IN AN INTERVIEW? I'VE GOT AN OPENING AT 2:00.
NOPE. JUST LOOKING FOR A BATHROOM.
JOB CENTER
WE OFFER A LIVING WAGE AND DECENT BENEFITS.
DON'T TELL MY BOSS, BUT I LOVE MY JOB.
NONE OF THE RUMORS YOU'VE HEARD ARE TRUE!
THAT'S USUALLY MY LINE DURING JOB INTERVIEWS. AND DATES.
BB

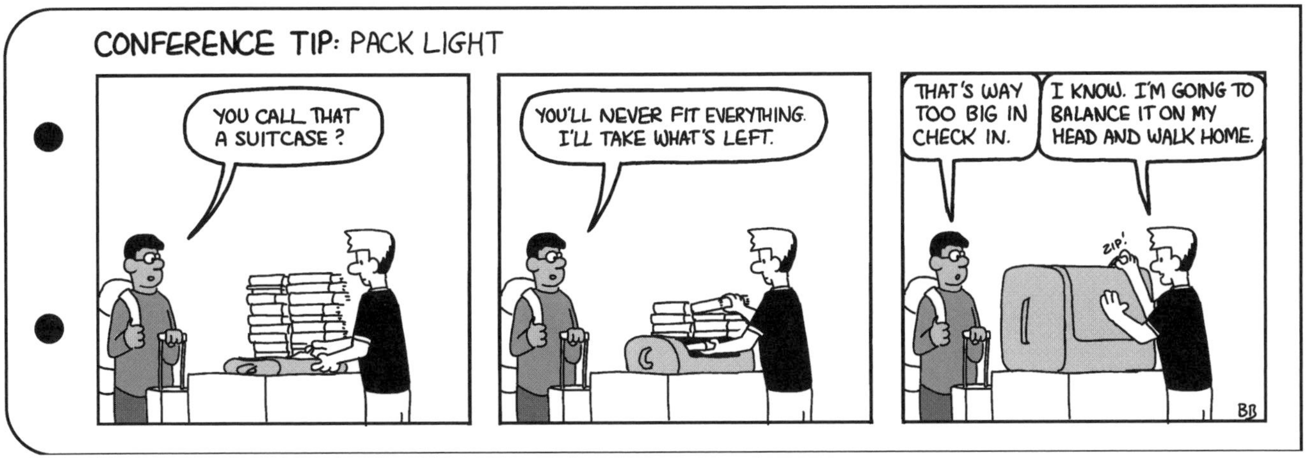
CONFERENCE TIP: PACK LIGHT
YOU CALL THAT A SUITCASE?
YOU'LL NEVER FIT EVERYTHING. I'LL TAKE WHAT'S LEFT.
THAT'S WAY TOO BIG IN CHECK IN.
I KNOW. I'M GOING TO BALANCE IT ON MY HEAD AND WALK HOME.
ZIP!
BB

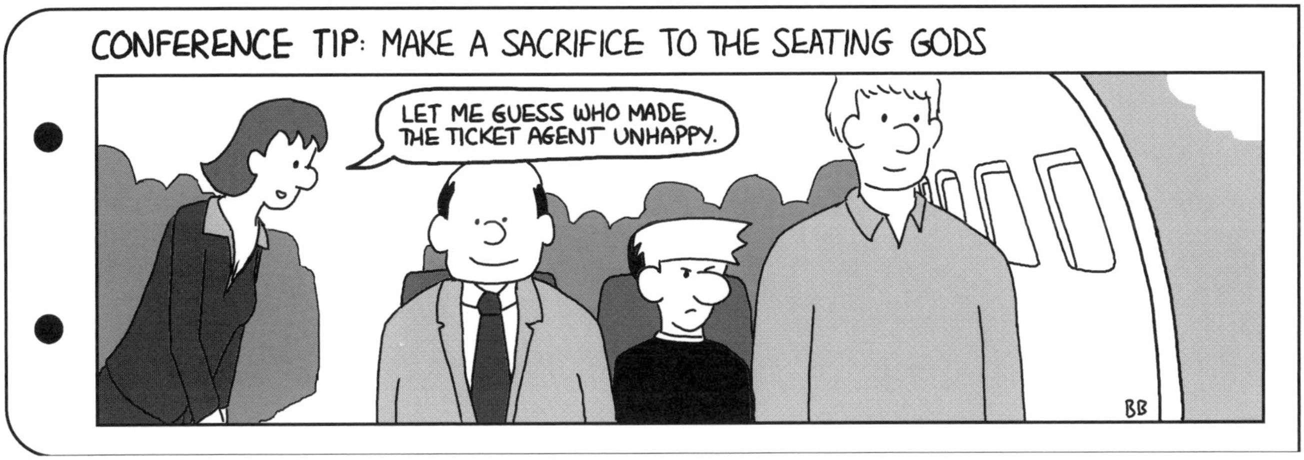
CONFERENCE TIP: MAKE A SACRIFICE TO THE SEATING GODS
LET ME GUESS WHO MADE THE TICKET AGENT UNHAPPY.
BB

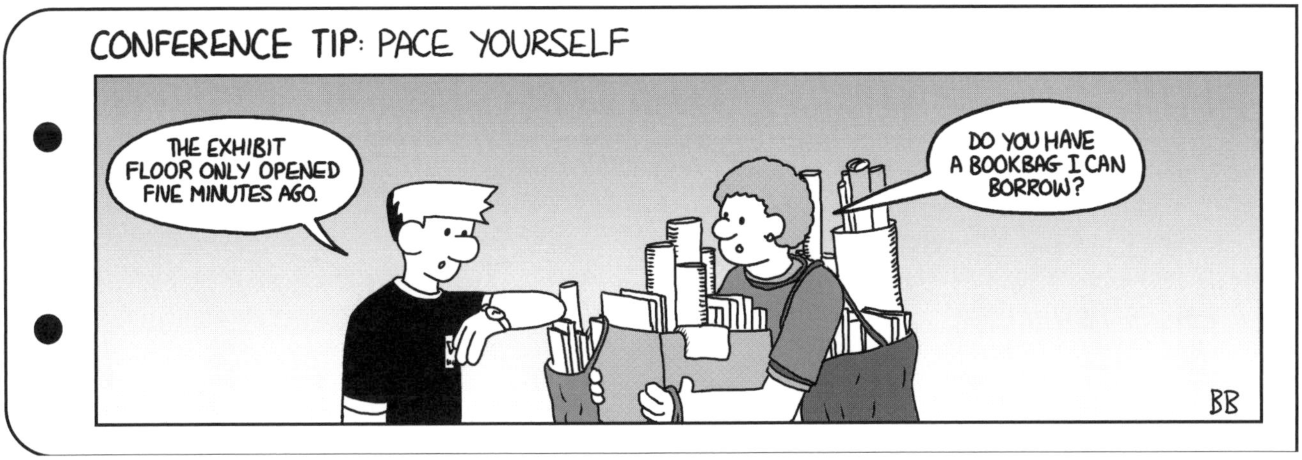
CONFERENCE TIP: PACE YOURSELF
THE EXHIBIT FLOOR ONLY OPENED FIVE MINUTES AGO.
DO YOU HAVE A BOOKBAG I CAN BORROW?
BB

CONFERENCE TIP: REMEMBER THE FOOD PYRAMID

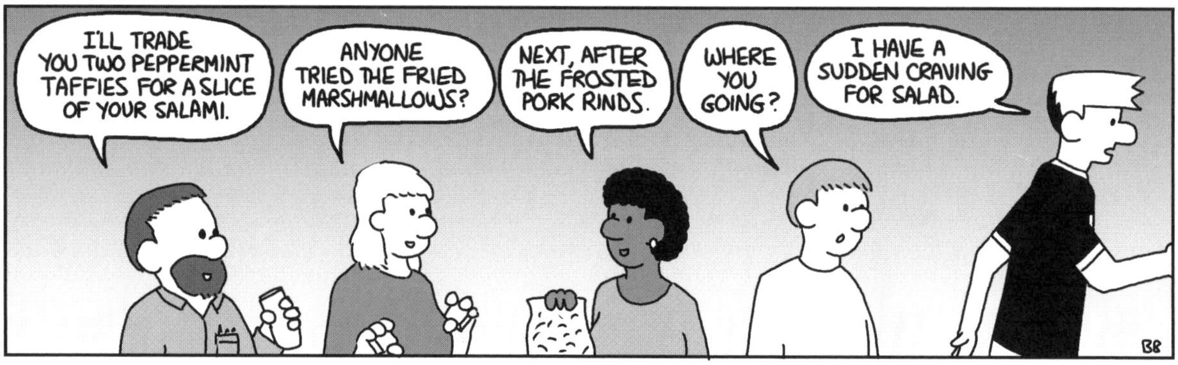
I'LL TRADE YOU TWO PEPPERMINT TAFFIES FOR A SLICE OF YOUR SALAMI.
ANYONE TRIED THE FRIED MARSHMALLOWS?
NEXT, AFTER THE FROSTED PORK RINDS.
WHERE YOU GOING?
I HAVE A SUDDEN CRAVING FOR SALAD.
BB

CONFERENCE TIP: PLAY "SPOT THE DAY JOB"

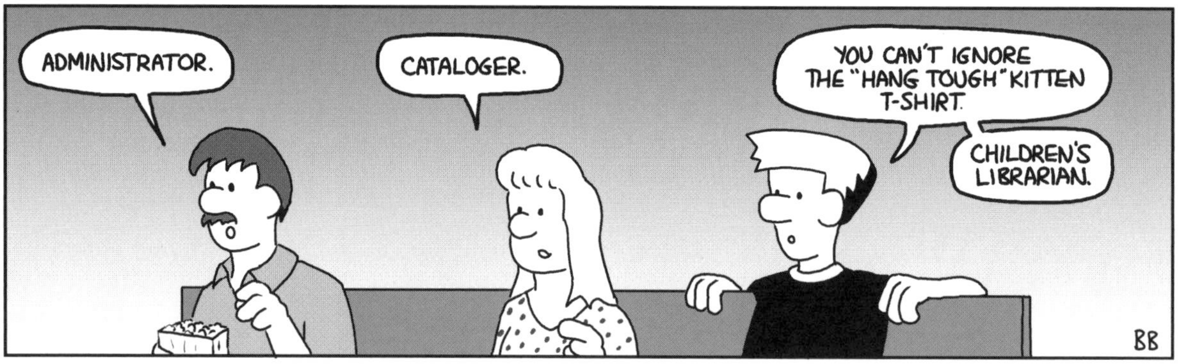
ADMINISTRATOR.
CATALOGER.
YOU CAN'T IGNORE THE "HANG TOUGH" KITTEN T-SHIRT.
CHILDREN'S LIBRARIAN.
BB

CONFERENCE TIP: BRING GIFTS BACK TO YOUR COWORKERS

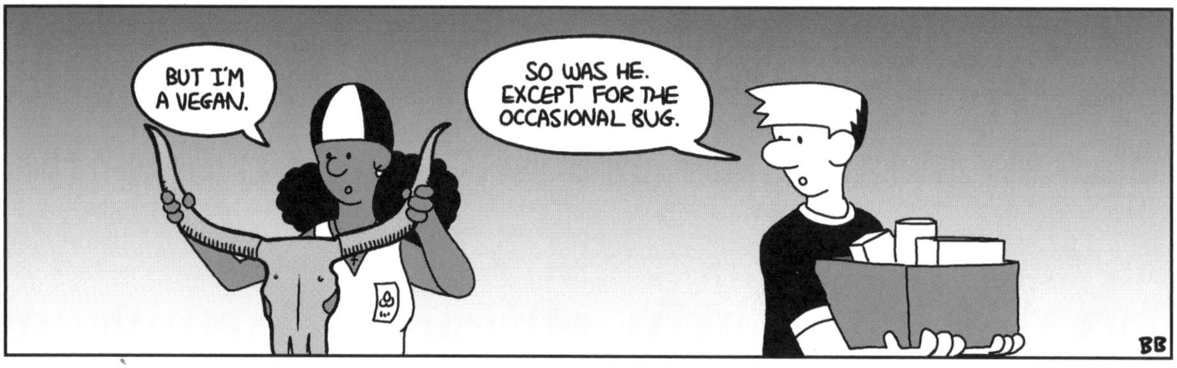
BUT I'M A VEGAN.
SO WAS HE. EXCEPT FOR THE OCCASIONAL BUG.
BB

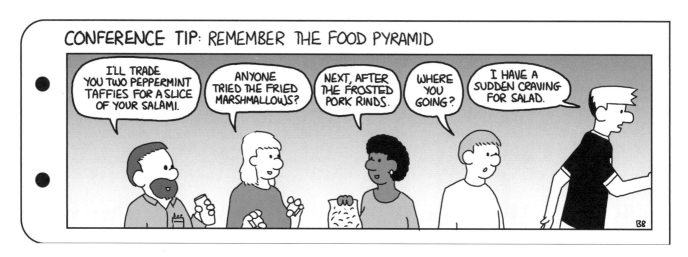

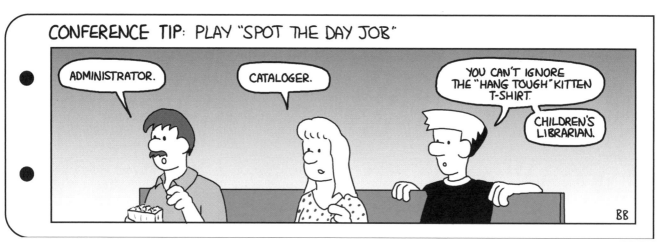

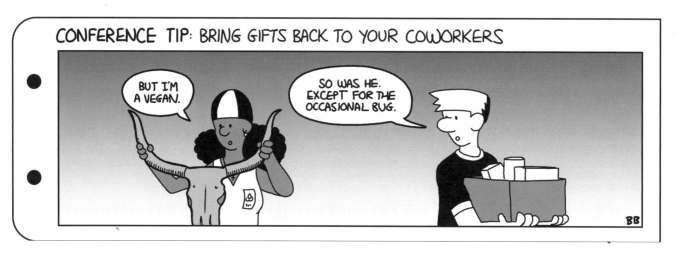